Command Responsibility and its Applicability to Civilian Superiors

Command Responsibility and its Applicability to Civilian Superiors

by

Maria L. Nybondas

T.M.C. Asser Press

ISBN 978-90-6704-327-4

FOREWORD

This year – 2010 – the First Review Conference of the Rome Statute of the International Criminal Court (ICC) will be held in Uganda. The Review Conference gives the State Parties to the Rome Statute the opportunity to propose and discuss amendments to the Statute, in order to enhance the work of the ICC. This important event draws renewed attention to the fact that international criminal law in general, and the Rome Statute in particular, are still very much in development.

While immense efforts have been made by international courts and tribunals, most specifically during the past 15 years, to build up a working international criminal justice system, it is apparent that international criminal law should be subject to additional thinking and practice, before it becomes an adequate and fully accepted body of law. Scholarly efforts concerning broader issues, such as the future of international criminal justice and the direction in which international criminal law should be steered, should be encouraged. Further research is also still needed in relation to specific substantive aspects of the law, so as to ensure the best possible foundation for future decisions that will have to be taken in cases before international – and national – courts.

In her book on command responsibility and its applicability to civilian superiors, Maria Nybondas intelligently explores an aspect of international criminal law that has preoccupied the minds of scholars and practitioners for years, not least since the start of the trials before the International Criminal Tribunal for the former Yugoslavia and the International Criminal Tribunal for Rwanda. As the principle of command responsibility is now accepted in (many) national Penal Codes, as well as in the Rome Statute, the doctrine will remain a highly important subject in the field of international criminal law. Therefore, the appearance of this thought provoking book is very timely.

What immediately springs to mind when reading this study is that the author does not only analyse command responsibility as an accepted doctrine of international criminal law. She is also concerned with the fundamental question of war – how war can be governed by laws and more specifically how a principle, which is accepted practice by warriors, can be made compatible with presently applicable international criminal justice provisions. Her mission, in which she has succeeded, has been to put forward a thesis and well founded arguments to support the position that command responsibility in international law is, first and foremost, a doctrine applicable to military commanders. The doctrine can provide an effective tool in international and national criminal justice systems, provided that command responsibility is not considered as a wide net to catch the big (civilian) fish on charges of, for instance, the crime of genocide.

In order for the international criminal justice system to become an effective complement to the various national systems, it is of utmost importance that practitioners and academics, both at the international and the national level, are involved in the discussion as to how the law can be improved and the practice enhanced. This book is a useful contribution to that discussion. This study will also be of interest to military officers, not least because it contains an interesting chapter on the issue of command responsibility as a purely military concept. The reader will be reminded of the fact that even an accepted principle of international criminal law should be applied in a way that makes adherence to the rules, in the heat of a conflict, possible. International criminal law and the Rome Statute will become truly effective only when the law is accepted as the law.

The Hague, January 2010

Judge Erkki Kourula
International Criminal Court

ACKNOWLEDGEMENTS

The initial idea of writing this book was introduced to me by Mr. Morten Bergsmo. Now that the project is completed, I would like to express my gratitude to him for his suggestions and his support over the years.

I am indebted to the T.M.C. Asser Institute for facilitating this project, and to T.M.C. Asser Press for agreeing to publish my book. I would like to express my gratitude to Mr. Dick Blom, who cycled endless kilometres during the last few years to provide me with books from the Peace Palace library. I am also very grateful for all the comments and the friendly advice from Mr. Hans Thijssen, who edited the book.

I would like to thank Major General (ret) Cammaert and Colonel Van Harskamp for their willingness to contribute to this project. I am particularly indebted to Professor Harmen van der Wilt and Professor Terry Gill of the University of Amsterdam. Harmen, I thank you for pointing me in the right direction and for giving me all the reasons to always trust your judgement. Terry, I appreciate all your support and the discussions we have had, not least the hypothetical and other examples of cases involving WW II bridges and American Secretaries.

I would like to express my gratitude to Ms. Chiseche Mibenge and Ms. Simone Eysink who have offered both moral and practical support during the process of completing this book.

I am thankful to my parents, who gave me a solid basis and always believe in me. I dedicate this book to Jeroen and Madeleine. From the first thought to the last letter, Jeroen was always there for me. Madeleine, who entered into my life four years ago, has shown me that things have to be put into perspective and to be given the right priority, and that by taking a day by day approach to things instead of focusing on a distant goal, there is so much to enjoy along the way.

Voorburg, February 2010 Maria L. Nybondas-Maarschalkerweerd

TABLE OF CONTENTS

ABBREVIATIONS

AC	Appeals Chamber
AJIL	American Journal of International Law
AP I	First Additional Protocol to the 1949 Geneva Conventions
Art(s).	Article(s)
BFSP	British and Foreign State Papers
EJIL	European Journal of International Law
FYROM	Former Yugoslav Republic of Macedonia
GAOR	General Assembly Official Records
ICC	International Criminal Court
ICJ	International Court of Justice
ICRC	International Committee of the Red Cross
ICTR	International Criminal Tribunal for Rwanda
ICTY	International Criminal Tribunal for the former Yugoslavia
IHL	International humanitarian law
ILC	International Law Commission
ILM	International Legal Materials
IMT	International Military Tribunal (Nuremberg Tribunal)
IMTFE	International Military Tribunal for the Far East (Tokyo Tribunal)
JCE	Joint Criminal Enterprise
LDP	Landmacht Doctrinepublikaties (Army Doctrine Publication)
LJIL	Leiden Journal of International Law
NATO	North Atlantic Treaty Organization
NJ	Nederlandse Jurisprudentie
PMC	Private Military Company
POW	Prisoners of War
RUF	Revolutionary United Front
SCSL	Special Court for Sierra Leone
Stb.	Staatsblad (Netherlands Bulletin of Acts, Orders and Decrees)
STL	Special Tribunal for Lebanon
TC	Trial Chamber
TWC	Trials of War Criminals
UCLA Law Review	Law Review of the University of California, Los Angeles
UN	United Nations
UN Doc.	United Nations Document
UNTS	United Nations Treaty Series
UNWCC	United Nations War Crimes Commission
US	United States Supreme Court Report
YIHL	Yearbook of International Humanitarian Law

Chapter 1
Introduction

> 'Command is a sacred trust. The legal and moral responsibility of commanders exceed those of any other leader of similar position or authority.'[1]

1.1 Command responsibility – a narrow and a broad concept

This book is devoted to the command responsibility doctrine under international law. The best way of showing what brought me, the present author, to enter into a study on this topic is by citing a particular scene from the book Band of Brothers, followed by a citation from the Trial judgement in the *Musema* case of the International Criminal Tribunal for Rwanda (ICTR). First, a scene from the Second World War:

> 'Winters ordered him to take the prisoners back to the battalion CP and then get himself tended by Doc Neavles.
> Then he remembered that Liebgott, a good combat soldier, had a reputation of "being very rough on prisoners." He also heard Liebgott respond to his order with the words, "Oh, Boy! I'll take care of them."
> "There are eleven prisoners", Winters said, "and I want eleven prisoners turned over to battalion." Liebgott began to throw a tantrum. Winters dropped his M-1 to his hip, threw off the safety, pointed it at Liebgott, and said, "Liebgott, drop all your ammunition and empty your rifle." Liebgott swore and grumbled but did as he was ordered.
> "Now", said Winters, "you can put *one* round in your rifle. If you drop a prisoner, the rest will jump you." Winters noticed a German officer who had been pacing back and forth, obviously nervous and concerned over Liebgott's exuberance when he first got the assignment. Evidently the officer understood English; when he heard Winters's further orders, he relaxed.
> Liebgott brought all eleven prisoners back to battalion HQ. Winters knew that for certain, as he checked later that day with Nixon.'[2]

Secondly, a quotation from the *Musema* judgement:

---

[1] See 'Doctrine of Command Responsibility in U.S. Human Rights Cases', 96 *AJIL* (2002) pp. 719-723, at p. 720, where reference is made to Art. 1-61 of the U.S. Army Field Manual of 31 August 1999.

[2] S.E. Ambrose, *Band of Brothers – E Company, 506th Regiment, 101st Airborne from Normandy to Hitler's Eagle's Nest* (New York, Simon & Schuster 2001) p. 150.

'*Witness R* testified about an attack which took place around the end of April, or the beginning of May, on Rwirambo hill opposite Muyira hill in Bisesero, during which he was injured.
He explained that this attack started in the morning and came from Gisovu. The leaders of the attack were Aloys Ndimbati, the *bourgmestre* of Gishyita, and Musema, the Director of the tea factory. Musema, who was armed with a rifle of unspecified length, was within rifle range of the witness. Musema had arrived in his red Pajero, followed shortly afterwards by the vehicle of Ndimbati. Other vehicles seen by the witness were 4 tea factory Daihatsu "*camionettes*" aboard which were *Interahamwe*. The witness was able to identify the *Interahamwe* as they wore blue uniforms, on the back of which was printed "*Usine à thé de Gisovu*". Two of the *camionettes* were green, one was yellow and one was white. All had "*Usine à thé Gisovu*" printed on their side panelling.
The witness said he saw that the attackers were armed with clubs, rifles and spears. While in a nearby valley looking for water, Witness R was injured from a shot which came from the direction of Ndimbati and Musema.'[3]
'With respect to the Prosecutor's argument that Musema could also be held responsible under Article 6 (3) of the Statute, the Chamber finds, firstly, that among the attackers at Rwirambo were persons identified as employees of the Gisovu Tea Factory. The Chamber is of the view that their participation resulted, inevitably, in the commission of acts referred to under Articles 2 to 4 of the Statute, including, in particular, causing serious bodily and mental harm to members of the Tutsi group.
The Chamber finds that it has also been established, as held *supra*, that Musema was the superior of said employees and that he held not only *de jure* power over them, but also *de facto* power. Noting that Musema was personally present at the attack sites, the Chamber is of the opinion that he knew or, at least, had reason to know that his subordinates were about to commit such acts or had done so. The Chamber notes that Musema, nevertheless, failed to take the necessary and reasonable measures to prevent the commission of said acts by his subordinates, but rather abetted in their commission, by his presence and by his personal participation.
Consequently, the Chamber finds that, for the acts committed by the employees of the Gisovu Tea Factory during the attack on Rwirambo Hill, Musema incurs individual criminal responsibility, as their superior, on the basis of the basis of [sic] Article 6(3) of the Statute.'[4]

The common denominator of these two citations is command responsibility. Can that concept cover situations that seemingly do not have much in common? This was the question that triggered the author. The military commander in the first scene avoids the committing of war crimes by the soldier in his unit when taking the necessary measures to ensure that the prisoners are not harmed before being handed over to the battalion. The witness in the *Musema* case provided evidence resulting in a legal finding according to which the accused fulfilled the requirements of the command responsibility doctrine as laid down in Article 6(3) of the Statute of the ICTR. Indeed, the scene picturing an event during the Second World War and the factual recollection of certain events by a witness together with the legal findings of the Trial Chamber in the *Musema* case, share some

[3] *Prosecutor* v. *Alfred Musema*, Judgement and Sentence, Case No. ICTR-96-13-T, 27 January 2000, paras. 396-398.
[4] Ibid., paras. 898-900.

common features. In both situations there is a person in a position of authority, there are (potential) perpetrators who are not in the same position of authority and the event takes place in an armed conflict. For the purposes of this study, however, what is of particular interest is the fact that two situations, two cases that show even more differences than commonalities, can both be described as cases of command responsibility. In the first case, the superior is a military commander. The perpetrator is a *de jure* subordinate of the superior. The aim of the commander is to bring the enemy soldiers back to the battalion safely. Had the commander not been as sharp and experienced as he was, resulting in war crimes being committed by the soldier, the aim of the commander would still have been the same. In the second case, however, the superior is a civilian, whose power is based on a civilian hierarchical relationship. As it was established that the superior was present and personally participated in the events, his aim cannot have been to ensure the safety of the Tutsi civilians.

The above-mentioned scenes show that, at present, command responsibility may cover a great variety of situations and relationships. While the first example describes an event of a purely military character in a traditional international armed conflict, the second example concerns a more recent situation of a mass atrocity, involving civilians both as the superior, as perpetrators and as victims. How far does the command responsibility doctrine reach? Much attention has been given to this topic in legal writings. At the same time it is recognised that command responsibility is still developing and, therefore, should be given the attention it needs by scholars, including authors of legal literature.

1.2 Terminology

This section aims at explaining concepts and terms that are used frequently throug hout the book. A correct understanding of the terminology at the beginning of the book is necessary, as certain concepts with a slightly different meaning are often used interchangeably.

The subject of this study will be referred to as the command responsibility doctrine. Preference is given to command responsibility instead of superior responsibility, as the doctrine is also frequently referred to. Based on the thesis and the findings of the author, as well as on the findings of other authors, the term command responsibility gives a more accurate impression of the origin and purpose of the doctrine. Whereas the term superior responsibility has been preferred during the last decade because of its neutrality, encompassing both civilian and military superiors, the term command responsibility points to its applicability primarily to military commanders or superiors who act with authority very similar to that of a military commander.

When discussing the subject-matter of this study in the legal literature, reference is often made to 'the principle of command responsibility'. For the purposes of the International Criminal Court (ICC), command responsibility is considered as a general principle of criminal law, together with the principle of individual criminal responsibility, the defences and the general principles in the strict sense, including *nullum crimen sine lege* and *nulla poena sine lege*.[5] Cassese did not consider the status of command responsibility as a general principle of criminal law necessarily restricted to the Rome Statute, where he held that the general principle had crystallised from Article 86(1) of the First Additional Protocol to the Geneva Conventions (AP I).[6] The author will refer to command responsibility as the command responsibility doctrine, to emphasise its status as an 'officially approved teaching based on accumulated experience.'[7]

Whereas the distinction between the terms 'liability' and 'responsibility' will be elaborated in Chapter 3, it is of relevance in this context to point out that where the term command responsibility is used without any further explanation or specification, it should be understood as the criminal responsibility of military commanders or other superiors for their failure to prevent or repress crimes committed by their subordinates. It is also of interest to note that while certainly connected to command responsibility, the state responsibility that may arise from crimes perpetrated by subordinates, where these are members of state organs, is not considered in the present study.[8]

It may also be pointed out here that throughout this study the author refers to the superior or commander as 'he'. Considering the still limited number of women in superior or command positions and the relatively speaking even smaller number of female war criminals, the author finds this preference for the masculine form justified. At the same time, it is recognised that two women (out

[5] For a more detailed account of the general principles, see K. Ambos, 'General Principles of Criminal Law in the Rome Statute', 10 *Criminal Law Forum* (1999) pp. 1-32.

[6] A. Cassese, *International Criminal Law* (Oxford, Oxford University Press 2003) pp. 200-201.

[7] See I.B. Holley, Jr., 'Concepts, Doctrines, Principles: Are You Sure You Understand These Terms?', 35 *Air University Review* (July – August 1984), available at <http://www.au.af.mil/au/cadre/aspj/airchronicles/aureview/1984/jul-aug/holley.html> (accessed 26 May 2009).

[8] While state responsibility for acts of members of the armed forces is not discussed in this study, the proximity of this form of responsibility to command responsibility may be illustrated by an excerpt from the judgement in the *Case Concerning Armed Activities on the Territory of the Congo* (*DRC* v. *Uganda*), where the International Court of Justice addressed Uganda's alleged responsibility for acts and omissions committed by Ugandan armed forces in the DRC, as referred to by Brownlie: '213. The Court turns now to the question as to whether acts and omissions of the UPDF and its officers and soldiers are attributable to Uganda. The conduct of the UPDF as a whole is clearly attributable to Uganda, being the conduct of a State organ. According to a well-established rule of international law, which is of customary character, 'the conduct of any organ of a State must be regarded as an act of that State' […]. The conduct of individual soldiers and officers of the UPDF is to be considered as the conduct of a State organ. In the Court's view, by virtue of the military status and function of Ugandan soldiers in the DRC, their conduct is attributable to Uganda. The contention that the persons concerned did not act in the capacity of persons exercising governmental authority in the particular circumstances, is therefore without merit. 214. It is furthermore irrelevant for the attribution of their conduct to Uganda whether the UPDF personnel acted contrary to the instructions given or exceeded their authority. According to a well-established rule of a customary nature, as reflected in Article 3 of the Fourth Hague Convention respecting the Laws and Customs of War on Land of 1907 as well as in Article 91 of Protocol 1 additional to the Geneva Conventions of 1949, a party to an armed conflict shall be responsible for all acts by persons forming part of its armed forces.' See ICJ Reports 2005, p. 168, at p. 242, as referred to in I. Brownlie, *Principles of Public International Law*, 7th edn. (Oxford, Oxford University Press 2008) p. 450.

of the approximately 100 accused in total) have been charged before the *ad hoc* tribunals.

1.3 The applicability of command responsibility in focus

The focus of this publication is on the command responsibility doctrine as established in international criminal law. As is revealed by the background to the doctrine as presently applicable, command responsibility has not met with difficulties in relation to its recognition. However, recognition indicates a general acceptance of a concept but may leave some openings for various interpretations. Consider the following statement by Sir Arnold McNair in the case concerning the International Status of South-West Africa:

> 'International law has recruited and continues to recruit many of its rules and institutions from private systems of law [...]. The way in which international law borrows from this source is not by means of importing private law institutions "lock, stock and barrel", ready-made and fully equipped with a set of rules. It would be difficult to reconcile such a process with the application of the "general principles of law". In my opinion, the true view of the duty of international tribunals in this matter is to regard any features of terminology which are reminiscent of the rules and institutions of private law as an indication of policy and principles rather than as directly importing these rules and institutions.'[9]

The kind of recruitment of rules described here corresponds to the way in which also command responsibility became part of international law. As stated above, and as is well-established, the principle of command responsibility was taken from national military practice and was applied by states to their armed forces. Consequently, when introducing the principle in international law, it was not 'ready-made and fully equipped with a set of rules'. It was recognised as a feature and principle of military organisation, but not as a criminal law concept.

By now, a significant amount of judgements has been rendered by international tribunals in cases involving the command responsibility doctrine. Considering the rather skeletal features of the doctrine before the first judgements, the tribunals have managed to add a great deal of meat to the bare bones of this concept. Adding to that an ever growing mass of academic papers, including some in the category of 'teachings of the most highly qualified publicists of the various nations', there is enough support for applying the doctrine of command responsibility as a fully-fledged rule of international criminal law.

Nevertheless, a systematic reading of the case law reveals some inconsistencies in the application of the doctrine. Further analysis shows that most of the hurdles and in particular the issues examined in this book relate to the under-

[9] See Separate Opinion by Sir Arnold McNair in *International Status of South-West Africa*, Advisory Opinion, ICJ Reports 1950, p. 128, at p. 148. May and Wierda pointed to this same statement in relation to rules of evidence applicable to international tribunals. See R. May and M. Wierda, *International Criminal Evidence* (Ardsley, Transnational Publishers 2002) p. 101.

standing of the purpose of command responsibility. What is it that one wants to obtain by applying command responsibility? Is the doctrine suitable for convicting those most responsible for international crimes?

The purpose of command responsibility becomes particularly relevant in relation to the applicability of the doctrine to civilian superiors, as civilians make up a distinct category of actors in international humanitarian law (IHL). The starting point is that a civilian is a person who is not participating in acts related to the waging of war and is thus not a combatant. It is a fact, however, that civilians can carry out certain tasks that contribute to the war effort. Since a few years, an in-depth discussion has been ongoing in relation to the topic of direct participation in hostilities.[10] A side-effect of this discussion has been the question as to who can be considered a civilian in the context of hostilities. To some extent the same discussion is brought to mind when analysing the command responsibility of civilians. For the purposes of IHL it is important to retain the distinction between combatants and civilians, despite the fact that the acts of a civilian may be identical to those of a combatant. For the purposes of command responsibility, the fact that the acts or rather the omissions of the civilian may be identical or similar to those of the military commander raises questions regarding the applicability of the doctrine in relation to civilian superiors. In both cases the question to be asked is what is reasonable when it comes to the function/position of a civilian. The author takes the view that a successful prosecution of a civilian superior can only be obtained in a very limited number of cases, due to the inherent difference between the military organisation and the civilian society and the different roles that usually are played by the military commander and the civilian superior in an armed conflict.

The lack of consistency in the present application and interpretation of the command responsibility doctrine complicates the effort of ensuring legal certainty in cases of command responsibility. Any misconceptions result in instability concerning the doctrine as a whole, and this works through to the 'exceptional' cases of civilian superior responsibility. Therefore, the central questions of this study can be formulated as follows: Which approach should be taken when considering the applicability of the command responsibility doctrine to civilian superiors? When applying the command responsibility doctrine, is a differentiation between military and civilian superiors justified? The aim of the study is to establish whether command responsibility is an effective basis for the prosecution of civilian superiors in relation to international crimes. Factors that should be taken into consideration are the origin of the doctrine; the recent case law relating to civilian superiors; the role of the superior, as this could have an impact on whether command responsibility or another partly overlapping mode of liability is applicable; and the nature of the underlying crime, as most specifically the

---

[10] Expert meetings, jointly initiated by the ICRC and the T.M.C. Asser Institute, were held on a yearly basis from 2003-2008 and the ICRC conducted research into the topic during the same period, all of which resulted in the *Interpretive Guidance on the Notion of Direct Participation in Hostilities under International Humanitarian Law* (Geneva, IRCR 2009).

crimes of aggression and genocide involve civilian superiors but because of their nature are not easily compatible with the command responsibility doctrine.

1.4 Applicable law and sources

The case law of the *ad hoc* tribunals plays a central role in this book. The research on which the analysis is based covers the relevant judgements from the *ad hoc* tribunals as well as some other international judicial decisions that shed light on the present subject-matter. Following the list of sources of international law included in Article 38 of the Statute of the International Court of Justice (ICJ), judicial decisions are a 'subsidiary means for the determination of rules of law',[11] but even if they are 'not strictly speaking a formal source'[12] of international law, 'they are regarded as authoritative evidence of the state of the law.'[13] Indeed, the literature on the command responsibility doctrine provides support for the view that judicial decisions are important evidence of the state of the law, as case law is heavily relied upon for the interpretation of various aspects of the concept. To a limited extent, reference has also been made to decisions of national courts.

In addition to case law, this study makes use of other formal, 'important sources' of law, where the label 'important sources' is based on the use of the sources in practice by the ICJ.[14] These sources are international conventions and customary international law, in the present study most prominently represented by the Rome Statute of the International Criminal Court (Rome Statute or ICC Statute).[15] The importance of Additional Protocol I to the Geneva Conventions of 12 August 1949 for this study should also be noted here, as this instrument contains two provisions – Articles 86 and 87 – that have been valuable for the development of the command responsibility doctrine. As for customary international law, the status of command responsibility as a rule of customary law is addressed in Chapter 2.

While a subsidiary source, at most, the author of this study has frequently made reference to the writings of publicists. Only teachings of the most qualified publicists of the various nations are mentioned in Article 38 ICJ, but in the present study the use of an opinion has not been based on the status or record of a publicist, but on the reasonableness and utility of the arguments presented by him

---

11 Art. 38(1)(d) Statute of the ICJ.

12 Brownlie, p. 19.

13 Ibid.

14 Ibid., p. 5.

15 UN Doc. A/CONF.183/9, 17 July 1998, 37 *ILM* (1998) p. 999. The statutes of the ICTY and ICTR do not enjoy the same status as a source of international law as does the Rome Statute, as the *ad hoc* tribunals were established under Chapter VII of the United Nations Charter. 'The fact that the Security Council is not a legislative body mandated that the subsidiary organ it created would not be endowed with competence the parent body did not have. Likewise it could not be seen as creating a new international law binding upon the parties to the conflict.' See D. Shraga and R. Zacklin, 'The International Criminal Tribunal for the Former Yugoslavia', 5 *EJIL* (1994) pp. 360-380, at p. 363.

or her. The author has also used materials other than those explicitly included in Article 38 ICJ. Most of these documents could be categorised as 'sources analogous to the writings of publicists', such as draft articles of the International Law Commission (ILC).[16]

In the opinion of the author, while any legal analysis is based on written sources in the categories mentioned above, a profound understanding of the mind set of military commanders and of the environment in which military commanders operate cannot be obtained purely through an analysis of legal sources. Considering the argument in this study that command is unique to military commanders, as is the responsibility it brings with it, it is essential, also for a civilian scholar, to at least make an attempt to comprehend the particularities of the military system, which confirm its uniqueness. In order to get a first hand impression of the thoughts and opinions on the command responsibility doctrine from those who have held command positions in conflict situations, the author discussed the topic with some prominent Dutch commanders. The result of the analysis of the essence of these interviews can be found in the annexes.[17] The interviews serve purely as an illustration of the views of these commanders on certain aspects of the command responsibility doctrine, and are not necessarily to be considered as representative of the views of commanders in general.

1.5 Scope and structure

The subject-matter of this book is limited to the international level. Insofar as the discussion concerns command responsibility as a form of criminal liability, the publicists who hold the view that command responsibility is 'an original creation of international criminal law' are correct.[18] Of course, command responsibility figured in national military legal systems before it was applied by international tribunals. However, the role of national military case law will not be given separate consideration here, since in the post-WWII period, especially in the last decade, the developments of the doctrine of command responsibility have come primarily, if not exclusively, through its codification and interpretation in international (case) law. It is logical and inevitable that any application of the command responsibility doctrine by national courts over the past decade has been and in the nearby future will be heavily influenced by the developments that have taken place at the international level. Both case law and literature analysing and commenting on the application of international courts and tribunals serve as a reference point when applying the doctrine at the national level. Whereas national systems may adhere to differing views regarding the applicability of international

[16] Brownlie, p. 25.

[17] See Annexes I and II.

[18] See G. Werle, 'General Principles of International Criminal Law', in A. Cassese, ed., *The Oxford Companion to International Criminal Justice* (Oxford, Oxford University Press 2009) pp. 54-62, at p. 58. Werle refers to K. Ambos, *Der Allgemeine Teil des Völkerstrafrechts – Ansätze einer Dogmatisierung* (Berlin, Duncker & Humblot 2002) p. 667.

law in national cases, there is ample evidence of references made by national courts to the command responsibility doctrine as applied by international tribunals.[19] Perhaps most notable are the judgements rendered by the Court of Bosnia and Herzegovina, in which the doctrine is regularly applied.[20] While recent and future judgements from national courts may affect the doctrine as applied at the international level, this study is limited to the international level and to the decisions and judgements rendered by international courts and tribunals.

Having introduced the topic and presented the relevant research questions in the present chapter, Chapter 2 addresses the legal basis for command responsibility. The chapter begins with exploring the existing treaty provisions and continues by addressing the status of command responsibility in customary law. Setting a basis for the rest of the study, the chapter sets out the present interpretation of individual criminal responsibility and command responsibility by international courts and tribunals. Chapter 2 also examines the *actus reus* and the *mens rea* of command responsibility.

Chapter 3 gets to the core of the matter as it explores the concept of command responsibility in armed conflict. In this chapter command responsibility is not a concept of criminal law, but a principle that is part of the military system and tradition. Different meanings of responsibility and various aspects of command are examined. Chapter 3 finally addresses the compatibility of the military concept of command responsibility with international criminal law. The view defended by the author throughout this book has its foundation in this chapter. The unique character of command responsibility as a military concept should be understood and accepted before entering into further analysis in Chapters 4 and 5, as it directly influences the approach that should be taken when considering the applicability of the command responsibility doctrine to civilian superiors.

Chapter 4 examines the application of the command responsibility doctrine to civilian superiors. First, the concept of the civilian superior is explored. Subsequently, cases concerning civilian superiors charged with command responsibility before the *ad hoc* tribunals are analysed. The cases are divided into two categories, the first of which consists of cases that resulted in a conviction of the accused based on his command responsibility. The second category consists of cases which resulted in an acquittal under command responsibility charges. The reasons for the acquittal are explored in more detail. The last part of Chapter 4 offers some observations on the application by the *ad hoc* tribunals of the command responsibility doctrine to civilian superiors.

---

[19] See, for example, the *Fujimori* case as decided by the Supreme Court of Peru: Corte Suprema de Justicia de la República, Sala Penal Especial, Caso *Fujimori*, Asuntos Varios 0019-2001 (Barrios Altos, Cantuta, Sotanos SIE), Sentencia: Fundamentos y fallo, 7 April 2009, at Parte IV – Decisión, § 4. La autoría mediata y la responsabilidad del superior en el Derecho Penal Internacional.

[20] See, *inter alia*, *Prosecutor's Office of Bosnia and Herzegovina* v. *Mitar Rašević and Savo Todović*, Verdict, Case No. X-KR/06/275, 28 February 2008; and *Prosecutor's Office of Bosnia and Herzegovina* v. *Paško Ljubičić*, Verdict, Case No. X-KR-06/241, 29 April 2008. It should be noted that the Court of Bosnia and Herzegovina is an extraordinary domestic court, as it includes international judges and prosecutors, and as many of the cases are referred to the Court from the ICTY, pursuant to Rule 11*bis* of the Statute of the ICTY.

In Chapter 5, the remaining hurdles in the application of the command responsibility doctrine are identified and analysed. Having explored the unique function of the military commander in Chapter 3 and having realised the difficulties in trying civilian superiors in the case law of the *ad hoc* tribunals in Chapter 4, Chapter 5 addresses contentious issues that are of significance to both military and civilian superiors. The issues elaborated are the nature of command responsibility, the possible overlap between individual criminal responsibility and command responsibility and the nature of the crime underlying the charges of command responsibility. The chapter follows logically on from the two previous chapters as the choices proposed are based on the findings in these chapters. The findings give additional support for the view held by the author that the applicability of the command responsibility doctrine in practice is limited to situations that are more likely to involve military commanders than civilian superiors.

Finally, Chapter 6 combines the ideas and findings presented in the previous chapters, and it offers some answers to the question whether the differentiation between military and civilian superiors in codified provisions of the doctrine and as applied by international tribunals is justified. The chapter addresses the consequences of these answers to cases charging civilian superiors pursuant to the command responsibility provision and provides a future perspective on the command responsibility doctrine in international criminal law.

Chapter 2
The Legal Basis for Command Responsibility

2.1 Introduction

The present chapter explores the legal basis of the command responsibility doctrine as it presently stands and the most recent historical developments of the principle, which have contributed to the legal provisions applicable today. The emergence of the doctrine in the statutes of the *ad hoc* tribunals and the immediate charges under the command responsibility principle against accused before the tribunals brought a number of publicists to delve into the legal history of the doctrine. Basing themselves on the most comprehensive article on command responsibility before the appearance of the *ad hoc* tribunals, written by W.H. Parks, several authors use the writings of the Chinese Sun-Tzu as the first 'legal' source for the doctrine. However, it seems that these writings discuss and recognise the responsibilities of the commander rather than the criminal liability based on the command responsibility principle as we know it today. On the other hand, the fact that writings that date back hundreds or even thousands of years mention the responsibilities of commanders and even kings and princes, in relation to their subordinates, shows that the development of an international criminal law doctrine of command responsibility as it is known today was based on a common understanding that in armed conflicts, superiors have certain responsibilities towards their subordinates.

The first part of the chapter aims at setting out the phases of the development of the command responsibility doctrine that have directly contributed to the present understanding of the principle and therewith constitutes the legal basis for command responsibility. The latter part of the chapter sets out the presently applicable definitions and interpretation of the principle. These should serve as the foundation for the more complex analysis of the doctrine in the subsequent chapters. This chapter is not aimed at repeating the historical research done by others, but the author recognises the importance of earlier research[1] and appreciates the availability of detailed documentation of the history of the doctrine.[2]

---

[1] For a significant contribution to the discussion on the command responsibility doctrine, see E. van Sliedregt, *The Criminal Responsibility of Individuals for Violations of International Humanitarian Law* (The Hague, T.M.C. Asser Press 2003); and G. Mettraux, *The Law of Command Responsibility* (Oxford, Oxford University Press 2009).

[2] The writings of Sun-Tzu have been referred to as one of the first written records dealing with the responsibility of the commander. While demonstrating a military strategy to his King, Sun-Tzu stated the following: 'If the instructions are not clear, if the explanations and orders are not trusted, it is the general's offense. When they [the soldiers, MLN] have already been instructed three times,

2.2 Codification by treaty

2.2.1 Emerging treaty provisions

For the purposes of this study, one international legal provision predating the Second World War is of particular importance for the understanding of the command responsibility doctrine. That is Article 1 of the Hague Regulations annexed to Hague Convention IV of 1907. Article 1 of the Hague Regulations[3] sets out the 'laws, rights and duties of war' applying to armies, militia and volunteer corps if they, among other things, fulfil the condition of being 'commanded by a person responsible for his subordinates.' This provision reflected the idea of a 'responsible command'[4] but did not explicitly set out the responsibility of a superior for criminal acts committed by subordinates. The normative importance of the concept of responsible command was and continues to be the condition that it sets for the legitimacy of a party to the conflict and the status of a combatant as 'lawful'. At the time of the adoption of the Additional Protocols to the 1949 Geneva Conventions the provision, Article 1 of the Hague Regulations, served to show that the responsibility of superiors who failed to prevent their subordinates from committing crimes was not new in treaty law, although the existing treaty provisions did not treat this responsibility as a criminal concept imposing penal sanctions.

The post-WWII courts based their jurisdiction and decisions regarding the responsibility of superiors for crimes committed by their subordinates above all on national laws and earlier national court decisions, as well as on general

---

and the orders explained five times, if the troops still do not perform, it is the fault of the officers.' See Sun-Tzu, *The Art of War*, transl. by R.D. Sawyer (Oxford, Westview Press 1994) p. 81. According to Parks, one of the earlier legal instruments recognising the idea of superior responsibility was the Article of Military Lawwes to be Observed in the Warres, by King Gustavus Adolphus of Sweden in 1621. Together with the 1775 Massachusetts Articles of War, Article 11 of which dealt with the responsibility of commanders for 'knowing and omitting to punish or prevent' offences committed by their subordinates, these show the recognition in national laws of the principle of command responsibility. However, in the case of the military laws by King Gustavus Adolphus, Article 46 as referred to by Parks expresses the rule that a commander should not order his soldiers to commit crimes, which of course does not correspond to the narrow meaning of command responsibility today. See W.H. Parks, 'Command Responsibility for War Crimes', 62 *Military Law Review* (1973) pp. 1-104, at p. 5. Beside legal instruments, Grotius in his *De Jure Belli ac Pacis* set out the responsibility of rulers for their failure to prevent or punish unlawful acts committed by their subjects. See H. Grotius, *De Jure Belli Ac Pacis* (1646), Vol. 2, transl. by F.W. Kelsey et al. (New York/London, Oceana Publications Inc./ Wildy & Son 1964) p. 523.

[3] Regulations Respecting the Laws and Customs of War on Land, annexed to the 1907 Hague Convention (IV) Respecting the Laws and Customs of War on Land, 100 *BFSP* 338, reprinted in 2 *AJIL* (1908) Supp. p. 90.

[4] In the *Hadžihasanović* case, the Appeals Chamber used the term 'responsible command' to explain its opinion that regardless of the conflict, where there is an organised military force, there is responsible command. In turn, responsible command implies command responsibility. See *Prosecutor* v. *Enver Hadžihasanović et al*., Decision on Interlocutory Appeal Challenging Jurisdiction in Relation to Command Responsibility, Case No. IT-01-47-AR72, 16 July 2003, paras. 14-17.

principles of law or even morality, but not on explicit international treaty provisions.[5] Neither the Statute of the Nuremberg Tribunal nor that of the Tokyo Tribunal included provisions on command responsibility. Neither did the four Geneva Conventions, adopted on 12 August 1949 and dealing with the protection of various groups of persons during armed conflicts, explicitly mention any criminal responsibility that should be borne by commanders and superiors for acts of their subordinates. An implicit reference to crimes of omission was, however, made in Article 13 of the Third Geneva Convention:

> 'Any unlawful act or omission by the Detaining Power causing death or seriously endangering the health of a prisoner of war in its custody is prohibited and will be regarded as a serious breach of the present Convention.'[6]

The provision was a general prohibition on unlawful acts or omissions against prisoners of war, but pointed to the responsibility of the Detaining Power as a whole and did not address the personal responsibility of superiors. The previous article of the Convention, Article 12, provided as follows:

> 'Prisoners of war are in the hands of the enemy Power, but not of the individuals or military units who have captured them. Irrespective of the individual responsibilities that may exist, the Detaining Power is responsible for the treatment given them.'

The Geneva Conventions set out provisions on the individual responsibility of those who commit crimes or order crimes to be committed, but did not go into specific provisions on the responsibility for acts of omission:

> 'Each high Contracting Party shall be under the obligation to search for persons alleged to have committed, or to have ordered to be committed, such grave breaches, and shall bring such persons, regardless of their nationality, before its own courts.'[7]

The Geneva Conventions have served as a firm legal basis, both as treaty law and customary law, for the later codification of individual responsibility, but the Conventions did not provide a legal basis for command responsibility, and an important element of that responsibility, the failure to act. The Convention on the Non-Applicability of Statutory Limitations,[8] adopted in 1968, included a provision according to which the provisions of the convention should also apply to

---

[5] With regard to the legal basis for the crimes charged in the indictment presented to the Nuremberg Tribunal, Goodhart in 1946 found that there was such a basis in existing international law, or else the crime was 'in accord with the principles found in every civilised system of law.' See A.L. Goodhart, 'The Legality of the Nuremberg Trials', in G. Mettraux, ed., *Perspectives on the Nuremberg Trial* (Oxford, Oxford University Press 2008) pp. 626-637, at pp. 632-636.

[6] Geneva Convention III of 12 August 1949, 75 *UNTS* p. 135.

[7] See the provisions concerning Grave Breaches of the 1949 Geneva Conventions I-IV, Arts. 49, 50, 129 and 146, respectively.

[8] Convention on the Non-Applicability of Statutory Limitations to War Crimes and Crimes Against Humanity of 26 November 1968, 754 *UNTS* p. 73.

superiors who tolerate the commission of crimes. Article 2 of the Statutory Limitations Convention has the following wording:

> 'If any of the crimes mentioned in Article I is committed, the provisions of this Convention shall apply to representatives of the State authority and private individuals who, as principals or accomplices, participate in or who directly incite others to the commission of any of those crimes, or who conspire to commit them, irrespective of the degree of completion, and to representatives of the State authority *who tolerate their commission.*'[9]

The immediate purpose of the Statutory Limitations Convention is not to oblige states to prosecute violations, but to oblige them not to apply statutory limitations where prosecutions have taken place. Nevertheless, Article 2 sends the message that, under international law, not only those who participate in crimes, but also those who tolerate their commission could be held criminally responsible. According to the ICRC Commentary to the Additional Protocols of 1977, the regulation of acts of omission was considered a necessity, as this would bring the so-called Law of Geneva into line with other international law provisions, in particular Article 2 of the Statutory Limitations Convention.[10]

Command responsibility is understood as a basis for criminal responsibility where the superior did not physically commit or give an order to commit a crime, but where he omitted to stop the commission of any such crime, or where he did not take the necessary steps to punish the offenders. Accordingly, the provision in the Statutory Limitations Convention corresponds to the command responsibility concept, as it deals with the toleration of an offence, and mentions representatives of the state authority. The description fits a part of the command responsibility concept. However, as just mentioned, the purpose of the treaty is another one. It does not set a duty on a state to prosecute a superior in accordance with the command responsibility concept. It compels states to refrain from applying statutory limitations in a situation where a representative of the State authority has tolerated the commission of certain crimes, among which are war crimes and grave breaches of the 1949 Geneva Conventions. The treaty does not specify whether the ratifying states are bound to have included these crimes in their national legislation.

The literature recognises Additional Protocol I to the 1949 Geneva Conventions as the first instance of explicit treaty codification of the concept of command responsibility as it is currently understood: that a superior can be held criminally responsible for not preventing or punishing unlawful acts committed by his subordinates. AP I introduced two provisions with relevance to the concept of superior responsibility – Article 86 entitled 'Failure to Act' and Article 87 called 'Duty of Commanders'.

---

[9] Ibid. (emphasis added by MLN).

[10] C. Pilloud et al., *Commentary on the Additional Protocols of 8 June 1977 to the Geneva Conventions of 12 August 1949* (Dordrecht, Nijhoff 1987), paras. 3526-3527. See the Convention on the Non-Applicability of Statutory Limitations to War Crimes and Crimes Against Humanity of 26 November 1968, 754 *UNTS* p. 73.

Article 86 states as follows:

> '1. The High Contracting Parties and the Parties to the conflict shall repress grave breaches, and take measures necessary to suppress all other breaches, of the Conventions or of this Protocol which result from a failure to act when under a duty to do so.
> 2. The fact that a breach of the Conventions or of this Protocol was committed by a subordinate does not absolve his superiors from penal or disciplinary responsibility, as the case may be, if they knew, or had information which should have enabled them to conclude in the circumstances at the time, that he was committing or was going to commit such a breach and if they did not take all feasible measures within their power to prevent or repress the breach.'[11]

Article 87 of AP I provides as follows:

> '1. The High Contracting Parties and the Parties to the conflict shall require military commanders, with respect to members of the armed forces under their command and other persons under their control, to prevent and, where necessary, to suppress and report to competent authorities breaches of the Conventions and the Protocol.
> 2. In order to prevent and suppress breaches, High Contracting Parties and Parties to the conflict shall require that, commensurate with their level of responsibility, commanders ensure that members of the armed forces under their command are aware of their obligations under the Conventions and this Protocol.
> 3. The High Contracting Parties and Parties to the conflict shall require any commander *who is aware* that subordinates or other persons under his control are going to commit or have committed a breach of the Conventions or of this Protocol, to initiate such steps as are necessary to *prevent such violations* of the Conventions or this Protocol, and, where appropriate, to *initiate disciplinary or penal action* against violators thereof.'[12]

Accordingly, by 1977 States had come to agree on the necessity of possible penal sanctions for commanders who failed to prevent or repress crimes committed by subordinates. All the essential elements were included in the AP I provisions and explicitly listed in the Commentary to the Additional Protocols: the superior-subordinate relationship, the awareness requirement and the prevention or repression requirement. Herewith the modern international criminal law doctrine of command responsibility was codified in treaty law.

2.2.2 **Treaty definitions further developed**

The most significant treaty provisions in the history of the doctrine of command responsibility are, undoubtedly, those included in the Statute of the International Criminal Court, adopted in Rome in 1998. Their importance lies, among other things, in the broad acceptance of the Statute among States and the rapid entry into force of this multilateral convention. Through the ratification of the Statute,

---

[11] Protocol Additional to the Geneva Conventions of 12 August 1949, and relating to the Protection of Victims of International Armed Conflicts, 1125 *UNTS* p. 3.

[12] Ibid.

the States become bound by its provisions and accept the applicability of the Statute, the treaty, to a situation concerning that particular State. An obligation to bring their legislation into conformity with the Rome Statute was felt by many States, which led to amendments to several national Penal Codes and to the inclusion of the command responsibility doctrine in national legislation, therewith adding to the *opinio juris* character of the Rome Statute, including the command responsibility doctrine.[13]

As with other treaty projects, the elaboration of the ICC Statute did not stand on its own but was the consequence of a trend of accepting a broader role for international criminal law to stop horrific atrocities from (re)occurring and to avoid impunity for perpetrators of internationally condemned crimes. It was further a consequence of the earlier development of similar rules. What is true for the ICC Statute as a whole is comparable with the development of the ICC provisions relating to the doctrine of command responsibility. Both earlier codification and case law preceded the ICC provisions on command responsibility.

The most notable contributors to the development of the command responsibility definition, besides the ICC Statute, are the Statutes of the International Criminal Tribunals for the former Yugoslavia and for Rwanda and the judicial decisions delivered by these tribunals. However, as the *ad hoc* tribunals were not set up by a multilateral treaty, states are not bound by the provisions in these statutes in the same way as they are bound by a treaty through ratification.

The precedent for the ICC, or the first attempts to draw up a Draft Code of Offences Against the Peace and Security of Mankind were presented by the ILC in 1954.[14] The command responsibility doctrine was, however, not mentioned in this document. Over the years several versions of the Draft Code were elaborated by the ILC[15] before it adopted the Draft Code of Crimes Against the Peace and Security of Mankind in 1996.[16] In the adopted version the command responsibility doctrine was included as Article 6, together with a commentary.[17] The ILC defined command responsibility as follows:

---

[13] Of course, the acceptance and implementation of the doctrine by states are crucial for the *opinio juris* character of the doctrine, not the ratification of the treaty by a large number of states, as such. As stated by Heintschel von Heinegg: '[T]he *opinio juris* as a constitutive element of customary law has to be strictly distinguished from an *opinio juris conventionis*. While treaties may play an important role in the process of determining rules of customary law, they do not dispense with the necessity of proving that the States concerned do consider themselves bound also vis-à-vis States not parties/signatories to the treaty in question.' See W. Heintschel von Heinegg, 'Criminal International Law and Customary International Law', in A. Zimmermann, ed., *International Criminal Law and the Current Development of Public International Law* (Berlin, Duncker & Humblot 2003) p. 42.

[14] Draft Code of Offences Against the Peace and Security of Mankind, UN GAOR, 9th Sess., Supp. No. 9, UN Doc. A/2693 (1954), pp. 11-12.

[15] For all reports on this subject by the International Law Commission, see the Draft Code of Offences against the Peace and Security of Mankind, available at <http://www.un.org/law/ilc> (accessed 22 September 2008).

[16] Draft Code of Crimes Against the Peace and Security of Mankind, UN GAOR, 51st Sess., Supp. No. 10, UN Doc. A/51/10 (1996).

[17] Ibid., p. 19.

> 'The fact that a crime against the peace and security of mankind was committed by a subordinate does not relieve his superiors of criminal responsibility, if they *knew or had reason to know*, in the circumstances at the time, that the subordinate was committing or was going to commit such a crime and if they *did not take all necessary measures* within their power to *prevent or repress* the crime.'[18]

Two years later, the Rome Conference on the establishment of an International Criminal Court adopted another definition, included in Article 28 of the ICC Statute:

> 'In addition to other grounds of criminal responsibility under this Statute for crimes within the jurisdiction of the Court:
> (a) A military commander or person effectively acting as a military commander shall be criminally responsible for crimes within the jurisdiction of the Court committed by forces under his or her effective command and control, or effective authority and control as the case may be, as a result of his or her failure to exercise control properly over such forces, where:
> (i) That military commander or person either *knew or*, owing to the circumstances at the time, *should have known* that the forces were committing or about to commit such crimes; and
> (ii) That military commander or person *failed to take all necessary and reasonable measures* within his or her power to *prevent or repress* their commission or to submit the matter to the competent authorities for investigation and prosecution.
> (b) With respect to superior and subordinate relationships not described in paragraph (a), a superior shall be criminally responsible for crimes within the jurisdiction of the Court committed by subordinates under his or her effective authority and control, as a result of his or her failure to exercise control properly over such subordinates, where:
> (i) The superior either *knew, or consciously disregarded information which clearly indicated*, that the subordinates were committing or about to commit such crimes;
> (ii) The crimes concerned activities that were *within the effective responsibility and control* of the superior; and
> (iii) The superior *failed to take all necessary and reasonable measures* within his or her power to *prevent or repress* their commission or to submit the matter to the competent authorities for investigation and prosecution.'[19]

It is rather obvious that the ICC Statute offered the most elaborate definition of the command responsibility doctrine so far. The most significant novelty in the ICC definition is the explicit differentiation between military and civilian superiors. Comparing it to AP I, Article 86 used the broader concept of superior and Article 87 specifically provided for the responsibility of military commanders but did not mention non-military superiors. In these provisions, there was no explicit mention of superiors not being military commanders. Two remarks may be made in relation to the lack of a provision on civilian superiors, without speculating on the reasons why, at the time, there was no need to include such a provision.

---

[18] Ibid.

[19] Rome Statute of the International Criminal Court, UN Doc. A/CONF.183/9 (1998), 37 *ILM* (1998) p. 999.

On the one hand, the case law from the post-WW II period includes judgements in which civilian superiors were tried for their omissions. Accordingly, when the word superior was included in Article 86, there was an awareness of the fact that civilians had previously been prosecuted for omissions.[20] On the other hand, AP I is a codification of international humanitarian law in relation to international armed conflicts and it regulated the conduct, primarily, of states' armed forces and thus concerns primarily military commanders. Considering the development of the command responsibility doctrine since AP I and the different character of the instrument, it is understandable that the ICC Statute is more elaborate on this issue.[21]

2.3 Customary status of command responsibility

2.3.1 **Prior to the ICC**

> 'Prior to World War II, legal standards for commanders were practical articulation of the accepted practice of military professionals. This customary international law expressed soldier's [sic!] standards which were born on the battlefield and not standards imposed upon them by dilettantes of a different discipline. Undoubtedly, the practicality of these rules led to their general acceptance which in turn was responsible for their codification. Such practical rules were understood and enforced.'[22]

Eckhardt here describes superior responsibility, as it was understood and applied before the Second World War, as an expression of customary international law. There are several documented cases predating the Second World War which concerned omissions by a commander similar to those now falling under the command responsibility doctrine. One of the cases was that against Captain Henry Wirz, who held the position of commander of a POW camp at Andersonville, Georgia, in the United States of America, in the 1860s. He was held responsible before a military commission in Washington for the mistreatment and killing of prisoners at the camp.[23] However, like many of the pre-WW II cases, the case against Captain Wirz did not charge the accused on the basis of command responsibility or a similar notion, but for 'combining, confederating and conspiring' together with others and for 'perpetration'. Only the circumstances of the case were such that if the accused were to be prosecuted today, the principle of

[20] The *Commentary on the Additional Protocols* mentions the fact that 'people were convicted for omissions' in post-WW II cases. The *Commentary* does not, however, specifically point to cases concerning civilians. See Pilloud, para. 3531.

[21] Consider the more elaborate discussion in section 6.2.1 *infra*.

[22] W.G. Eckhardt, 'Command Criminal Responsibility: A Plea for a Workable Standard', 97 *Military Law Review* (1982) p. 1, at p. 3.

[23] L. Friedman, *The Law of War: A Documentary History*, Vol. I (New York, Random House 1972) pp. 783-798.

command responsibility may be thought of as a basis for his responsibility.[24] While this and most other pre-WW II cases that dealt with acts and failures by superiors do not fit the exact concept of command responsibility and, therefore, do not provide direct proof of a customary international law standard, they do show that there was a general acceptance of the responsibilities of a commander in relation to his subordinates and that these responsibilities could become the subject of a criminal prosecution.

A case which has been identified as directly concerning an omission to prevent or punish was the case against Emil Müller before the Supreme Court of Leipzig.[25] In addition to other charges, Captain Müller was convicted of the charge of having 'tolerated and approved of' ill-treatment of a prisoner by his subordinates.[26] The legal provision on the basis of which this kind of behaviour could be prosecuted was Section 143 of the Military Penal Code, which read as follows:

> 'Wer als Befehlshaber einer militärischen Wache, eines Kommandos oder einer Abtheilung, oder wer als Schildwache oder als Posten eine strafbare Handlung wissentlich begehen läßt, welche er verhindern konnte und zu verhindern dienstlich verpflichtet war, wird ebenso bestraft, als ob die Handlung von ihm selbst begangen wäre.'[27]

Interestingly, this provision addressed several of the elements of the present command responsibility doctrine that are presently debated by judges and publicists. It specifically defines the *mens rea* required, it requires a duty to act and it defines the nature of the responsibility of the commander.[28]

Considering the accepted view that customary law should be 'looked for primarily in the actual practice and *opinio juris* of States',[29] this case and the national law provision applied provide evidence of state practice and some support for the view that command responsibility as it is applied today was included in customary law even before the Second World War. While neither a piece of legislation, nor a judicial decision, also the report presented to the Preliminary Peace Conference at Versailles by the Commission on the Responsibility of the Authors of the War and on the Enforcement of Penalties deserves to be mentioned as a source of custom.[30] The Commission in its report recommended the establishment of a tribunal which could prosecute:

---

[24] Among others, the post-WW II cases against *Hirota* and *Roechling* have been considered in the context of command responsibility, but differ from the present understanding of the doctrine, and would probably not lead to a conviction if tried on the basis of Art. 28 ICC.

[25] Judgement in the Case of Emil Müller, 30 May 1921, 16 *AJIL* (1922) p. 684.

[26] Ibid., p. 691.

[27] Militär-Strafgesetzbuch für das Deutsche Reich, Vom 20. Juni 1872. Original source: Deutsches Reichsgesetzblatt, Band 1872, Nr. 18, Seite 174-204. Cited source: <http://www.documentarchiv.de/ksr/1872/militaerstrafgesetzbuch_deutsches-reich.html> (accessed 1 September 2008).

[28] Compare this to the discussion in Chapter 5 *infra*.

[29] *Continental Shelf case* (Libyan Arab Jamahiriya/Malta), Judgement, 3 June 1985, ICJ Reports 1985, p. 13, at p. 29.

[30] Brownlie, pp. 6-7.

> '[A]ll authorities, civilian or military, belonging to enemy countries, however high their position may have been, without distinction of rank, including the heads of states, who ordered, or with knowledge thereof and with power to intervene, abstained from preventing or taking measures to prevent, putting an end to or repressing violations of the laws or customs of war.'[31]

The Commission advocated criminal liability both on the part of those who had actively ordered violations of the laws and customs of war, and of those who had failed to prevent or punish the perpetrators of such violations. It may be concluded that by the time the proceedings against alleged war criminals began, in the aftermath of the Second World War, the concept of holding a superior criminally liable for a failure to prevent a subordinate from committing a crime was certainly not internationally unknown.

Additional support for the customary law character of command responsibility before the Second World War can be found when considering how customary law is established. In the *Asylum* case[32] the ICJ considered that an important part of the recognition of a rule as customary law is that there should not be many instances where state practice is inconsistent with the customary rule. Where there is 'fluctuation and discrepancy' in the application of a rule, 'it is not possible to discern [...] any constant and uniform usage, accepted as law.'[33] Of the well-known cases concerning acts and omissions of superiors both in the pre- and post-WW II period there are no instances of explicit decisions that would go against the concept of command responsibility. The absence of such cases thereby supports the existence of command responsibility as a rule of customary law in the relevant period. In addition to that, it has been argued that, '[W]here there is no practice which goes against an alleged rule of customary law, it seems that a *small* amount of practice is sufficient to create a customary rule.'[34]

Albeit controversial because of their victors' justice character, the post-WW II cases, and the *Yamashita* case[35] in particular, confirmed the principle of command responsibility as an accepted basis for criminal liability. The United States Military Commission at Manila, before handing down the verdict, addressed the accused and said:

> 'The Commission concludes: (1) That a series of atrocities and other high crimes have been committed by members of the Japanese armed forces under your command against people of the United States, their allies and dependencies throughout the Philippine Islands; that they were not sporadic in nature but in many cases were methodically supervised by Japanese officers and noncommissioned officers; (2) That during

[31] Commission on the Responsibility of the Authors of the War and on the Enforcement of Penalties, Report Presented to the Preliminary Peace Conference, Versailles, 29 March 1919, reprinted in 14 *AJIL* (1920) pp. 95-154, at p. 121.

[32] *Asylum case* (Colombia/Peru), Judgement, ICJ Reports 1950, p. 266.

[33] Ibid., p. 277.

[34] P. Malanczuk, *Akehurst's Introduction to International Law*, 7th rev. edn. (London, Routledge 1997) p. 42.

[35] In re *Yamashita*, UNWCC, Vol. IV, pp. 1-96.

the period in question you failed to provide effective control of your troops as was required by the circumstances.'[36]

The Military Commission reasoned that the fact that Yamashita failed to provide effective control over his troops justified a finding of criminal liability.[37] Subsequent post-WW II cases, such as those brought before the Nuremberg Military Tribunals under Control Council Law No. 10[38] and before other military courts,[39] may have strengthened the customary law status of command responsibility and

---

[36] L. Friedman, *The Law of War: A Documentary History*, Vol. II (New York, Random House 1972) p. 1598.

[37] Ibid., p. 1597. The United States Supreme Court, considering the Application for leave to file a petition for a writ of *habeas corpus* and a writ of prohibition, confirmed that the law of war imposed an affirmative duty to protect prisoners of war and the civilian population and that an unlawful breach of that duty could lead to personal criminal responsibility. In re *Yamashita*, 327 US 1, pp. 14-16.

[38] See in particular the following post-WW II cases:
Judgements rendered by the Nuremberg Military Tribunals under Control Council Law No. 10:
The Hostages case, TWC, Vol. XI, pp. 1230-1319; in Friedman, Vol. II, pp. 1303-1343. The accused were, *inter alia*, charged as principals or accessories to the murder of large numbers of civilians in several countries. With regard to the main defendant, Field Marshal Wilhelm List, the military tribunal held that '[h]is failure to terminate these unlawful killings and to take adequate steps to prevent their recurrence constitutes a serious breach of duty and imposes criminal responsibility. Instead of taking corrective measures, he complacently permitted thousands of innocent people to die [...]. He cannot escape responsibility by a claim of a want of authority. The authority is inherent in his position as commanding general of occupied territory. The primary responsibility for the prevention and punishment of crime lies with the commanding general; a responsibility from which he cannot escape by denying his authority over the perpetrators.' Friedman, Vol. II, pp. 1305 and 1324.

The High Command case, TWC, Vol. XI, pp. 462-697; in Friedman, Vol. II, pp. 1421-1470. The main accused, Field Marshal Wilhem von Leeb, was acquitted of some and convicted of other charges relating to crimes committed by subordinates under his command. The judgement shows that the tribunal considered the various elements of command responsibility in relation to each charge without assuming responsibility based on authority. Considering the criminal responsibility of commanders of occupied territory for crimes committed by various agencies, the military tribunal held that such responsibility is personal and not unlimited. According to the tribunal, '[m]ilitary subordination is [a] comprehensive but not conclusive factor in fixing criminal responsibility. [...] A high commander cannot keep completely informed of the details of military operations of subordinates [...]. He has the right to assume that details entrusted to responsible subordinates will be legally executed. [...] Criminal acts [...] cannot in themselves be charged to him on the theory of subordination. [...] Criminality does not attach to every individual in this chain of command from that fact alone. There must be a personal dereliction.' Friedman, Vol. II, pp. 1449-1450.

Application of the command responsibility principle can also be found in the *Pohl* case, TWC, Vol. V, pp. 958-1163, in Friedman, Vol. II, pp. 1254-1280; the *Medical* case, Judgement, TWC, Vol. II, pp. 171-300; and the *Flick et al.* case, Opinion and Judgement, TWC, Vol. VI, p. 1187-1223, in Friedman, Vol. II, pp. 1281-1302.

[39] Cases selected by the United Nations War Crimes Commission:
Schonfeld and Nine Others, UNWCC, Vol. XI, pp. 64-73. The accused were charged with committing a war crime in that they were 'concerned in the killing of' members of various Air Forces. The case neither charged nor found anyone guilty on the basis of command responsibility. However, the military court did give recognition to the principle by finding that '[c]ommand responsibility might also arise, in the case of a person occupying a position of authority, through culpable negligence', where that person 'had reasonable grounds for supposing that his men were going to indulge in committing a war crime against their opponents [...] and he failed to take all reasonable steps to prevent such an occurrence.'

provided some clarification to the application of the doctrine. However, it should be noted that post-WW II tribunals have been severely criticised for their lack of concern for providing sufficient proof when claiming that certain rules constituted international customary law.[40]

Considering whether the command responsibility indeed constituted international customary law, the Trial Chamber of the International Criminal Tribunal for the former Yugoslavia (ICTY) in the *Čelebići* case referred to the *Medical* case,[41] the *Hostages* case,[42] the *High Command* case[43] and the *Toyoda* case,[44] all of which explicitly set out that superiors who had stood by or did nothing when subordinates were about to or had committed violations of the laws of war were

---

Abbaye Ardenne case, UNWCC, Vol. IV, pp. 97-112. This case, against a military commander, Kurt Meyer, both charged and convicted the accused, although not using that term, on the basis of command responsibility. The accused was held responsible for the killing of POWs, who had been shot by 'troops under his command'. The Canadian Military Court even specified which facts and circumstances were of importance for determining the responsibility of the accused: 'The rank of the accused, the duties and responsibilities of the accused by virtue of the command he held, the training of the men under his command, their age and experience, anything relating to the question whether the accused either ordered, encouraged or verbally or tacitly acquiesced in the killing of prisoners, or wilfully failed in his duty as a military commander to prevent, or to take such action as the circumstances required to endeavour to prevent, the killing of prisoners [...].'

Sakai case, UNWCC, Vol. XIV, pp. 1-7. The accused was a military commander in China during the war of 1939-1945, and 'one of the leaders who were instrumental in Japan's aggression against China.' On one charge, concerning war crimes and crimes against humanity, the accused was found to have incited or permitted his subordinates to commit certain crimes, among which were the murder of POWs and the rape of civilians. That this case was decided on the basis of command responsibility seems doubtful when considering the 'inciting' and 'permitting' as a basis for liability. These modes of liability are on the borderline between today's individual criminal responsibility and command responsibility. On the other hand, the tribunal in its findings said the following: 'That a field Commander must hold himself responsible for the discipline of his subordinates, is an accepted principle. It is inconceivable that he should not have been aware of the acts of atrocities committed by his subordinates. [...]. All the evidence goes to show that the defendant knew of the atrocities committed by his subordinates and deliberately let loose savagery upon civilians and prisoners of war.' This shows that in the opinion of the tribunal the accused was culpable under the command responsibility principle, but the basis for his conviction was formulated as 'inciting or permitting'.

Masao case, UNWCC, Vol. XI, pp. 56-61. The accused was a military commander in Borneo from December 1944. He was convicted, among other things, of having failed 'to discharge his duty as a commander to control the members of his command', which led to the killing of 33 prisoners 'on the orders of an officer who was under the command of the accused.' According to the accused he did not hear about the killing until after the hostilities had ended.

[40] See H.H.G. Post, 'The Role of State Practice in the Formation of Customary International Humanitarian Law', in I.F. Dekker and H.H.G. Post, eds., *On the Foundation and Sources of International Law* (The Hague, T.M.C. Asser Press 2003) pp. 129-147, at p. 132.

[41] *United States* v. *Karl Brandt et al.* (the *Medical* case), Vol. II, Trials of War Criminals before the Nürnberg Military Tribunals under Control Council Law No. 10 (Washington, U.S. Govt. Printing Office 1950) p. 186, at p. 212.

[42] *United States* v. *Wilhelm List et al.* (*Hostages* case) Vol. XI, TWC, 1230, 1303.

[43] *UnitedS tates* v. *Wilhelm von Leeb et al.* (*High Command* case) Vol. XI, TWC, 462, 512.

[44] *UnitedState s* v. *Soemu Toyoda*, Official Transcript of Record of Trial, p. 5006.

to be held responsible.[45] According to the United States Military Tribunal in the *Medical* case:

> '[T]he law of war imposes on a military officer in a position of command an affirmative duty to take such steps as are within his power and appropriate to the circumstances to control those under his command for the prevention of acts which are violations of the law of war.'[46]

The cases served to show the existence of case law accepting the principle of command responsibility, while not all cases had found the accused guilty on the basis of this doctrine.[47]

While not entering into a thorough comparative study of the existing national legislation on command responsibility, the *Čelebići* Trial Chamber, by way of example, mentioned a few provisions which in its view provided evidence of the international customary law character of the principle at the time of the Second World War.[48] In fact, the *Čelebići* Trial Chamber leaned on the findings by the United States Military Commission in the *Yamashita* case, according to which at least France, Luxembourg, China and The Netherlands between 1943 and 1947 had enacted legal provisions that made prosecution under the command responsibility doctrine possible.[49]

The need to prove the customary law character of the command responsibility doctrine in 1998 when the *Čelebići* judgement was rendered, was a consequence of the requirement set out in the report of the UN Secretary-General pursuant to paragraph 2 of Security Council Resolution 808 (1993), according to which:

> '[T]he application of the principle *nullum crimen sine lege* requires that the international tribunal should apply rules of international humanitarian law which are beyond any doubt part of customary law so that the problem of adherence of some but not all States to specific conventions does not arise.'[50]

Accordingly, when the ICTY for the first time assessed the responsibility of an accused on the basis of the command responsibility principle, it was up to the *Čelebići* Trial Chamber to confirm the applicability of Article 7,[51] and more specifically Article 7(3) of the Statute, as a rule of customary law. As Article 6(3) of the ICTR Statute sets out the same standards of responsibility, this provision

---

[45] *Prosecutor* v. *Zejnil Delalić et al.* (*Čelebići*), Judgement, Case No. IT-96-21-T, 16 November 1998, para. 338.

[46] *United States* v. *Karl Brandt et al.* (the *Medical* case), Vol. II, Trials of War Criminals before the Nürnberg Military Tribunals under Control Council Law No. 10 (Washington, U.S. Govt. Printing Office 1950) p. 186, at p. 212.

[47] The Japanese Admiral Toyoda was acquitted on all charges. See *United States* v. *Soemu Toyoda*, Official Transcript of Record of Trial.

[48] *Čelebići*, TC Judgement, paras. 336-337.

[49] See In re *Yamashita*, UNWCC, Vol. IV, pp. 1-96, at pp. 87-88.

[50] *Report of the Secretary-General Pursuant to Paragraph 2 of Security Council Resolution 808 (1993)*, UN Doc. S/25704 (1993), reprinted in 32 *ILM* (1993) p. 1163, para. 34.

[51] Art. 7 ICTY, 32 *ILM* (1993) p. 1159.

equally reflects international customary law as it was at the time of the establishment of the Tribunals.[52]

It should be pointed out here that at present the customary law character of the doctrine of command responsibility in international law is generally accepted. However, Heintschel von Heinegg convincingly questions the customary law character of certain war crimes and the customary law status of the principle of individual criminal responsibility (including command responsibility), in particular in relation to non-international armed conflicts. In his opinion, too little evidence has been presented that supports such a finding, most significantly evidence of state practice.[53] At the same time, he recognises that the literature in the field has accepted the customary law status of individual criminal responsibility.[54]

An additional question that may be asked concerns the customary law status of the specific interpretation and elaboration of the doctrine. Since they began their work, the *ad hoc* tribunals have decided a large number of cases. They have had ample opportunity to develop the specific elements of this form of responsibility, and have done so. But has this particular interpretation of the doctrine also reached the status of customary law?

In this regard reference can be made to the same report by the Secretary-General of the United Nations, which set out the customary law requirement of the provisions applied by the ICTY. With respect to the content of the doctrine the Secretary-General held that:

> 'A person in a *position of superior authority* should, therefore, be held individually responsible for giving the unlawful order to commit a crime under the present statute. But he should also be held responsible for failure to prevent a crime or to deter the unlawful behaviour of his subordinates. This imputed responsibility or criminal negligence is engaged if the person in superior authority *knew, or had reason to know*, that his subordinates were about to commit or had committed crimes and yet *failed to take the necessary and reasonable steps to prevent or repress* the commission of such crimes or to punish those who had committed them.'[55]

These elements, which reflect those set out in the Commentary to the Additional Protocols, can be seen to correspond to the interpretation of the command responsibility by the *ad hoc* tribunals, in that they contain the requirement of a superior-subordinate relationship, the knowledge requirement and an element of the failure to prevent or punish the subordinates. As will be seen further on in this study, these elements are also subject to various possible interpretations. In its customary law study (ICRC study), the International Committee of the Red Cross (hereafter, ICRC) 'sought to analyse issues in order to establish what rules of customary international law can be found inductively on the basis of State prac-

---

52 Art. 6 ICTR, 33 *ILM* (1994) p. 1598.

53 Heintschel von Heinegg, pp. 27-47. See also Mettraux, pp. 22-23.

54 Ibid., p. 34.

55 *Report of the Secretary-General Pursuant to Paragraph 2 of Security Council Resolution 808 (1993)*, UN Doc. S/25704 (1993), reprinted in 32 *ILM* (1993) p. 1163, para. 56.

tice' in relation to a certain issue.[56] Based on the Additional Protocols, case law from the *ad hoc* tribunals, the statutes of these tribunals and the Special Court for Sierra Leone (SCSL), military manuals from various states and national case law, the ICRC study sets out that the interpretation of the command responsibility principle as included in customary law covers at least five points: i) Civilian command authority; ii) Commander/subordinate relationship; iii) The commander/superior knew, or had reason to know; iv) Investigation and reporting; and v) Necessary and reasonable measures.[57] These points will be explained and elaborated in section 2.4.2 of this chapter. Based on the findings of the ICRC study, there seems to be support for the view that all these points form part of the command responsibility principle as a rule of customary international law.[58]

On the other hand, it is recognised that because of the increase in the codification of international law ever since the Second World War, the role of international customary law has decreased.[59] Now that a period of more than ten years has passed since the establishment of the *ad hoc* tribunals, and the doctrine has been further developed and defined in many cases, and its existence has not been denied, the practical importance of defining the elements of superior responsibility in customary law prior to the decisions by the *ad hoc* tribunals has diminished. Codification of the doctrine in several Statutes, those of the ICC, ICTY, ICTR and the SCSL, reduces the relevance as perpetrators of war crimes subsequent to the establishment of these tribunals could probably not claim the lack of law regarding superior responsibility. Nevertheless, as investigations into and trials concerning crimes committed in the 1980s and even earlier still take place,[60] the question remains of some interest.

2.3.2 **From ICC until the present**

The ICC Statute introduced a provision on command responsibility that slightly differs from those existing before its creation. While the provision is more elaborate than earlier ones, there is no specification for Article 28 like the 'Elements of Crimes' document, which set out the more specific interpretation of the crimes under the jurisdiction of the Court.[61] It has been argued that because the ICC

---

[56] J.-M. Henckaerts and L. Doswald-Beck, *Customary International Humanitarian Law*, Vol. I (Cambridge, Cambridge University Press 2005) p. xxx.

[57] Ibid., pp. 561-563.

[58] It may be pointed out that one study, such as the ICRC study, should not be considered as proof of the status of a doctrine as a rule of international customary law. With regard to certain rules, however, a study may present documents showing state practice and *opinio juris*, which together seem to justify the customary law label given to the rule.

[59] A. Cassese, *International Law*, 2nd edn. (Oxford, Oxford University Press 2005) p. 165.

[60] Examples of such recent or still ongoing investigations are those concerning crimes committed by the former leader of Iraq, Saddam Hussain, and by the Khmer Rouge in Cambodia (then Democratic Kampuchea) in the 1970s. On some aspects of these trials, see S. Alford, 'Some Thoughts on the Trial of Saddam Hussein: The Realities of the Complementarity Principle', 8 *International Criminal Law Review* (2008) pp. 463-475; and R. Skilbeck, 'Defending the Khmer Rouge', 8 *International Criminal Law Review* (2008) pp. 423-445.

[61] Elements of Crimes, ICC-ASP/1/3(part II-B), 9 September 2002.

Statute has only been specified in relation to the crimes under its jurisdiction, in the separate Elements of Crimes document, there is 'room for interpretation' concerning the specific elements of 'liability by omission', or command responsibility.[62] For its exercise of jurisdiction, the ICC is to apply the ICC Statute as its primary source.[63] For the purposes of command responsibility, the Court should apply the principle as laid down in Article 28 of the Statute, but because of the lack of elaborated elements in the Statute, its provisions are insufficient.

But how much room for interpretation will there be? The Court will not only be dependent on the space provided by the lack of specific elements provided in the Statute, but also on the interpretative possibilities that are left when taking other sources of law into account. According to Article 21 ICC the Court should apply:

> '(b) In the second place, where appropriate, applicable treaties and the principles and rules of international law, including the established principles of the international law of armed conflict;'

As concluded above, the existing treaty provisions do not provide any guidance as to the specific interpretation of the doctrine. The Court will then have to turn to international customary law, where such rules can be of assistance.

The previous section showed that at least the ICRC Study found certain elements, or 'points', of the command responsibility doctrine to have become part of customary international humanitarian law. If the ICRC study is correct in its findings regarding the customary law status of command responsibility, these elements should be taken into account when applying the doctrine. Not doing so would be a breach of international customary law. However, the restriction that would be put on the Court as a consequence of these 'points' established as customary law, is probably marginal. The points mentioned are rather fundamental for the existence of the principle and can be found in Article 28 ICC. Thus, from the point of view of interpretation by the Court, any nuance to the elements would anyway be made on an even higher level of specification than that included in the elements of the ICRC Study. This is proven by the remaining challenges which the doctrine faces, among which is the application of the doctrine in relation to civilian superiors. As regards the 'room for interpretation' left for the Court, it will have to apply the elements that are both included in the formulation of Article 28 and correspond to those mentioned in the ICRC Study, but it may formulate its own opinion on issues that are still unclear or controversial, and thus, by definition have not become part of international customary law.

That being said, will customary law still have a role of importance to play after the codification of the doctrine in the ICC Statute? In order to identify the international rules applicable to a certain question, the primary source of law are international treaties. For the superior responsibility doctrine, the ICC Statute is the most relevant source. However, only States Parties to the treaty are bound by

[62] Van Sliedregt, p. 9.
[63] Art. 21 ICC (Applicable law).

these rules. Accordingly, for states not parties to the treaty it would be of interest to know whether the command responsibility doctrine as laid down in the ICC Statute reflects the current rule of international law because of its status as customary law. These states that are not parties to the treaty could be bound by the rules on command responsibility contained in the ICC Statute if the treaty has become customary law or if the command responsibility provision is said to be an expression of customary law or is intended to express a rule of customary law.[64] Taking into consideration the fact that several rather influential states, shown to be involved in events that may give rise to command responsibility, have not ratified the ICC Statute, the question is not just theoretical.

The Statute neither includes an explicit statement that the provisions included in it are an expression of customary law, nor was the Statute intended to be a codification of international customary law. Accordingly, the elements of command responsibility in present international customary law can be sought in the ICC Statute only if the provisions of the Statute have become customary law. The Statute was adopted by a majority of the states of the United Nations and has been ratified by more than the required number of States in order for it to enter into force. It might be argued that this fact gives the treaty a certain authority which in turn could mean that the provisions contained in the Statute might be considered as *opinio juris*. Certain States have also taken steps to implement the rules contained in the ICC Statute into their own legal system or have enacted new legislation corresponding to the provisions in the Statute,[65] expressing state practice. The acceptance and application of the provision might or might not be of such a degree as to express customary law.

It is worth noting, however, that also and in particular the international tribunals have rendered decisions, the arguments of which may have or are becoming expressions of international customary law. As long as the ICC has not applied the provisions included in its Statute, these are the only judicial decisions based on provisions of customary law. However, the provisions on command responsibility in the Statutes of the *ad hoc* tribunals differ from those in the ICC Statute. This means that in fact two different interpretations of the same doctrine may exist at the same time and seemingly both express the doctrine under international customary law.[66] To a state not party to the ICC Statute which has to comply with international customary law, this situation does not seem satisfac-

---

[64] Malanczuk, p. 40.

[65] See, for example, the recently implemented legislation in the following states: the Netherlands, International Crimes Act [*Wet internationale misdrijven*], 9 June 2003, Stb. (Staatsblad: Bulletin of Acts, Orders and Decrees) 2003, No. 270; Germany, Code of Crimes Against International Law (CCAIL) [*Gesetz zur Einführung des Völkerstrafgesetzbuches*], 26 June 2002, *Bundesgesetzblatt Jahrgang* 2002, Teil II, Nr. 42, 2254; Finland, Government Act No. 55/2007 proposing changes to the provisions of the Penal Code concerning war crimes and crimes against humanity and some laws connected thereto (translation by MLN), Law enacted on 11 April 2008, Entered into force on 1 May 2008, Finlands FörfS. (Statutes of Finland) 212/2008.

[66] On another issue, but with similar implications, see P. Gaeta, 'The Defence of Superior Orders: The Statute of the International Criminal Court versus Customary International Law', 10 *EJIL* (1999) pp. 172-191.

tory. On the other hand, the fact that the ICC has not applied the provisions to a real case and rendered a judgement in such a case means that it is still not clear whether this difference could become a practical challenge or whether applying different standards to the doctrine is just a hypothetical problem.

2.4 Present definitions by international courts and tribunals

2.4.1 **Individual criminal responsibility**

The jurisdiction of the international or internationalised tribunals and courts established since 1993, starting with the ICTY, has been restricted to natural persons, and has been based on the basic principle in criminal law that a person is criminally liable, where both 1) the requirements of conduct, which is defined in law and not justified by law; and 2) the requirements of personal culpability are fulfilled.[67]

The requirements of individual criminal responsibility were set out in Article 7 ICTY and Article 6 ICTR:

> '1. A person who planned, instigated, ordered, committed or otherwise aided and abetted in the planning, preparation or execution of a crime referred to in articles 2 to 4 of the present Statute, shall be individually responsible for the crime.
> 2. The official position of any accused person, whether as Head of State or Government or as a responsible Government official, shall not relieve such person of criminal responsibility nor mitigate punishment.
> 3. The fact that any of the acts referred to in articles 2 to 5 of the present Statute was committed by a subordinate does not relieve his superior of criminal responsibility if he knew or had reason to know that the subordinate was about to commit such acts or had done so and the superior failed to take the necessary and reasonable measures to prevent such acts or to punish the perpetrators thereof.
> 4. The fact that an accused person acted pursuant to an order of a Government or of a superior shall not relieve him of superior responsibility, but may be considered in mitigation of punishment if the International Tribunal determines that justice so requires.'

According to this article, both the commission of a crime referred to in the Statute and the omission to prevent or punish the commission of a crime referred to in the Statute may lead to individual criminal responsibility. The omission set out in paragraph 3 reflects the command responsibility principle, which in the ICC Statute is included as a separate provision. The ICC Statute limited its provision concerning individual criminal responsibility to the modes of participation where the perpetrator either commits or in some other way participates in the commission of the crime. The omission to prevent or punish the perpetrators of a crime was left for Article 28.

[67] N. Jareborg, *Allmän kriminalrätt* (Uppsala, Iustus Förlag 2005) pp. 33 and 37-39.

Accordingly, Article 25(3) of the ICC Statute provides that the jurisdiction of the Court for holding persons individually responsible for crimes committed covers situations where a person:

'(a) Commits such a crime, whether as an individual, jointly with another or through another person, regardless of whether that other person is criminally responsible;
(b) Orders, solicits or induces the commission of such a crime which in fact occurs or is attempted;
(c) For the purpose of facilitating the commission of such a crime, aids, abets or otherwise assists in its commission or its attempted commission, including providing the means for its commission;
(d) In any other way contributes to the commission or attempted commission of such a crime by a group of persons acting with a common purpose. Such contribution shall be intentional and shall either:
  (i) Be made with the aim of furthering the criminal activity or criminal purpose of the group, where such activity or purpose involves the commission of a crime within the jurisdiction of the Court; or
  (ii) Be made in the knowledge of the intention of the group to commit the crime;
(e) In respect of the crime of genocide, directly and publicly incites others to commit genocide;
(f) Attempts to commit such a crime by taking action that commences its execution by means of a substantial step, but the crime does not occur because of circumstances independent of the person's intentions. However, a person who abandons the effort to commit the crime or otherwise prevents the completion of the crime shall not be liable for punishment under this Statute for the attempt to commit that crime if that person completely and voluntarily gave up the criminal purpose.'

While individual criminal responsibility in theory is clearly different from command responsibility, there are situations in which the distinction between the two is not easily discernible. By way of example, this can be the case where a superior, who is on or in the vicinity of the crime scene at the time crimes are being committed, remains inactive in relation to the perpetrators of the crime. Support may be found for the prosecution of the superior for encouraging the act as a mode of participation. Depending on the circumstances, the command responsibility doctrine may also be applied. The lack of consistency in the application of the command responsibility doctrine that is of interest to this study is in many cases caused by the proximity of some modes of liability to command responsibility. The modes of participation that are of specific relevance to the subject-matter of the present study will be discussed in more detailed in subsequent chapters, in particular in section 5.3.2 on Joint Criminal Enterprise and in section 5.3.3 on aiding and abetting.

2.4.2 Command responsibility

The Statutes of the ICTY and the ICTR include provisions of command responsibility that for the relevant parts are identical. These are included in Articles 7(3) and 6(3) respectively:

> 'The fact that any of the acts referred to in articles 2 to 5 of the present Statute was committed by a subordinate does not relieve his superior of criminal responsibility if he knew or had reason to know that the subordinate was about to commit such acts or had done so and the superior failed to take the necessary and reasonable measures to prevent such acts or to punish the perpetrators thereof.'[68]

The *Akayesu* Judgement[69] of the ICTR was the first decision in which one of the *ad hoc* tribunals had to address the command responsibility doctrine. In the two earlier decisions rendered by the ICTY, the *Tadić* Judgement[70] and the *Erdemović* Judgement,[71] the accused were not charged with command responsibility, nor did their positions make any considerations as to their liability under the command responsibility doctrine necessary. Tadić himself physically committed the crimes charged or assisted others in the commission of crimes. He was not considered to be acting from a position of superior authority.[72] The same is true for Erdemović, who carried out the orders of his superiors.[73] Accordingly, the *Akayesu* Trial Chamber had primacy in considering command responsibility as a basis for criminal liability before an international court for the first time since the Second World War.

Considering paragraph 3 of the provision on individual criminal responsibility, the Trial Chamber noted the various elements of command responsibility. It pointed out that there were differing views concerning the *mens rea* of the superior and concluded that command responsibility should not be a form of strict liability. In order to incur responsibility, there had to be at least very serious negligence on the part of the accused. The Trial Chamber did not state what exactly the threshold should be in this regard. The other point addressed by the Trial Chamber was the question whether Article 6(3) should be applicable to both civilian and military superiors. The application of the principle to civilians was considered 'contentious' and was to be considered on a case by case basis.[74] Accordingly, it did not set a precedent as to how the doctrine should be applied.

---

[68] Statute of the International Criminal Tribunal for the former Yugoslavia, Annex to the *Report of the Secretary-General pursuant to paragraph 2 of Security Council Resolution 808 (1993)*, UN Doc. S/25704, 3 May 1993, reprinted in 32 *ILM* (1993) p. 1159; and Statute of the International Tribunal for Rwanda, Annex to *Security Council Resolution 955 (1994)*, UN Doc. S/RES/955, 8 November 1994, reprinted in 33 *ILM* (1994) p. 1598.

[69] *Prosecutor* v. *Jean-Paul Akayesu*, Judgement, Case No. ICTR-96-4-T, 2 September 1998.

[70] *Prosecutor* v. *Duško Tadić*, Judgement, Case No. IT-94-1-T, 7 May 1997.

[71] *Prosecutor* v. *Drazen Erdemović*, Sentencing Judgement, Case No. ICTY-96-22-T, 29 November 1996.

[72] *Akayesu*, TC Judgement, paras. 714 et seq.

[73] *Erdemović*, TC Sentencing Judgement, paras. 10 and 14-15.

[74] *Akayesu*, TC Judgement, paras. 487-491.

In its legal finding the Trial Chamber found that there was an insufficient basis to hold the accused responsible under Article 6(3). In a few sentences the Trial Chamber considered the elements that had to be fulfilled in order to incur responsibility under the command responsibility provision. It noted that under Article 6(3) a superior-subordinate relationship was one of the fundamental elements of command responsibility. There was evidence that showed such a relationship between the accused and the *Interahamwe*, the armed local militia, but because this relationship had not been alleged in the indictment, the Chamber did not consider the responsibility of the accused under this provision any further.[75]

Looked at in a chronological order, the subsequent case decided by the *ad hoc* tribunals was the *Kambanda* case before the ICTR.[76] The judgement was based on a guilty plea by the accused, in which he admitted guilt under Article 6(3). The Trial Chamber refrained from elaborating on the interpretation of the principle and did not refer to the considerations of the command responsibility doctrine by the *Akayesu* Trial Chamber. Interestingly, the accused thus admitted to his being responsible on the basis of a principle which had not yet been explained or interpreted by either tribunal.

It lasted until November 1998 before the ICTY in the *Čelebići* case elaborated on the command responsibility doctrine and discerned its elements, which have to be met in order for the accused to be held liable. These elements were very similar to those identified in the Commentary to Article 86(2) of Additional Protocol I.[77] The elements as identified by the *Čelebići* Trial Chamber have subsequently been referred to by the Trial Chambers in all other cases that have dealt with superior responsibility, as well as by the Trial Chambers of the ICTR. The elements introduced in the *Čelebići* judgement, together with the elaborated interpretations in subsequent judgements, serve as a good reference to the present interpretation of the command responsibility doctrine by the international courts.

The essential elements were found to be the following:

> '(i) the existence of a superior-subordinate relationship;
> (ii) the superior knew or had reason to know that the criminal act was about to be or had been committed; and
> (iii) the superior failed to take the necessary and reasonable measures to prevent the criminal act or punish the perpetrator thereof.'[78]

The elements may best be divided into objective and subjective elements, often referred to as *actus reus* and *mens rea* respectively. The objective elements of command responsibility can be found in subparagraphs (i) and (iii) of the definition, while the *mens rea* is the knowledge requirement of the superior, as laid down in subparagraph (ii).

---

[75] Ibid., para. 691.

[76] *Prosecutor* v. *Jean Kambanda*, Judgement and Sentence, Case No. ICTR-97-23-S, 4 September 1998.

[77] Pilloud, paras. 3543-3547.

[78] *Čelebići*, TC Judgement, para. 346.

2.4.2.1 *Actus reus*

In establishing when and where a superior-subordinate relationship exists between the accused and the perpetrator of the relevant crime, the *Čelebići* Trial Chamber pointed to several factors relevant to this relationship. It was recognised that in order to establish a superior-subordinate relationship, the accused must have been in a position of authority.[79] What was not defined, however, was the level of authority that the superior needs to have in order to incur superior responsibility, if any.

The position that the accused occupied could be either one of formal authority or a position that officially had not been established, but could de facto exist in a situation where, for example, a conflict had caused the normal societal or hierarchical structures to break down or at least temporarily to cease being applicable. It was thus established that merely a lack of formal authority could not render the command responsibility doctrine inapplicable.[80] However, a de facto position is as such not enough to incur command responsibility, but has to be substantiated by showing that the superior exercised control over his subordinates. On the other hand, a similar qualification is required of the de jure superior, as it has been established that the fact that a person exercised authority formally does not suffice to prove command responsibility. The Čelebići Appeals Chamber stated that, 'In general, the possession of de jure power in itself may not suffice for the finding of command responsibility if it does not manifest in effective control, although a court may presume that possession of such power prima facie results in effective control unless proof to the contrary is produced.'[81] The further assessment that has to be made is, thus, whether the superior had actual ability or powers to control the perpetrators of the crime, or as the recognised standard now states 'effective control' over the persons committing the crimes.[82]

The *de jure – de facto* discussion is obviously closely related to the question whether also civilians may incur command responsibility.[83] As stated by the *Kordić* Trial Chamber: 'A formal position of authority may be determined by reference to official appointment or formal grant of authority.'[84] All military positions are usually clearly defined and follow a formal, hierarchical structure and, accordingly, a military commander will operate from a *de jure* position of authority. Where it is argued that a person exercised *de facto* superior authority, the person will have been a military official who had not formally been appointed to the position but because of the circumstances did have the authority and effective control over other persons. In the alternative, the *de facto* superior could be a civilian who in the specific situation had a position of superior authority from

[79] Ibid, para. 354.

[80] Ibid.

[81] *Prosecutor* v. *Zejnil Delalić et al.* (*Čelebići*), Appeal Judgement, Case No. IT-96-21-A, 20 February 2001, para. 197. See also *Prosecutor* v. *Dario Kordić and Mario Čerkez*, Judgement, Case No. IT-95-14/2-T, 26 February 2001, para. 418.

[82] *Čelebići*, TC Judgement, para. 378.

[83] See Chapter 4 *infra*, for a more detailed discussion.

[84] *Kordić and Čerkez*, TC Judgement, para. 419.

which followed his liability as a superior for crimes committed by his subordinates. While, as mentioned above, the Trial Chamber in *Akayesu* held that the application of the command responsibility doctrine to civilians was contentious, the *Čelebići* Judgement and subsequent decisions have determined that the rule that civilians can be held liable under the superior responsibility doctrine cannot be considered controversial. Support for this view was found in post-WW II jurisprudence.[85]

Article 28 of the ICC Statute on the responsibility of commanders and other superiors further confirms the present view that also civilian superiors may incur responsibility under the command responsibility doctrine. The ICC Statute distinguishes between military commanders and civilian superiors by dividing the article into two paragraphs, each provision dealing with one category of superiors. Nevertheless, both military and civilian superiors should be in a position of 'effective control', a notion that was also referred to in the *Čelebići* Judgement. However, Article 28 includes a qualification regarding the two groups of superiors. While the military commanders should exercise 'effective command and control', the other group needs to have acted from a position of 'effective authority and control'. The underlying idea seems to be the same as that applied by the *ad hoc* tribunals. Article 28 makes no explicit reference to *de jure* and *de facto* superiors, but determines the applicability of the article to '[a] military commander or person effectively acting as a military commander', which clearly enough expresses the possibility of *de facto* superiors being held responsible as superiors. The same is true for the second group of superiors, which is described as 'superior and subordinate relationships not described in paragraph (a).' This paragraph (b) creates a possibility to hold civilians, who have not been appointed to a formal position of superior authority, responsible as a superior for crimes committed by their *de facto* subordinates.

The other objective element of the definition elaborated by the *Čelebići* Trial Chamber stated that command responsibility would arise where the superior failed to prevent the crimes from taking place or failed to punish the perpetrators of crimes already committed. The fact that a person exercises superior authority over his subordinates means that he has an inherent duty to keep his subordinates from carrying out illegal acts and to take measures where they have done so, in order to maintain order and discipline. Further, with regard to the element of a failure to prevent or punish, the *Blaškić* Appeal Judgement drew the following, rather obvious conclusion: 'The failure to punish and failure to prevent involve different crimes committed at different times: the failure to punish concerns past crimes committed by subordinates, whereas the failure to prevent concerns future crimes of subordinates.'[86] The issue at stake was whether the failure to punish could be 'a separate head of responsibility' or whether it was a sub-category of the superior's liability for failure to prevent. The Appeals Chamber considered that a superior could be held responsible solely on the basis of his failure to

[85] *Čelebići*, TC Judgement, paras. 359-363.

[86] *Prosecutor* v. *Tihomir Blaškić*, Appeal Judgement, Case No. IT-95-14-A, 29 July 2004, para. 83.

punish and that finding him so responsible was not dependent on whether he had also failed to prevent crimes.[87]

The *Čelebići* Trial Chamber pointed out that a failure on the part of the superior cannot amount to strict liability, liability in all cases regardless of whether the superior in fact had a possibility to prevent or punish the crimes.[88] The definition recognises that a superior can be expected to take the necessary and reasonable measures to prevent or punish crimes by his subordinates. Accordingly, in the opinion of the *Blaškić* Trial Chamber, 'it is a commander's degree of effective control, his material ability, which will guide the Trial Chamber in determining whether he reasonably took the measures required either to prevent the crime or to punish the perpetrator.'[89] It has also been recognised that a determination *in abstracto* of the meaning of the terms 'necessary' and 'reasonable' is not desirable and should be done separately for each case.[90]

With regard to this specific issue, the case law of the *ad hoc* tribunals has developed in a different direction compared to the Draft Code of the ILC, which suggested that the responsibility of a superior should be restricted to situations where the superior had the 'legal competence to take measures.'[91] The cases before the ICTY referred to above established that where the superior had the ability, be it informal, to prevent or punish, there should not be a threshold to holding a superior liable for his failure to take measures. The ICC Statute, on the other hand, corresponds to the definitions of the *ad hoc* tribunals in this regard, referring to necessary and reasonable measures without mentioning the legal competence of the superior.

2.4.2.2 *Mens rea*

Liability under the command responsibility doctrine as interpreted by the *Čelebići* Trial Chamber arises only where the superior knew or had reason to know that his subordinates were going to or had committed crimes.

i) Actual knowledge

There seems to be little controversy around the knowledge requirement of the definition, as far as the actual knowledge of the superior is concerned. It has been broadly recognised that the evidence that the superior knew about crimes being planned or crimes having been committed can be both direct and circumstantial. A list of the indicia that may be used to establish that the superior knew of the crimes, drawn up by the Commission of Experts Established pursuant to Security

---

[87] Ibid., paras. 78-85.
[88] *Čelebići*, TC Judgement, para. 383.
[89] *Prosecutor* v. *Tihomir Blaškić*, Judgement, Case No. IT-95-14-T, 3 March 2000, para. 335.
[90] *Čelebići*, TC Judgement, para. 394.
[91] Draft Code of Crimes Against the Peace and Security of Mankind, UN GAOR, 51st Sess., Supp. No. 10, UN Doc. A/51/10 (1996), pp. 38-39.

Council Resolution 780 (1992) in its Final Report,[92] was applied by the *Čelebići* Trial Chamber and was referred to in several other cases.[93] At the same time, the *Čelebići* Judgement followed the Final Report also in concluding that there cannot be absolute responsibility on the part of the superior and, accordingly, if there is no direct evidence of the knowledge, it may not be presumed but must be based on circumstantial evidence. However, the Trial Chamber in the *Aleksovski* Judgement held that, '[A]n individual's superior position *per se* is a significant indicium that he had knowledge of the crimes committed by his subordinates.'[94] This supports the view that although the superior position alone is not enough to prove the superior's actual knowledge of the crimes, the evidence that will have to be brought forward in order to prove superior responsibility may vary depending on the position of authority and level of responsibility of the superior.[95]

The views expressed by the ICTY on the actual knowledge of the superior reflect the present interpretation of the issue. The ICC definition lacks further provisions on how actual knowledge by the superior should be established.[96]

ii) Imputed knowledge

The Statutes of the *ad hoc* tribunals have clearly laid down that where the superior did not know about the crimes being committed, he can also be held responsible if he 'had reason to know' that crimes by his subordinates were going to be or had been committed. Nevertheless, the meaning of the 'had reason to know' has remained unclear in relation to other standards of knowledge, most significantly the 'should have known' standard, as laid down in Article 28 ICC.[97] Dif

---

[92] *Final Report of the Commission of Experts Established pursuant to Security Council Resolution 780 (1992)*, UN Doc. S/1994/674, 27 May 1994, Annex.

[93] The following indicia were listed in paragraph 58 of the Final Report:
(a) number of illegal acts;
(b) type of illegal acts;
(c) scope of illegal acts;
(d) time during which the illegal acts occurred;
(e) number and type of troops involved;
(f) logistics involved, if any;
(g) geographical location of the acts;
(h) widespread occurrence of the acts;
(i) tactical tempo of operations;
(j) modus operandi of similar illegal acts;
(k) officers and staff involved; and
(l) location of the commander at the time.
See references to the list in *Čelebici*, TC Judgement, para. 386; *Blaškić*, TC Judgement, para 307; and *Kordić and Čerkez*, TC Judgement, para. 427.

[94] *Prosecutor* v. *Zlatko Aleksovski*, Judgement, Case No. IT-95-14/1-T, 25 June 1999, para. 80.

[95] *Kordić and Čerkez*, TC Judgement, para. 428.

[96] In the only case in which the ICC has addressed responsibility under Art. 28, the *Bemba* case, Pre-Trial Chamber III did not at this stage examine the interpretation of the provision in any detail. See *Prosecutor* v. *Jean Pierre Bemba Gombo*, Decision Adjourning the Hearing pursuant to Art. 61(7)(c)(ii) of the Rome Statute, Case No. ICC-01/05-01/08-388, 3 March 2009.

[97] Van Sliedregt 2003, pp. 159-164.

fering views were presented in the judgements of the two *ad hoc* tribunals.[98] In particular with regard to this discussion it is worth keeping in mind the fact that the ICC Statute had been adopted before any of the judgements relevant to the superior responsibility discussion had been rendered. Although it is not clear what role the ICC Statute may have played in the decision-making process of the Trial Chambers, the judges were at least aware of the different definition in the ICC Statute from that applicable to the *ad hoc* tribunals in this regard.

The *Čelebići* Trial Chamber started out from the assumption that a superior may not have known of the crimes being committed by his subordinates. However, if he himself had remained blind to information which would have given him the knowledge, had he wanted to, the superior could in the opinion of the Chamber not be excluded from superior responsibility.[99] In order to establish a correct interpretation of the 'had reason to know' provision, consideration was given to Additional Protocol I, Article 86(2) of which provides that superiors can be held responsible 'if they knew or had information which should have enabled them to conclude in the circumstances at the time' that their subordinates were about to commit or had committed crimes. As interpreted by the Trial Chamber and confirmed by the Appeals Chamber, this provision should be understood to mean that:

> '[A] superior can be held criminally responsible only if some specific information was in fact available to him which would provide notice of offences committed by his subordinates. This information need not be such that it by itself was sufficient to compel the conclusion of the existence of such crimes. It is sufficient that the superior was put on further inquiry by the information, or, in other words, that it indicated the need for additional investigation in order to ascertain whether offences were being committed or about to be committed by his subordinates.'[100]

While not explicitly stated by the *Čelebići* Trial Chamber, the Appeals Chamber concluded that 'had reason to know' effectively means the same as 'had information which should have enabled them to conclude', the latter however expressing the content of the provision more clearly.[101] The *Kordić* Trial Chamber concluded that therewith the stricter 'should have known' standard was rejected.[102] While both the *Blaškic* Trial Chamber[103] and the ICTR Trial Chambers in the *Akayesu*[104] and *Kayishema and Ruzindana*[105] Judgements expressed views differing from that expressed in the *Čelebići* Judgement, it seems that the Appeals Chambers decision in *Čelebići* settled the 'had reason to know' issue.

---

[98] See the discussion in section 5.2.1 *infra*.
[99] *Čelebići*, TC Judgement, para. 387.
[100] Ibid., para. 393.
[101] *Čelebići*, AC Judgement, para. 232.
[102] *Kordić and Čerkez*, TC Judgement, para. 435.
[103] *Blaškić*, TC Judgement, paras. 309-332.
[104] *Akayesu*, TC Judgement, para. 489.
[105] *Prosecutor* v. *Clément Kayishema and Obed Ruzindana*, Judgement, Case No. ICTR-95-1-T, 21 May 1999, para. 227.

With regard to the relationship between the 'had reason to know' standard pursuant to Article 6(3)ICTR/7(3)ICTY and the 'should have known' standard, as applicable to military commanders under Article 28 ICC, it might be of help to sum up and highlight some of the views expressed by the *ad hoc* tribunals when discussing the *mens rea* standard: 1) The 'should have known' standard equals negligence;[106] 2) the 'had reason to know' standard does not equal negligence;[107] and 3) 'criminal negligence is not a basis of liability in the context of command responsibility.'[108] Considered together, these findings do not provide any clarity about the two standards. If negligence cannot result in liability under the command responsibility doctrine and if the 'should have known' standard expresses negligence, only 'had reason to know' or a higher standard could be used in cases concerning command responsibility. If this is the case and the ICC standard for military commanders is considered stricter, i.e., setting a lower threshold for a conviction, than the 'had reason to know' standard,[109] the ICC will have to define what the 'should have known' standard implies for the purposes of the cases before the court. In *Blaškic* support was expressed for the application of the 'should have known' standard and the *Kayishema and Ruzindana* Judgement favoured a distinction between military and other superiors. While these judgements favoured an interpretation that would be closer to the ICC provision, the prevailing interpretation by the *ad hoc* tribunals shows that the relationship between the 'had reason to know' standard and that of the ICC provision is not yet settled. A useful comparison between the 'had reason to know' standard in comparison with the knowledge standard of the ICC Statute – 'knew, or consciously disregarded information which clearly indicated' – as applicable to other superiors, i.e., civilian superiors, has not been made by the *ad hoc* tribunals.

2.5 Conclusion

The present chapter has laid out the basis for the principle on command responsibility both in treaty law and as an accepted doctrine in international law. As the codification of the principle took place relatively recently, in Additional Protocol I, the application of the principle has relied heavily on the customary law character of the doctrine. Several post-WW II cases, most importantly the *Yamashita* case, convicted superiors on the basis of the command responsibility principle before the principle had been codified by international treaty. Some of the cases show that the elements that form part of the doctrine today were applied in a similar manner to the application at the *ad hoc* tribunals. On the other hand, in relation to other cases that have been referred to as proving the application of command responsibility in the period after the Second World War, it is doubtful

[106] *Blaškić*, TC Judgement, para. 332.
[107] *Čelebići*, AC Judgement, para. 241.
[108] *Prosecutor* v. *Sefer Halilović*, Judgement, Case No. IT-01-48-T, 16 November 2005, para. 71.
[109] See the criticism of this standard by Mettraux, in Mettraux, pp. 210-213.

whether brought before an international court or tribunal today, these accused would or should even be prosecuted under the command responsibility provision.

While there is an ongoing debate regarding the emergence of international customary law, in particular concerning rules of international humanitarian law,[110] the *ad hoc* tribunals accepted the customary law status of the command responsibility principle, at the same time confirming the applicability of the doctrine under the jurisdiction of these tribunals. The constitutive elements of the principle as defined in the *Čelebići* case were essentially the same as those formulated in the Commentary to the Additional Protocols, and as there seems to be no disagreement as to the necessity of these elements for the application of the command responsibility principle, it is likely that also these elements are part of international customary law. Establishing the superior-subordinate relationship, the *mens rea* and the failure to prevent or punish the perpetrators of the crimes have shown to be essential for the existence of the command responsibility doctrine as a basis for criminal liability.

Herewith the basis is set for a further elaboration of more specific aspects of the application of the doctrine in the following chapters. While there is agreement among those presently and previously applying the principle as to its most fundamental elements, the existing treaty provisions, customary law and case law have still not reached the stage of general agreement in relation to certain aspects of its application.

[110] See the following articles as contributions to this debate: T. Meron, 'The Geneva Conventions as Customary Law', 81 *AJIL* (1987) pp. 348-370; M. Koskenniemi, 'The Pull of the Mainstream', 88 *Michigan Law Review* (1990) pp. 1946-1962; Heintschel von Heinegg, pp. 27-47.

Chapter 3
Command Responsibility in Armed Conflict

3.1 Introduction

It is generally recognised that there are two forms of command responsibility resulting in criminal liability, both mentioned in the previous chapter. The first form of responsibility is the direct responsibility of superiors for orders to commit breaches of international law.[1] The second form is the superior responsibility *strictu sensu*, the criminal responsibility for omitting to prevent or punish subordinates who are about to commit or who have committed crimes under international law. Both forms of command responsibility, however, originate from the general responsibility of command inherent in the positions of military commanders within the armed forces and their duty to control their troops.

In his widely consulted article on command responsibility from 1973, Parks submitted that looked at from a historical perspective, the concept of command responsibility developed along two paths, one covering the general responsibility of command, just mentioned, and another path encompassing the criminal responsibility of the commander. At the same time he made an interesting submission, stating that either '(a) the natural development of the former would lead to inevitable inclusion of the latter' or '(b) there was in fact an intertwining of the development of the two from the outset.'[2] He further submitted that, '[T]he development of an international standard was incidental in nature, occurring only where states manifested such conduct as to make it apparent that no satisfactory municipal standard was to be applied, and the other parties to the conflict were in a position to impose what was considered to be an appropriate international standard on culpable commanders of the offending state.'[3]

Although Parks did not go into an analysis of what exactly is meant by this general responsibility of command, in the conclusion to his article he noted that, '[A]ccepting the position of commander, an officer accepts massive responsibility – responsibility to see that his troops are fed, clothed, and paid; responsibility for their welfare, morale and discipline; responsibility for his unit's tactical training and proficiency; responsibility for close coordination and cooperation with adjacent and supported or supporting units; and responsibility for accomplishment

[1] This form of superior responsibility has been mentioned both in international case law and by international legal scholars. See *Čelebići*, TC Judgement, para. 333; and L. Zegveld, *Armed Opposition Groups in International Law: The Quest for Accountability* (Ph.D. Dissertation, Utrecht University 2000) p. 229.

[2] Parks, pp. 1-104, at p. 2.

[3] Ibid., pp. 2-3.

of his mission.' Almost ten years later Eckhardt asked what 'command criminal responsibility' is, and pointed out that this term refers specifically to the criminal responsibility of the commander. Most importantly, he noted that it is not the same as the general responsibility of command, referring to Parks.[4] These authors, both of them military officers, argued that there is this general responsibility of command that is certainly connected with 'command criminal responsibility' and is involved in the history of the command responsibility doctrine, but is a different concept with different implications for the commander.

As command responsibility is a doctrine under international criminal law, most of the literature only concentrates on the command responsibility that leads to criminal liability. Considering the fact that not much attention has been given to the concept of the general responsibility of command that does not involve criminal liability it is of interest to elaborate on this concept and to determine whether the acceptance of general responsibility of command as being a part of the command responsibility doctrine possibly influences the applicability of the doctrine. The thesis of the author is that the origin of the doctrine in general command responsibility explains why the command responsibility doctrine lends itself more easily to the prosecution of military commanders and why the applicability of the doctrine in relation to civilian superiors is limited.

The present chapter explores the general responsibility of command as a military concept. It refers to the concept as general command responsibility, to distinguish it from command responsibility *stricto sensu* – command responsibility for a failure to prevent or punish crimes by subordinates under international criminal law. For the purposes of establishing the meaning of general command responsibility, two concepts have to be defined – command and responsibility. First, the chapter discusses various aspects of the concept of command. Secondly, a distinction will be made between role responsibility and liability responsibility. The subsequent section elaborates on general command responsibility and the fact that it does not constitute liability responsibility. Then the moral component of command responsibility will be discussed. Finally, the link will be made between general command responsibility and command responsibility under international criminal law.

3.2 The concept of command

3.2.1 Introduction

According to ancient Chinese military thinking, war was to be appraised in terms of five fundamental factors, the first of which was moral influence. By moral influence was meant, '[T]hat which causes the people to be in harmony with their leaders, so that they will accompany them in life and unto death without fear of mortal peril.'[5] In order to attain such harmony, strict discipline was needed, and was therefore

[4] Eckhardt, p. 4.

[5] M. van Creveld, *The Art of War – War and Military Thought* (London, Cassell & Co 2000) p. 24.

considered as 'a basis for all military action.'[6] Strict discipline is the military virtue of an army, and in the words of Van Creveld: '[S]ince necessity is not for every private to judge, discipline is the general's way to impose necessity on his troops.'[7] In order to exercise the art of war, the armed forces need to be led by commanders who can enforce discipline. This fundamental principle has stayed throughout history, despite the development of technology and the changing strategies used to win wars. The fact that an army needs a structure of responsible command was not even altered by the change from war belonging to the province of art to war being considered as a science, from the end of the 19th century onwards.[8]

The size of the armed forces and the weaponry and technology used in battle have differed, but the logics behind having 'officers whose function is to lead or direct and men whose job is to kill and be killed'[9] have not changed, at least not with regard to states' armed forces. An exception to the hierarchical military structure was mainly offered by the medieval armies that were made up exclusively of 'equal' officers, knights, but at least in principle also these armies were commanded by a commander in chief.[10]

While the command structure as an established and efficient system is still recognised by state armed forces, it is increasingly recognised that in so-called 'new wars',[11] which are not fought as classic conflicts between states, the fighting units are less dependent on structure, discipline and chains of command.[12] In these 'new wars' the combating parties taking part in the conflict may, except for regular armed forces, be paramilitary organisations, mercenaries and local militias.[13] The less strict structures of such organisations are said to have changed the way wars are conducted and to have caused increasing numbers of violations against the laws of war.[14] Rather than having a clear chain of command, these organisations seem to be under the direct command of an individual, as opposed to a state or a political grouping.[15] That some authors refer to 'new wars' is by no means a statement that such conflicts constitute a novelty, but are rather referred to in these terms because they represent the typical, most frequent type of conflict of the last decades.[16] While

---

6 Ibid., p. 25.

7 Ibid.

8 M. van Creveld, *Command in War* (Cambridge, Harvard University Press 1985) p. 150. Although Van Creveld recognises that war is thought of as a science, he still talks about exercising the art of war, which shows that there is another element to war than the strictly scientific one. Ibid., p. 274.

9 Ibid., p. 50.

10 Ibid., pp. 49-50.

11 M. Kaldor, 'Old Wars, Cold Wars, New Wars, and the War on Terror', 42 *International Politics* (2005) pp. 491-498, at pp. 492-493.

12 H. Born and D. Verweij, 'Het hobbesiaanse karakter van zogeheten 'nieuwe oorlogen', 55 *Internationale Spectator* (2001) p. 26.

13 An example of a conflict in which all these groups took part in the fighting is the war in the former Yugoslavia. See Born and Verweij, p. 24.

14 Ibid., pp. 24-25.

15 Ibid., p. 24.

16 Kaldor argued that 'new wars' are not entirely new, as they show similarities with pre-modern war in Europe, but that they are new because they 'take place in the context of the disintegration of

the fighting units may be structured in a different way in these types of conflicts, this is not to say that command is completely absent.

For the purposes of this study in general and this chapter in particular, command as a unique phenomenon of military fighting units is elaborated. While the point of departure is command as a function of the regular armed forces, this is not to say that command must contain the same elements or features in all armed groups.

3.2.2 **Definition of command**

The assumption that a commander is a military officer who exercises command raises the question as to what exactly command means. A definition of command can be found in the Glossary of Terms and Definitions of the North Atlantic Treaty Organization (NATO Glossary), in which the term command has been given five different meanings:

1. The authority vested in an individual of the armed forces for the direction, coordination and control of military forces;
2. An order given by a commander; that is, the will of the commander expressed for the purpose of bringing about a particular action;
3. A unit, group of units, organization or area under the authority of a single individual;
4. To dominate an area of [sic!] situation;
5. To exercise command.[17]

It is the exercise of command, in conjunction with the authority vested in an individual of the armed forces for the direction, coordination and control of military forces that will be considered here. The exercise of command, as part of military conduct, means to lead a military organisation towards achieving a military goal.[18] Military conduct comprises many functions – manoeuvre, firepower, intelligence and military information, protection and logistics. The exercise of command is an additional function that links and integrates the other functions. Where this is successful, there will be more synergy in the conduct of the forces, which in turn means an increase in military power.[19] Thus, not only command, but effective command is essential for a successful operation, or for attaining the desired goal.[20]

The need for command depends on the complexity of the army and 'increases with the sophistication of the forces.'[21] Van Creveld has identified two main

---

states' as opposed to the old wars that 'were linked to the rise of the modern nation-state and were state-buiding.' See Kaldor, pp. 492-493.

[17] NATO Glossary of Terms and Definitions, available at <http://www.nato.int/docu/stanag/aap006/aap-6-2009.pdf>, p. 2-C-9 (accessed 2 July 2009).

[18] *Leidraad Commandovoering*, LD I (The Hague, Doctrinecommissie van de Koninklijke Landmacht 2000) p. 43.

[19] Ibid.

[20] *Militaire Doctrine*, LDP 1 (The Hague, Doctrinecommissie van de Koninklijke Landmacht 1996) p. 79.

[21] Van Creveld 1985, p. 6.

responsibilities of command, the first being the task to ensure the availability of food, sanitation and other necessities without which the army cannot operate. The second responsibility of command includes the 'gathering of information and the planning and monitoring of operations'; in other words, everything that is related to the carrying out of the assigned mission by the armed forces.[22]

The function of war that Van Creveld calls command consists of command, control and communications together.[23] In other words, the exercise of command is a process that includes several elements. While Van Creveld calls them command, control and communications, the NATO definition identifies direction, coordination and control as the relevant elements of the same process. The Dutch Army in *Militaire Doctrine* talks about direction, decision-making and control.[24]

Van Creveld has described the process of command as follows:

> 'There is, in the first place, the gathering of information on the state of one's own forces – a problem that should not be underestimated – as well as on the enemy and on such external factors as the weather and the terrain. The information having been gathered, means must be found to store, retrieve, filter, classify, distribute, and display it. On the basis of the information thus processed, an estimate of the situation must be formed. Objectives must be laid down and alternative methods for attaining them worked out. A decision must be made. Detailed planning must be got under way. Orders must be drafted and transmitted, their arrival and proper understanding by the recipients verified. Execution must be monitored by means of a feedback system, at which point the process repeats itself.'[25]

The same process is well-illustrated in *Militaire Doctrine* as consisting of three intertwined circles, all containing one of the elements. The commander is to ensure that action is taken or that his unit refrains from taking action, in order to reach the desired goal. He also motivates and leads subordinates towards taking action. At the same time he has to make informed decisions and control his unit.

3.2.3 **Levels and types of command**

In order to ensure an effective process of command, command is exercised on different levels. Four general levels of command have been identified, these being: policy command, strategic command, operational command and tactical command.[26] On the level of policy command, command is exercised by state leaders. Command on this level relates to the commission and withdrawal of the armed forces as well as to making policy decisions on the objectives aimed at. At the strategic command level, the highest military commanders draw up a plan to achieve the objectives set out on the policy level. Commanders belonging to the operational command level

---

[22] Ibid.

[23] Ibid., p. 1.

[24] *Militaire Doctrine*, pp. 103-104.

[25] Van Creveld 1985, p. 7.

[26] I. Bantekas, *Principles of Direct and Superior Responsibility in International Humanitarian Law* (Manchester, Manchester University Press 2002) p. 75.

are senior military officers who are responsible for the implementation of the military plan at the actual scene of the war. Commanders on the operational level give orders to commanders on the tactical command level, who in turn exercise direct command over the troops.[27]

The levels of command are sometime referred to using slightly different terms. The Dutch Army uses the term High Command for the highest and Battle Command for the lowest command level. These are said to correspond to strategic command on the one end and tactical command on the other. While differing from the earlier terminology, Battle Command means direct command on the level of the soldiers carrying out an operation.[28]

In addition to the general levels of command, there are a number of other types of command, which focus on the function exercised or a geographical area, rather than the level of command in terms of the hierarchy of the armed forces. These may overlap with the levels of command identified.

In particular on the operational and tactical command levels, the terms operational control and tactical control are also interesting. According to the NATO Glossary, control in this respect has the following meaning: 'That authority exercised by a commander over part of the activities of subordinate organizations, or other organizations not normally under his command, which encompasses the responsibility for implementing orders or directives. All or part of this authority may be transferred or delegated.'[29] As compared to command, control here involves a more specific, more limited authority than where the commander exercises command on the same level. Control is authority that is delegated to a certain commander.[30]

3.2.4 **Commanders**

While the perception of a 'commander' may have changed over time, there are studies that point to the '[c]ommonality of traits and behaviour' of military commanders, regardless of the period or place in which they operate.[31] According to an ancient description of a good commander, that is someone who is 'temperate, self-restrained, vigilant, frugal, hardened to labour, alert, free from avarice, neither too young nor too old, indeed a father of children if possible, a ready speaker and a man with a good reputation.'[32] All good characteristics combined in one man, seemed to be the ideal. This picture of an ancient commander does have some things in common with the ideal commander of today, although a number of the characteristics listed, like that of being a father of children, are not to be considered as requirements for a good commander today.

---

27 Ibid.

28 *Militaire Doctrine*, p. 105.

29 NATO Glossary of Terms and Definitions, available at <http://www.nato.int/docu/stanag/aap006/aap-6-2007.pdf>, p. 2-C-14.

30 *Militaire Doctrine*, pp. 83-84.

31 J. Keegan, *The Mask of Command – A Study of Generalship* (London, Pimlico 2004) p. 1.

32 Van Creveld 2000, p. 44.

Present-day commanders should, preferably, also have certain qualities: vision and intelligence, originality, insight and an ability to assess a situation,[33] intuition, initiative, integrity and exemplary behaviour.[34] The overarching quality is the commander's leadership quality. The way in which the commander acts and exercises his leadership has great influence on the morale of his troops and on the functioning of those troops in difficult, highly dangerous circumstances.[35] The commander should have the courage to take risks and resolute decisions, as military operations are characterised by being unique every time and by the lack of sufficient information, which would allow for the optimal decision. It is considered better to take a quick decision that may be risky than waiting for more information and ideal solutions.[36]

The commander exercises command at the various levels mentioned above. He makes the decisions and exercises control at his level. At the lower levels a commander might be able to do this on his own, but where the troops are larger in number or command is exercised at a higher level, the commander is assisted by staff.[37]

3.2.5 **Staff officers**

A significant distinction is that between military officers who issue direct orders and those belonging to the staff – commanding officers and staff officers. For an accurate picture of the difference between the two, the following summary of the structure of the armed forces is very illustrative:

> 'Armies generally adopt a hierarchical structure, divided horizontally into formations, e.g. army, corps, division, and so on. Each formation consists of a specific number of operational fighting units whose activities are directed and coordinated by particular headquarters (HQ). The formation commander, a general, commands the formation but generally delegates command of the headquarters to a deputy chief of staff. Various sections of the formation HQ assist the commander in making his plans and provide a variety of support to the fighting units in carrying them out. The commander of each of these sections is a member of the "staff". The term "staff" can have a narrow or broad meaning. The former refers to those senior officers who form the commanders' think-tank, while the latter covers the much larger group of people who work in the various departments that these officers head up. The staff is therefore the nerve-centre of the HQ.'[38]

Accordingly, staff can be divided into the broader concept of 'staff' and the narrower concept of 'staff officers'. In the past, when the concept of staff was still being developed, the division of labour between staff officers and commander,

[33] Dutch: 'inzicht en inschattingsvermogen'.
[34] *Militaire Doctrine*, pp. 117-120.
[35] Ibid., pp. 114 and 116-117.
[36] *Leidraad Commandovoering*, p. 50.
[37] *Militaire Doctrine*, pp. 121-122.
[38] Bantekas, p. 75 n. 25.

i.e., officers with 'line duties', was not that rigid, in particular where operations in the field were carried out.[39] Nowadays, the staff has an established position. A commander is assisted by staff in the command process at the control stage. The staff provides support in organising, directing and coordinating the troops about to or already carrying out an operation. It makes a contribution at the decision-making stage and in bringing about the plans made.

Staff officers in general do not have command authority, but using the wording of Keijzer: '[A]lthough they may not be authorized to intervene directly, staff officers have often so much power that in practice their advice has the weight of executive orders. Their rank, together with their position as a member of the commander's staff and the knowledge and the derived distinction inherent in that position, give them an authority which cannot be ignored.'[40] According to Keijzer, the fact that junior staff officers may sometimes issue orders in the name of their commanders to higher officers and communicate with members of superior staff, thereby bypassing the commander, implies that the principle of the unity of command has lost some of its importance. However, with regard to some operational functions, a linear command structure is still preferred.[41]

There are also examples of cases where it is difficult to establish the exact position of an officer as being a staff officer or an officer commanding a certain formation.[42]

3.2.6 The human factor in the command process

Command structures and the responsibilities at each stage can in theory be well-defined. However, to completely understand the process of command in warfare and the realities on the ground is less straightforward, in particular without practical experience of the armed forces. Keegan pointed out that warfare in one society may differ significantly from warfare in another society.[43] The differences have an impact on the traits and behaviour of the commanders,[44] and on the command process itself. There is the lack of very specific statistical data on the information flow within the command system.[45] Another, no less important reason, is the difficulty of grasping the information that is informally or tacitly communicated within the command system. In addition to that, there is the commander himself and the mental processes in his head that are unknown to the outsider, and there is 'the tone

---

[39] Van Creveld 1985, p. 141.

[40] N. Keijzer, *The Military Duty to Obey* (Amsterdam, Vrije Universiteit 1977) p. 40.

[41] Ibid., pp. 40-41. As an example of such an operational function, Keijzer mentions 'the officer on duty on the bridge of a warship'. While other officers may outrank him, only the commander of the ship is superior to him as long as he acts within the scope of his tasks. Ibid., p. 41.

[42] For example, in the *Halilović* case, the ICTY Trial Chamber was not able to clearly establish what the role of the accused was at a certain point in time. See *Prosecutor* v. *Sefer Halilović*, Indictment, Case No. IT-01-48-I, 12 September 2001, para. 1, and *Halilović*, TC Judgement, para. 111.

[43] Keegan, p. 1.

[44] Ibid.

[45] Van Creveld 1985, p. 262.

of voice with which a report is delivered, or an order issued; the look on a man's face, the glimmer in his eye, when handed this or that message.'[46]

Osiel has pointed out that, 'When the superior wants his troops to engage in atrocities, he has a strong interest in letting them get or appear to get out of his control, for their conduct can then no longer be easily attributable to him. He can accomplish this in many ways, such as by brutalizing them shortly before contact with the enemy, then letting their hostile emotions carry them away in what will appear to be the heat of combat.'[47] This illustrates the fact that command structures can be described and the responsibilities of the commander defined, but that the command process in reality is a human activity, which depends on the performance and the qualities of the persons taking part in it.

For historians who want to reconstruct past events and come to understand the outcome of an event, the human factor is, in a way, a hindrance. It is difficult to know exactly why certain events took place, because the reasons for certain decisions were only known to the commander himself or to persons within the command process. For international criminal tribunals which have to establish whether one particular military officer was responsible for certain acts, an understanding of the command process is essential. Problems occur in particular where an omission or permission on the part of the commander has to be established. Understanding the informal communication within the command system and the mental processes of the commander can be crucial, but is very difficult to establish.

The concept of command can be made even more complex if one considers the other factors on which the process of command is dependent. The effective exercise of command may depend on: the motivation of the men; the character of the conflict – conventional warfare, war on land, at sea, in the air; weaponry; forces in the field or at base; the level at which command takes place – tactical level to policy level; psychological factors – effective presentation of information within the command system.[48]

What is easily overlooked when considering the exercise of command is that the authority held by a commander, in combination with his personality and personal charisma, constitutes one of the critical factors that enable ordinary people to carry out their tasks in war, even where orders include killing.[49] The authority serves to make the soldier overcome 'an inner and usually unrealised resistance towards killing a fellow man'[50] and to ensure the carrying out of tasks in general. It is held that even if some human beings kill other human beings from time to time, the ordinary man, soldier, wants to avoid killing as much as possible.[51] According to Grossman,

[46] Ibid., pp. 262-263.

[47] M.J. Osiel, *Obeying Orders* (New Brunswick, Transaction Publishers 1999) p. 234.

[48] Van Creveld 1985, pp. 263-264.

[49] D. Grossman, *On Killing – The Psychological Cost of Learning to Kill in War and Society* (New York, Back Bay Books/Little, Brown and Company 1995) p. 143.

[50] Ibid., p. 29. The citation is a part of a quote by S.L.A. Marshall. Also Keijzer mentions 'the general inhibition against killing other human beings' as a value existing in most civilisations. This value is in sharp contrast to armed military action that expects the soldier to be prepared to kill and even to be killed. See Keijzer, pp. 32-33.

[51] Grossman, p. 87.

who based his findings largely on earlier research into the behaviour of soldiers in war, the soldier – the subordinate – in war is faced with a Catch-22 situation:

> 'If he overcomes his resistance to killing and kills an enemy soldier in close combat, he will be forever burdened with blood guilt, and if he elects not to kill, then the blood guilt of his fallen comrades and the shame of his profession, nation, and cause lie upon him.'[52]

The order by and authority of a commander constitute triggers to carry out an act which the subordinate in his private life would normally refrain from doing.[53] But most interestingly, it is not the position of authority, as such, that influences the subordinate. Grossman listed four subfactors that are crucial when an order that meets with moral or other resistance has to be carried out:

1. proximity of the authority figure to the subject, i.e., the subordinate;
2. respect for the authority figure;
3. intensity of the authority figure's demands; and
4. the authority figure's legitimacy.[54]

Where the leader is present, where the subordinates identify themselves with the leader and respect him, where the leader clearly communicates what is expected of the subordinates, and where the leaders expresses legitimate, lawful demands, the chances of obedience are the greatest.[55] Keegan came to a similar conclusion, his findings being based on research into successful military leadership in the past. According to him, there are five imperatives of command: the imperative of kinship, the imperative of prescription, the imperative of sanction, the imperative of action and the imperative of example.[56] Successful command is dependent on a bond of kinship between the commander and his followers; on the ability of the leader to speak directly to his subordinates, to raise their spirits and to inspire them; on the courage to impose sanctions; on the commander knowing when to act; and on the commander being present or sharing the risk that he imposes on others.[57]

It is not just the position of authority of the commander that makes the subordinates comply with orders to carry out violent acts, inherent in the conduct of war. The way he communicates, his personality and charisma will influence the decision of the subordinate/soldier and the whole command process.

---

[52] Ibid.

[53] Ibid., p. 143. The impact of authority on the willingness of people to inflict even lethal harm on other people was studied by Milgram. For a practical example of what impact authority can have on a solider, Milgram used an interview, published in the New York Times in 1969, in which a participant in the My Lai massacre explained how he was able to kill civilian men, women and children. See S. Milgram, *Obedience to Authority* (New York, Harper Collins Publishers 2004) pp. 179-189.

[54] Grossman, p. 144.

[55] Ibid., pp. 144-145.

[56] Keegan, pp. 315-338.

[57] Ibid.

3.2.7 Command and management

A comparison is sometimes made between command and management. A manager is someone who initiates and steers the activities of people within an organisation. He/she is a superior who makes decisions on the work that has to be done, how it is to be done and by whom. A manager should also be able to explain why something has to be done. The manager exercises direct authority over some of the employees, at the same time being dependent on the performance of the subordinate employees.[58] To this extent there are important similarities between the tasks and responsibilities of the civilian superior in a peace situation and those of a military commander.

The similarities, however, do not justify a comparison of command with management. Van Creveld has said the following on this issue: 'Although modern works on military matters are as fond of comparing command with management as their predecessors were of comparing war with science, management and command are by no means identical. Quite apart from the problem of motivation, the difference between them consists precisely in the greater uncertainty governing war, the most confused and confusing of all human activities.'[59] Managers are dependent on several external factors, such as the economic, demographic, technological and political environment in which the organisation operates.[60] Thus, a manager has to ensure the desired result despite some uncertainties. This uncertainty, however, cannot be compared with the uncertainties of war, as these come on top of the uncertainty that is present in all peacetime human activity. 'War is the realm of uncertainty; three quarters of the factors on which action in war is based are wrapped in a fog of greater or lesser uncertainty.'[61]

Comparing command responsibility with purely civilian activities is difficult for the same reason. One author considered that civilians are subjected to superior-subordinate relationships in the same way as servicemen are, in the tax authorities – taxpayer relationship, for example.[62] However, the issue of command is then not being considered. In the words of Van Creveld: 'For the exercise of command to be possible there must be somebody to obey orders.'[63] Although used in a different context, the same holds true here. If command is to be exercised, there has to be someone to give the order to. While the relationship between the tax authorities and taxpayers is certainly one of constraint, the taxpayer is not under command, nor subjected to the disciplinary measures only present in the armed forces. According to Holmes Armstead: 'The commander both assigns roles and duties as a command function and enforces criminal law upon the military personnel under his or her command. This is purposefully a powerful relationship and is in many ways

[58] D. Keuning and D.J. Eppink, *Management & Organisatie: Theorie en toepassing* (Groningen, Wolters-Noordhoff 2004) pp. 9-10.

[59] Van Creveld 1985, pp. 186-187.

[60] Keuning and Eppink, pp. 464-475.

[61] C. von Clausewitz, 'Ethics and Military Strategy', in G.M. Reichberg, H. Syse and E. Begby, eds., *The Ethics of War* (Malden, Blackwell Publishing 2006) pp. 553-561, at p. 557.

[62] Bantekas, p. 70.

[63] Van Creveld 1985, p. 50.

anathema to the constitutionally guaranteed individual liberty we so jealously guard through the many institutions of civil society.'[64]

A commander, unlike a manager, 'must be able to compel obedience in a fashion totally distinct from organizations recognized in civil society.'[65] The commander is faced with teaching and training soldiers to obey authority, including orders to kill other human beings.[66] However, the training of the subordinates and the obedience must not only serve the purpose of enabling the subordinates to carry out violent acts, but also of compelling the subordinates to refrain from acting, in particular acting in violation of the law. The commander has to be able to use his authority to make subordinates obey his orders not to commit crimes – subordinates who are trained to fight and kill, who may be subjected to fear for their lives, and who may look differently at the world, due to their war experience.[67] This constitutes a substantial difference as compared to the manager in a purely civilian peacetime superior-subordinate relationship.

That being said, there are organisations in which civilians are organised in hierarchical structures resembling that of the military. One example of such an organisation is the police. While the responsibilities of the police commander may correspond to those of the military commander more than those of the purely civilian manager, the most essential differences, still, are the situations in which they operate and, at least to a certain extent, their mandate and authority.

3.3 The concept of responsibility

Familiarity with the command responsibility doctrine presupposes the understanding of the kind of responsibility that is of concern in that specific context. The term 'responsibility', however, can be seen to cover a multiplicity of distinguishable 'senses', or in other words, the meaning of the term depends on the way and the context in which it is used.[68] There are several ways in which these 'senses' can be divided in order to distinguish what is meant by the term in various situations. Hart speaks of 'role responsibility', 'causal responsibility', 'liability responsibility' and 'capacity responsibility'.[69] For the purposes of the present study, the role responsibility and the liability responsibility deserve further consideration. Role responsibility will be explored more in detail in section 3.4 of this chapter. In short, role responsibility arises, '[W]henever a person occupies a distinctive place or office in a social organization, to which specific duties are attached to provide

[64] J. Holmes Armstead, 'The Chain of Command', in L. Rothfield, ed., *Antiquities under Siege – Cultural Heritage Protection after the Iraq War* (Lanham, Rowman & Littlefield Publishers 2008) pp. 117-124, at p. 120.

[65] Ibid.

[66] See section 3.2.6 *supra*.

[67] Keegan, p. 311.

[68] H.L.A. Hart, *Punishment and Responsibility* (Oxford, Clarendon 1968) p. 211.

[69] Ibid., pp. 211-212.

for the welfare of others or to advance in some specific way the aims and purposes of the organization.'[70]

First, however, attention should be paid to the meaning of responsibility and how it differs from liability, or as Hart calls it – liability responsibility.[71] More specifically, as the study concerns the doctrine of command responsibility, the general concept of responsibility in relation to *criminal* liability is of interest here.[72] It should also be mentioned that the relationship between the concept of responsibility and liability is explored from the point of view of the individual, not from the perspective of other entities, such as states or corporations.[73]

According to Duff: 'We should understand responsibility as a matter of being responsible (i.e. answerable) *for* something, *to* some person or body, within a responsibility-ascribing practice. Liability – to criminal punishment or to moral blame – is grounded in responsibility.'[74] In clarifying the distinction between responsibility and liability, Duff considers that, 'The relationship between responsibility and liability can be simply stated: responsibility is a necessary but not a sufficient condition of liability. I am liable to conviction or blame for *X* only if I am responsible for *X*; but I can be responsible for *X* without being thus liable.'[75] For the purpose of illustrating the correctness of this relationship, it is warranted to cite Duff's example:

> 'If I wound an assailant, this being the only way to ward off his unlawful attack on me, I have a justification for what I do – a moral justification that saves me from moral condemnation for injuring him, and a legal justification that should save me from a criminal conviction for wounding. In offering this justification, I do not deny responsibility for using violence on *V*, or for *V*'s wound. I admit responsibility for that action and its result, as something that I had reason not to do (for we always have reason not to use violence on fellow human beings, and to avoid acting in ways that will injure them). I thus admit that I must answer for my action and its result: I must answer morally to anyone whose business it is, and legally in a criminal court. But, I claim, I have an exculpatory answer: that my action was, in its context, justified as an act of self-defence.'[76]

To be answerable does not imply liability, but both Hart and Duff recognise that in some contexts and to some people responsibility and liability may be almost

---

[70] Ibid., p. 212.

[71] Ibid., pp. 215-222.

[72] Accordingly, in examining the concept of liability, the author will not consider other forms of liability, such as liability to pay taxes or liability to pay maintenance for one's children. See R.A. Duff, *Answering for Crime – Responsibility and Liability in the Criminal Law* (Oxford, Hart Publishing 2007) p. 19.

[73] See the discussion on state criminal responsibility in N. Reid, 'Bridging the Conceptual Chasm: Superior Responsibility as the Missing Link between State and Individual Responsibility under International Law', 18 *LJIL* (2005) pp. 795-828. For an example of the responsibility of states for international crimes, as considered by the ICJ, see T.D. Gill, 'The 'Genocide' case: Reflections on the ICJ's Decision in Bosnia and Herzegovina v. Serbia', 2 *Hague Justice Journal* (2007) pp. 43-47.

[74] Duff, pp. 15-16.

[75] Ibid., p. 20.

[76] Ibid., p. 21.

equivalent.[77] However, Duff explicitly advocates a distinction between the two notions, in order to recognise criminal responsibility – liability – 'as a special species of responsibility'.[78]

Concerning liability responsibility in relation to omissions, Ashworth explains why there is and why it is understandable that there is a certain amount of hesitation regarding such responsibility. Criminal law normally prohibits certain acts, which means that as long as one refrains from committing such acts, there will be no criminal responsibility.[79] There is usually no obligation to act. In relation to omissions, however, the criminal law imposes a duty to act.[80] That refraining from acting can lead to criminal responsibility seems to be the exception to the rule. According to Ashworth, there are three reasons as to why that exception should be maintained.[81] First, while a prohibition can be quite clearly defined, a crime of omission can only be defined in vague terms. Whether a failure to act constitutes a crime of omission will be more dependent on the circumstances of the case, which in turn will create more uncertainty regarding the legal obligations of persons. Secondly, because of the uncertainty, the prosecutorial discretion in such cases will be heavily relied on, which may be said to weaken the rule of law. The scarcity of cases concerning omissions in Swedish case law is said to confirm the prudence observed or hesitation by prosecutors in pressing charges in such cases.[82] The third reason for being careful when criminalising omissions is related to the duty to act that is imposed on a person and to the feeling of a 'moral distinction between acts and omissions.' These two factors led to a need for a greater justification for imposing criminal responsibility for omissions.[83] While there is a moral distinction between an act and omissions, this is not to say that omissions cannot be morally reprehensible. Usually omissions would be considered less serious than acts, but not necessarily without moral blame. The duty to act that an omission imposes is clearly considered as even more problematic. Normally a person is at liberty to 'pursue one's own ends'[84] and if a person is asked to do something, a recognition or

[77] Hart 1968, pp. 216-217; and Duff, p. 22.

[78] Duff, p. 36.

[79] A. Ashworth, *Principles of Criminal Law*, 5th edn. (Oxford, Oxford University Press 2006) pp. 45-46.

[80] Jareborg, p. 181.

[81] Ashworth, pp. 45-46.

[82] Jareborg, p. 186.

[83] Ashworth, pp. 45-46. Interestingly, the ICTR in the *Rutaganira* case (guilty plea) found that there could be participation in a crime against humanity through complicity by omission. The Trial Chamber pointed out that 'determining omission under Article 6(1) of the Statute is a more complex task than showing omission under Article 6(3).' In order to determine liability for an omission under Art. 6(1), the Chamber found it necessary to consider three factors: 1) 'Did the Accused have authority and did he choose to not exercise it?'; 2) 'Did the Accused have a moral authority over the principals such as to prevent them from committing the crime and did he choose not to exercise it?'; and 3) 'Was the Accused under a legal duty to act which he failed to fulfill?' The Chamber answered all questions in the affirmative, but clearly wanted to provide a well grounded finding where liability was based on an omission. See *Prosecutor* v. *Vincent Rutaganira*, Judgement and Sentence, Case No. ICTR-95-1C-T, 14 March 2005, paras. 61-84.

[84] Ibid., p. 46.

compensation will usually be expected in exchange.[85] Where an omission leads to criminal liability, this liberty of a person is restricted. As stated earlier, this thought is exceptional in criminal law, which normally imposes a duty on persons to refrain from acting in a certain way.[86]

In some situations, however, demanding action may be less intrusive than a prohibition of a certain act. Fletcher asked whether statutes that require an act are fundamentally wrong, and gave the example of laws prohibiting homosexual sodomy, on the one hand, and promoting a culture of safe sex, including an affirmative duty to use condoms, on the other.[87] It may be claimed that, if enforced, the law prohibiting an act intrudes more upon the liberty of an individual than the duty to act in a certain way.[88] The answer to Fletcher's question should arguably be no. While liability for an omission is exceptional in criminal law, there is not necessarily something fundamentally wrong about it.

One way of limiting the possibilities of criminalising omissions has been to limit this liability to certain categories of people – to those who hold a position in which other people are particularly dependent on their good care or in which they most obviously can avoid danger or crime. This idea that there is a duty to act in certain positions is recognised in several national systems and is known by the term *Garantenstellung*.[89] It is, however, not always clearly defined which categories of people could be in such a position or which omissions can constitute a crime. The hesitation to hold those to whom even *Garantenstellung* applies liable for omissions is proven by the fact that considerably lesser sentences are imposed for crimes of omission in national legal systems.[90]

The idea of *Garantenstellung* proves the proximity of Hart's role responsibility to liability responsibility. While role responsibility can be either moral or legal, or neither of the two, by applying the *Garantenstellung* theory to people with role responsibility, an omission on their part may lead to liability responsibility. This thought is interesting when considering how the responsibilities of commanders (general command responsibility) relate to liability under the command responsibility doctrine, which will be discussed in the following sections.

3.4 'General command responsibility' as role responsibility

Although admittedly a generalisation, Hart expressed the view that, '[W]henever a person occupies a distinctive place or office in a social organization, to which specific duties are attached to provide for the welfare of others or to advance in some specific way the aims or purposes of the organization, he is properly said

[85] Jareborg, p. 181.

[86] Ibid.

[87] G.P. Fletcher, *Basic Concepts of Criminal Law* (New York, Oxford University Press 1998) p. 48.

[88] Ibid.

[89] C. Roxin, *Täterschaft und Tatherrschaft*, 7th edn. (Berlin, De Gruyter 2000) pp. 458-526.

[90] Jareborg, pp. 194-195.

to be responsible for the performance of these duties, or for doing what is necessary to fulfil them. Such duties are a person's responsibilities.'[91] This definition of role responsibility corresponds to the responsibilities of military commanders. By accepting a position of command, the military officer is bound by certain obligations that are set out by the armed forces for which he engages in military activities. Inherent in his position as a commander is the authority to demand certain action from his subordinates. In short, it is his duty to exercise command. As explored above, to command is to carry out a number of tasks, to direct, to coordinate and to control his subordinates or the task that has to be performed in order to attain the expected goal.[92]

A military commander holding a certain position of command is aware that the justification for his position is the general command responsibility that the person accepts when embarking upon his or her duties. Significant in respect of general command responsibility is that it cannot be delegated. A certain position carries with it a certain responsibility within the military organisation. While a commander may give certain responsibilities to his subordinates, who may themselves be commanders at a lower level, the delegation of his own responsibilities would mean that the responsibility moves from that specific superior to someone at a lower level. That is not the case.[93] It is this basis for leadership within the armed forces that explains why command criminal responsibility may, at least theoretically, be applied at all levels, not just at the lowest or the highest level.

General command responsibility comes with the position to which a commander is appointed or otherwise acquires. But what makes commanders comply with their general command responsibility? Does general command responsibility, comprising of the duty to exercise command and its possible consequences, have its origin in a legal norm or are there other motives for complying with a commander's general command responsibility?

The explanatory memorandum to the Dutch International Crimes Act notes that the origin of the responsibility/liability of superiors is to be found in the laws of war, but also in the fact that military commanders bear a great responsibility for the behaviour of soldiers under their command, including a corresponding supervisory task and authority in relation to their subordinates.[94] This observation points to the issue at stake in the present section. The history of command responsibility as a part of the laws of war is well-documented. But as the explanatory memorandum rightly points out, the general responsibility of commanders is a fact, a given. Command-

---

[91] Hart 1968, p. 212.

[92] See section 3.2 *supra*.

[93] C.P.M. van Egmond, 'Leiderschap in the praktijk', in Th.A. van Baarda, A.H.M. van Iersel and D.E.M. Verweij, eds., *Praktijkboek Militaire Ethiek* (Budel, DAMON 2004) pp. 49-71, at p. 70.

[94] See the Explanatory Memorandum to the Dutch International Crimes Act [Regels met betrekking tot ernstige schendingen van het international humanitair recht (Wet internationale misdrijven), Memorie van toelichting], Tweede Kamer, vergaderjaar 2001-2002, 28337, nr. 3, p. 30 ('De figuur van de aansprakelijkheid van de meerdere vindt zijn oorsprong in het oorlogsrecht en in het gegeven dat militaire bevelhebbers een grote verantwoordelijkheid dragen voor – en een daarmee corresponderende toezichthoudende taak en bevoegdheid hebben ten aanzien van – het gedrag van de aan hun bevel onderworpen militairen'.).

ers have a duty to exercise command and acknowledge that they may be blamed if something goes wrong. That is how it is and how it always has been. General command responsibility is essential for the exercise of effective command, and as mentioned previously, effective command is invaluable for attaining a military goal.[95]

Parks argued that, 'Command has always imposed responsibility; yet few instances are recorded prior to the end of World War II where that responsibility was either criminal or international in nature.'[96] History shows that command responsibility was neither a criminal law concept, nor an international law concept for the greatest part of history. It is obvious that general command responsibility was a basic requirement for the conduct of war before becoming either a criminal law or an international law concept. According to Eckhardt: 'Prior to World War II, legal standards for commanders were practical articulation of the accepted practice of military professionals. This customary law expressed soldier's [sic!] standards which were born on the battlefield and not standards imposed upon them by dilettantes of a different discipline.'[97] Accordingly, legal norms were drawn from the 'accepted practice of military professionals' and expressed 'standards born on the battlefield'. This suggests that before legal standards were developed, the armed forces functioned on the basis of accepted practice and battlefield standards. In Eckhardt's view, it was the practicality of these rules that 'led to their general acceptance which in turn was responsible for their codification.'[98]

Parks has concluded that as long as there has been war, '[T]he commander has received the glories of victory and the burden of defeat, whether deserved or not.'[99] The picture sketched here applies to the commander-in-chief, but interpreted to the commanders at all levels of the armed forces, this statement points to an obligation that all commanders have in attaining the goals set out for them.[100] Unless they do so they will receive 'the burden of defeat'. But where does the obligation stem from?

Eckhardt mentioned that the practice and the standards on the battlefield constituted rules, but in his view these were rules that only later developed, through acceptance and codification, into legal rules. In his book *The Concept of Law*, H.L.A. Hart states that if one can say that someone 'has or is under an obligation', this implies 'the existence of a rule'.[101] According to Hart rules impose obligations, '[W]hen the general demand for conformity is insistent and the social pressure brought to bear upon those who deviate or threaten to deviate is great.'[102] General command responsibility fits this description. It is in the interest of everyone within the armed forces, or a part thereof, that the commander acts in conformity with his general command responsibility, in order to attain the expected goal or to maintain

[95] See section 3.2.2 *supra*.
[96] Parks, pp. 1-104, at p. 19.
[97] Eckhardt, p. 3.
[98] Ibid.
[99] Parks, pp. 101-102.
[100] *Militaire Doctrine*, p. 103.
[101] H.L.A. Hart, *The Concept of Law* (Oxford, Oxford University Press 1984) p. 83.
[102] Ibid., p. 84.

stability among the troops. General command responsibility also corresponds to Hart's two additional characteristics of an obligation. A rule imposes an obligation when the rule is considered 'necessary to the maintenance of social life or some highly prized feature of it.'[103] Examples of rules that are thought of in terms of an obligation are those which 'restrict the free use of violence' or 'require honesty or truth or require the keeping of promises, or specify what is to be done by one who performs a distinctive role or function in the social group.'[104] Such an obligation is most certainly applicable to commanders. The third characteristic of a rule imposing an obligation, according to Hart, is that, '[T]hese rules may, while benefiting others, conflict with what the person who owes the duty may wish to do.'[105] Also the third characteristic corresponds to the reality of a commander. For example, the commander knows that he has an obligation to carry out a certain operation, while that may put himself and his subordinates in danger.

Based on this analysis, the obligation felt by commanders to act in accordance with their general command responsibility is imposed by a rule. The next question is what kind of rules are we talking about? What kinds of rules form the origin of the concept of command responsibility? Hart argues that, '[T]here are many types of social rule and standard lying outside the legal system.'[106] In his view:

> 'Such non-legal rules may be distinguished and classified in many different ways. Some are rules of very limited scope concerning only a particular sphere of conduct (e.g. dress) or activities for which there are only intermittent opportunities, deliberately created (ceremonies and games). Some rules are conceived as applying to the social group in general; others to special sub-groups within it, either marked off by certain characteristics as a distinct social class, or by their own choice to meet or combine for limited purposes. Some rules are considered to be binding by virtue of agreement and may allow for voluntary withdrawal: others are thought not to have their origin in agreement or any other form of deliberate choice.'[107]

General command responsibility would fit the description of such social rules as it applies to a specific group of people, the armed forces. One could also see the similarities regarding some rules not being based on agreement or deliberate choice, bearing in mind the Dutch view that command responsibility has its origin in the 'fact' that commanders are expected to behave in a certain way.

Instead of calling the basis for the concept of command responsibility a social rule, could it not be argued that general command responsibility was born out of tradition, that it is a habit, after all general command responsibility as described in the previous section has always been part of the conduct of war? Following the reasoning by Hart, there are some reasons why the origin of general command responsibility cannot be called a military habit or tradition. A social rule distinguishes itself from a habit in that deviation from a social habit does not result

---

[103] Hart 1984, p. 85.
[104] Ibid.
[105] Ibid.
[106] Ibid., p. 165.
[107] Ibid., p. 166.

in criticism, while deviation from a social rule does. We have established that inadequate performance by a commander leads to some form of consequence, a sanction, or in other words, criticism. With regard to a social rule, this criticism is considered justified. Another distinguishing feature of a social rule compared to a social habit is that it is considered as a general standard of behaviour within the group. While a habit, like going to the cinema every week, can be observed as a standard by an outsider, a social rule, like the rules of a game, is considered by the social group as 'a general standard to be followed by the group as a whole.'[108] In a similar way, command responsibility cannot be considered a tradition or a social habit, as the whole system of a responsible command is accepted by the armed forces as a whole.

3.5 The moral component of command responsibility

Signs of a moral component of general command responsibility can be found when observing how the behaviour of medieval commanders is pictured. It is said that they fought in person and thereby filled a moral function.[109] Van Creveld has established that the knightly ethos among commanders prevailed as long as commanders continued to fight in person,[110] and only changed with the development of the weaponry used to fight the wars. When killing took place from a distance and made the engagement of the knight/the commander in the fight impractical and unnecessary, the knightly ethos declined.[111] That seems like a natural development, considering the fact that the commander's personal involvement in the battle diminished when being distanced from the immediate impact of the war and the suffering caused by the war. However, it is still considered that the remnants of chivalry have an impact on a commander, who is 'a representative of a proud military profession lineage and tradition.'[112] This knightly ethos, together with considerations of military necessity and humanity, is part of the decision-making and the responsibilities, the general command responsibility, of the modern commander.[113] One should keep in mind that only the commander-in-chief and high-level, strategic commanders, were distanced from the front when weaponry developed. Commanders at a lower level, in particular at the technical or the battle-command level, are still involved in carrying out a task together with their units.[114] The remnants of chivalry still have an impact on all commanders, regardless of the level at which the commander acts.

The Dutch Army seems to confirm this in its book *Militaire Doctrine*, where it discusses various qualities demanded of a commander, in particular integrity and

[108] Ibid., pp. 55-56.
[109] Van Creveld 1985, p. 50.
[110] Ibid., p. 51.
[111] Ibid., pp. 52-53.
[112] Eckhardt, p. 3.
[113] Ibid.
[114] *Militaire Doctrine*, pp. 105-106.

exemplary behaviour. It points out that these qualities are necessary for upholding morale and discipline among the troops and that by showing the subordinates the high demands he expects of himself he wins respect. Interestingly, the book states that these high demands are based on professional and personal values and norms. The examples mentioned are honesty, loyalty and moral courage.[115] Thus, a good commander is not guided solely by necessity or by pragmatic and functional considerations. It is recognised that there are professional values, moral values, or as some may say, the remnants of the knightly ethos, that should influence the behaviour of the commander.

Could one say that the concept of command responsibility is at least partly based on a moral rule? Hart found that in 'all societies which have developed a legal system'[116] there are some social rules 'to which supreme importance is attached, and which in spite of crucial differences have many similarities to its law.'[117] These are moral rights, moral duties or moral obligations, or simply moral rules. 'Moral obligations, like most legal obligations, are within the capacity of any normal adult. Compliance with these moral rules, as with legal rules, is taken as a matter of course, so that while breach attracts serious censure, conformity to moral obligation, again, like obedience to the law, is not a matter for praise except when marked by exceptional conscientiousness, endurance, or resistance to special temptation.'[118]

In the previous section arguments were presented in support of the idea that the origin of the concept of command responsibility can be found in a social rule. Does this social rule attach such supreme importance that one could speak of the concept of command responsibility as a moral obligation? Hart argues that moral rules vary in different societies and at different times.[119] At least the general command responsibility shares some characteristics of a moral rule. It has what Hart calls 'immunity from deliberate change'. General command responsibility cannot be 'changed or repealed by deliberate enactment'. Armies have always functioned on this basis and there seems to be no workable alternative to the concept. However, this is a practical rather than a moral issue. There is no obvious moral reason why an army could not function on another basis than on the basis of general command responsibility, if such a system was functional. On the other hand, the concept of command responsibility shares some characteristics of a moral rule in that moral blame will only be a consequence of the commander's action where he had a choice in acting differently.[120] It is also true that a failure to act in accordance with the general command responsibility may lead to blame of a moral character. However, as set out earlier in this chapter, the consequences may also be of another character, disciplinary measures, for example.

---

[115] Ibid.
[116] Hart 1984, p. 166.
[117] Ibid.
[118] Ibid., p. 167.
[119] Ibid.
[120] Although this resembles a legal rule, Hart identifies some distinctions between a moral and a legal rule also with regard to this issue. This discussion is restricted to the characteristics of a moral rule.

The origin of the concept of command responsibility may not be a moral rule, as described by Hart, but there is a moral component to it. Various armies and some commanders explicitly point out that general command responsibility encompasses more than formal rules and requirements. Command is also exercised with one's heart.[121] Van Baarda refers to the US Field Manual which covers command responsibility and describes it as being, '[T]he ethical and legal obligation a commander assumes for the actions, accomplishments, or failures of a unit.'[122]

The moral element of command responsibility is emphasised in situations where the commander does not incur liability responsibility because the omission on his part is not criminalised, but where the 'feeling' remains that what the commander has done or has failed to do was wrong, at least morally wrong. The moral element may be illustrated by two examples:

1. Some soldiers commit rape. An investigation shows that the commander failed in training his subordinates in accordance with the requirements of the armed forces. International case law has not found commanders liable under the command responsibility doctrine for a failure to train their subordinates.[123] Nonetheless, the general command responsibility is breached and the consequence is that, at the very least, the commander is morally blamed for the crimes committed.
2. Guerillas fighting for a warlord commit war crimes, while members of a peacekeeping mission who are aware of this do nothing to stop them.[124] The commander failed to take action, but he is not prosecuted. There may have been a lack of mandate, the elements under the command responsibility doctrine may not be fulfilled or there may be some other reason why the commander is not criminally liable. However, there is a moral responsibility on the part of the commander to prevent war crimes, which is felt as being independent of his legal duty to act.

For the commander, the same obligation arises regardless of whether he could be held criminally responsible or not. He should take all necessary and reasonable measures to prevent war crimes from being committed, also where his part is limited to training his subordinates to act in compliance with the laws and customs of war, or where he only has *de facto* power to prevent crimes. Even in situations where the inaction of the commander is supported by legal norms, there may be a moral responsibility to act. The foregoing shows that the moral component of command responsibility is inextricably bound up with the rest of the concept.

---

[121] See *Leidraad Commandovoering*, pp. 54-56; and Van Egmond, pp. 60-61. See also the interview with Colonel Van Harskamp, Annex I.

[122] Th.A. van Baarda, 'Ethiek, commandantenverantwoordelijkheid en enkele dilemm's bij militaire operaties', in Th.A. van Baarda, A.H.M. van Iersel and D.E.M. Verweij, eds., *Praktijkboek Militaire Ethiek* (Budel, DAMON 2004) pp. 73-123, at p. 97.

[123] See *Halilović*, TC Judgement, paras. 87-88; and *Prosecutor* v. *Enver Hadžihasanović et al.*, TC Judgement, Case No. IT-01-47-T, 15 March 2006, para. 151.

[124] Example taken from Van Baarda, p. 100.

3.6 The relationship between general command responsibility and command criminal responsibility

If the concept of command responsibility has its origin in the practice of military professionals and battlefield standards, and constitutes a social rule of the armed forces, where is the link to the legal concept of command responsibility? In other words, what is the relationship between social and legal rules? Following the reasoning of Hart, a primitive society may exist relying solely on such social or primary rules. When that society gets more complex there is a need for secondary rules, which are, in fact, rules familiar to a legal system.[125] The origin of command responsibility lies in the primitive army which acted on the basis of a responsible command. As pointed out earlier, legal standards applicable to commanders and to the conduct of war in general were first accepted as applicable standards and then codified. This fits well within the ambit of Hart's role responsibility. Hart argues that responsibilities 'may be either legal or moral or fall outside this dichotomy.'[126] The responsibilities may, thus, also be social. Where general command responsibility could lead to disciplinary or other legal sanctions under national military law, society had obviously reached a high level of complexity which required legal sanctions for a breach of the responsibilities. In international law, Article 1 of the Hague Regulations, which provides that one of the qualifications for being a belligerent is 'to be commanded by a person responsible for his subordinates',[127] confirmed the legal normative basis for general command responsibility.

As was found in the previous sections, general command responsibility corresponds to role responsibility. Where role responsibility is considered a legal responsibility, the consequence of not fulfilling the responsibilities may be liability responsibility. Applying this theory to general command responsibility, a very specific breach – the failure to prevent subordinates from committing crimes or to punish those subordinates who have committed crimes – may lead to command criminal responsibility. That specific breach has become subjected to liability responsibility. This, however, does not mean that other breaches by the commander of his general command responsibility led to liability responsibility. The general command responsibility as role responsibility may also encompass moral responsibilities. It may be the moral responsibility of a commander to inform the parents of the death of their son during a military exercise. A failure by the commander to do so does not fall under the command responsibility principle and the consequence of this failure may not at all be liability responsibility. Another example can be taken from the failed protection of important architectural and cultural sites in Iraq during the armed conflict that commenced in 2003. The level of violence, the lack of planning and staffing and not having set cultural protection as a priority led to the inability of the commanders on the ground

[125] Hart 1984, pp. 89-96.

[126] Hart 1968, p. 213.

[127] Regulations Respecting the Laws and Customs of War on Land, annexed to the 1907 Hague Convention (IV) Respecting the Laws and Customs of War on Land.

to provide protection at various cultural sites.[128] Although it is considered that commanders have a responsibility in this regard as part of their general command responsibility, the protection of cultural property in Iraq was not one of the priorities of combat.[129] At least the commanders on the ground could not be more than, perhaps, morally responsible for this failure.

Section 3.3 found that criminal law is generally very careful when the liability responsibility concerns an omission. As command responsibility concerns the omission of a commander to prevent or punish subordinates from committing or for committing international crimes, the same hesitation as in national criminal law should apply when finding liability responsibility under the command responsibility doctrine. The general command responsibility of commanders implies certain duties in relation to their subordinates, which gives reason to hold that the theory of *Garantenstellung* can be applied to military commanders. This makes it more easily justifiable to hold a category of people criminally liable, but as mentioned in section 3.3, even where *Garantenstellung* applies, the scarcity of case law in some states indicates that liability for crimes of omission should be charged and imposed with great care.

As such, this is nothing new. In the 1970s Röling, who served as a judge in the Tokyo Tribunal, pointed out that an attitude had developed according to which society could forbid acts, and thereby consider them as crimes, but also require action by people, meaning that a lack of action – an omission – could be considered a crime. Having said that, he continued by noting that the question as to how far the criminal responsibility for an omission goes, was a very difficult one to answer.[130] In his Opinion to the Tokyo Judgement, Judge Röling held that the scope of the responsibility for omissions was extensive and that it should be applied with care. He considered the Tokyo Judgement to have gone too far, in this respect, extending the responsibility for mistreatment of POWs to all members of the government, while the Japanese government had an established division of labour.[131] Although this warning was voiced at a time when the principle of command responsibility as a basis for international criminal liability was relatively new, it is – nevertheless – topical as it stresses the importance of finding a balance between the need to prosecute and the need to keep the principle within reasonable, justifiable limits, and also to pay attention to the realities of war, or in other words, a balance between the interests of criminal law and the interests of the commander and the armed forces.

Section 3.2.2 above showed that the purpose of the exercise of command is to ensure that the military goal is reached. With a commander who exercises command, the efficiency of the armed forces is increased. The responsibilities of

---

128 Holmes Armstead, pp. 117-124, at p. 118.

129 Ibid., p. 119.

130 B.V.A. Röling, 'Criminal Responsibility for Violations of the Laws of War', 12 *Revue belge de droit international* (1976) pp. 8-26, at p. 15.

131 B.V.A. Röling and C.F. Rüter, eds., *The Tokyo Judgment: The International Criminal Tribunal for the Far East (IMTFE), 29 April 1946 – 12 November 1948*, Vol. II (Amsterdam, APA – University Press Amsterdam 1977) p. 1064.

the commander exist, first and foremost, to make the military organisation run more smoothly. The commander is expected to make decisions and give orders that benefit the military operation. The purpose of this general command responsibility is clearly different from the purpose of and justification for criminal law and punishment, which are described as being twofold. First, criminal law and punishment are a 'deserved response to culpable wrongdoing'. Secondly, criminal law is a 'necessary institution to deter such wrongdoing'.[132] The justification for international criminal law seems to be essentially the same. The purpose of having international criminal law can be found in the Preamble to the ICC Statute, where the States Parties express their determination to put an end to impunity for the perpetrators of the most serious crimes of concern to the international community as a whole and to contribute to the prevention of such crimes.[133] Although the ICC Statute may not be perceived of as an international penal code, the preamble gives an impression of what the majority of states consider to be the purpose of international criminal law. If we transfer this thought to the subject of the present study, command responsibility as a part of international criminal law should be applied as a response to culpable wrongdoing and it should serve to prevent international crimes from occurring.

International criminal law expects that the commander is aware of the requirements of the laws of war. This is generally also the case. According to Best, even officers in 18th and 19th century Europe were well-aware of the *jus in bello*. The responsibility for observing the *jus in bello* lay almost exclusively with these officers and, accordingly, 'it was simply part of their professional ethic and way of life.'[134] Manuals and other materials may have provided the officers with some knowledge of the subject, but the laws and customs of war were mostly 'something the young officer picked up on the job, part of the way his elders thought and talked.'[135]

At the beginning of the 21st century, military officers in most countries are being educated in the laws and customs of war, as part of their training as commanders. Also the consequences of committing breaches of the laws and customs of war are being discussed, which includes the subject of command responsibility as laid down in international criminal law. Commanders and military lawyers are the ones who have to make sure that activities of the military forces are exercised in accordance with the laws of war. In addition to that, commanders are bound by national military law applicable to them as well as other codes of conduct. Every military officer, in his role as a commander, on the basis of the nature of his position, must know and must have considered what his responsibilities as a commander imply.

If criminal liability for an omission is to be imposed with care, as suggested by Röling, not only the interests and expectations of international criminal law

---

[132] Ashworth, p. 17.

[133] Preamble to the Rome Statute of the International Criminal Court, UN Doc. A/CONF.183/9, 17 July 1998, 37 *ILM* (1998) p. 999.

[134] G. Best, *War and Law since 1945* (Oxford, Oxford University Press 1994) p. 20.

[135] Ibid.

should be observed, but also the fact that it should be possible to exercise the art of war without constant fear of prosecution. Just as with *Garantenstellung* in national criminal law, international criminal law should be reluctant to put categories of people in a position which imposes a duty to act.

In general there is an unwillingness or reluctance on the part of governments to prosecute commanders, exactly for this reason. The commander is considered to make a sacrifice and serves the nation in times of war. The main duty of the commander is to bring the military operation to a successful end. In his article on the evolution of command responsibility, Lippman mentioned the *Goldman* case, which illustrates this reluctance to prosecute. In this case Captain Goldman, a commander during the Vietnam War, 'countenanced the rape, sodomy and murder of two Vietnamese nurses by members of his company.'[136] 'The court martial determined that Goldman was an exemplary officer and sentenced him to a reprimand and forfeiture of one hundred dollars pay per month for twelve months, an insignificant sentence given the gravity of his crimes.'[137] Lippman rightly criticised the outcome of this case as not reflecting the seriousness of the misconduct.[138] On the other hand, the case reflects the unwillingness to prosecute commanders for omissions in times of war, even where the crimes committed by subordinates were obvious war crimes.

An important role in ensuring that the link between role responsibility and liability responsibility as laid down in the command responsibility doctrine in international criminal law is maintained is logically played by the prosecutors exercising their prosecutorial discretion and by the judges who decide on which issues emphasis should be placed. A reasonable and justifiable application with attention to the reality of commanders and other superiors is dependent on the decision as to whom, to what crimes and when the command responsibility principle is applied.

3.7 Conclusion

If looked at from a military perspective, the command responsibility concept is not, first and foremost, a principle of international criminal law. Command responsibility, or general command responsibility as opposed to criminal command responsibility, encompasses all responsibilities held/exercised by the commander, while criminal command responsibility concerns a very specific basis for sanctioning a commander whose failure to exercise his general command responsibility is connected to the commission of violations of international humanitarian law. In a sense, command criminal responsibility is the very last step of a commander's general command responsibility.

---

136 M. Lippman, 'The Evolution and Scope of Command Responsibility, 13 *LJIL* (2000) p. 155.

137 Ibid.

138 It should be pointed out here that the fact that the commander 'countenanced' the crimes committed by his subordinates could be interpreted as permission and, hence, the commander might be charged on the basis of his individual criminal responsibility before any of the international tribunals.

The present chapter serves as a basis for the subsequent chapters and shows that the general command responsibility as exercised by commanders is something unique to the armed forces. Any application of the criminal command responsibility doctrine to civilians, or an attempt to 'broaden' the scope of command responsibility, will be faced with that uniqueness. The chapter has illustrated that relationships outside the armed forces are seldom comparable to those brought about by the command exercised in the military context. The responsibilities that are implicitly or explicitly connected to the various levels of command are not necessarily based on legal provisions, but have their basis in tradition and even in moral rules. The fact that this general command responsibility forms the foundation for the functioning of military commanders points to the link between command responsibility as exercised by military commanders and the international criminal law concept of command responsibility. The compatibility of the military concept with the corresponding notion in international criminal law can only be reached if the latter notion takes the reality of the military commanders into account and also serves the purposes of international criminal law. Rules of international criminal law in general, and the criminal command responsibility concept in particular, will only reduce the number of excesses of warfare if they are not experienced as a threat to the efficient and effective conduct of war.

Chapter 4

Applying command responsibility to civilian superiors

4.1 Introduction

The previous chapter analysed command responsibility as a military concept and found that the international criminal law concept is interwoven with the general command responsibility that serves as a tool for the armed forces to ensure a more efficient conduct of war. The purpose of this chapter is to explore the interpretation and applicability of the command responsibility doctrine specifically in relation to civilian superiors.

When considering the normative basis for the application of command responsibility to civilian superiors, there are two different paths that should be explored. First, there is the practical application of the doctrine to civilian superiors. Secondly, there is the codification of the applicability of command responsibility to civilian superiors in Article 28 ICC. This needs some further explanation.

In the *Čelebići* Judgement, which was the first judgement rendered by the ICTY that addressed command responsibility, the Trial Chamber considered the applicability of the command responsibility doctrine to civilian superiors.[1] The Trial Chamber noted that the text of Article 7(3) does not limit the scope of the article to cover only military commanders,[2] which means, first, that civilian superiors are also covered by the provision and, secondly, that there are no separate requirements or limitations when applying the provision to civilian superiors.[3]

---

[1] *Čelebići*, TC Judgement, paras. 355-363.

[2] Ibid., para. 356. The provision on command responsibility in the Statutes of the ICTY and ICTR, and the provision in the Statute of the Special Court for Sierra Leone, make no specific mention of civilians. They mention the responsibility of the superior, not the commander, which indicates a neutral approach as to whether the superior may be a civilian or a military superior. The Final Report of the Commission of Experts Established pursuant to Security Council Resolution 780 (1992) also avoids the use of the term civilian superior. Discussing the applicability of the command responsibility principle, the report notes that '[t]he doctrine of command responsibility is directed primarily at military commanders' and that '[m]ost legal cases in which the doctrine of command responsibility has been considered have involved military or paramilitary accused.' According to the report, also '[p]olitical leaders and public officials have been held liable under this doctrine in certain circumstance.' The civilian superior is not mentioned.

In the commentary to the Draft Code of Crimes Against the Peace and Security of Mankind the International Law Commission in its 1996 report considered the word superior as included in the article on command responsibility and stated the following: 'The reference to 'superiors' is sufficiently broad to cover military commanders or other civilian authorities who are in a similar position of command and exercise a similar degree of control with respect to their subordinates.'

[3] The view that it is not the distinction between civilians and military commanders that should be the determining factor in relation to command responsibility is supported by scholars. See, for

The Trial Chamber sought for confirmation of the applicability of the doctrine to civilian superiors as accepted customary law in Second World War jurisprudence, making reference to the Tokyo judgement – the cases against Hirota and Shigemitsu, and to other cases like the *US* v. *Flick and others*, and the *Roechling* case.[4] All these cases concerned civilian superiors who were held accountable for crimes that were committed during the Second World War.[5] Having established that such an application of the provision was indeed supported by customary law, the ICTY has since the *Čelebići* Judgement accepted that Article 7(3) applies equally to military commanders and civilian superiors. The initial hesitation of the ICTR to apply superior responsibility to civilian superiors that appeared in *Akayesu*,[6] according to some resulted in a 'split of authority'[7] between the ICTR and the ICTY, but changed into frequent reference to the doctrine in later cases, also by the Rwanda Tribunal.

---

example, R. Cryer, 'The Boundaries of Liability in International Criminal Law, or "Selectivity by Stealth"', 6 *Journal of Conflict and Security Law* (2001) pp. 3-31, at p. 29; and Zegveld, p. 237.

[4] See, for example, *Čelebići*, TC Judgement, paras. 357-363.

[5] It should be noted here that the IMTFE tried several civilian superiors for omissions in relation to international crimes. Hirota (Foreign Minister), Koiso (Prime Minister) and Shigemitsu (Foreign Minister), high level civilian superiors, were convicted for disregarding their legal duty to prevent crimes. Despite these convictions, which could be said to prove the applicability of the command responsibility doctrine to civilian superiors, the Tokyo Judgement confirms the difficulties to apply the doctrine to civilians. Hirota and Shigemitsu, in their position as Foreign Minister, were not in a superior-subordinate relationship with the perpetrators of the crimes, as presently required by the command responsibility doctrine. Koiso, as the Prime Minister, could perhaps more easily have taken measures to put a halt to the atrocities than those accused who held the position of Foreign Minister. However, the case against Koiso is also an example of why the command responsibility doctrine is not well suited for cases against civilian superiors. Koiso was convicted for disregarding his duty to prevent crimes, but by the time he became the Prime Minister the commission of war crimes by the Japanese troops had become notorious. He played a leading role in the Japanese plans for expansion in the 1930s, which led to a conviction for the waging of a war of aggression. By accepting the position of Prime Minister while aware of atrocities being committed and by staying in office for six months without taking action, he played a different role in the events than the superior who under the command responsibility doctrine omitted to prevent or repress crimes. His failure amounted to a deliberate disregard of his duty, which today might be considered as approving of the crimes committed, amounting to aiding and abetting the crime. The fact that the Tokyo Tribunal convicted many of the civilian superiors for the waging a war of aggression and for ordering, authorizing or permitting crimes (Tojo, Head of the War Ministry), but only in a few contentious cases for disregarding their duty to prevent breaches of the laws of war, arguably supports the thesis that the liability of the civilian superior for atrocities within an armed conflict is not very often to be labelled as command responsibility. See the Verdict in the Tokyo Judgement, in N. Boister and R. Cryer, eds., *Documents on the Tokyo International Military Tribunal – Charter, Indictment and Judgments* (Oxford, Oxford University Press 2008) pp. 598-628.

[6] *Akayesu*, TC Judgement.

[7] G.R. Vetter, 'Command Responsibility of Non-Military Superiors in the International Criminal Court', 25 *Yale Journal of International Law* (2000) pp. 89-141, at p. 133; K. Roberts, 'The Use of the Tokyo Trial in Determining the Applicability of the Doctrine of Command Responsibility to Civilians', in K. Koufa, *The New International Criminal Law*, 2001 International Law Session, Thesaurus Acroasium, Vol. XXXII (Thessaloniki, Sakkoulas Publications 2003) pp. 1045-1063, at pp. 1047-1048.

Thus, on the one hand, the existing case law is based on a provision that covers all superiors and on the basis of which there is no need to make a distinction regarding the civilian or military status of the superior. On the other hand, there is Article 28 ICC, which has so far not served as the basis for any judgement. This article provides explicitly for the application of command responsibility to civilians. In contrast with the ICTY, the ICC does not have to consider whether the doctrine applies to civilian superiors; just as the Statute, its primary source is drafted to include this possibility. In this respect, the ICC will be able to build on the existing case law, be that from the *ad hoc* tribunals or from the Special Court for Sierra Leone. A complicating factor is the provision – Article 28 – itself. Where the *ad hoc* tribunals did not have to pronounce on the civilian or military status of the superior, the ICC will have to first establish this status of the superior, before turning to the evidence on the elements. In addition to the status definition, Article 28 contains two separate knowledge requirements that depend on the civilian or military status of the superior.[8] With regard to these two aspects, the ICC will not be able to build on the experience of the *ad hoc* tribunals, but will have to develop a new way of applying the command responsibility doctrine and to decide on the importance of the different standards.

Taking this as a starting point, the present chapter first discusses the 'civilian superior', or in other words, the superior who does not fit the description of the military commander in Article 28(a) ICC. Secondly, the application of the doctrine to superiors who are not military commanders in the case law of the *ad hoc* tribunal will be analysed. Several cases have come before the *ad hoc* tribunals, in which the defendant or defendants were civilians, charged under the command responsibility provision. Some accused have been acquitted under the command responsibility charges and a few have been held criminally liable, either in combination with responsibility for their personal participation in crimes or solely on the basis of command responsibility. The aim is to discover the basis for the convictions or for the even more frequent acquittals. Finally, the chapter aims at drawing some conclusions regarding the present basis for the application of the command responsibility doctrine to civilian superiors.

The whole chapter is considered in the light of Article 28 ICC, both because that provision is a widely accepted standard when prosecuting international crimes and because it offers a clearly set division between a military commander, a *de facto* military commander and purely civilian commanders. This is not to say that Article 28 ICC offers the only possible way forward, nor that that article may not be subjected to changes in the future.

[8] On *mens rea*, see section 2.4.2.2 *supra*.

4.2 The civilian superior

4.2.1 Identifying the civilian superior

In the previous chapter the issue of command was explored and the commander identified. It was argued that command responsibility in the military context has a particular meaning and position, which explains why command responsibility is particularly suitable for the prosecution of military commanders. How can the civilian superior be identified?

A basic assumption could be that the opposite of the military superior is the civilian superior, that those who do not exercise command within an armed group organised in a hierarchical manner are civilian superiors. This starting point is problematic, though, as the grey area between the commander and the civilian superior is too big for such a black and white division. On the basis of case law that has been produced since the Second World War, it is clear that there are military superiors who do not fit the description of a commander and that there are civilian superiors who, in fact, operate as if they were military commanders. The *ad hoc* tribunals have to a certain extent avoided the difficulty of establishing which kind of superior is at stake by simply requiring that the superior needs to exercise effective control over his subordinates, whoever the superior is and whoever the subordinates are. In some cases, however, they have paid attention to the civilian/military status of the superior when considering the evidence of a superior-subordinate relationship between the accused and the actual perpetrators.[9]

At the same time, the fact that the various tribunals do not distinguish between civilian and military superiors means that the case law is not particularly enlightening with regard to the identification of the civilian superior. As both civilian and military superiors may incur command responsibility, the establishing of *de facto* control has not required the *ad hoc* tribunals to make findings concerning the civilian or military status of the superior in question.

However, now that the ICC Statute not only recognises that the superior responsibility doctrine is applicable to civilians, but also distinguishes between civilians and military commanders in its Article 28, the practical question of who falls under which category of superiors will arise. Without a distinction in the definition, it would be enough to prove the constituent elements of this responsibility. With the distinction, it will become necessary to decide whether the superior in the specific case is a civilian or a military. On the other hand, the statute provides that where the superior is a civilian, another knowledge requirement will apply. This provision which compels the Court to categorise the accused is directly related to the concern that, '[A] Tribunal should be very careful in holding civil government officials responsible for the behaviour of the army in the field.'[10] While it is apparent that the application of command responsibility to

[9] See section 4.2.4 *infra*.

[10] The Trial Chamber included a direct quote by Röling. See *Akayesu*, TC Judgement, para. 490.

civilians is accepted, it is equally recognised that the application of the principle to civilians constitutes an extension of its original field of application.[11]

But who is the civilian superior? What should be kept in mind here is the context in which we are trying to identify the civilian superior. It is a context in which international crimes are committed and even if the requirement of an armed conflict is not absolute, the context is not a peaceful one with only incidental occurrences of violations.

The understanding that where a superior is not a military commander he is a civilian, is based on the basic idea in international humanitarian law that distinguishes between two categories only, combatants and non-combatants, or civilians. Those who are not combatants are civilians.[12] Despite the fact that the reality of societies in armed conflicts does not correspond to this black and white

---

[11] W. Zhu, 'The Doctrine of Command Responsibility as Applied to Civilian Leaders: The ICTR and the *Kayishema* Case', in S. Yee and W. Tieya, eds., *International Law in the Post-Cold War World, Essays in Memory of Li Haopei* (London, Routledge 2001) p. 374.

[12] 1977 Protocol Additional to the Geneva Conventions of 12 August 1949, and relating to the Protection of Victims of International Armed Conflicts (Protocol I), 8 June 1977, 1125 *UNTS* p. 3. Art. 50 of Additional Protocol I to the 1949 Geneva Conventions (AP I) provides a definition of civilians. Art. 50(1) provides as follows: 'A civilian is any person who does not belong to one of the categories of persons referred to in Article 4A(1), (2), (3) and (6) of the Third Convention and in Article 43 of this Protocol. In case of doubt whether a person is a civilian, that person shall be considered to be a civilian.' The article refers to Art. 4A(1), (2), (3) and (6) of the Third Geneva Convention, which have the following wording:

'Art 4. A. Prisoners of war, in the sense of the present Convention, are persons belonging to one of the following categories, who have fallen into the power of the enemy:

(1) Members of the armed forces of a Party to the conflict, as well as members of militias or volunteer corps forming part of such armed forces.

(2) Members of other militias and members of other volunteer corps, including those of organized resistance movements, belonging to a Party to the conflict and operating in or outside their own territory, even if this territory is occupied, provided that such militias or volunteer corps, including such organized resistance movements, fulfil the following conditions:

(a) that of being commanded by a person responsible for his subordinates;

(b) that of having a fixed distinctive sign recognizable at a distance;

(c) that of carrying arms openly;

(d) that of conducting their operations in accordance with the laws and customs of war.

(3) Members of regular armed forces who profess allegiance to a government or an authority not recognized by the Detaining Power.

[...]

(6) Inhabitants of a non-occupied territory who, on the approach of the enemy, spontaneously take up arms to resist the invading forces, without having had time to form themselves into regular armed units, provided they carry arms openly and respect the laws and customs of war.'

As stated in Art. 50 of Additional Protocol I, civilians are also those persons who do not belong to the armed forces and other armed groups defined in Art. 43 AP I:

'1. The armed forces of a Party to a conflict consist of all organized armed forces, groups and units which are under a command responsible to that Party for the conduct of its subordinates, even if that Party is represented by a government or an authority not recognized by an adverse Party. Such armed forces shall be subject to an internal disciplinary system which, "inter alia", shall enforce compliance with the rules of international law applicable in armed conflict.

2. Members of the armed forces of a Party to a conflict (other than medical personnel and chaplains covered by Article 33 of the Third Convention) are combatants, that is to say, they have the right to participate directly in hostilities.

definition of actors or groups, the idea that these groups should be divided rests on a firm historical basis.[13] According to Best, a reference to this idea can be found in Rousseau's work, who asserted that there is an 'unbridgeable conceptual divide between non-combatants and combatants.'[14] The divide is based on the recognition by those who conducted war that it was 'possible and desirable not to hurt' persons who were not involved in the fighting and who were 'innocent'.[15] Not all civilians are that obviously innocent, however, and 'their moral entitlement to exclusion from attack or the risks of attack is not so clear.'[16] The fact that the divide as pointed out by Rousseau was set out in legal provisions has made the distinction more problematic. From having been someone 'who formed no part of an enemy country's armed strength and made no contribution to it', the civilian is now 'an enemy person not dressed in a markedly military way and not enlisted in a designated military organization.'[17] The present picture of a civilian seems to focus more on formal characteristics than the former one, which was based on the reality that the combatant met on the scene of the war.

Article 28 of the ICC Statute which explicitly distinguishes between military commanders and other superiors is not more helpful in this respect. While the *ad hoc* tribunals and scholars use the 'either/or' division between military commanders and civilian superiors, Article 28 provides as follows: '(a) A military commander or person effectively acting as a military commander shall be criminally responsible [...]; (b) With respect to superior and subordinate relationships not described in paragraph (a), a superior shall be criminally responsible [...].' Thus, all superiors who hold the position of a military commander or who are effectively acting as military commanders fall under paragraph (a), while all other superiors fall under paragraph (b). The provision does not explicitly distinguish between military and civilian superiors, but simply leaves paragraph (b) open for all other superior-subordinate relationships. In theory, these relationships could be of whatever kind, but as IHL knows of no other categories than the combatant and the civilian, it is legitimate to call superiors under paragraph (b) civilian superiors.

Accordingly, those who are not military commanders and, thus, may be called civilian superiors whose acts, or rather omissions, as to the rest correspond to the requirements laid down can be held criminally responsible under this superior responsibility provision. This distinction, which retains the traditional division between military commanders and those who cannot be characterised as such, was considered desirable during the negotiating process leading to the present formulation of the article.[18]

---

3. Whenever a Party to a conflict incorporates a paramilitary or armed law enforcement agency into its armed forces it shall so notify the other Parties to the conflict.'

[13] Best, pp. 258-259.

[14] Ibid., p. 258.

[15] Ibid., p. 257.

[16] Ibid., p. 258.

[17] Ibid.

[18] Van Sliedregt 2003, p. 180.

As there is no explicit definition of the civilian superior and as the civilian superior on the basis of the above sources seems to be the superior who does not qualify as a military commander, some authors have made an attempt, making reference to the case law, to identify categories of civilians to which the title civilian superior would apply. Analysing Article 28 of the ICC Statute, Fenrick held that those superiors falling under Article 28(b) 'can include political leaders, business leaders, and senior civil servants.'[19] It is clear, however, that Fenrick does not want to make any definite statement when he says that the category of superior *can* include those leaders mentioned. Thus, it is possible that also others may fall under this paragraph of Article 28 ICC. Fenrick also holds that the category of 'superior' resembles that of a military organisation in that also these superiors 'may have varying degrees of responsibility' and in that there may be superiors who have authority over other superiors at a lower level.[20]

Zhu, on the other hand, found that, 'Military leaders are considered to be those who hold absolute control over the formulation of military policy. But a person will be considered a civilian leader when he was a member of the government, army officer or not, who fulfilled his official duty without a direct relation to or control over or by the armed forces.'[21] If this is the correct definition of a civilian superior, does that not mean that such a superior could also qualify for the superiors intended for Article 28(b) of the ICC Statute? If even an army officer does not automatically fall under Article 28(a), the determination of who is considered a superior for the purposes of paragraph (b) seems to be dependent on the judges' case by case evaluation of the sort of superior the leader accused in the case at hand was.

4.2.2 **Level of authority**

The provisions on command responsibility in international instruments are silent as to the level of authority a superior ought to have in order to incur responsibility under the command responsibility principle. Case law from the *ad hoc* tribunals further shows that the level of authority is not one of the decisive elements when establishing command responsibility. It has also been explicitly stated that a position of influence and authority alone cannot be considered as proof of an existing superior-subordinate relationship. The decisive factor is the effective power of control that the superior exercises over his subordinates.[22] On the other hand, the effective command issue is closely linked to the level of authority of the superior and much of the discussion concerning command responsibility in case law and

[19] W.J. Fenrick, 'Article 28', in O. Triffterer, ed., *Commentary on the Rome Statute* (Baden-Baden, Nomos 1999) pp. 515-522, at p. 521.

[20] Ibid.

[21] Zhu, p. 375.

[22] *Čelebići*, TC Judgement, para. 377.

by learned scholars and the general public centres around the position and the level of authority of the superior.[23]

The function and position of a superior is of particular interest with regard to civilian superiors. Within the military command structure the level of authority logically depends on how high on the hierarchical ladder the superior has climbed. Based on his rank and his duties, his level of authority can be estimated. Consequently, a commander on the tactical level, with the lowest rank in a position of command, may be held responsible under the command responsibility principle. The settings in which civilian superiors could become liable under the command responsibility principle are not that clearly defined. In principle, anyone who exercises effective control in a superior-subordinate relationship is in a position that could lead to command responsibility. Does that mean that also lower 'ranking' civilians are potential command responsibility 'candidates'?

According to Zhu: 'In reality, the structure of social society is not as rigid as in the military.'[24] As opposed to the military command structure, civilian society knows no equivalent to, for example, a non-commissioned officer exercising command authority at the tactical level of operations. While a lower ranking commander will know that he has a general command responsibility in relation to his subordinates, a breach of which will have some form of consequence, the same situation would be less likely in a civilian setting.

The list of potential civilian superiors in Fenrick's commentary to Article 28 ICC included business leaders, political leaders and senior civil servants.[25] This list indicates that a certain level of authority is needed, but is open to a case by case interpretation. A better indication regarding the level of authority of the civilian superior is reached when considering the fact that where there is a superior, there must also be a subordinate. According to Fenrick: 'Any person who has a superior who can direct his work or work related activities may be a subordinate to that superior.'[26] Following this definition, some persons may be both a superior and a subordinate in a large organisation. At the same time, this definition suggests that any person within a civilian organisation who has a subordinate, may become a civilian superior for the purposes of command responsibility. The requirement of a clear leadership position is thereby removed, at least theoretically.

Ambos found that post-WW II jurisprudence required that defendants had been leaders, planners or belonged to the policy level, with regard to aggressive war and that the IMTFE 'limited the responsibility to cabinet members'.[27] However, these findings give no indication whatsoever as to what, if any, level is necessary in order to incur command responsibility. The question is whether the

---

[23] K. Ambos, 'Superior Responsibility', in A. Cassese, P. Gaeta and J.R.W.D. Jones, eds., *The Rome Statute of the International Criminal Court: A Commentary*, Vol. I (Oxford, Oxford University Press 2002) pp. 823-872, at pp. 855-857.

[24] Zhu, p. 382.

[25] Fenrick, p. 521.

[26] Ibid.

[27] Ambos 2002, 'Superior Responsibility', p. 855.

command responsibility principle as applied to civilians requires any theoretically distinguishable level of authority of the civilian superior.

Rather than looking at any possible theoretical requirements inferred from 60-year old case law, it may prove more credible to conclude that the level of authority required of civilian superiors depends on more practical factors. First, the command responsibility principle as defined in international criminal law has almost exclusively been considered and applied in the context of international crimes. After the Second World War as well as after the conflicts in the former Yugoslavia and in Rwanda, the level of authority of the superiors prosecuted has depended more on the availability of the accused and the financial resources and mandate of the tribunals, than on theoretical considerations. In other words, where all alleged war criminals cannot be prosecuted, prosecutorial discretion is a significant factor. While this is not *per se* specific to the prosecution of civilian superiors, it is a fact that on the international level, many of those considered most responsible for cruelties having taken place in a certain conflict, and therefore 'suitable' for prosecution at the international level, have been and will be the highest governmental and other leaders, i.e., civilians. The ICC is no different in this respect. The Prosecutor will have to make a choice as to which alleged perpetrators will be prosecuted and, secondly, charged under the command responsibility principle. The level of authority test can only be done when lower level, 'Corporal-like', civilian superiors are prosecuted under the command responsibility principle.

Secondly, the level of authority of civilian superiors prosecuted and, more importantly, convicted under the command responsibility principle, is very much related to the issue of commission versus omission. The indictments from the *ad hoc* tribunals show that almost all of the civilian superiors prosecuted have been charged under the command responsibility provision.[28] Evidently, the command responsibility provision is being associated with criminal responsibility of the highest government officials and political leaders.[29] Even more so than in relation to the military commanders, the question with regard to civilian superiors at that level is whether such leaders would not best be prosecuted under the individual criminal responsibility provisions. Where the superior is the highest government official in the region, it is more likely that he committed, rather than omitted to prevent or punish crimes, where commission includes leading, planning, encouraging and assisting in the commission of crimes.

[28] Both indictments from the early years of the tribunals' existence and those of a later date include charges on the basis of command responsibility in relation to civilian superiors. See, for example, *Prosecutor* v. *Jean-Paul Akayesu*, Amended Indictment, Case No. ICTR-96-4-I, 17 June 1997; and *Prosecutor* v. *Jadranko Prlić*, Second Amended Indictment, Case No. IT-04-74-T, 11 June 2008, para. 228.

[29] This is most notably proven by the fact that Slobodan Milošević, who was the President of Serbia, was indicted pursuant to Art. 7(3). See, among other indictments related to him, the indictment related to crimes in Bosnia and Herzegovina: *Prosecutor* v. *Slobodan Milošević*, Amended Indictment, Case No. IT-02-54-T, 22 November 2002. Another prominent accused who faces charges of command responsibility is Charles Taylor, at the time of the atrocities the President of Liberia. See *Prosecutor* v. *Charles Ghankay Taylor*, Amended Indictment, Case No. SCSL-03-01-I, 16 March 2006.

These two considerations, the 'most responsible' factor and the 'commission' factor, seem contradictory. On the one hand, there is no interest in prosecuting the 'small fish' and, on the other hand, where the level of authority is too high, the role of the superior might be more suitable for prosecution under the individual criminal responsibility provisions. Is it rather the group of superiors 'in the middle' that should be the object of this form of responsibility? These superiors may from a political perspective be interesting enough for prosecution. There is also a greater likelihood that these superiors were actually not involved in the crimes, and due to failing supervision or the like, omitted to prevent or punish crimes by subordinates. It is interesting here to note the view expressed by Zhu that the command responsibility principle is applicable to civilian superiors, 'so long as the degree of authority is similar to that of a military commander.'[30] While the degree of authority is not the same as the level of authority here, it is interesting to compare also the level of authority with the military commanders, i.e., 'so long as the level of authority is similar to that of a military commander.' As was analysed in Chapter 3, the military concept of command responsibility is not limited to the highest level of superiors. However, even if it was possible, in the abstract, to consider the civilian superiors 'in the middle', the most suitable objects of the command responsibility principle, the problem of identifying such civilians, except on a case by case basis, remains.

As for the problem with regard to the possible individual rather than command responsibility of the highest level civilian superiors, there is always the possibility of allowing both individual and command responsibility at the same time. Issue solved. Judging by the development of the principle this, however, will not be the preferred solution, which means that there is no simple answer to the problem of the prosecution of the highest level civilian superiors under the command responsibility principle.

4.2.3 **Categories of civilians**

4.2.3.1 *Article 28(a) ICC* – de jure

In the above we came to the conclusion that the identification of the civilian superior is not possible through exclusion, or by applying the IHL division of combatants and civilians, nor by making lists of positions of which one can assume that the holder may become a civilian superior for the purposes of command responsibility. All these methods focus on what kind of position the superior has. As stated above, it is not the position of the superior or the authority that the position may bring with it that is of importance when applying the command responsibility doctrine. Rather, the important focal point should be what the superior actually does.

It is possible to distinguish between three categories of civilians. While, of course, these categories are also connected to the position that the superior holds,

[30] Zhu, p. 377.

the focus is on what he/she does, instead of what position the superior holds. Considering these categories in terms of Article 28 ICC, we can distinguish between the following superiors:

1. The superior who holds a typically civilian position but who is a *de jure* military commander;
2. The superior who holds a typically civilian position but who is a *de facto* military commander;
3. The superior who holds a civilian position and who does not exercise other than civilian duties.

The first category is that of civilians who hold a civilian position but who are *de jure* charged with duties of a military commander. Schmitt has given some examples of this category of civilians:

> 'Civilians often fill *de jure* positions relative to the armed forces. As an example, by Article II of the US Constitution, the President is the "Commander-in-Chief". Similarly, the Queen of England is the British Commander-in-Chief pursuant to the unwritten constitution of the United Kingdom, and each of the royals serves as a regimental "Colonel-in-Chief". In fact, British officers swear an oath of allegiance to the Queen, not the State, and it is the Queen who issues their commission.'[31]

Not all civilian *de jure* military commanders may have the same practical importance in carrying out military tasks. While the role of the Queen of England as the Commander-in-Chief is a symbolic role, the President of the United States of America and some other presidents also *de facto* fulfil a role as Commander-in-Chief, in particular during an armed conflict.[32]

The division of superior into military and other superiors in Article 28 ICC does not correspond nicely to this category of superiors. While the reason for the inclusion of Article 28(b) was the concern during the negotiations leading to the adoption of the ICC Statute that particularly heads of state could be too easily tried under the command responsibility doctrine, the question is whether such accused would even fall under Article 28(b). As was just mentioned, where the Head of State has *de jure* powers as Commander-in-Chief and also exercises these powers, he is both a *de jure* and a *de facto* commander, despite his civilian function. By definition, Article 28(b) cannot be applicable to him, as *de facto* commanders are to be tried under Article 28(a). Of course, in states where the Head of State is not entrusted with the powers of a *de jure* military commander, he remains a civilian, unless on the basis of the facts of the particular case it appears that the Head of State in relation to the crimes committed was a *de facto* military commander.

---

31 M.N. Schmitt, 'Targeting and Humanitarian Law: Current Issues', 34 *Israel Yearbook on Human Rights* (2004) pp. 59-104, at p. 77.

32 Fenrick, p. 517.

On the basis of this analysis it seems that the purpose of the (b) provision is not being served. The division and the separate standard under Article 28(b) do not apply to this particular category of civilians who hold *de jure* military authority and also exercise such authority. This is of course not to say that no superiors fall under the (b) provision. This category of superiors will be considered below.

4.2.3.2 *Article 28(a) ICC* – de facto

From the first cases of the *ad hoc* tribunals onwards, the judgements have recognised that the *de jure* authority of the accused superior over the alleged subordinates is neither enough nor necessary in order to prove superior responsibility. Where a superior exercises *de jure* authority, but where at the time of the crimes the *de facto* effective control over the subordinates was exercised by someone else, the *de jure* superior does not incur responsibility under the command responsibility doctrine. On the other hand, where a superior has not been appointed to or does not on any other basis occupy a *de jure* superior position, he might still be held criminally liable under the command responsibility provision if he *de facto* exercised control over the subordinates at the time of the crimes. In such cases the *de jure* authority is not a necessary requirement. Accordingly, the *de facto* superior plays a crucial role when establishing command responsibility. As we know by now, the effective control is the decisive factor for showing a superior-subordinate relationship.

The role of the *de facto* superior is emphasised by the fact that Article 28 of the ICC Statute divides the superiors who may incur responsibility under the command responsibility principle into 1) military commanders; 2) persons effectively acting as a military commander; and 3) superiors who do not fit into either of the first two categories. The second category serves to cover the *de facto* superior who cannot *de jure* be defined as a military commander. In other words, the second category concerns a civilian *de facto* exercising the powers of a military commander.

Fenrick found that the category of superiors 'effectively acting as a military commander' is a wide category which 'may include police officers in command of armed police units, persons responsible for paramilitary units not incorporated into the armed forces, and persons who have assumed de facto control over the armed forces, armed police units, or paramilitary units.'[33] This is not an exhaustive list but gives an impression of those superiors which, in Fenrick's opinion, could be effectively acting as military commanders. Thus, superiors in similar positions may also be considered as *de facto* military commanders. If these categories are used, a large number of those civilian superiors who would qualify for command responsibility fall under Article 28(a).

Also Schmitt has identified civilians who exercise authority in relation to the armed forces:

[33] Fenrick, pp. 517-518.

> 'At times, individuals without a *de jure* position in the chain of command also exercise influence over military operations. For example, Congress must approve all military funding in the United States. This makes Senators and Congressmen, particularly those on committees dealing with the military, enormously influential *vis-à-vis* defense policy. Or consider individuals tied to a dictator who exercise great influence over particular aspects of a conflict, such as certain members of Saddam Hussein's family or other highly placed members of his tribe from Tikrit.'[34]

In identifying the civilian superior, in particular the civilian who is a *de facto* military commander, the problem is that the lists of possible superiors are of no actual relevance when trying the civilian superior under the command responsibility provision. Only the facts established in each case may give reason to hold that a civilian superior exercised authority which was comparable to that of a military commander.

4.2.3.3 *Article 28(b) ICC*

The list by Fenrick, which includes political leaders, business leaders, and senior civil servants as possible civilian superiors, shows that although a certain number of civilians would better qualify as *de facto* commanders under Article 28(a), there are superiors who do fit under Article 28(b). However, when considering the further requirement of 'effective authority and control' which is demanded of both the *de facto* military commander and the civilian superior, there is no difference between the two categories of superiors in this regard. Both differ from the military commander for which the requirement is 'effective command and control'. This means that for the purposes of the ICC Statute effective authority and control is demanded of both the *de facto* military commander and the civilian superior.

Outside the context of international and internationalised tribunals and their case law, one conflict and in particular certain events in the context of this conflict brought the identification of the civilian superior for the purposes of command responsibility to the forefront. This was the conflict in Iraq, which began in 2003. The mistreatment of prisoners in the Abu Ghraib prison by members of the US armed forces and allegedly also by private military contractors led to questions regarding the command responsibility in relation to these perpetrators. Although there are many conflicts in which the identification of civilian superiors may be necessary, the command responsibility issue in relation to private military contractors is different in that the characteristics of this group of potential civilian superiors do at least not at a first glance correspond to the groups of civilian superiors identified at the *ad hoc* tribunals. Another reason for considering this issue briefly here is the general impression that command responsibility is hardly applicable in relation to these actors/possible perpetrators of international crimes.

---

[34] Schmitt 2004, 'Targeting', p. 78.

At the time of the scandals surrounding the mistreatment of prisoners at the Abu Ghraib prison in Iraq, the question was raised who, except for the perpetrators themselves, could be held responsible for the fact that these crimes could take place.[35] As far as the identification of civilian superiors is concerned, the status of the political leaders at the highest level in the US is not of particular interest here. A Minister or the Head of State as civilian superiors for the purposes of command responsibility have been discussed earlier. Difficulties in identifying the civilian superior also arise at a lower level. Applying command responsibility, the responsibility is not necessarily to be found only on a ministerial level.

The categories of persons listed by Fenrick as possible civilian superiors for the purposes of command responsibility traditionally hold positions that are easily defined as civilian. Political leaders, businessmen and senior civil servants are mostly concerned with civilian affairs or are at least easily distinguished from military commanders. With regard to private military contractors the situation is different, and as was found above, this is why the identification of the civilian superior for the purposes of command responsibility should focus on what the superior does, rather than which position he or she holds. The difficulty concerning private military contractors is twofold. First, there is still the ongoing debate as to whether PMCs are civilian or military actors in the conflict. Secondly, the question is whether the superior of the perpetrator acted as a *de jure* or a *de facto* military commander or as a purely civilian superior, as laid down in Article 28 ICC. While this study is not aimed at establishing the difference between civilians and combatants, the ongoing discussion on this topic can be used in this context to establish whether the perpetrators themselves, being PMCs, are civilians.[36]

Analysing the status of PMCs as either civilians of combatants, Schmitt summarised his findings as follows: 'Since civilian employees and private contractors do not wear uniforms denoting combatant status, seldom fall under the formal command of military personnel, and generally lie beyond the reach of military discipline that the armed forces use to enforce adherence to the 'laws and customs of war', it would be a stretch to style them members of the armed forces.'[37] His conclusion with regard to private contractors fulfilling the requirements of Article 4A(2) of Geneva Convention III is similar. Schmitt considered it 'highly unlikely that private contractors could qualify for Article 4A(2) combat-

[35] G.G.J. Knoops, 'De Abu Ghraib vervolgingen. Strafrechtelijke "victor's justice" voor militaire leiders?', *Nederlands juristenblad* (2005) pp. 778-783.

[36] It is clear that while private military contractors do not constitute an entirely new category of actors in armed conflict, the level of the impact that their acts may have has never been so prominent. Any conclusions by Schmitt were based on the behaviour and structure of private military companies at present, in particular in the conflict in Iraq, in which the use of private contractors reached an unprecedented level. Accordingly, there is no general agreement regarding the status of PMCs, but the conclusion by Schmitt offers a well-reasoned opinion.

[37] M.N. Schmitt, 'Humanitarian Law and Direct Participation in Hostilities by Private Contractors or Civilian Employees', 5 *Chicago Journal of International Law* (2004) pp. 511-546, at p. 526.

ant status.'[38] Schmitt's findings lead him to conclude that PMCs must fall under the other category of actors: civilians.

What is problematic about this approach is the fact that private military companies fulfil different tasks and may have differing structures and ways of operating. In his article from 1998, Zarate discussed the features and roles of private international security companies, in general, and some companies which had been operating in African conflicts and in the conflict in the former Yugoslavia, in particular. According to him, these private security companies had only been working with legitimate governments and 'restricted their activities to training national militaries as opposed to serving as infantry in battle.'[39] However, he recognised that this was a situation that might change and that there were certain risks in making use of these private security companies.[40] In more recent studies, it is recognised that private military contractors engage in activities that make them direct participants in hostilities,[41] thereby increasing the likelihood of these contractors being responsible for international crimes to the same extent as members of the armed forces may be so responsible.

McDonald identified a number of tasks carried out by private military contractors in present-day armed conflicts, some of which involve direct participation in hostilities.[42] Examples of such functions are the interrogation at prisons and the operation of weapons systems. The Abu Ghraib scandal, again, is a good example of such a function. For the purposes of establishing command responsibility, these functions are most interesting, in that persons in combat-like activities are most likely to end up in a situation where international crimes are committed.

Having concluded that PMCs in general have to be considered as civilian actors in the conflict, the logical assumption would be that where the superior of a perpetrator of international crimes is accused under the command responsibility doctrine, that superior would be considered a civilian superior, if he/she works for the enterprise that is engaged as a PMC. Following the division in Article 28 ICC, he is a civilian superior within a civilian enterprise who supervises civilian employees.

On the other hand, could a superior in an enterprise that as a PMC carries out conflict-related activities similar to those of the armed forces in such circum-

---

[38] Ibid., p. 531.

[39] J.C. Zarate, 'The Emergence of a New Dog of War: Private International Security Companies, International Law, and the New World Disorder', 34 *Stanford Journal of International Law* (1998) pp. 75-162, at p. 78.

[40] Ibid.

[41] *Interpretive Guidance on the Notion of Direct Participation in Hostilities under International Humanitarian Law* (Geneva, ICRC 2009) p. 37.

[42] The functions identified by McDonald include the following: '[P]roviding security for civilian objects; developing and maintaining weapons systems; interrogation at prisons; driving, […]; translation, interpretation and linguistics; training armies and police; maintenance of military supply chains and guarding military convoys; computer and technological support; procurement; catering; and other logistics functions, […] guarding military objectives […]; force protection; rescue operations for US forces; combat and combat service support; operating weapons systems […]; and some types of intelligence gathering.' See A. McDonald, 'Dogs of War Redux? Private Military Contractors and the "New Mercenarism"', 7 *Militair Rechtelijk Tijdschrijft* (2007) pp. 210-228, at pp. 218-219.

stances become a *de facto* military commander, or would he at all times remain a civilian leader because his company does not fulfil the qualifications of a combatant? As long as the perpetrators are not considered as combatants, thus civilians, and the superior is a civilian, the superior must be considered a civilian superior also for the purposes of Article 28 ICC, as he does not even *de facto* command members of armed forces. If the PMCs were to be considered as combatants, the superior himself would also be a military commander from the outset. In media reporting one PMC, whose employees allegedly abused and tortured prisoners in the Abu Ghraib prison, had its own chain of command.[43] This still says nothing about the status of the superior, but it does give the impression that some PMCs are organised like an armed group.

A specific problem for the application of command responsibility to superiors of PMCs is the fact that even if the PMCs have their own chains of command they do not usually fall under the chain of command of the armed forces.[44] The PMCs work for the armed forces, but if a PMC does not fall under the chain of command, the question is whether there is a superior-subordinate relationship between the military commander who is in command of an operation and the PMC which carries out tasks within the same operation. It would be fair to say that where the military commander does not have *de facto* effective control over the PMC, he cannot be held responsible under the command responsibility doctrine. However, the fact that a situation is not clearly regulated may not lead to a situation in which no one can be held responsible. The responsibility would then have to be sought higher up, at the political level, in which case the superior would be a civilian superior. Whether in such cases command responsibility could be proven is questionable. The present interpretation and application of the command responsibility doctrine makes proving liability in relation to PMC only feasible if the civilian superior within the PMC enterprise is charged. A determination of whether a specific PMC acts under the supervision and discipline of his own superior within the enterprise or that of the military commanders of one of the parties to the conflict will be case-specific.[45]

As has just been set out, in theory it is possible to think of types of superiors that may fall under Article 28(a) as *de facto* commanders and types that may fall under Article 28(b). The interesting question is whether the existing theoretical

---

[43] See 'Judge Allows Abu Ghraib Lawsuit Against Contractor', available at <http://www.washingtonpost.com/wp-dyn/content/article/2007/11/06/AR2007110602025.html> (accessed 12 December 2008).

[44] Schmitt 2004, 'Humanitarian', p. 526. On this problem, see also Zarate, pp. 75-162, at p. 77, where he stated that, 'Concern about these SCs [Security Companies, MLN], like concern about mercenaries, pirates, and terrorists, stems from the inherent violence of their profession combined with a lack of control over and accountability for their actions. Since these are private companies, countries which recommend or export them arguably can disavow any connection to SCs' activities.' On the necessity of regulating Private Military Companies in general, see P. van der Kruit, 'Noodzakelijke regulering van Private Military Compagnies [sic!]. Enkele mogelijkheden', 7 *Militair Rechtelijk Tijdschrift* (2007) pp. 252-263.

[45] Schmitt 2004, 'Humanitarian', p. 530.

difference between the *de facto* military commander under Article 28(a) and the civilian superior under Article 28(b) will also be a practical one.

4.2.4 Civilian superiors identified

Also recent armed conflicts have proven that armed conflicts have different actors and, consequently, different potential perpetrators of international crimes, in addition to the armed forces, depending on the place and context in which the conflict takes place. The *ad hoc* tribunals have rendered judgements in cases concerning crimes that were committed in two very different conflicts, both as regards the context and the manner in which the crimes were perpetrated. Both civilian and military superiors have been identified as having played an important role in the conflicts.

The judgements rendered by the *ad hoc* tribunals reveal that the Chambers have encountered some difficulties when applying the command responsibility doctrine, which is clearly geared towards the prosecution of military commanders, to civilians. In relation to some accused, the identification of their civilian or military status has been an issue, despite the lack of an explicit requirement and a need to do so in the command responsibility provisions. A few cases may be highlighted in this respect.

Beginning with the ICTY, the Trial Chamber in the case against *Kordić* found that the accused 'was the political leader of the Bosnian Croats in Central Bosnia with particular authority in the Lašva Valley and although having no formal position in the chain of command he was associated with the military leadership; as such he participated in the HVO[46] take-over of the municipalities and the attacks on Busovača [...].'[47] However, his position as a *de facto* military commander was never established. The case shows that in armed conflicts, the civilian or military function of a person, in this case the superior, may not be clearly distinguishable. The finding of the Trial Chamber is an indication of this. Of course, the problem is also that of a lack of evidence in certain cases. With regard to Kordić, the Appeal Judgement in the *Blaškić* case, which concerned crimes committed in the same area, mentions new evidence according to which Kordić was in command of certain perpetrators, more specifically the Military Police.[48] For the purposes of identifying the civilian superior, it is interesting to note this attempt to prove that Kordić was a *de facto* military commander. As such, there is no theoretical need to prove his *de facto* military position, as the Statute does not distinguish between civilian and military superiors. In practice, however, there may very well have been a need to establish his role as a military commander. How, otherwise, should the prosecution convince the judges of the effective control of a political leader over the perpetrators of the crimes?

The *Aleksovski* case is of interest in this specific instance because of the fact that it was not determined whether he was a civilian or a military superior. In this

---

[46] The Croatian Defence Council.

[47] *Kordić and Čerkez*, TC Judgement, para. 829.

[48] *Blaškić*, AC Judgement, paras. 350, 352 and 395-400.

case, the Appeals Chamber specifically pointed out that for the purposes of the case it was not necessary to determine whether the accused, as a commander of a prison, was a civilian or a military commander. The Appeals Chamber stated as follows:

> 'In the instant appeal, the Appellant contends that, because he was appointed by the Ministry of Justice rather than the Ministry of Defence, he did not have such powers over the guards as a civilian prison warden, whereas the Trial Chamber finds that he was the superior to the guards by reason of his powers over them. The Appeals Chamber takes the view that it does not matter whether he was a civilian or military superior, if it can be proved that, within the Kaonik prison, he had the powers to prevent or to punish in terms of Article 7(3). The Appeals Chamber notes that the Trial Chamber has indeed found this to be proven, thus its finding that the Appellant was a superior within the meaning of Article 7(3).'[49]

Regrettably, the Appeals Chamber did not indicate whether commanders of prisons should be considered as *de facto* military commanders or civilian superiors.

For the purposes of the discussion as to who is considered to be a civilian superior under Article 28(b) ICC only, reference may be made to the existing case law of the *ad hoc* tribunals. So far, Plavsić is the only political leader who has arguably been convicted by the ICTY under the superior responsibility provision. The conviction was based on a guilty plea, and therefore, on the basis of existing ICTY case law, it is difficult to establish whether political leaders are those superiors which fall under Article 28(b) ICC. Although, the Sentencing Judgement in the case against Plavsić states, among other things, that, 'The Presidency [of which Plavsić was a member, MLN] also had authority over the Bosnian Serb police, TO [territorial defence forces, MLN] and civilian authorities.'[50] The position held by the accused shows more characteristics of a *de facto* military commander than of a purely civilian superior for the purposes of Article 28(b) ICC.

The *Brđanin* case is illustrative in this respect. Had Brđanin been found to have exercised *de facto* control over the municipal authorities, the police and the paramilitary units, he would best be described as a *de facto* military commander under Article 28(a) ICC, as suggested by Fenrick. His control would resemble that of a military commander, as a person who has 'assumed *de facto* control over the armed forces, armed police units, or paramilitary units.'[51]

The next question is had the Trial Chamber found that Brđanin only exercised *de facto* control over the municipal authorities, would he then qualify as a civilian superior under Article 28(b) ICC? He could be considered a regional political leader with effective authority and control over civil servants, not organised in chains of command like the police or paramilitary units. However, even if that

---

[49] *Prosecutor* v. *Zlatko Aleksovski*, Appeal Judgement, Case No. IT-95-14/1-A, 24 March 2000, para. 76.

[50] *Prosecutor* v. *Biljana Plavšić*, Sentencing Judgement, Case No. IT-00-39&40/1, 27 February 2003, para. 14.

[51] Fenrick, pp. 517-518.

superior was to qualify for Article 28(b) in theory, the question is whether the division will have any practical implications. As has been pointed out earlier, those who fit the description of a pure civilian superior very often play a role in the conflict and crimes, which is best prosecuted under the provisions on individual criminal responsibility.

While not having been tried, the case against Karadžić and Mladić illustrates the problem related to the question of how superior responsibility should be applied to civilians, in particular if this case was to be dealt with by the ICC, as the Rome Statute makes use of an explicit differentiation between the two groups of superiors.

In its Review of Indictment Pursuant to Rule 61 of the Rules of Procedure and Evidence in the case against Karadžic and Mladić the Trial Chamber found that, 'Karadžić, as president of the SDS and then of the so-called Serbian Republic of Bosnia and Herzegovina, acceded to broad institutional powers making him the head of a political organisation and of the armed forces throughout Bosnian Serb-held territory of Bosnia and Herzegovina.'[52] As for Mladić, the Trial Chamber held that he was the 'highest-ranking officer in the army of the self-styled Bosnian Serb Republic' and that he had 'repeatedly demonstrated absolute control over his troops.'[53] However, his power 'extended to the political level. He played an essential part in decisions by the Bosnian Serb Administration and on the latter's behalf participated in negotiations and signed several agreements, which were all subsequently implemented by his troops.'[54]

The first of the two categories of superiors mentioned in Article 28 deals with '[a] commander or person effectively acting as a military commander.' The second category defined in Article 28 is 'superior and subordinate relationships not described in paragraph (a)', where the perpetrators were 'under his or her effective authority and control.' Based on the Rule 61 decision, both Karadžić and Mladić would fit the definition of a commander or a person effectively acting as such. On the other hand, the Trial Chamber in its decision concluded that the responsibility of both accused could better be characterised as Article 7(1) responsibility.[55]

To the general public it seems clear that both Karadžić and Mladić are responsible for a number of crimes and should be tried by the ICTY. Considering the description of the positions and roles of these two highly authoritative persons, it is apparent that both Karadžić and Mladić were in a position to influence the course of events in Bosnia and Herzegovina at the time of the alleged crimes. What the description of these accused shows is that Article 28 of the ICC Statute complicates matters in that it demands a distinction between civilians and *de facto* military superiors.

---

[52] *Prosecutor* v. *Radovan Karadžić and Ratko Mladić*, Review of Indictment Pursuant to Rule 61 of the Rules of Procedure and Evidence, Case No. IT-95-5-R61, IT-95-18-R61, 11 July 1996, para. 70.

[53] Ibid., para. 77.

[54] Ibid., para. 78.

[55] Ibid., para. 83.

The case against Karadžic and Mladić also illustrates the issue of the level of authority involved in command responsibility. The Trial Chamber in its review of the indictment concluded that the basis for responsibility should be Article 7(1), which shows that it is not plausible to suggest that superiors at a certain level only failed to prevent or punish their subordinates, as opposed to having played some other role in the preparation or commission of the crimes.

The ICTR jurisprudence is somewhat more helpful when considering who could be a civilian superior for the purposes of Article 28(b) ICC. One case has been decided in which the accused was a political leader and incurred responsibility under Article 6(3) of the ICTR Statute. The case at issue is the case against Jean Kambanda, who was the Prime Minister of the interim government of Rwanda in the period when the crimes charged took place.[56] Kambanda pleaded guilty to genocide, conspiracy to commit genocide, direct and public incitement to commit genocide, complicity in genocide, murder as a crime against humanity and extermination as a crime against humanity.[57] Kambanda was held responsible under Article 6(1) and 6(3) for all crimes charged, except for the crime of conspiracy to commit genocide, for which he was convicted under Article 6(1).[58]

With regard to Article 28(b) ICC, the case against Kambanda is interesting but 'disappointing'. The accused acknowledged that he incurred command responsibility in relation to the crimes committed by his subordinates. The perpetrators were members of the armed forces, militia and civilians. As the accused admitted his guilt under Article 6(3), the Trial Chamber did not have to prove his *de facto* control beyond a reasonable doubt. The case shows that the accused, while being a political leader, at the time of the killings acted as a *de jure* or a *de facto* military commander. The 'other superiors' qualification under Article 28(b) ICC would not apply to Kambanda.

Using the categories of civilian superiors listed by Fenrick, the accused in the *Kayishema and Ruzindana* case[59] would qualify as a civilian superior in the group of civil servants. At the time of the crimes, Kayishema was the prefect of the Kibuye prefecture. Kayishema was charged and convicted under Article 6(1) and 6(3). The Appeals Chamber upheld the Trial Chamber's ruling on Kayishema's Article 6(3) responsibility. According to the Trial Chamber the accused had 'effective control over the communal police and the *gendarmerie*, as evidenced by legislative provisions, and the actual control he wielded over all the assailants including the *gendarmes*, soldiers, prison wardens, armed civilians and members of the *Interahamwe* as demonstrated by the identification of Kayishema as leading, directing, ordering, instructing, rewarding and transporting them to carry out the attacks.'[60] The findings indicate that Kayishema exercised 'actual control'

---

[56] *Prosecutor* v. *Jean Kambanda*, Judgement and Sentence, Case No. ICTR-97-23-S, 4 September 1998.

[57] Ibid., para. 40.

[58] Ibid.

[59] *Kayishema and Ruzindana*, TC Judgement.

[60] *Prosecutor* v. *Clément Kayishema and Obed Ruzindana*, Appeal Judgement, Case No. ICTR-95-1-A, 1 June 2001, para. 299.

or, in other words, *de facto* control over gendarmes, militia and other 'organised' perpetrators. Logically, Kayishema would be considered a *de facto* military commander for the purposes of Article 28 ICC.

The ICTR has also convicted a business leader under the command responsibility provision. *The Prosecutor* v. *Alfred Musema* concerned crimes committed in the Kibuye *préfecture* in Rwanda in the context of the widespread attacks against Tutsi and moderate Hutu civilians in 1994. The accused, Musema, was charged and convicted under Article 6(1) and 6(3). The accused was the director of the Gisovu Tea Factory. In this function and because of the poverty in the region, Musema wielded considerable authority in relation to the people he employed, but also in relation to the communal authorities, which were dependent on the tax income from the Tea Factory employees.[61] The Trial Chamber came to the following conclusion:

> 'The Chamber finds that it has been established beyond reasonable doubt that Musema exercised *de jure* authority over employees of the Gisovu Tea Factory while they were on Tea Factory premises and while they were engaged in their professional duties as employees of the Tea Factory, even if those duties were performed outside factory premises. The Chamber notes that Musema exercised legal and financial control over these employees, particularly through his power to appoint and remove these employees from their positions at the Tea Factory. The Chamber notes that Musema was in a position, by virtue of these powers, to take reasonable measures, such as removing, or threatening to remove, an individual from his or her position at the Tea Factory if he or she was identified as a perpetrator of crimes punishable under the Statute. The Chamber also finds that, by virtue of these powers, Musema was in a position to take reasonable measures to attempt to prevent or to punish the use of Tea Factory vehicles, uniforms or other Tea Factory property in the commission of such crimes. The Chamber finds that Musema exercised *de jure* power and *de facto* control over Tea Factory employees and the resources of the Tea Factory.'[62]

Accordingly, Musema exercised *de facto* control over the Tea Factory employees, i.e., civilian perpetrators. The Trial Chamber did not find it proven beyond a reasonable doubt that Musema exercised *de jure* or *de facto* authority in relation to other members of the population of the region. The Trial Chamber used the following wording: 'In relation to other members of the population of Kibuye *Préfecture*, including *thé villageois* plantation workers, while the Chamber is satisfied that such individuals perceived Musema as a figure of authority and as someone who wielded considerable power in the region, it is not satisfied beyond reasonable doubt on the basis of the evidence presented to it that Musema did, in fact, exercise *de jure* power and *de facto* control over these individuals.'[63] Accordingly, Musema only exercised *de facto* control over civilians. As such, this means that Musema would qualify as a superior under Article 28(b) ICC.

---

[61] *Prosecutor* v. *Alfred Musema*, Judgement and Sentence, Case No. ICTR-96-13-T, 27 January 2000, para. 873.

[62] Ibid., para. 880.

[63] Ibid., para. 881.

Interestingly, the Trial Chamber, considering the applicable law in the case at hand, stated that the command responsibility principle was also applicable where a civilian superior only exercised *de facto* control The question in the case of Musema was to what extent he exercised control over persons 'who *a priori* were not under his authority during the period from April to July 1994, namely, the soldiers, the Gisovu Commune police, and the *Interahamwe*.'[64] In its findings, however, the Trial Chamber only made the above-mentioned statement as to Musema's control over 'the other members of the population of Kibuye *Préfecture*',[65] making no mention of soldiers, members of the police or the militia. The conclusion, of course, is that Musema's *de facto* control reached only those perpetrators who were employees of the Tea Factory, but for a complete picture the Trial Chamber should have clarified Musema's relationship with perpetrators belonging to the armed forces, the police or the militia.

Up until now, Musema is the only convicted civilian who could fit the category 'other superiors' under Article 28(b) ICC. That one case indicates, however, that the distinction between *de facto* military commanders and other superiors may become of practical importance. On the other hand, in the *Musema* case, the accused was convicted under both Article 6(1) and 6(3) in relation to the same events. Trial and Appeals Chambers in more recent judgements have decided in favour of an Article 7(1)/6(1) conviction where both bases for responsibility have been proven. That means that only where the superior incurred responsibility solely on the basis of the command responsibility principle, would the distinction between *de facto* military commanders and other superiors be relevant. The remaining question is whether such a situation is imaginable. The civilian superior would not be involved in the crimes by planning, inciting, ordering, aiding or abetting them. His subordinates, most likely civilians in order not to make him a *de facto* military commander, would commit genocide, crimes against humanity or war crimes 'while they were engaged in their professional duties',[66] as the civilian superior would not be responsible for crimes committed by someone in his personal capacity. The likelihood of that actually happening without the personal involvement of the superior seems rather small.

On the basis of the foregoing analysis and using the categories of persons who, according to Fenrick, could be considered as *de facto* military commanders, it seems that only where the relationship is similar to that of a military commander can the civilian superior be accountable under the command responsibility principle.[67] In other words, a civilian superior will in practice only fulfil the requirements of the command responsibility principle where he shares the characteristics of a *de facto* military commander.

---

[64] Ibid., paras. 143-144.

[65] Ibid., para. 881.

[66] Ibid., para. 880.

[67] In support of this view, see, for example, A. Zahar, 'Command Responsibility of Civilian Superiors for Genocide', 14 *LJIL* (2001) p. 591 ('While there is no doubt that civilian superiors are liable to prosecution for command responsibility, the doctrine will be properly operative only in cases where the superior's control of subordinates resembles that enjoyed by military commanders').

The Trial Chamber in the case against Barayagwiza was puzzled by the potential superior responsibility of members of political parties. It pointed to the following: 'A political party is unlike a government, military or corporate structure in that its members are not bound through professional affiliation or in an employment capacity to be governed by the decision making body of the party. Nevertheless, the Chamber considers that to the extent that members of a political party act in accordance with the dictates of that party, or otherwise under its instruction, those issuing such dictates or instruction can and should be held accountable for their implementation.'[68] Thus, the finding by the Chamber indicates that also leaders of political parties may incur command responsibility as civilian superiors.

In general, the cases against civilian superiors decided by the ICTR have been criticised by scholars. Among others, Zahar criticised the conviction of Kayishema under the command responsibility provision. According to him, the tribunal applied the wrong test for establishing command responsibility, the test simply requiring a 'standard of mere influence'. The problem with that was that 'an influential civilian administrator, such as a Rwandan prefect, is thereby transformed into a kind of universal superior – thousands within his sphere of influence become his subordinates in the eyes of the law.'[69] The level of authority was, at least indirectly, also an issue in the case against Kayishema. Zahar, who criticised the judgement, asked the following question: 'How *could* Kayishema have taken measures to prevent the attack when he was *the leader of it*?'[70] 'and how could he have later punished the perpetrators, when he was a perpetrator himself.'[71]

According to Zahar, also the Musema Trial Judgement was erroneous.[72] The Trial Chamber in the *Musema* case found that the accused exercised *de jure* and *de facto* power over the Tea Factory employees, and thereby also found him responsible under the superior responsibility provision. According to Zahar, such reasoning was misguided and did 'not distinguish Musema from any ordinary factory director.' Furthermore, he held that, '[I]t cannot be that all business managers stand liable to be convicted for international crimes perpetrated by their employees for the reason only that they were linked to them through commonplace ties of labour.'[73]Accordingly, while Fenrick identified both senior civil servants and business leaders as potential civilian superiors, the practical application of the command responsibility principle to these categories has been criticised.

---

[68] *Prosecutor* v. *Ferdinand Nahimana, Jean-Bosco Barayagwiza and Hassan Ngeze*, Judgement and Sentence, Case No. ICTR-99-52-T, 3 December 2003, para. 976.

[69] Zahar, p. 600.

[70] Ibid., pp. 591-616, at p. 598.

[71] Ibid., p. 598.

[72] Ibid., pp. 601-604.

[73] Ibid., p. 602.

These examples from case law give an indication of the difficulty in defining which civilian superiors may be rightly prosecuted under the command responsibility provisions.

4.3 Civilian superiors as objects of the command responsibility principle in the judgements rendered by the *ad hoc* tribunals

4.3.1 Introduction

As set out in the introduction to this chapter, there is no obligation on the part of the *ad hoc* tribunals to establish the civilian or military status of the accused before rendering a decision under the command responsibility provision. While the ICC will have to determine the status of the superior for the purposes of Article 28(a) or 28(b), the *ad hoc* tribunals did not need to overcome this hurdle when trying the accused. Nevertheless, the *ad hoc* tribunals have faced some difficulties when trying cases charging command responsibility in respect of superiors who cannot be considered as military commanders. From the point of view of a successful prosecution on the basis of the command responsibility provision, the problem has been the vast amount of acquittals on these charges. The number of unsuccessful trials of civilian superiors supports the thesis that the command responsibility doctrine is most suitable for the prosecution of military commanders. However, the fact that the command responsibility charges have not been effective does not in itself explain why the *ad hoc* tribunals have only convicted a few civilian superiors under Article 6(3)/7(3). The present section pinpoints the reasons for the convictions rendered and for the acquittals.

Zhu expressed the hope that, '[T]he limits of superior responsibility for acts of omission that are attributable to civilian leaders […] be articulated and elaborated in the case law, including that of the *ad hoc* tribunals.'[74] Such limits have not been explicitly set by the tribunals and, accordingly, it will be useful to analyse the findings in some of the cases concerning civilian superiors, with the intention of discovering whether these limits have been implicitly set out in the case law.

4.3.2 Convictions under Article 7(3)/6(3)

4.3.2.1 *ICTY*

In a majority of the cases brought before the ICTY the accused exercised military or 'semi-military' functions. Examples of the latter accused are prison guards who were not necessarily members of the armed forces.[75] In most of the cases concerning clearly civilian accused, the persons charged have been political leaders at various levels. Thus far, only two civilian superiors have been convicted by

---

[74] Zhu, p. 375.

[75] See, for example, *Prosecutor* v. *Duško Sikirica et al.*, Second Amended Indictment, Case No. IT-95-8-PT, 3 January 2001.

the ICTY under the command responsibility provision. In both cases the accused pleaded guilty to a certain count in the indictment, thereby accepting his/her command responsibility in relation to that specific crime.

The first case in which the Trial Chamber convicted a civilian superior under the command responsibility provision was the case of the *Prosecutor* v. *Stevan Todorović*.[76] At the time of the crimes referred to in the *Todorović* case, the accused was the Chief of Police in Bosanski Šamac. He was also a member of the Serb Crisis Staff 'which took the place of the duly-elected municipal assembly and maintained control over all aspects of the municipal government.'[77] Todorović was charged on the basis of Article 7(1) and 7(3),[78] with persecutions on political, racial and religious grounds, deportation, murder, inhumane acts, rape and torture, as crimes against humanity. He was also charged with several grave breaches of the Geneva Conventions and violations of the laws and customs of war, including murder and torture.[79] In the plea agreement, the prosecution withdrew all charges except the charge of persecution, laid down in count 1 of the indictment. In relation to one allegation of torture, as included in the same count,[80] the prosecution pursued liability only under Article 7(3). Accordingly, the accused pleaded guilty to various crimes, together making up the crime of persecution, under both Article 7(1) and 7(3), but for separate facts.

Because of the fact that the case was decided by way of a plea agreement, it differs from cases where the accused denies the charges and the Trial Chamber has to decide whether the facts have been proven beyond a reasonable doubt.[81] As in all cases where a plea agreement is resorted to, the accused, Todorović, made an agreement with the prosecution agreeing that certain facts were true and constituted the factual basis for his guilty plea. In the agreement the accused also acknowledged that as the Chief of Police he had a position of superior authority in relation to all other police officers in Bosanski Šamac and, at the same time, that he bore 'responsibility for the acts of his subordinates under Article 7, paragraph 3, of the Statute.'[82]

The second case in which the accused was charged under both Article 7(1) and Article 7(3) and entered a guilty plea in relation to one of the charges is the case against Biljana Plavšić, a political leader, who among other functions held the position of member of the three-member Presidency of the Serbian Republic.

[76] *Prosecutor* v. *Stevan Todorović*, Case No. IT-95-9/1.

[77] *Prosecutor* v. *Stevan Todorović*, Second Amended Indictment, Case No. IT-95-9-PT, 25 March 1999, para. 11.

[78] Ibid., paras. 25 and 27.

[79] Ibid., paras. 29-49.

[80] *Todorović*, Second Amended Indictment. Only para. 34(d) of count 1 concerned the crime of torture, although it was not specified which crime the prosecution referred to. In the Sentencing Judgment, however, the Trial Chamber clarified that superior responsibility was charged for the torture of Omer Nalic and that this fell under count 1 of the indictment. See *Prosecutor* v. *Stevan Todorović*, Sentencing Judgement, Case No. IT-95-9/1-S, 31 July 2001, para. 5.

[81] W. Schabas, *Introduction to the International Criminal Court*, 2nd edn. (Cambridge, Cambridge University Press 2004) p. 155.

[82] *Todorović*, Sentencing Judgement, para. 14.

The indictment charged Plavšić with genocide; complicity in genocide; persecutions, extermination, murder, deportation and inhumane acts as crimes against humanity; and murder as a violation of the laws and customs of war.[83]

The Sentencing Judgement in this case does not explicitly state whether the basis for responsibility was Article 7(1), Article 7(3) or both. The Trial Chamber in its judgement simply convicted Plavšić of persecutions and sentenced her to eleven years' imprisonment. However, in the plea agreement, Plavšić agreed to plead guilty to the crime of persecution as included in Count 3 of the indictment, and recognised that her crimes constituted either acts or omissions.[84] Count 3 of the indictment explicitly charged Plavšić on the basis of individual criminal responsibility and command responsibility.[85] In the document called Factual Basis for Plea of Guilt, Plavšić admitted to having ignored allegations of ethnic cleansing and to having been aware that other key leaders of the Bosnian Serb Republic ignored crimes that were committed against non-Serbs. No measures were taken to stop the violations 'despite the power and responsibility of the collective and the expanded collective Presidencies or the Ministries to prevent and punish such crimes.'[86] By admitting these facts, the accused showed that she incurred responsibility on the basis of Article 7(3). Altogether the statements and admissions by the accused give reason to believe that Plavšić's conviction was based on both her individual criminal responsibility and her command responsibility.

The two cases discussed are, on the one hand, a confirmation of the applicability of the command responsibility doctrine to civilian superiors. On the other hand, the guilty pleas do not give a truthful picture of the possibilities in a full trial of applying the command responsibility provision to civilian superiors.

4.3.2.2 *ICTR*

The number of civilians accused before the ICTR is far higher than that at the ICTY. Out of some 74 arrestees by December 2008, only about 14 people had held clearly military positions. A few accused had held 'semi-military' positions as leaders of the *Interahamwe* militia, but the large majority were political leaders, senior government administrators, religious leaders and businessmen. A small number of the accused had held other civilian positions, such as a journalist, a medical doctor, a prosecutor or a youth organiser.[87] As many of these civilians were charged under Article 6(3), the ICTR has actually put the application of the command responsibility doctrine to civilians to the test, more so than the

[83] *Prosecutor* v. *Biljana Plavšić*, Amended Consolidated Indictment, Case No. IT-00-39&40-PT, 7 March 2002, paras. 15-27.

[84] *Prosecutor* v. *Biljana Plavšić*, Plea Agreement, Case No. IT-00-40-PT, 30 September 2002, paras. 3 and 5.

[85] *Plavšić*, Amended Consolidated Indictment, in particular, para. 23.

[86] *Prosecutor* v. *Biljana Plavšić*, Factual Basis for Plea of Guilt, Case No. IT-00-39&40-PT, 30 September 2002, para. 21. See also *Plavšić*, Sentencing Judgement, para. 18.

[87] See 'ICTR Detainees – Status on 2 December 2008', available at <http://69.94.11.53/ENGLISH/factsheets/detainee.htm> (accessed 18 December 2008).

ICTY. In this section some of the convictions under Article 6(3) and the particular reasoning in each case are discussed.

i) Kambanda

The first civilian superior to be convicted by the ICTR on the basis of command responsibility was Jean Kambanda, at the time of the crimes the Prime Minister of Rwanda. The conviction in this case was based on a plea agreement.[88] Jean Kambanda pleaded guilty to all six counts of the indictment.[89] He was convicted of genocide, conspiracy to commit genocide, direct and public incitement to commit genocide, complicity in genocide, murder as a crime against humanity and extermination as a crime against humanity.[90] Kambanda was sentenced to life imprisonment.[91] Kambanda was held responsible under Article 6(1) and 6(3) for all crimes charged, except for the crime of conspiracy to commit genocide, for which he was convicted under Article 6(1).

Just as in the *Todorović* and *Plavšić* cases, the *Kambanda* case adds to the statistics of cases against civilian superiors convicted under the command responsibility doctrine. The conviction being based on a guilty plea, the judgement is not informative of the judges' approach to the liability of the accused in this case.

ii) Nahimana, Barayagwiza and Ngeze

In the case of the *Prosecutor* v. *Nahimana, Barayagwiza and Ngeze*, all the accused were civilians. Nahimana had been a professor of history and the Dean of the Arts Faculty at the National University of Rwanda. He was one of the founders of the *Radio Télévision Libre des Milles Collines* (RTLM), which played a crucial role in the events covered in this case. Barayagwiza was the Director of Political Affairs at the Ministry of Foreign Affairs and he was also one of the founders of RTLM, and a founder of the *Coalition pour la Défense de la République* (CDR), a party which promoted unity and solidarity among the Hutu and was closed to Rwandans of Tutsi ethnicity. The CDR was a significant player in the events of this case. The accused Ngeze had worked as a journalist and in 1990 he founded a newspaper called *Kangura*, a well-known newspaper within Rwanda and internationally. Ngeze held the position of Editor-in-Chief of this newspaper. Accordingly, the accused all held civilian positions.

All accused were charged with superior responsibility under Article 6(3) in respect of genocide, either on counts of the crime of genocide proper, or of direct and public incitement to commit genocide or complicity in genocide. They were

[88] See section 4.3.2.1 *supra*.

[89] *Prosecutor* v. *Jean Kambanda*, Judgement and Sentence, Case No. ICTR-97-23-S, 4 September 1998, para. 5.

[90] Ibid., para. 40.

[91] Ibid., at IV. Verdict.

also charged with crimes against humanity under Article 6(3).[92] While Ngeze, the Editor-in-Chief of *Kangura*, was not found liable on any count on the basis of his command responsibility, both Nahimana and Barayagwiza were convicted under Article 6(3).

In this case the findings on the command responsibility of Nahimana and Barayagwiza are interesting, if not peculiar. Prior to its findings on the individual criminal responsibility of each accused, the Trial Chamber found that the genocidal intent of all the accused was established beyond a reasonable doubt.[93] With regard to Barayagwiza the Trial Chamber found that he had publicly expressed his readiness to exterminate the Tutsi population. It held that, 'From his words and deeds, Barayagwiza's ruthless commitment to the destruction of the Tutsi population as a means by which to protect the political gains secured by the Hutu majority from 1959 is evident.'[94] Accordingly, by 'words and deeds' Barayagwiza had made clear that he supported or encouraged the extermination of the Tutsi ethnic group.

The Trial Chamber continued by making its findings on the individual criminal responsibility of each accused. In relation to genocide, the findings only concern Barayagwiza, as Nahimana was not charged on the basis of command responsibility. The Trial Chamber found that, 'Nahimana and Barayagwiza were, respectively, 'number one' and 'number two' in the top management of the radio', the RTLM.[95] The Trial Chamber continued by stating that the accused 'represented the radio at the highest level in meetings with the Ministry of Information; they controlled the finances of the company; and they were both members of the Steering Committee, which functioned in effect as a board of directors for RTLM.'[96] The Chamber recognised that Nahimana and Barayagwiza did not make decisions with regard to particular broadcasts, but it found that such decisions 'reflected an editorial policy for which they were responsible.'[97] The Chamber held that, 'The broadcasts collectively conveyed a message of ethnic hatred and a call for violence against the Tutsi population', and that, 'Nahimana and Barayagwiza were responsible for this message and knew it was causing concern.'[98] The Chamber considered it established that, 'Nahimana and Barayagwiza knew what was happening at RTLM and failed to exercise the authority vested in them as office-holding members of the governing body of RTLM, to prevent the genocidal harm that was caused by RTLM programming.' An earlier intervention by Nahimana to stop attacks by RTLM on UNAMIR and General Dallaire contributed to the finding that the accused, Nahimana and Barayagwiza, had *de facto* authority to prevent the 'genocidal harm'.[99] The role and authority

---

[92] *Prosecutor* v. *Ferdinand Nahimana, Jean-Bosco Barayagwiza and Hassan Ngeze*, TC Judgement Summary, Case No. ICTR-99-52-T, 3 December 2003, para. 5.

[93] *Nahimana et al.*, TC Judgement and Sentence, para. 969.

[94] Ibid., para. 967.

[95] Ibid., para. 970.

[96] Ibid.

[97] Ibid.

[98] Ibid., para. 971.

[99] Ibid., para. 972.

of the accused convinced the Chamber that, 'Nahimana and Barayagwiza had superior responsibility for the broadcasts of RTLM.'[100] As Nahimana was not charged with genocide pursuant to Article 6(3), the Trial Chamber made the following finding in relation to Barayagwiza only: 'For his active engagement in the management of RTLM prior to 6 April, and his failure to take necessary and reasonable measures to prevent the killing of Tutsi civilians instigated by RTLM, the Chamber finds Jean-Bosco Barayagwiza guilty of genocide pursuant to Article 6(3) of its Statute.'[101]

Why is it necessary to include such a thorough review of the findings? The findings on these specific points raise two issues with regard to command responsibility that deserve some more attention. The first issue concerns the genocidal intent of the accused and the subsequent finding on his command responsibility. As the accused was charged with genocide, the Trial Chamber had to establish the special intent required on the part of the accused. However, by doing so the Chamber showed that Barayagwiza not only knew of genocidal acts taking place, but in fact that the accused himself supported the idea of committing these crimes. On the other hand, the Chamber found that the accused bore command responsibility in relation to the broadcasts of RTLM, which led to 'genocidal harm'. There is a contradiction here, which as such is not specific to this case but concerns the whole issue of command responsibility for the crime of genocide. In this case, how could one expect that the accused would prevent or punish the acts of his subordinates if, in fact, the extermination of the Tutsi population was exactly what he wanted? The issue of genocide and command responsibility is not exclusively a point of discussion in cases against civilian superiors, but the fact that this controversial line of reasoning was used here partly contributed to another conviction of a civilian superior under Article 6(3).

The second issue concerns Barayagwiza's *de facto* authority to prevent the 'genocidal harm' from occurring. As has been discussed earlier in this study, the *ad hoc* tribunals have interpreted the command responsibility provisions so as to require not only authority in relation to subordinates, but effective control over those subordinates. In the present case, a causal connection was found between the broadcasts and the actual killings.[102] Groups of perpetrators were also identified. But did Barayagwiza exercise effective control over these perpetrators? It was found that the accused could have used his authority to stop the broadcasts or intervene and change the message of the broadcasts and thereby prevent the crimes. However, it is very questionable, to say the least, whether one can consider all the possible listeners who were possibly carrying out crimes as a consequence of the broadcasts as subordinates of the accused. What authority would Barayagwiza have had to punish the perpetrators for committing crimes or to bring them before the authorities, in accordance with the requirements of the command responsibility principle, as he had no direct hierarchical, professional or personal relationship with all the listeners? Applying the command

[100] Ibid., para. 973.
[101] Ibid.
[102] Ibid., para. 949.

responsibility provision in relation to these specific facts and to the crime of genocide is stretching the principle too far.

Considering the responsibility of Barayagwiza in relation to direct and public incitement to commit genocide, which the Trial Chamber did, seems more convincing. Indeed, the Chamber found that the broadcasts of RTLM constituted direct and public incitement to commit genocide and it referred to its earlier finding that Barayagwiza had the specific intent required for genocide. Accordingly, the Chamber found 'beyond a reasonable doubt that Barayagwiza was responsible for RTLM programming pursuant to Article 6(3) of the Statute of the Tribunal.'[103] Unfortunately, the arguments concerning his Article 6(3) responsibility are not well set out. It was established that the broadcasts constituted incitement to commit genocide. However, if the accused was to incur responsibility on the basis of Article 6(3), his superior-subordinate relationship should have been in relation to those who carried out the crime of direct and public incitement to commit genocide, i.e., those who worked at RTLM, not the actual perpetrators of the crime of genocide. As set out earlier, Barayagwiza was the 'number two' at RTLM and thereby undoubtedly exercised authority over those who actually brought the 'information' to the listeners. However, finding out whether he exercised effective control over those persons committing the crime of incitement to commit genocide is secondary to the earlier argument concerning the crime of genocide and Barayagwiza's genocidal intent. Where the accused supported the thought of and encouraged the killing of members of the Tutsi ethnic group, it may be considered incongruous, in fact illogical, to contend that he should have prevented and punished those committing the crime.[104] Therefore, the command responsibility principle does not constitute the correct basis for liability in relation to these facts and crimes. The arguments concerning command responsibility for direct and public incitement to commit genocide in relation to RTLM broadcasts would also apply to Nahimana.

In relation to the crimes of extermination and persecution as crimes against humanity the Trial Chamber referred to its findings on genocide and applied the same basis as set out above for finding Barayagwiza responsible under Article 6(3).[105] Article 6(1) and Article 6(3) liability for crimes against humanity was established in relation to RTLM broadcasts (Nahimana) and in relation to actions of the CDR and the Impuzamugambi[106] (Barayagwiza).[107] The Trial Chamber found Nahimana responsible under both provisions on the basis of the facts established in relation to genocide.[108] Barayagwiza was said to have directed and

[103] Ibid., para. 1034.

[104] The same logic was articulated in *Blaškić*, TC Judgement, para. 337, where the Trial Chamber stated the following: 'It would be illogical to hold a commander criminally responsible for planning, instigating or ordering the commission of crimes and, at the same time, reproach him for not preventing or punishing them.'

[105] *Nahimana et al.*, TC Judgement and Sentence, paras. 1064 and 1082.

[106] The Impuzamugambi was the youth wing of the CDR.

[107] *Nahimana et al.*, TC Judgement and Sentence, paras. 1063-1067, 1081 and 1083.

[108] Ibid., paras. 1063 and 1081.

planned extermination carried out by the CDR.[109] His active role in promoting the killing of Tutsi civilians by the CDR and the Impuzamugambi was established in relation to genocide and was used as a basis for his Article 6(1) responsibility for persecution as a crime against humanity.[110] At the same time, the Trial Chamber found that the two accused failed to take the necessary and reasonable measures to prevent the killing of Tutsi civilians and thereby incurred command responsibility with respect to the same events. The same argument as mentioned above applies here; it is illogical to hold the accused responsible for their active role in planning, directing, supporting or otherwise assisting the killing of the Tutsi population and, at the same time, to reproach them for not having taken the necessary and reasonable measures to prevent the crimes.

The Appeals Chamber reversed the convictions to a considerable degree in this case. The main issue was the error made by the Trial Chamber in finding that the broadcasts of RTLM before 6 April 1994 contributed to the acts of genocide, which, according to the Appeals Chamber, they did not. In the case of Nahimana, the consequence of the finding was that all the findings of guilt under Article 6(1) were reversed. The convictions under Article 6(3) were upheld, as far as they concerned acts caused by RTLM broadcasts after 6 April 1994. With regard to Barayagwiza, the Appeals Chamber reversed some findings under Article 6(1) relating to his activities within the CDR, while affirming others. His conviction under Article 6(3) for genocide was reversed, with regard to the RTLM, because the effective control of the accused was only established for the period before 6 April 1994. With regard to the finding of guilt on genocide in relation to the CDR, the Appeals Chamber held that an accused could not be convicted under Article 6(1) and 6(3) on the same count and for the same acts. As regards the conviction for direct and public incitement to commit genocide under Article 6(3) in relation to acts committed by the CDR militants and *Impuzamugambi*, the Appeals Chamber found that the Trial Chamber had erroneously found that effective control between the accused and the perpetrators was established.[111]

The outcome of the case was altered by the findings of the Appeals Chamber. However, the issues raised above as a consequence of the Trial Chamber judgement remain issues of concern as these were not explicitly addressed by the Appeals Chamber. As stated, the reversal of the convictions was based on more factual arguments.

iii) Musema

The case against Alfred Musema was thoroughly analysed above in relation to the question whether Musema, the director of a tea factory, could qualify for the category 'other superiors' under Article 28(b) of the ICC Statute. As stated

[109] Ibid., paras. 1065 and 1067.

[110] Ibid., para. 1083.

[111] *Prosecutor v. Ferdinand Nahimana, Jean-Bosco Barayagwiza and Hassan Ngeze*, AC Judgement Summary, Case No. ICTR-99-52-A, 28 November 2007. The findings in relation to Hassan Ngeze were not of direct relevance to the discussion concerning Art. 6(3).

in that context, Musema was charged and convicted under both Article 6(1) and Article 6(3) in relation to the same events.[112] As in the *Barayagwiza* case, the Trial Chamber in the *Musema* case held that the accused should incur both individual criminal responsibility and command responsibility for the same crimes. On one charge of rape as a crime against humanity, the accused was found guilty only on the basis of Article 6(1). The reason for this finding was the fact that the accused himself had raped a woman and while this was proven beyond a reasonable doubt, it could not be established that his subordinates had committed any such act,[113] or more accurately that those who, in concert with Musema, raped the woman, were his subordinates.[114] Evidence to that effect would most likely have led to a conviction in line with the rest of the findings in relation to the other charges, i.e., both under Article 6(1) and Article 6(3).

Later case law dismissed the conviction of an accused under both provisions in relation to the same facts. While presently judgements from the *ad hoc* tribunals would not very likely contain this approach, this finding on cumulative convictions in the Musema judgement and other judgements is not of great concern for future cases. However, the fact that Musema was convicted under both provisions for the same facts again adds to the impression of the command responsibility doctrine as being equally applicable to military commanders and civilian superiors.

iv) Kayishema

In the *Prosecutor* v. *Clément Kayishema and Obed Ruzindana* the accused were charged with genocide; murder, extermination and other inhumane acts as crimes against humanity; and violations of Article 3 common to the Geneva Conventions and of Additional Protocol II, under Article 4(a) of the ICTR Statute. The indictment concerned massacres of members of the Tutsi population that took place at a church complex and at a stadium in Kibuye town, at the church in Mubuga and in the area of Bisesero, all places that were part of the *Prefécture* of Kibuye.[115] At the time of the events concerned in the indictment, Clément Kayishema was the *Prefect* of the Kibuye *Préfecture*.[116] Both accused were civilians.[117] While Ruzindana was charged on the basis of Article 6(1), his co-accused Kayishema was charged under both Article 6(1) and Article 6(3). The Trial Chamber found that Kayishema incurred both individual and command responsibility for the crime of genocide.[118] It held that, ‘It is clear that for all crime sites denoted in

[112] See section 4.2.4 *supra*.

[113] *Prosecutor* v. *Alfred Musema*, Judgement and Sentence, Case No. ICTR-96-13-T, 27 January 2000, para. 968.

[114] Ibid., paras. 846-853 and 861.

[115] *Prosecutor* v. *Clément Kayishema and Obed Ruzindana*, First Amended Indictment, Case No. ICTR-95-1-I.

[116] *Kayishema and Ruzindana*, TC Judgement, para. 9.

[117] *Kayishema and Ruzindana*, First Amended Indictment, paras. 23-34.

[118] *Kayishema and Ruzindana*, TC Judgement, paras. 568-569. In relation to the crimes against humanity charged the Trial Chamber found that a conviction under the genocide provision absorbed

the Indictment, Kayishema had *de jure* authority over most of the assailants, and *de facto* control of them all. It has also been proved beyond reasonable doubt that the attacks that occurred were commenced upon his orders (Mubuga Church excepted). They were attacks clearly orchestrated by him, and only executed upon his direction.'[119] The Chamber continued by considering the knowledge requirement of the command responsibility provision and found that 'his identification at the site both before and during the attacks leave the Trial Chamber in no doubt that Kayishema knew of the crimes that were being committed by his subordinates.'[120] With regard to the third element, the omission to prevent and punish, the Trial Chamber was of the opinion that, 'No evidence was adduced that he attempted to prevent the atrocities that he knew were about to occur and which were within his power to prevent.'[121] Finally, the Chamber stated as follows:

> 'It is unnecessary to elaborate upon Kayishema's punishment of these perpetrators, or lack thereof, in any further detail. The task would be a superficial one in light of the Trial Chamber's findings that Kayishema exercised clear, definitive control, both *de jure* and *de facto*, over the assailants at every massacre site set out in the Indictment. It has also been proved beyond a reasonable doubt that Kayishema ordered the attacks or, knowing of their imminence, failed to prevent them.'[122]

Therewith, the Trial Chamber considered it proven that Kayishema incurred responsibility under Article 6(3).

In its conclusion to the findings on Kayishema's command responsibility, the Trial Chamber stated that, 'The inherent purpose of Article 6(3) is to ensure that a morally culpable individual is held responsible for those heinous acts committed under his command.' The Chamber found that, 'Kayishema not only knew, and failed to prevent, those under his control from slaughtering thousands of innocent civilians; but he orchestrated and invariably led these bloody massacres'. It concluded by saying that, '[I]n order to adequately reflect his culpability for these deaths, Kayishema must be held responsible for the actions and atrocities committed.'[123]

The findings of the Trial Chamber are remarkably contradictive. If the accused orchestrated and led the massacres, he is undoubtedly to be held liable under Article 6(1). Regardless of whether a conviction under Article 6(1) is possible or not, there is at least no role for command responsibility here. The

the crimes charged as crimes against humanity. The Chamber found it to be in the interest of justice not to find the accused guilty of other inhuman acts as crimes against humanity, as the accused had not been properly informed of the specific charges under these counts. As regards the violations against Art. 3 common to the Geneva Conventions and Additional Protocol II, the Trial Chamber stated that it had not been proven beyond a reasonable doubt that the crimes were 'committed in direct conjunction with the armed conflict.' See *Kayishema and Ruzindana*, TC Judgement, paras. 577, 587 and 623.

119 *Kayishema and Ruzindana*, TC Judgement, para. 504.

120 Ibid., para. 510.

121 Ibid., para. 513.

122 Ibid., para. 515.

123 Ibid., para. 516.

purpose of the command responsibility doctrine is to hold persons accountable who failed to carry out their duty to prevent or punish crimes. Orchestrating and leading are clearly a way of contributing to the commission of the crimes. The Trial Chamber here obviously did not pay attention to the object and purpose of the doctrine, despite the fact that they discussed the 'inherent purpose' of Article 6(3). To say that the purpose of Article 6(3) is to hold 'a morally culpable individual' criminally liable is in contradiction with the various meanings of the term responsibility, which was discussed in Chapter 3 of this study. The fact that an accused may be considered as morally culpable for heinous international crimes is not sufficient in a criminal trial, where the legal requirements as set out in the Statute are not fulfilled.

The Appeals Chamber dismissed the appeals in the case and upheld the conviction of Kayishema and Ruzindana, including the conviction of Kayishema under Article 6(3).[124] However, the Appeals Chamber did consider whether the Trial Chamber had erred in finding that the accused had effective control over his subordinates. The Appeals Chamber upheld the view of the Trial Chamber. Interestingly, it pointed out that, 'Kayishema was also found to have effective control over the communal police and the *gendarmerie*, as evidenced by legislative provisions, and the actual control he wielded over all the assailants including the *gendarmes*, soldiers, prison wardens, armed civilians and members of the *Interahamwe* as demonstrated by the identification of Kayishema as leading, directing, ordering, instructing, rewarding and transporting them to carry out the attacks.'[125] The finding shows that proof of the civilian superior position of the accused was based on facts indicating that the accused carried out acts falling under Article 6(1). This supports the idea presented earlier in this chapter that whether a civilian is a civilian superior for the purposes of the command responsibility provisions should be determined on the basis of what the person in a certain position does, instead of simply on the basis of what position the person has. This approach by the Trial Chamber is to be applauded. On the other hand, by showing what acts the superior carried out, there is no doubt that he was actively involved in the events. As stated earlier, it is doubtful whether the command responsibility is at all applicable in such a case.

The findings in this case are in line with those in the *Musema* case, in which case the Trial Chambers similarly convicted the accused under both Article 6(1) and Article 6(3) in relation to the same events.

v) Rugambarara

The initial indictment charged Juvénal Rugambarara, the 'bourgmestre' (mayor) of Bicumbi commune, Kigali-Rural prefecture, with genocide, complicity in genocide, conspiracy to commit genocide, direct and public incitement to commit genocide, extermination, torture and rape as crimes against humanity and serious violations of common Article 3 to the Geneva Conventions, under Articles 6(1)

[124] *Kayishema and Ruzindana*, AC Judgement, para. 372.
[125] Ibid., para. 299.

and 6(3).[126] However, on 12 June 2007 the prosecution filed a motion in which it sought leave to amend the indictment. The amended indictment was reduced to one count of extermination as a crime against humanity on the basis of Article 6(3).[127] Interestingly, the prosecution and the accused a day later jointly filed a motion for consideration of a plea agreement.[128] The reason for the amended indictment was not a lack of evidence, but seems to have been a measure to reach a guilty plea, which, of course, contributes to the expeditiousness of the proceedings.[129]

The accused, Rugambarara, entered a guilty plea in which he accepted his responsibility for 'having failed in his duty to take the necessary and reasonable steps to ensure the punishment of his subordinates for the crimes they committed.'[130] He thereby 'admitted that he had effective control over his subordinates and the material ability to punish the perpetrators or commission an investigation into the said crimes.'[131] This means that he admitted the existence of a superior-subordinate relationship between himself and 'all the conseillers, communal policemen, local administrators, and armed militiamen located in Mwulire, Mabare and Nawe secteurs in Bicumbi commune', as alleged in the amended indictment.[132]

Together with the other cases decided by way of a guilty plea the *Rugambarara* case does not contribute much to the discussion on the applicability of the command responsibility doctrine to civilian superiors. As the case adds another civilian to the list of superiors convicted by an international tribunal under the command responsibility doctrine, it may be considered that guilty pleas are a convenient way for the prosecution to ensure a conviction on the basis of Article 6(3)/7(3). While effective control on the part of the civilian superior is difficult to argue convincingly, a guilty plea on the basis of Article 6(3) ensures that a person who is, as stated in *Kayishema*, at least 'morally culpable' agrees to his criminal liability under the command responsibility provision.

4.3.2.3 *Discussion*

All the convictions under Article 6(3)/7(3) discussed above may be criticised for various reasons. The guilty pleas are regrettable, from the point of view of command responsibility, because they did not give the prosecution and the defence, and ultimately the judges, the possibility to weigh the evidence and the arguments for and against a conviction of a civilian superior under the command responsi-

[126] *Prosecutor* v. *Juvénal Rugambarara*, Judgement and Sentence, Case No. ICTR-00-59-T, 16 November 2007, para. 2.

[127] Ibid., para. 3.

[128] Ibid., para. 4.

[129] *Prosecutor* v. *Juvénal Rugambarara*, Decision on the Prosecution Motion to Amend the Indictment, Case No. ICTR-00-59-T, 28 June 2007, para. 7.

[130] *Rugambarara*, TC Judgement and Sentence, para. 5.

[131] Ibid., para. 45.

[132] *Prosecutor* v. *Juvénal Rugambarara*, Amended Indictment, Case No. ICTR-2000-59-I, 2 July 2007, para. 10.

bility provision. The other judgements discussed contain clearly contradicting arguments as regards the active/passive relationship between the superior accused and the crimes committed. His active role in the events is used to prove the superior-subordinate relationship with the perpetrators of the crime. The manner in which the arguments are brought forward reduces the validity of the command responsibility provision as a basis for criminal liability. In short, the cases discussed do not offer credible support for the applicability in practice of the command responsibility doctrine to civilian superiors.

4.3.3 Acquitted of Article 7(3)/6(3) charges

An acquittal under the superior responsibility principle may be the consequence of different circumstances, one of the main reasons being the lack of evidence in relation to the superior, which evidently means that the superior is not responsible under the applicable law.[133] However, a simple but (for the purposes of this study) important consequence of an acquittal of a civilian superior in a case where superior responsibility was charged, is that the applicability of the principle to civilians or at least to the specific civilian in that specific case is not shown. On the other hand, an acquittal may also shed some light on why the principle was not applied or applicable to that specific civilian superior. For this reason, analysing some interesting cases of acquittal may contribute to a complete picture of the applicability of the command responsibility principle to civilian superiors.

In the cases before the *ad hoc* tribunals concerning clearly civilian superiors, the reasons for the acquittal of the accused have varied. One category of cases led to a finding of not guilty because of the lack of specificity in the indictments or related technical issues in the indictments. Another reason for a failing charge under the superior responsibility provision is the plea agreements and guilty pleas entered by the accused. An obvious, but yet interesting category of cases is that which concerns the accused in relation to which the available or presented evidence at some stage posed a problem for establishing the command responsibility of the accused beyond a reasonable doubt. The last category of acquittals identified here concerns the cases where Articles 7(1)/6(1) and 7(3)/6(3) were unsuccessfully charged at the same time in relation to the same facts.

4.3.3.1 *Vague indictments*

The lack of sufficient detail in the indictments has caused problems in a few cases against civilian superiors before the ICTR. A vague indictment has not been iden-

---

[133] An example of such a case is that against Ljube Boškoski, who was the Minister of the Interior of the former Yugoslav Republic of Macedonia (FYROM). Having established the superior-subordinate relationship and the knowledge requirement for the purposes of Art. 7(3), the prosecution did not show that the accused failed to take the necessary and reasonable measures to punish the perpetrators of the crimes, as he was informed that reports about the atrocities had been sent to the judicial authorities and that an investigation was being attempted. See *Prosecutor* v. *Ljube Boškoski and Johan Tarčulovski*, Judgement, Case No. IT-04-82-T, 10 July 2008, paras. 419-536.

tified as the main reason for a finding of not guilty under the superior responsibility provision in relation to a civilian accused before the ICTY.

i) Akayesu

In 1994, at the time relevant to the crimes charged, the accused in the *Akayesu* case served as the bourgmestre of Taba commune and, accordingly, held a civilian position. Akayesu was charged with genocide, crimes against humanity and violations of Article 3 common to the 1949 Geneva Conventions in relation to events in Taba commune, including the killing of Tutsi civilians. In its judgement, the Trial Chamber stated that the accused was charged under Article 6(1) for the crimes alleged in the indictment. With regard to three counts of the indictment, concerning crimes of sexual violence, the Chamber stated that the accused was additionally or alternatively charged under Article 6(3) of the Statute.[134]

The Chamber found that the accused 'had reason to know and in fact knew that acts of sexual violence were occurring on or near the premises of the bureau communal and that he took no measures to prevent these acts or punish the perpetrators of them.'[135] Accordingly, there was enough evidence to establish the mental element of the superior responsibility provision. In addition, the Chamber noted that, '[T]he evidence supports a finding that a superior/subordinate relationship existed between the Accused and the *Interahamwe* who were at the bureau communal',[136] and who were the physical perpetrators of the crimes. Nevertheless, Akayesu was acquitted under Article 6(3).

The Chamber pointed to the fact that the superior-subordinate relationship between the accused and the perpetrators, which was proven, was not alleged in the indictment, although such a 'relationship is a fundamental element of the criminal offence set forth in Article 6(3).'[137] In addition to this, the Chamber drew a rather oddly formulated conclusion: 'The amendment of the Indictment with additional charges pursuant to Article 6(3) could arguably be interpreted as implying an allegation of the command responsibility required by Article 6(3).'[138] What the Trial Chamber seems to have said was that if the indictment is amended to include charges pursuant to Article 6(3), the accused could also be held responsible under that provision, which is self-evident. Following these two observations, the Chamber concluded that it would not be fair to the accused to make inferences in this regard.

The judgement has been criticised for being too technical regarding the fact that the superior-subordinate relationship was not explicitly laid down in the indictment.[139] In addition to that, however, what made the conclusions as regards

[134] *Akayesu*, TC Judgement, para. 471.

[135] Ibid., para. 691.

[136] Ibid.

[137] Ibid.

[138] Ibid.

[139] W. Schabas, 'Commentary', in A. Klip and G. Sluiter, eds., *Annotated Leading Cases of International Criminal Tribunals*, Vol. 2 (Antwerp, Intersentia/Hart 2001) p. 553.

superior responsibility and especially the second observation mentioned above sound odd is the fact that the Chamber refers to additional charges pursuant to Article 6(3) in the indictment, while pointing out the lack of explicit charges referring to the superior-subordinate relationship between the accused and the perpetrators. In fact, neither of these allegations was explicitly set out in the amended indictment. However, the amended indictment did add some charges to the initial indictment, more specifically those charges of crimes of sexual violence, with reference to which the Chamber discusses superior responsibility. The relevant paragraph of the indictment reads as follows:

> '12B Jean Paul Akayesu knew that the acts of sexual violence, beatings and murders were being committed and was at times present during their commission. Jean Paul Akayesu facilitated the commission of the sexual violence, beatings and murders by allowing the sexual violence and beatings and murders to occur on or near the bureau communal premises. By virtue of his presence during the commission of the sexual violence, beatings and murders and by failing to prevent the sexual violence, beatings and murders, Jean Paul Akayesu encouraged these activities.'[140]

There is, however, no explicit mention in this paragraph or elsewhere in the indictment of charges on the basis of superior responsibility, whereas it was explicitly stated in the indictment that the accused allegedly incurred individual responsibility and what forms of participation in a crime leads to such responsibility under Article 6(1).[141] Whether the prosecution presented oral arguments to the effect that the accused was charged under Article 6(3) was not mentioned in the judgement, which leads to the conclusion that the Chamber need not have considered, or could have decided not to consider, the superior responsibility of the accused in the first place.

Paragraph 12B of the indictment mentioned that Akayesu 'facilitated' the commission of the crimes 'by allowing' the crimes to occur. Furthermore, 'by virtue of his presence' during the commission of the crimes and by 'failing to prevent' the crimes, the accused 'encouraged' the criminal acts. As in other cases before the *ad hoc* tribunals, this description of the role of the accused could also have constituted a mode of participation in the crimes, such as aiding and abetting, which falls under Article 6(1). Although the *Akayesu* case was the first case before the ICTR, even the early indictments of accused before the ICTY included an explicit mention of the basis of responsibility, either individual, superior or both, under which the accused was charged.

This is not the right place to elaborate on the modes of participation or the right form of an indictment, and so the analysis only serves to show that while the *Akayesu* case is considered as the first case before the *ad hoc* tribunals in which the principle of command responsibility was examined, the superior responsibility of the civilian superior accused in the case was not even mentioned in the indictment. Accordingly, the Chamber should have avoided the discussion on

---

140 *Akayesu*, Amended Indictment, para. 12B.
141 Ibid., para. 11.

superior responsibility because it knew that such responsibility was not charged, instead of finally in its decision acquitting the accused under the superior responsibility provision in fairness to the accused, a technicality.

The *Akayesu* case is usually described as the first case of superior responsibility before the *ad hoc* tribunals and as a case in which hesitation was expressed in relation to civilian superiors.[142] While it is assumed that the hesitation concerned the superior responsibility of the accused, Akayesu, the judgement reveals that the Chamber did not base its hesitation on the case before it, but on one case decided by the Tokyo Tribunal in the post-WW II period.[143] As is well-known, the approach of the *Akayesu* Trial Chamber in relation to civilians has been overturned in subsequent ICTR cases.[144] As a consequence, the *Akayesu* judgement offers very little guidance as to why and how the superior responsibility principle should be applied to civilian superiors.

ii) Ntagerura

André Ntagerura was charged jointly with two others, Emmanuel Bagambiki and Samuel Imanishimwe,[145] in relation to attacks against the Tutsi population in the Cyangugu prefecture, during which one hundred thousand or more people were killed.[146] Ntagerura was charged with genocide; conspiracy to commit genocide; complicity in genocide; extermination as a crime against humanity; and violence to life, health and the physical or mental well-being of persons as serious violations of Article 3 common to the Geneva Conventions and Additional Protocol II.[147] All counts, except one, charged the accused on the basis of Article 6(1). Under one count of complicity in genocide, Ntagerura was charged solely on the basis of Article 6(3).[148]

At the time relevant to the indictment, Ntagerura was the Minister of Transport and Communications of the Republic of Rwanda and a prominent member of the ruling party, the *Mouvement republican national pour la démocratie et le développement* (MRND).[149] Ntagerura allegedly had 'strong political and community ties in Cyangugu *préfecture*.'[150]

The Trial Chamber acquitted the accused on all counts. Considering the charge of complicity in genocide under Count 6 of the indictment, the Trial Chamber simply found that the prosecution had not proven the allegations related

[142] Schabas 2001, p. 553.
[143] *Akayesu*, TC Judgement, paras. 490-491.
[144] See, for example, *Musema*, TC Judgement, paras. 135-136.
[145] *Prosecutor* v. *André Ntagerura, Emmanuel Bagambiki and Samuel Imanishimwe*, Judgement and Sentence, Case No. ICTR-99-46-T, 25 February 2004.
[146] *Prosecutor* v. *André Ntagerura*, Amended Indictment, Case No. ICTR-96-10-I, 29 January 1998.
[147] Ibid., at Charges.
[148] Ibid., at Count 6.
[149] Ibid., paras. 6-8.
[150] Ibid., para. 9.1.

to this count beyond a reasonable doubt.[151] In its legal findings, the Chamber considered it unnecessary to consider whether Ntagerura incurred command responsibility 'as a superior over civil servants of the Ministry of Transport and Communications', considering its earlier decision that the provisions of the indictment that were relevant to the charge on command responsibility were both vague and failed to identify any criminal conduct on the part of the accused. The vagueness concerned the failure to specify a superior-subordinate relationship between the accused and the perpetrators, the knowledge of the accused, as well as the failure to take necessary and reasonable measures to prevent or punish the perpetrators. Consequently, for the Trial Chamber a vague indictment was sufficient for completely refraining from discussing the command responsibility of Ntagerura.[152] While technically a correct decision, a lack of specificity in the indictment led the Trial Chamber to dismiss a very rare, if not the only, case that charged a civilian superior solely on the basis of command responsibility under one count.

4.3.3.2 *Guilty pleas*

As discussed earlier in this chapter, some convictions of civilian superiors on the basis of command responsibility were entered following a guilty plea by the accused. Interestingly, other plea agreements have excluded that provision and have focussed on a guilty plea on the basis of the individual criminal responsibility of the accused.

i) Serugendo

Joseph Serugendo was a member of the governing board of *Radio Television de Mille Collines* (RTLM) and an adviser to the RTLM radio station. He also held a position at the *Office Rwandais d'Information* and was a member of the 'enlarged National Committee of the *Interahamwe za MRND* that exercised authority over the *Interahamwe* of Kigali.'[153] Serugendo was charged with conspiracy to commit genocide; genocide or alternatively complicity in genocide; direct and public incitement to commit genocide; and persecution as a crime against humanity. All charges, except that on conspiracy to commit genocide, were brought under both Article 6(1) and Article 6(3).[154]

Serugendo entered into a plea agreement with the prosecution and pleaded guilty to direct and public incitement to commit genocide and persecution as a crime against humanity, on the basis of Article 6(1).[155] The guilty plea and

---

[151] *Ntagerura et al.*, TC Judgement and Sentence, para. 667.

[152] Ibid., paras. 624, 42 and 69.

[153] *Prosecutor* v. *Joseph Serugendo*, Judgement and Sentence, Case No. ICTR-2005-84-I, 12 June 2006, para. 16.

[154] *Prosecutor* v. *Joseph Serugendo*, Corrigendum of Indictment, Case No. ICTR-2005-84-I, 21 July 2005.

[155] *Serugendo*, Judgement and Sentence, paras. 3-5.

the withdrawal of the other charges meant that Serugendo was not convicted under Article 6(3). As in most cases, the Trial Chamber did consider the superior position of the accused at the sentencing stage and stated the following: 'At all relevant times, Serugendo had no formal position within the government, military, or political structures of Rwanda. In addition, Serugendo did not personally broadcast any anti-Tutsi messages during the relevant period. However, his technical and managerial role was important to the ability of the RTLM to continue to transmit such messages.'[156] The Chamber continued by saying that, 'Although Serugendo's crimes are grave, the Chamber is not satisfied that he is deserving of the most serious sanction available under the Statute.'[157] Serugendo was sentenced to six years' imprisonment.[158]

ii) Bisengimana

Paul Bisengimana was the bourgmestre of Gikoro commune in the period of the events concerned in this case.[159] Bisengimana was charged with genocide under Article 6(1) and 6(3), complicity (Art. 6(1)), murder (Art. 6(1)), extermination (Art. 6(1)) and rape (Art. 6(1) and 6(3)) as crimes against humanity,[160] crimes that were committed in relation to attacks on the Tutsi population in Gikoro commune, part of the Kigali-Rural prefecture.[161] Bisengimana pleaded guilty to aiding and abetting murder and extermination as crimes against humanity, under Article 6(1).[162] The Trial Chamber withdrew and dismissed the counts to which the accused had not pleaded guilty.[163] Accordingly, the charges under Article 6(3) were also dismissed.

Interestingly enough, in the plea agreement the accused agreed to the following description of his superior position:

> 'By his own account, the Accused's position as *bourgmestre* meant that he exercised both *de jure* and *de facto* authority over all public servants and other holders of public office within Gikoro *commune*, including, but not limited to, the *conseillers de de secteur*. The *conseillers de secteur* represented executive power at the *secteur* level and were responsible for maintaining law and order in their respective *secteurs*.
>
> Paul Bisengimana acknowledges that he had a duty to protect the population, prevent or punish the illegal acts of the perpetrators of the attacks at Musha Church and Ruhanga Complex but that he failed to do so. He admits that he had the means to oppose the killings of Tutsi civilians in Gikoro *commune*, but that he remained indifferent to the attacks. With respect to the Musha Church massacres, Paul Bisengimana

---

156 Ibid., para. 84.

157 Ibid., para. 85.

158 Ibid., at VI. Disposition.

159 *Prosecutor* v. *Paul Bisengimana*, Judgement and Sentence, Case No. ICTR-00-60-T, 13 April 2006, para. 37.

160 Ibid., para. 7.

161 *Prosecutor* v. *Paul Bisengimana*, Indictment, Case No. ICTR-00-60-I, 10 July 2000.

162 *Bisengimana*, TC Judgement and Sentence, para. 19.

163 Ibid., para. 12.

acknowledges that his presence during the attack would have had an encouraging effect on the perpetrators and given them the impression that he endorsed the killing.'[164]

In other words, according to the plea agreement, Bisengimana admittedly fulfilled all the elements necessary to prove command responsibility. There existed a superior-subordinate relationship between him and the perpetrators, he had the means to prevent the crimes and was aware of the perpetrators' intentions to commit crimes, but he remained indifferent and failed to prevent or punish the crimes of the perpetrators. Nevertheless, the Trial Chamber accepted a guilty plea according to which the accused was responsible for aiding and abetting crimes under Article 6(1) of the Statute. There was no subsequent mention of Article 6(3).

iii) Discussion

While the guilty pleas do not add much to the discussion on the application of the command responsibility doctrine by the *ad hoc* tribunals, they do illustrate the 'safety-net function' that the command responsibility charges have had in many cases, in particular in the early cases brought before the tribunals. In relation to both Serugendo and Bisengimana, the accused were clearly involved in the events in a manner that justified a conviction on the basis of their individual criminal responsibility. That they were also charged under Article 6(3) was to be certain that there would be a conviction. Consequently, that the plea agreements left out Article 6(3) is understandable, as the cases did not constitute 'pure' command responsibility cases.[165]

4.3.3.3 *Insufficient proof of the elements*

4.3.3.3.1 Effective control

i) Kordić and Čerkez

Where the superior position and authority of a civilian has been established, the Trial Chamber has in some cases based its acquittal of the superior on the lack of effective control of the superior over his subordinates. As has been mentioned earlier, this constitutes one of the crucial factors in establishing the existence of a superior-subordinate relationship, which, in turn, constitutes one of the three elements of superior responsibility. As will be shown below, the effective control requirement has become one of the main reasons for acquitting civilian superiors under superior responsibility.

An interesting case in this respect is the case against Dario Kordić and Mario Čerkez,[166] and in particular the considerations with regard to Kordić, a regional

[164] Ibid., paras. 38-39.
[165] See the references to 'pure' command responsibility in sections 5.3.2.2 and 6.2.3 *infra*.
[166] *Kordić and Čerkez*, TC Judgement.

political leader in Central Bosnia and, hence, a civilian. Kordić was charged with crimes against humanity, grave breaches and violations of the laws or customs of war, including the persecution and murder of Bosnian Muslim civilians, in several different places within Central Bosnia. The prosecution alleged that Kordić was both individually responsible for the crimes charged, and as a superior. The accused was said to have been instrumental in the campaign of persecution and in launching attacks on Bosnian Muslim towns and villages. Importantly, the prosecution case was that although, admittedly, the accused was a political leader, he 'acted as an HVO Commander, gave orders to local commanders and was known as "Colonel".'[167] The accused was found guilty under Article 7(1) of the Statute for planning, instigating and ordering crimes.

The Trial Chamber found that while Kordić 'played an important role in military matters, even at times issuing orders, and exercising authority over HVO forces, he was, and remained throughout the Indictment period, a civilian, who was not part of the formal command structure of the HVO.'[168] Although Kordić allegedly held the rank of Colonel during the war, the Trial Chamber considered that this indicated 'a military role, but no more'.[169] Consequently, the Trial Chamber turned to consider whether Kordić could be held responsible under Article 7(3) as a civilian.

It was admitted that as a civilian, Kordić had tremendous influence and power in Central Bosnia and occupied an important position in the leadership of the HZ H-B.[170] Nevertheless, relying on the Appeals Chamber Judgement in the *Čelebići* case, the Trial Chamber stressed that even substantial influence was no indication of effective control. Kordić did not have a material ability to prevent or punish crimes, which according to the Trial Chamber meant that he was neither a commander nor a superior in respect of the HVO and, therefore, he was not liable under Article 7(3).[171]

The reasoning of the Trial Chamber could be seen as a straightforward interpretation of earlier case law being applied to the case at hand. On the other hand, the outcome of the case in respect of Kordić raises questions with regard to the object and purpose of the superior responsibility principle. Although the *Kordić* case is not unique, in this respect, it illustrates a specific problem in applying superior responsibility to civilians.

The reference that was made in the *Kordić* case to the *Čelebići* case concerned the accused Delalić. The Trial Chamber agreed with the Appeals Chamber in *Čelebići* that the influence of a person, as such, did not fulfil the requirement of effective control, the now widely accepted element of superior responsibility. That such an interpretation of this element of superior responsibility is not accurate, would at present, not least considering the case law, be difficult to sustain.

[167] Ibid., para. 13.
[168] Ibid., para. 839.
[169] Ibid., para. 772.
[170] The Croatian Community of Herceg-Bosna.
[171] *Kordić and Čerkez*, TC Judgement, paras. 838-841.

Accordingly, the problem is not the theoretical interpretation of how effective control should be established, but the application of this theory in practice.

The problem of an acquittal based on the argument of a lack of effective control is more apparent in relation to the accused, Kordić, than, for example, with regard to Delalić in the *Čelebići* case. While Kordić was a regional leader with, admittedly, 'tremendous influence and power',[172] and he also 'played an important role in military matters',[173] the Trial Chamber in *Čelebići* concluded that Delalić was simply a 'well-placed influential individual', but that he did not have any 'political or military authority.'[174] All allegations to the contrary were rejected by the Trial Chamber. It is clear from the judgements that the role and authority of Kordić were of significant importance for the commission of the criminal acts, while the evidence did not support such findings in relation to Delalić. The problem of the object and purpose of the superior responsibility of civilians in relation to these two cases is that the assessment of the facts in relation to the effective control of the superior seems to have been the same, despite the significantly different roles and circumstances of the accused. But even if the assessment in both cases was right, the question is when would the effective control factor have been met?

Delalić was acquitted on all counts, both under Article 7(1) and 7(3). Kordić, on the other hand, was sentenced to 25 years' imprisonment on the basis of his individual criminal responsibility. The prosecutor did not appeal against the acquittal of Kordić on superior responsibility and the Appeals Chamber upheld Kordić's sentence and did not consider his superior responsibility any further.

It seems easier to accept that someone who was acquitted on all counts and had no part in any of the criminal acts charged, was not responsible under the superior responsibility provision either. As for Kordić, the question from the point of view of the superior responsibility principle is, if the assessment in his case was correct, the following: What does it take to make a civilian superior responsible under the superior responsibility principle? As stated above, the problem may not be the effective control requirement, as such, but how to reach the level of acceptance that a civilian superior indeed had this effective control over the physical perpetrators of the crimes. It could simply be argued that this is a question of evidence, and that in cases where enough evidence has been gathered to prove the effective control, the civilian superior will be found liable under the superior responsibility provision. However, when considering the case law, in particular the cases decided by the ICTY, this argument has proven unsatisfactory, as very few civilians have been actually convicted under Article 7(3).

The reasoning in *Kordić* was that he was not a commander, nor a superior (or this was not shown to be the case). Also in the *Brđanin* case, the accused was not considered to have had effective control over the 'physical perpetrators'. During the period in which the crimes charged were committed, Radoslav Brđanin occupied a political position in the Bosanska Krajina Municipalities Assembly and the

---

172 Ibid., para. 838.

173 Ibid., para. 839.

174 *Čelebići*, TC Judgement, para. 658.

position of President of the Autonomous Region of Krajina (ARK) Crisis Staff. With regard to the command responsibility charges, the Trial Chamber found that the ARK Crisis Staff had *de facto* authority over the municipal authorities and the police. The ARK Crisis Staff also exercised influence over the army and Serbian paramilitary units.[175] Although the municipal authorities, the police, the army and the paramilitary organisations implemented the decisions and executed the orders given by the ARK Crisis Staff, the Trial Chamber found that the accused did not exercise *de facto* effective control over the members of these groups, as he did not have the material ability to prevent or punish crimes committed by them.[176]

On the other hand, the Trial Chamber held that, 'In the instant case, the Trial Chamber is satisfied that the Accused held positions of authority at the highest level in the ARK and that he abused this authority in a way which discriminated against Bosnian Muslims and Bosnian Croats and brought them great harm and misery. The Trial Chamber therefore agrees with the Prosecution that it is appropriate to consider the Accused's senior position and his abuse of authority as an aggravating factor of considerable weight.' Accordingly, the accused was found to have fulfilled positions of authority, but not to an extent which justified a finding of command responsibility. In this regard, the *Brđanin* case is similar to the case against Kordić.

As for the more recent judgements, it seems that the Trial Chambers have chosen an easier way to avoid the problematic 'effective control' argument in relation to both civilian and military superiors. They have come up with the 'not necessary to consider' argument, which will be elaborated upon in the sub-chapter on unsuccessful cumulative charges.

ii) Kamuhanda

The 'lack of effective control' argument has also been used in a number of cases against civilian superiors in the context of the Rwandan genocide. The *Prosecutor* v. *Jean de Dieu Kamuhanda* concerned the crimes committed against the Tutsi population in the Gikomero commune, Kigali-Rural prefecture. The accused, Kamuhanda, held the office of Minister of Higher Education and Scientific Research in the interim government of Rwanda from late May 1994 to mid-July 2004. He was also an influential member of MRND in Kigali.[177]

The indictment charged Kamuhanda under Article 6 in general, making no specification as to whether the charges concerned Article 6(1) or Article 6(3).[178] The Trial Chamber convicted the accused of instigating, ordering and aiding

[175] *Prosecutor* v. *Radoslav Brđanin*, Judgement, Case No. IT-99-36-T, 1 September 2004, paras. 200-229.

[176] Ibid., paras. 370-377.

[177] *Prosecutor* v. *Jean de Dieu Kamuhanda*, Indictment, Case No. ICTR-99-54A-I, 14 November 2000, para. 4.2.

[178] *Kamuhanda*, Indictment.

and abetting genocide[179] and extermination as a crime against humanity,[180] under Article 6(1). The AC affirmed the conviction for genocide and extermination as a CAH, but overturned the convictions for instigating and aiding and abetting genocide and extermination.[181]

The Trial Chamber made the following finding with regard to the superior position of the accused:

> 'The Chamber finds that no specific evidence has been brought to it as regards the nature of the relationship between the Accused and the attackers of the Gikomero Parish Compound. There has been no clear evidence presented by the Prosecution that the Accused had a superior-subordinate relationship with these attackers nor that he maintained effective control over them during the period relevant to the Indictment.
> This finding is not inconsistent with the Chamber's earlier finding that the Accused was in a position of authority over the attackers, for purposes of his responsibility under Article 6(1) for ordering the attack at the Gikomero Parish Compound. The finding of a position of authority for purposes of "ordering" under Article 6(1) is not synonymous with the presence of "effective control" for purposes of responsibility under Article 6(3). It is settled that the two provisions are distinct: and, in our view, so are the considerations for responsibility under them.
> Therefore the Chamber does not find that the Accused can bear criminal responsibility as a superior under article 6(3) of the Statute for the crimes that occurred in Kigali-Rural préfecture between 1 January 1994 and July 1994.'[182]

According to the Trial Chamber, there was a lack of proof as to the effective control of the accused in relation to his subordinates. The fact that the accused was in a position which showed that he had the authority to order an attack, was not equivalent to concluding that he exercised effective control over the perpetrators. The reasoning by the Trial Chamber is problematic. It is true that the two provisions, Article 6(1) and Article 6(3), are distinct and, therefore, need distinct considerations, but this finding raises the following question: If the accused had the authority to order the perpetrators to attack the civilians, did he not have the authority to prevent the attacks by ordering the perpetrators not to attack the Tutsi population? Whether command responsibility is the right basis for responsibility in the case of Kamuhanda is a different issue, as he obviously incurred responsibility under Article 6(1). However, the reasoning of the Trial Chamber is unsatisfactory when asking what, then, would have been required to establish the effective control of the accused, if his authority to 'order' was not to be considered when establishing whether the accused exercised effective control over the perpetrators.

---

[179] *Prosecutor* v. *Jean de Dieu Kamuhanda*, Judgement and Sentence, Case No. ICTR-99-54A-T, 22 January 2004, paras. 651 and 750.

[180] *Kamuhanda*, TC Judgement and Sentence, paras. 700 and 750.

[181] *Prosecutor* v. *Jean de Dieu Kamuhanda*, Appeal Judgement, Case No. ICTR-99-54A-A, 19 September 2005, at XIII. Disposition.

[182] *Kamuhanda*, TC Judgement and Sentence, paras. 611-613.

iii) Niyitegeka

In the case against Eliezer Niyitegeka the accused was charged with genocide, complicity in genocide, conspiracy to commit genocide, direct and public incitement to commit genocide, crimes against humanity, and with serious violations of Article 3 common to the Geneva Conventions and of Additional Protocol II,[183] in relation to events that for the most part took place in the Kibuye prefecture. Niyitegeka was charged on the basis of individual and command responsibility in relation to all charges, except conspiracy to commit genocide (Art. 6(1) only).[184] At the time relevant to the indictment, the accused held the position of Minister of Information of the interim government. By profession he was a journalist and a radio presenter on Radio Rwanda. Niyitegeka was also a member of the *Mouvement Démocratique Républicain* (MDR) and the chairman of the same party in the Kigali prefecture between 1991 and 1994, as well as a member of the national political bureau.[185] The Trial Chamber found the accused guilty on all counts except for the crime of complicity in genocide and rape as a crime against humanity.[186] The basis for his responsibility was Article 6(1).

The Trial Chamber found that there was no proven superior-subordinate relationship between the accused and the perpetrators of the crime; there was not enough evidence to show that the accused exercised effective control over the actual perpetrators.[187] The Chamber held that as the Minister of Information, the accused had no *de jure* or *de facto* control over 'bourgmestres and conseillers, Interahamwe, gendarmes, soldiers, communal police and armed civilians in Kibuye *Préfecture*', as alleged by the prosecution. The evidence showed that the accused had been the leader of attacks, but according to the Chamber there was no evidence indicating that he was in a superior-subordinate relationship with the attackers.[188] While the evidence did show that the attackers followed the orders of the accused, there was no evidence that, '[T]hey did so in a superior-subordinate hierarchy, or that the Accused had the ability to prevent or punish them for crimes committed.'[189] There was evidence that at some point the accused had 'persuaded the Interahamwe to leave after quoting a Rwandan proverb, and talking to them for approximately ten minutes', but this exchange was not seen as proof of a superior commanding his subordinates. Accordingly, the existence of a superior-subordinate relationship had not been proven, a finding which led the

---

183 *Prosecutor* v. *Eliézer Niyitegeka*, Judgement and Sentence, Case No. ICTR-96-14-T, 16 May 2003, para. 7. The charges concerning serious violations of Art. 3 common to the Geneva Conventions and of Additional Protocol II were later withdrawn.

184 Ibid., para. 8.

185 Ibid., para. 6.

186 Ibid., para. 480. The Appeals Chamber dismissed the appeal by Niyitegeka in its entirety. See *Prosecutor* v. *Eliezer Niyitegeka*, Appeal Judgement, Case No. ICTR-96-14-A, 9 July 2004, para. 270.

187 *Niyitegeka*, TC Judgement and Sentence, paras. 473-478.

188 Ibid.

189 Ibid., para. 477.

Chamber to consider it unnecessary to 'examine the other elements of superior responsibility'.[190]

The arguments in the *Niyitegeka* case are similar to those in the case against Kamuhanda. While the actual perpetrators of the crimes followed orders given by the accused, the Trial Chamber did not find the 'effective control' element to have been proven, and consequently did not find it necessary to consider the remaining elements of the principle.

iv) Semanza

The indictment against Laurent Semanza contained charges of genocide, crimes against humanity and serious violations of Article 3 common to the Geneva Conventions and of Additional Protocol II.[191] The accused had been the bourgmestre of Bikumbi commune, but was replaced in 1993. He remained a member of the MRND and was nominated as a representative of that party to the National Assembly, which was to be established pursuant to the Arusha Accords.[192] Semanza was found guilty of complicity in genocide as well as rape, torture, murder and extermination as crimes against humanity,[193] on the basis of Article 6(1).

The Trial Chamber found that the Prosecutor had failed to establish a superior-subordinate relationship between the accused and the perpetrators of the crimes. Therefore, it considered it unnecessary to consider whether the accused fulfilled the knowledge requirement or whether he took the necessary and reasonable measures to prevent the crimes.[194] In the opinion of the Trial Chamber, the prosecution had not established that a parliamentarian exercised *de jure* authority over militiamen and other persons, the principal perpetrators of the crimes.[195] It also rejected the assertion that based on his influence in the community he exercised *de facto* authority over the perpetrators.[196] Subsequently, the Trial Chamber rejected the evidence according to which the accused appeared to be 'commanding' or 'coordinating' principal perpetrators and 'to have given orders or permission to kill or rape Tutsis.'[197] The Chamber did not consider this evidence 'credible or reliable' for the purposes of establishing Semanza's effective control.[198] The Chamber indicated that, '[W]itnesses who are outside of or

---

[190] Ibid., paras. 477-478.

[191] *Prosecutor* v. *Laurent Semanza*, Judgement, Case No. ICTR-97-20-T, 15 May 2003, para. 7.

[192] Ibid., para. 15.

[193] Ibid., para. 553.

[194] Ibid., para. 418.

[195] Ibid., para. 412.

[196] Ibid., para. 413. The influence of the accused was illustrated by: '(i) his more than twenty years of service as bourgmestre ending in 1993; (ii) the support and good will he enjoyed from the majority of the community based on his prior good works; (iii) his "promotion" to serve in parliament for the Kigali-Rural prefecture; (iv) his continued public presence alongside the new bourgmestre, Rugambarara, and many people's belief that he was still the bourgmestre; (v) his alleged role as chairman of the MRND party in Kigali-Rural; (vi) his alleged close connections to President Habyarimana and other high government officials; and (vii) his wealth.'

[197] Ibid., para. 414.

[198] Ibid., para. 416.

unfamiliar with an alleged formal or informal hierarchy do not necessarily provide the best indication of an individual's actual superior authority.'[199] In addition, the Trial Chamber was of the view that the prosecution had not presented sufficient evidence as to the material ability of the accused to prevent the crimes or to punish the perpetrators.[200]

The arguments as to why 'effective control' on the part of the accused was not shown beyond a reasonable doubt differ slightly from the arguments in the *Niyitegeka* and *Kamuhanda* cases. In *Niyitegeka* and *Kamuhanda* the Trial Chamber doubted that proof of the accused giving orders to the perpetrators could be used to show effective control, while in Semanza the Trial Chamber doubted the credibility and reliability of certain witnesses on such specific details as the nature of a superior-subordinate relationship.

v) Ntakirutimana, Gérard

Gérard Ntakirutimana, a medical doctor at the hospital of the Seventh Day Adventist Church, at Mugonero Complex, Gishyita commune,[201] was charged on the basis of Article 6(1) and Article 6(3) in relation to the massacres at Mugonero Complex and on the basis of Article 6(1) in relation to the massacres in the area of Bisesero, in the Gisovu and Gishyita communes.[202] The prosecution alleged that on or about 10 April 1994, the accused became the *de facto* director of Mugonero Hospital and that in this capacity he had effective control over certain members of personnel of the hospital, who attacked Tutsi refugees at the Mugonero Complex.[203] The accused was found guilty of genocide and murder as a crime against humanity under Article 6(1).[204]

The findings with regard to the command responsibility of Gérard Ntakirutimana seem well-reasoned. The Chamber observed that even if there was evidence which established that the accused assumed the directorship of Mugonero Hospital, this evidence, alone did not demonstrate that he exercised effective control over hospital staff. On the other hand, the Chamber pointed out that the fact that there was no administrative relationship between the accused and one of the perpetrators (an employee of the nursing school, which was part of the Mugonero Complex), did not preclude that the accused had effective control over that perpetrator. The Trial Chamber considered that the evidence adduced was decisive

---

199 Ibid.

200 Ibid., para. 417.

201 *Prosecutor* v. *Elizaphan and Gérard Ntakirutimana*, Judgement and Sentence, Cases No. ICTR-96-10 & ICTR-96-17-T, para. 38.

202 *Ntakirutimana*, TC Judgement and Sentence, paras. 13 and 15. Gérard Ntakirutimana was charged with genocide, complicity in genocide, conspiracy to commit genocide, crimes against humanity, and serious violations of Art. 3 common to the Geneva Conventions and of Additional Protocol II. Gérard Ntakirutimana's co-accused and father, Élizaphan Ntakirutimana, was not charged under Art. 6(3).

203 Ibid., paras. 431-432.

204 Ibid., para. 878.

in this respect.[205] Having considered the testimonies given, the Trial Chamber found that very little evidence had been introduced that would have clarified the relationship between the accused and the principal perpetrators. The accused had been seen in the company of the perpetrators, but no information was provided which would have established that the accused exercised effective control over the perpetrators. Consequently, the Trial Chamber concluded that the prosecution had failed to show that Gérard Ntakirutimana exercised effective control over the perpetrators of the crimes.[206]

4.3.3.3.2 Knowledge

i) Bagilishema

Ignace Bagilishama was the bourgmestre of Mabanza commune, Kibuye prefecture. Bagilishema was accused under both Article 6(1) and Article 6(3) in relation to crimes committed against Tutsi in several communes of the Kibuye prefecture.[207] The Trial Chamber acquitted the accused on all counts,[208] and the Appeals Chamber affirmed the acquittal.[209]

The prosecution appeal included allegations of errors relating to the finding of the Trial Chamber under Article 6(3), more specifically as to whether the Trial Chamber considered the 'had reason to know' test, as to the finding that it was established beyond a reasonable doubt that the accused 'had reason to know' as required by Article 6(3). The prosecution also alleged errors regarding the analysis by the Trial Chamber of the superior-subordinate relationship between the accused and the perpetrators.[210]

The Appeals Chamber found that the Trial Chamber had rightly established that Bagilishema 'neither knew nor possessed information which would have enabled him to conclude, in the circumstances at that time', that his subordinates had committed or were about to commit crimes.[211] Although not invalidating the judgement of the Trial Chamber, the Appeals Chamber on this issue admitted that the Trial Chamber had committed an error of law when applying the 'had reason to know' test. The Appeals Chamber found that the Trial Chamber had applied a 'criminal negligence' test, which in the opinion of the Appeals

---

205 Ibid., para. 436.

206 Ibid., paras. 437-438.

207 *Prosecutor* v. *Ignace Bagilishema*, Amended Indictment, Case No. ICTR-95-1A-I, 17 September 1999, para. 5. The accused was charged with: genocide; complicity in genocide; murder, extermination and other inhuman acts as crimes against humanity; and serious violations of Art. 3 common to the Geneva Conventions and of Additional Protocol II, under Art. 6(1) and 6(3).

208 *Prosecutor* v. *Ignace Bagilishema*, Judgement, Case No. ICTR-95-1A-T, 7 June 2001, at VI. Verdict.

209 *Prosecutor* v. *Ignace Bagilishema*, Appeal Judgement (Reasons), Case No. ICTR-95-1A-A, 3 July 2002, at VI. Disposition.

210 Ibid., para. 24.

211 Ibid., paras. 37 and 45-46.

Chamber 'cannot be the same as the 'had reason to know' test in terms of Article 6(3) of the Statute.'[212] The Appeals Chamber made the following statement:

> 'References to "negligence" in the context of superior responsibility are likely to lead to confusion of thought, as the Judgement of the Trial Chamber in the present case illustrates. The law imposes upon a superior a duty to prevent crimes which he knows or has reason to know were about to be committed, and to punish crimes which he knows or has reason to know had been committed, by subordinates over whom he has effective control. A military commander, or a civilian superior, may therefore be held responsible if he fails to discharge his duties as a superior either by deliberately failing to perform them or by culpably or wilfully disregarding them.
>
> Depending on the nature of the breach of duty (which must be a gross breach), and the gravity of the consequences thereof, breaches of duties imposed by the laws of war may entail a disciplinary rather than a criminal liability of a superior who is subject to military discipline. The line between those forms of responsibility which may engage the criminal responsibility of the superior under international law and those which may not can be drawn in the abstract only with difficulty, and the Appeals Chamber does not need to attempt to do so in the present Judgement. It is better, however, that Trial Chambers do not describe superior responsibility in terms of negligence at all.'[213]

As stated earlier, the wrongly applied test did not invalidate the finding of the Trial Chamber that the accused did not have knowledge of the crimes as required by Article 6(3), and should, therefore, be acquitted. The same outcome was upheld even after additional findings of two errors of law made by the Trial Chamber. First, the Appeals Chamber found that the Trial Chamber had made an error with regard to the notion of 'effective control', 'to the extent that it suggested that the control exercised by a civilian superior must be of the same nature as that exercised by a military commander.'[214] According to the Appeals Chamber it is 'sufficient that, for one reason or another, the accused exercises the required 'degree' of control over his subordinates, namely, that of effective control.'[215] 'It is not suggested that 'effective control' will necessarily be exercised by a civilian superior and by a military commander in the same way, or that it may necessarily be established in the same way in relation to both a civilian superior and a military commander.'[216] Secondly, the Appeals Chamber found that the Trial Chamber had failed to consider the *de facto* authority of the accused. The Trial Chamber erroneously held that, '[B]oth *de facto* and *de jure* authority need to be established before a superior can be found to exercise effective control over his or her subordinates.'[217]

All things considered, the conclusion of the Appeals Chamber was that even if a *de facto* superior-subordinate relationship had been found when applying the

---

[212] Ibid., para. 37.
[213] Ibid., paras. 35-36.
[214] Ibid., para. 55.
[215] Ibid.
[216] Ibid., para. 52.
[217] Ibid., para. 61.

right test, the lack of knowledge of the accused would anyway have led to an acquittal under Article 6(3).

4.3.3.3.3 Necessary and reasonable measures

At the time of the events referred to in the indictment in the *Ntagerura, Bagambiki and Imanishimwe* case, one of the accused, Emmanuel Bagambiki, was the prefect of the Cyangugu prefecture. He was charged under Article 6(1) and 6(3) in relation to crimes committed in Cyangugu prefecture.[218] Bagambiki was acquitted on all counts.[219]

According to the prosecution, Bagambiki was the *de jure* and *de facto* superior of 'sub-prefects, bourgmestres, all government employees in the prefecture, gendarmes and soldiers.'[220] The Trial Chamber considered the alleged superior-subordinate relationship between the accused and each group of subordinates in turn. With regard to the gendarmes, Rwandan law provided that a prefect could requisition the gendarmes to participate in operations in a prefecture. However, an ability to requisition was not the same as *de jure* authority over the gendarmes, as the control of the gendarmes stayed with the officer in charge. While there was evidence to show that Bagambiki did requisition the gendarmes, there was insufficient evidence that the accused would have exercised *de facto* control over how the gendarmes carried out their mission.[221] The same reasoning applied to the soldiers. While a prefect had authority to requisition their participation, the Trial Chamber found that the accused had neither *de jure* authority over them, nor *de facto* authority, based on the evidence available.[222] With regard to the other officials, the Trial Chamber found that Rwandan law provided for a *de jure* relationship of authority between the prefect and the bourgmestre and the communal police. As the accused did not refute that he had effective control over these officials, the Chamber considered that established. No other *de jure* or *de facto* superior-subordinate relationships between the accused and the perpetrators were established.[223]

The Trial Chamber continued by considering whether the accused fulfilled the knowledge requirement in relation to the crimes committed by his subordinates, the bourgmestre of Kagano commune and the communal police. There was evidence to show that the accused was neither present nor was he informed about a certain attack in which the bourgmestre and the communal police participated, until after its completion. The Chamber concluded that the accused did not have advance knowledge of the attack and, therefore, could not have prevented it. In

[218] *Prosecutor* v. *Emmanuel Bagambiki and Samuel Imanishimwe*, Indictment, Case No. ICTR-97-36-I, 13 October 1997, para. 3.31. Bagambiki was charged with genocide, complicity in genocide, conspiracy to commit genocide (Art. 6(1) only), crimes against humanity and serious violations of Art. 3 common to the Geneva Conventions and of Additional Protocol II.

[219] *Ntagerura et al.*, TC Judgement and Sentence, para. 805.

[220] Ibid., para. 631.

[221] Ibid., paras. 633-639.

[222] Ibid., paras. 640-643.

[223] Ibid., paras. 644-646.

addition, there was insufficient evidence to establish whether Bagambiki 'should have known' that the communal police were involved in the attack. With regard to the knowledge of the accused in relation to the bourgmestre, the Chamber found that items looted during the attack were found in the possession of the bourgmestre and, consequently, that Bagambiki 'should have known' that the bourgmestre participated in the attack.[224] That having been established, the Trial Chamber finally found that the prosecution had failed to prove beyond reasonable doubt that the accused did not take the necessary and reasonable measures to punish the bourgmestre for his role in the attack. Bagambiki was shown to have suspended the bourgmestre and according to the Chamber, this was the correct available disciplinary measure for a prefect under the applicable law. As the prosecution did not submit any evidence as to what other punitive measures the accused could have taken, the Trial Chamber found that Bagamibiki did take the necessary and reasonable measures as required by the command responsibility principle.[225] The Appeals Chamber dismissed the appeal by the prosecution on Bagamibiki's responsibility under Article 6(3).[226]

The *Bagambiki* case is one of very few cases in which the *ad hoc* tribunals found the superior-subordinate relationship and the knowledge requirement proven and then went on to consider whether there was an actual failure on the part of the superior. In this sense the reasoning in the case is not inconsistent or contradictory.

There may be a discussion as to whether the dismissal of the bourgmestre constituted the necessary and reasonable measures to be taken by a superior. If the dismissal of a subordinate who has committed international crimes is a sufficient measure to escape command responsibility, the case sets a disturbing precedent for future cases. Where it is not necessary that the superior ensures the initiation of a criminal procedure against the subordinate, it seems that the necessary measure needed for the purposes of the command responsibility provision is not in proportion with the harm caused. The civilian superior finds out that a subordinate has committed international crimes, simply dismisses the subordinate and knows that he will not incur responsibility under the command responsibility provision.

On the other hand, it may be argued that a dismissal is, indeed, the only measure available for a civilian superior in the position of prefecture in relation to the bourgmestre in the Rwandan context. If that is the case, the *Bagambiki* judgement is a clear illustration of why the command responsibility principle is more suitable for the prosecution of military commanders. The military law system enables a commander to either impose disciplinary measures or to report the crime of a subordinate to a prosecuting authority. In other words, a military commander cannot that easily fulfil the necessary and reasonable measures

[224] Ibid., para. 649.

[225] Ibid., para. 650.

[226] *Prosecutor* v. *André Ntagerura, Emmanuel Bagambiki, and Samuel Imanishimwe*, Appeal Judgement, Case No. ICTR-99-46-A, 7 July 2006, paras. 339-352.

requirement, which in turn ensures that the hierarchical responsibility system of the armed forces is maintained.

4.3.3.4 *Unsuccessful 'cumulative charges'*

In some cases the accused have been cumulatively charged both under Article 7(1)/6(1) and Article 7(3)/6(3), but the tribunals have found that a conviction under the individual criminal responsibility provision is the preferred basis for a conviction, leading to an 'acquittal' under the command responsibility charges. There have been two alternative ways of reasoning. In some cases the tribunal has found both individual and command responsibility established by the prosecution but has decided that the command responsibility incurred is subsumed by the individual criminal responsibility, or in other words, where responsibility under Article 7(1) and 7(3) has been established, an Article 7(1) conviction will be entered. The second option applied by the tribunals was to consider a finding under Article 7(3) unnecessary where Article 7(1) responsibility was established. Accordingly, in these cases the tribunal refrained from making any finding at all under the command responsibility provision, which means that the question whether the civilian superior could have been held responsible under Article 7(3) was left unsettled.

4.3.3.4.1 Article 7(1) and 7(3) = 7(1)

For a short period relevant to the indictment, Juvénal Kajelijeli, the accused, was the officially appointed bourgmestre of Mukingo commune. During that period, he allegedly exercised *de facto* authority as bourgmestre of the same commune.[227] Kajelijeli was further alleged to be one of the founders and a leader of the *Interahamwe*-MRND. According to the prosecution he had close connections to the national secretary general of the MRND, whom he consulted regarding 'military training, distributions of weapons and uniforms to *Interahamwe* and distribution of lists of Tutsi to be eliminated.'[228] Kajelijeli was charged in relation to his participation in and his failure to prevent and punish assaults and killings of members of the Tutsi population.[229]

The Trial Chamber convicted Kajelijeli of genocide and crimes against humanity under both Article 6(1) and 6(3). Kajelijeli appealed against his conviction under Article 6(3) in relation to crimes committed by the *Interahamwe*. The Appeals Chamber overturned the decision of the Trial Chamber and quashed the convictions under these counts in so far as they were based on Article 6(3), but

---

227 *Prosecutor* v. *Juvénal Kajelijeli*, Amended Indictment pursuant to the Tribunal Order Dated 25 January 2001, Case No. ICTR-98-44A-I, 25 January 2001, paras. 3.5 and 4.6.1.

228 *Prosecutor* v. *Juvénal Kajelijeli*, Judgement and Sentence, Case No. ICTR-98-44A-T, 1 December 2003, para. 19.

229 Ibid., paras. 20-22. Kajelijeli was charged with conspiracy to commit genocide, genocide or alternatively complicity in genocide, direct and public incitement to commit genocide, and murder, extermination, rape, persecution and other inhumane acts as crimes against humanity, under both Art. 6(1) and Art. 6(3).

not on the basis of an error made by the Trial Chamber concerning the superior-subordinate relationship between Kajelijeli and the perpetrators, as argued by the appellant. Instead the Appeals Chamber based its decision to quash the convictions under Article 6(3) on findings by the ICTY Appeals Chamber, according to which responsibility under both Article 7(1) and Article 7(3) should lead to a conviction on the basis of Article 7(1) only:[230]

> 'The ICTY Appeals Chamber has held that in relation to a particular count where a Trial Chamber has convicted an accused under the legal requirements of both Articles 7(1) and 7(3) of the ICTY Statute, "a Trial Chamber should enter a conviction on the basis of Article 7(1) only, and consider the accused's superior position *as an aggravating factor* in sentencing." Indeed, "where the Trial Chamber finds that both direct responsibility and responsibility as superior are proved [...] the Trial Chamber *must* take into account the fact that both types of responsibility were proved in its consideration of the sentence." Clearly, before taking an accused's superior position into account at sentencing, the Trial Chamber must have found that the accused's superior position was proven at trial. As held by the ICTY Appeals Chamber, "only those matters which are *proved beyond reasonable doubt* against an accused may be the subject of an accused's sentence or taken into account in aggravation of that sentence".'[231]

The formulation by the Appeals Chamber is somewhat peculiar in that, on the one hand, it considered a conviction under Article 6(1) to be sufficient, but on the other hand, it found that proof beyond reasonable doubt of the superior position of the convicted person was necessary when considering the aggravating circumstances at the sentencing stage. The Appeals Chamber did not explain what it meant by proving a 'superior position' 'beyond reasonable doubt'. In several other cases an established position of authority has been considered an aggravating circumstance, without having gone through the process of establishing the superior-subordinate relationship beyond reasonable doubt.[232] The purpose of the doctrine is not to be used as a requirement which has to be fulfilled for the purposes of finding the superior position as an aggravating circumstance at the sentencing stage.

---

[230] *Prosecutor* v. *Juvénal Kajelijeli*, Appeal Judgement, Case No. ICTR-98-44A-A, 23 May 2005, para. 81.

[231] Ibid., para. 82.

[232] See, for example, *Kamuhanda*, TC Judgement and Sentence, para. 764; and *Prosecutor* v. *Laurent Semanza*, Appeal Judgement, Case No. ICTR-97-20-A, 20 May 2005, para. 336, where the Appeals Chamber stated the following: 'The question of criminal responsibility as a superior is analytically distinct from the question of whether an accused's prominent status should affect his or her sentence. It was within the Trial Chamber's competence and reasonable for it to conclude that the Appellant did not hold a hierarchical position sufficient to render him liable for criminal responsibility as a superior while also finding that his influence was substantial enough to constitute an aggravating factor.'

4.3.3.4.2 Article 7(1), so no Article 7(3)

One of the main reasons for the acquittal of civilians under the superior responsibility principle by the ICTY is that Article 7(1) responsibility has been established before even considering the charges under Article 7(3). According to both ICTY and ICTR case law, such a finding renders it unnecessary to consider any responsibility under Article 7(3).

i) Kvočka et al.

An example of this interpretation of the individual responsibility provision of the Statute can be seen in the *Kvočka* case, where the prosecution had brought charges under both Article 7(1) and Article 7(3).[233] Except for the accused Zigić, all the accused were charged under Article 7(3). However, the Chamber found that because liability had already been established for the role of the accused in a joint criminal enterprise under Article 7(1), there was no need to further consider the issue of responsibility as a superior.[234] In relation to one of the accused, the Chamber held that, '[H]is participation in the joint criminal enterprise of Omarska camps renders him liable for crimes committed therein and arguably makes Article 7(3) liability duplicative.'[235] The Chamber did not elaborate on the reason for its decision.

ii) Stakić

A similar decision was made in the *Stakić* case. At the time of the events described in the case, the accused, Stakić, who by profession was a physician,[236] was the President of the self-proclaimed Assembly of the Serbian People of the Municipality of Prijedor. He further assumed the positions of President of the Prijedor Municipal People's Defence Council, President of the Prijedor Municipal Crisis Staff and later on the position of President of the Municipal Assembly of Prijedor.[237] Accordingly, at all times relevant to the case, the accused was a civilian, who held high positions within the municipality, and according to the Chamber, who was 'a figure of greatest authority'.[238]

However, the Trial Chamber found that the accused had participated in the crimes committed, within the meaning of Article 7(1), and that his mode of participation could best be described as 'co-perpetratorship'.[239] As in the *Kvočka*

[233] The accused had a civilian background and occupied various positions with the police before taking up duty at the Omarska, Keraterm and Trnopolje prison camps in the Prijedor region, Bosnia and Herzegovina.

[234] *Prosecutor* v. *Radislav Kvočka et al.*, Judgement, Case No. IT-98-33-T, 2 November 2001, paras. 412, 466-467, 570 and 683.

[235] Ibid., paras. 412.

[236] *Prosecutor* v. *Milomir Stakić*, Judgement, Case No. IT-97-24-T, 31 July 2003, para. 3.

[237] Ibid., para. 336.

[238] Ibid., paras. 912-913.

[239] Ibid., para. 468.

case, the Chamber in *Stakić* concluded that as such individual responsibility under Article 7(1) was found, any findings under Article 7(3) were unnecessary. The Chamber reasoned that it was 'in general not necessary in the interest of justice and of providing an exhaustive description of individual responsibility to make findings under Article 7(3).'[240] It even stated that it would be a waste of judicial resources to enter into a debate on Article 7(3) knowing that Article 7(1) responsibility subsumes Article 7(3) responsibility. However, the Chamber specified that this was the case where the Chamber was satisfied beyond reasonable doubt of 'both responsibility under 7(1) and the superior positions held by the accused.'[241]

iii) Ngeze

Prior to and during the events relevant to the indictment the accused, Hassan Ngeze, was the editor-in-chief of the Kangura Newspaper. He was a former member of the political party MRND and one of the founding members of the Coalition for the Defense of the Republic (CDR). Ngeze exercised political control over the *Interahamwe* militia groups. He was charged with crimes in relation to the newspaper *Kangura* under both Article 6(1) and Article 6(3).[242] The Trial Chamber found Ngeze guilty of conspiracy to commit genocide, genocide, direct and public incitement to commit genocide and persecution and extermination as crimes against humanity on the basis of Article 6(1).[243] The Trial Chamber made reasoned arguments as to why Ngeze did or did not incur individual criminal responsibility. However, nowhere in its legal findings did the Chamber present any arguments as to why it did not even consider whether the accused fulfilled the elements of the command responsibility principle. One explanation for this may be that in the opinion of the Chamber, a conviction under Article 6(1) makes a finding under Article 6(3) superfluous.

iv) Gacumbitsi

During the period covered by the indictment, the accused, Sylvestre Gacumbitsi, held the position of bourgmestre of Rusumo commune, Kibungo prefecture.[244] He was charged under both Article 6(1) and Article 6(3) in relation to crimes committed against the Tutsi population in the Kibungo prefecture.[245] The Trial

240 Ibid., para. 466.

241 Ibid.

242 *Nahimana et al.*, TC Judgement and Sentence, para. 10. The accused was charged with conspiracy to commit genocide, genocide, direct and public incitement to commit genocide, complicity in genocide and persecution, extermination and murder as crimes against humanity. Conspiracy to commit genocide was charged under Art. 6(1) only. All the other alleged crimes were based on both Art. 6(1) and Art. 6(3).

243 Ibid., para. 1094.

244 *Prosecutor* v. *Sylvestre Gacumbitsi*, Indictment, Case No. ICTR-01-64-I, 20 June 2001, part II.

245 Ibid., part III. Gacumbitsi was charged with genocide (Art. 6(1) and 6(3)) or alternatively complicity in genocide (Art. 6(1)), and extermination, murder and rape as crimes against humanity (Art. 6(1) and 6(3)).

Chamber found the accused guilty of genocide, and extermination and rape as crimes against humanity.[246] The Trial Chamber made its findings under Article 6(1) and, due to the similarity of the acts charged, considered it unnecessary to enquire whether the accused also incurred responsibility under Article 6(3).[247] In addition to the similarity of the acts charged under Article 6(1) and Article 6(3), the Trial Chamber mentioned the lack of evidence of a superior-subordinate relationship as a reason for not considering the Article 6(3) responsibility of the accused.[248]

In its appeal, the prosecution contended that the Trial Chamber had made an error in not convicting Gacumbitsi under Article 6(3) of the Statute. The Appeals Chamber found that the Trial Chamber had erred in only considering the *de jure* authority of the accused, and that it should have considered whether the accused exercised *de facto* authority over the perpetrators. However, the Appeals Chamber found that the prosecution at the trial stage had only presented evidence of the general authority of the accused to impose law and order in the commune and of the accused playing a leading role in the genocidal campaign. In the opinion of the Appeals Chamber, this did not prove that the accused exercised effective control over the perpetrators. The Appeals Chamber dismissed the appeal on this point.[249]

4.3.3.4.3 Discussion

The attractive aspect of charging civilian superiors and military commanders cumulatively under Articles 6(1)/6(3) and 7(1)/7(3) is its 'safety-net function'. If the prosecution cannot prove individual criminal responsibility there is always the chance of a command responsibility conviction. But in relation to civilian superiors in particular, how successful or meaningful has this approach been? Individual criminal responsibility is preferred in all instances, of course not because of some possibility of actually choosing between the two, but because the facts of the cases show that the responsibility of the civilian superior corresponds to that set out in Article 6(1)/6(3). As will be discussed in Chapter 5, there are situations where the individual and command responsibility is not clearly distinguishable, which could justify charges under both provisions. On the other hand, in cases where a superior-subordinate relationship was proven, the effective control requirement has often been established on the basis of facts that show that the superior ordered crimes to be committed. The existence of such proof is an indication of the bigger involvement in the crimes than the involvement of the superior for the purposes of command responsibility. Accordingly, that cumula-

---

[246] *Prosecutor* v. *Sylvestre Gacumbitsi*, Judgement, Case No. ICTR-01-64-T, 17 June 2004, para. 334.

[247] Ibid., paras. 290, 315 and 332.

[248] Ibid., para. 332.

[249] *Prosecutor* v. *Sylvestre Gacumbitsi*, Appeal Judgement, Case No. ICTR-01-64-A, 7 July 2006, paras. 141-146.

tive charges in relation to the same facts would be decided 'in favour of' a command responsibility conviction is unlikely.

4.4 Conclusion

The present chapter has shown that just as IHL does not clearly define a civilian, there is no meaningful definition of a civilian superior for the purposes of command responsibility. More important than the definition is the understanding of whether the superior carries out such activities and exercises such powers that the perpetrators committing crimes will be considered as subordinates for the purposes of command responsibility and that the person holding the position may be held criminally liable in relation to the acts committed by these subordinates.

The level of authority of a superior is not an element of command responsibility, but it certainly influences the possibilities of and interest in prosecuting a certain superior under the command responsibility provision. The position and level of authority also constitutes an indication of the 'effective control' element that has to be established. A survey of *ad hoc* tribunal case law indicates that most accused identified as non-military commanders would qualify as *de facto* military commanders if tried under the ICC provision. The survey also shows that most cases against civilian superiors have ended in an 'acquittal', the acquittal, however, not always being based on their lack of effective control. In fact, the bases for the 'acquittals' have varied to a great extent. While some command responsibility charges were thrown out because of insufficient information in the indictment, other command responsibility charges were set aside when the accused pleaded guilty under charges of individual criminal responsibility. The effective control of some civilian superiors was established, but in these cases sufficient proof was lacking in relation to the *mens rea* requirement or in relation to the alleged failure of the superior to take the necessary and reasonable measures. The single most important reason for the dismissal of command responsibility charges has been the preference given by the judges to a conviction under the individual criminal responsibility provision, where both bases of responsibility were charged cumulatively.

It may be concluded that despite the fact that the *ad hoc* tribunals have not had to establish criteria for who qualifies as a civilian superior and, thus, have applied the command responsibility provision as being identically applicable to both military commanders and civilian superiors, the result has been very meagre. What does this say about the application of the doctrine to civilian superiors? An obvious conclusion is that so far all cases, whether charging military or civilian superiors, have been based on the same requirements. In theory, there is no higher threshold for holding civilian superiors liable, but in practice case law shows that proving the elements of the command responsibility doctrine in relation to civilian superiors is far from easy. Another conclusion that can be drawn on the basis of the existing case law is that where command responsibility 'competes' with individual criminal responsibility in relation to the same facts, there is usually an indication of the superior's involvement in the crimes, which gives reason to convict him on the basis of his individual responsibility.

As applied and as formulated in Article 28 ICC, the command responsibility doctrine is clearly geared towards military commanders who, indeed, only failed to prevent or punish crimes committed by their subordinates and did not play any other role in carrying out atrocities. There may be superiors in situations that have not been tried by the international tribunals that are suitable for prosecution under the command respons ibility provision, but up until now the reality seems to be that where civilians are charged, they occupy high-level positions in which the superior is somehow involved in the events. If the purpose is to hold superiors liable who should have known or even knew about crimes but failed to do anything about this situation, then that is what the superior should have done – failed to prevent or punish – nothing more.

Chapter 5

Remaining hurdles in the application of the command responsibility doctrine

5.1 Introduction

The present chapter addresses the remaining hurdles in the application of the command responsibility doctrine, relevant to all commanders or superiors who may become objects of charges based on command responsibility. In Chapter 3 the author analysed command responsibility in armed conflict and pointed to the unique features of the military commander and the military organisation. Chapter 4 addressed the applicability of the command responsibility doctrine to civilian superiors, based on the outcome of the cases tried before the *ad hoc* tribunals. Both chapters illustrate that the command responsibility doctrine does not lend itself very easily to the prosecution of civilian superiors. The analysis of certain contentious issues in Chapter 5 is an essential part of demonstrating the limited applicability of the command responsibility in practice, which gives additional support to the view that the doctrine will only lead to a conviction of a civilian superior in exceptional cases.

There are three themes in this chapter which cover the issues most frequently debated in the case law and the legal literature and in relation to which there seems to be the highest degree of uncertainty. First, this chapter discusses the nature of command criminal responsibility. Is the commander/superior who fails to prevent or punish crimes committed by his/her subordinates an accomplice in the crime or should the failure to prevent or punish be considered as a crime of its own? Does either of these approaches satisfactorily describe the role of the commander/superior in the events and the extent to which he is culpable?

While in most cases tried before the *ad hoc* tribunals it was generally held that a superior convicted under Article 7(3)/6(3) was responsible for the crimes committed by his/her subordinates, more recent judgements, however, show a clear shift in the way the responsibility of the superior is perceived, towards command responsibility as responsibility of its own kind – *sui generis* responsibility. Considering the variety of ideas both in case law and in scholarly writings, a more detailed analysis of what it is that the superior is held responsible for, is warranted.

Secondly, the chapter discusses the overlap between certain modes of liability that lead to individual criminal responsibility and liability under the command responsibility provision. The modes of liability concerned here are the concepts of joint criminal enterprise (hereafter, JCE) and aiding and abetting, both of which may apply in circumstances similar to those to which command responsibility is applicable. Both case law and literature show signs of inconsistency and uncertainty regarding the distinction between the three concepts and their applicability in relation to superiors' acts of omission.

The relationship between command responsibility and the modes of liability leading to individual criminal responsibility is not only important when considering when and whether JCE, aiding and abetting or command responsibility should be applied, but also in relation to the question as to whether individual criminal responsibility (as set out in Article 6(1) ICTR/ 7(1) ICTY/25 ICC) and command responsibility (Article 6(3) ICTR/7(3) ICTY/ 8 ICC) may be applied cumulatively in relation to the same facts. While the development in the case law has moved towards not allowing 'cumulative convictions', this issue still needs consideration, in particular as the attention has moved towards considering the superior position or even established command responsibility as an aggravating circumstance at the sentencing stage of the case.

Thirdly, the nature of the crime underlying the charges of command responsibility will be considered. Those international courts and tribunals which have incorporated a provision on command responsibility in their statutes have not restricted the applicability of the provision to specific crimes, which means that the doctrine should apply regardless of the nature of the crime. Existing case law shows that applying command responsibility in relation to the crime of genocide is rather questionable. The fact that the crime of aggression belongs to the subject-matter jurisdiction of the ICC has raised questions similar to those concerning the applicability of command responsibility in relation to the crime of genocide. As the crimes under the jurisdictions of the various international courts and tribunals vary slightly, the question arises whether command responsibility is applicable only to certain international crimes. What makes the command responsibility doctrine problematic in relation to the prosecution of crimes not qualifying as international crimes?

5.2 THE NATURE OF COMMAND RESPONSIBILITY

5.2.1 **Liability for an international crime**

Both national and international criminal law recognise that criminal conduct consists either of an act or an omission.[1] That omissions may lead to criminal liability under international criminal law is explicitly set out in the various provisions on command/superior responsibility. It is also recognised in both national legal systems and in international criminal law that criminal responsibility may arise for the perpetration of as well as participation in a crime. The responsibility arising from perpetration is called principal or direct responsibility, whereas participation leads to derivative or indirect responsibility. As set out by Van Sliedregt, direct and indirect responsibility are technical rather than normative terms, as the

[1] Fletcher, pp. 45-50.

'principal' who incurs direct responsibility may be less culpable than a 'secondary party' who will be indirectly responsible, if the latter is an instigator and does not actually commit the crime.[2]

As far as command responsibility is concerned, the subordinates are the perpetrators, the principals, of the international crime for which charges have been laid. The Statutes of the *ad hoc* tribunals as well as some of their case law give reason for interpreting the superior who failed to prevent or punish the perpetrators as being a participant in the underlying crime, as he/she omitted to prevent or punish the perpetrators.[3] For instance, when the Trial Chamber rendered its judgement in the *Čelebići* case, it found Mucić guilty of, among other crimes, wilful killings as a grave breach of Geneva Convention IV, with respect to murders committed in Čelebići camp. The basis for his responsibility was Article 7(3) of the Statute. The Trial Chamber concluded as follows: 'Mr. Mucić is accordingly criminally responsible for the acts of the personnel in the Čelebići prison-camp, on the basis of the principle of superior responsibility.'[4]

This way of applying the concept was and still is understandable, both when considering the history of the principle and when reading the international and semi-international statutes in which the principle was codified. The historical case always referred to in this respect is that against Yamashita, who was held primarily responsible for the grave and large-scale crimes that had taken place in the Philippines at the time in question. The crimes had taken place and Yamashita was considered to be the main culprit. It would be difficult to sustain that Yamashita was not blamed for the crimes committed and that it was in fact simply his failure in carrying out his duty which justified the conviction and the resulting sentence of capital punishment. The Yamashita case thereby provides support for the line of reasoning of the *ad hoc* tribunals.

According to Swart, who was a member of the Trial Chamber in the *Hadžihasanović* case, the structure and formulation of Article 7 ICTY/6 ICTR invite application that holds the superior responsible as a participant in an international crime, where the conditions of the command responsibility provision are fulfilled. However, Swart himself, together with many others, supports the recent 'development' of the doctrine, which dissociates itself from the 'liability for an international crime' view. The reason for the general change of opinion is related to the biggest downside of that approach – the problems it creates in relation to the principle of culpability.[5] Several authors have challenged the application

[2] Van Sliedregt 2003, pp. 53-61.

[3] For an analysis and also a criticism of this approach, see, for example: I. Bantekas, 'The Contemporary Law of Superior Responsibility', 93 *AJIL* (1999) pp. 573-595, at pp. 575-577; M. Damaška, 'The Shadow Side of Command Responsibility', 49 *American Journal of Comparative Law* (2001) pp. 463-464; A.H.J. Swart, 'De strafrechtelijke aansprakelijkheid van meerderen in het internationale humanitaire recht', in M.M. Dolman, P.D. Duyx and H.G. van der Wilt, eds., *Geleerde lessen. Liber amicorum Simon Stolwijk* (Nijmegen, Wolf Legal Publishers 2007) pp. 213-234, at pp. 217-218; and Van Sliedregt 2003, pp. 59-60.

[4] *Čelebići*, TC Judgement, para. 775.

[5] See, for example, the commentary to the *Hadžihasanović* case, H.G. van der Wilt, 'Commentary', in A. Klip and G. Sluiter, eds., *Annotated Leading Cases of International Criminal Tribunals*, Vol. XIV (Antwerp, Intersentia 2008) pp. 115-122, at pp. 120-122.

of command responsibility as liability for an international crime, among them Ambos, who noted that if applied in this way, the superior under the command responsibility doctrine is blamed for the fact that he failed in his supervisory duty, but in addition he is also held liable for the violations carried out by his subordinates.[6] This problem was also noted by Rogers, who was of the opinion that the superior is not to be held responsible for the specific crimes committed by his subordinates. Accordingly, he should not be considered a murderer where others have actually committed the murder.[7] On the other hand, when commenting on the articles relevant to command responsibility of the Additional Protocols, Rogers stated that a commander 'becomes liable for a breach committed by a subordinate [...].'[8] The hesitation by Rogers does not give a clear answer regarding the character of superior responsibility in international criminal law, which exactly illustrates the situation of the principle in international law at present with regard to this specific point.

Damaška, whose criticism of the doctrine made a deep impression on both judges and scholars, found that considering the understanding of the culpability principle under national criminal law, the command responsibility doctrine under international criminal law created a gap between the liability of the superior and his guilt.[9] In other words:

> '[A] commander's liability is divorced from his culpability to such a degree that his conviction no longer mirrors his underlying conduct and his actual *mens rea*.'[10]

While recognising that not all national systems may contain the same requirements, Damaška firmly opined that:

> '[C]onviction for egregious crimes, such as murder or rape, can never result from attribution to a negligent actor of someone else's wrongdoing.'[11]

The culpability problem was considered particularly problematic because the ICTY Trial Chamber in *Blaškić* found negligence to be a sufficient *mens rea* standard under the 'had reason to know' requirement of Article 7(3).[12] The Appeals Chamber corrected this interpretation in its 2004 judgement and held, referring to the Čelebići Appeal Judgement, that:

---

[6] K. Ambos, 'Joint Criminal Enterprise and Command Responsibility', 5 *Journal of International Criminal Justice* (2007) pp. 159-183, at p. 176.

[7] A.P.V. Rogers, *Law on the Battlefield*, 2nd edn. (Manchester, Manchester University Press 2004) p. 193.

[8] Ibid., p. 198.

[9] Damaška, pp. 463-464. See also Van der Wilt, 'Commentary', pp. 115-122, at p. 120.

[10] Damaška, p. 464.

[11] Ibid.

[12] Van der Wilt, 'Commentary', pp. 115-122, at p. 120.

'Neglect of a duty to acquire such knowledge [...] does not feature as a provision [Article 7(3)] as a separate offence, and a superior is not therefore liable under the provision for such failures but only for failing to take necessary and reasonable measures to prevent or to punish.'[13]

The points of criticism mentioned above specifically concentrated on the application of the doctrine under Article 6(3) ICTR/7(3) ICTY, as these provisions have been applied in practice. While recognising that the ICC Statute contains a higher *mens rea* standard for civilian superiors, Damaška noted that a 'should have known' standard will be retained for military commanders.[14] Of course, the 'should have known' standard has so far not been defined by the ICC.

Triffterer, one of the few proponents of command responsibility as participation in the crime, underlines the view that in particular under the ICC Statute, command responsibility is not based on negligence on the part of the superior and, therefore, the superior may very well be held partly liable for the crime committed. Following his interpretation of Article 28, the provision that the superior shall be criminally responsible 'as a result of his or her failure to exercise control properly' suggests that the failure of the superior is twofold.[15] In order to become criminally liable, the superior first failed to exercise control and secondly failed to take all necessary and reasonable measures. According to Triffterer, the first failure should fulfil the mental element in Article 30 ICC, 'with intent and knowledge'.[16] This approach solves the causality demand, as the crimes would not have occurred without the failure of the superior to control properly, and at the same time the culpability issue.[17] In addition, Article 28 of the ICC Statute could clearly be considered to provide that the superior who fails to prevent or punish his subordinates will be held responsible for the international crimes under the jurisdiction of the ICC. The exact wording is, 'shall be criminally responsible for crimes within the jurisdiction of the Court.' In other words, it is in accordance with the letter of the law that command responsibility judgements have found a superior criminally liable for a certain crime under the command responsibility provision of the article.[18]

Interestingly, a very recent example from national law shows that the culpability issue has not constituted an obstacle for implementing Article 28 ICC as a provision which leads to responsibility for the international crime committed by the subordinates. According to the new provision of 11 April 2008 on superior responsibility in Chapter 11 of the Finnish Penal Code, the superior will be held responsible as a perpetrator or for participation in the international crime committed by his subordinates where he fails to exercise control over these persons

---

13 *Blaškić*, AC Judgement, para. 62.

14 Damaška, p. 494.

15 O. Triffterer, '"Command Responsibility" – *Crimen sui generis* or Participation as "otherwise provided" in Article 28 Rome Statute?', in J. Arnold et al., eds., *Menschengerechtes Strafrecht – Festschrift für Albin Eser zum 70. Geburtstag* (Munich, Beck 2005) pp. 901-924, at pp. 910 and 919.

16 Ibid., p. 910.

17 Ibid., p. 919.

18 Ibid., pp. 904-905.

and where the *mens rea* requirement and the element of necessary and reasonable measures, corresponding to those of Article 28 ICC, were fulfilled.[19] This implementation of the ICC Statute is of much later date than both the German provisions and the *Halilović* case, but seems to have encountered no problems with regard to the issue of the personal guilt of the superior. However, the provision only concerns the failure of the superior to prevent his subordinates from committing the crime. His failure to report the crimes or to submit the matter to the authorities is considered as a lesser crime and the superior will be held liable for an omission to report a crime.[20] This specific example is worth mentioning in that this piece of legislation is based on existing international legal provisions on the principle, and in that it postdates the *Halilović* and the *Hadžihasanović* cases, which were the first to turn away from interpreting command responsibility as the responsibility of a superior for the crime committed by his subordinates.

5.2.2 An act *sui generis*

Where criminal conduct consists of an omission, a differentiation may be made between a genuine crime of omission (*echtes Unterlassungsdelikt*) and commission by omission (*unechtes Unterlassungsdelikt*). Where the commander under the command responsibility doctrine is considered to be liable for an international crime, as in the previous section, the superior commits an act by omission. The present section discusses command responsibility as a genuine crime of omission, an *echtes Unterlassungsdelikt*, where the omission itself constitutes the crime. In the previous section, a slight distinction was noted between the formulation of the command responsibility provisions in the ICTY/ICTR Statutes and that of the ICC Statute. With regard to the discussion on command responsibility as a *crimen sui generis*, this distinction should be kept in mind. The focus will first be on the reasoning of the *ad hoc* tribunals.

Despite the Appeals Chamber's dismissal of the idea accepted by the Trial Chamber in the *Bagilishema* case that the accused superior could be found criminally responsible under a 'third basis of liability' based on gross negligence,[21] the prevalent view since the *Halilović* Trial Judgement has been that command responsibility is a genuine crime of omission. Instead of considering that the superior was a participant in the underlying crime, the *Halilović* Trial Chamber held that what the superior should be held liable for was the failure to prevent or punish. That the existing jurisprudence of the tribunal found the superior responsible 'for the acts of his subordinates'[22] according to the *Halilović* Trial Chamber:

---

[19] Finnish Penal Code, Chapter 11, para. 12.
[20] Ibid., para. 13.
[21] *Bagilishema*, TC Judgement, para. 897; and *Bagilishema*, AC Judgement, paras. 32-37.
[22] *Halilović*, TC Judgement, para. 54.

'[D]oes not mean that the commander shares the same responsibility as the subordinates who committed the crimes, but rather that because of the crimes committed by his subordinates, the commander should bear responsibility for his failure to act.'[23]

By reading the discussion on the nature of command responsibility in international law in the *Halilović* Trial Judgement, it becomes clear that there is admittedly a desire to leave behind the idea of the superior being partly responsible for the crimes committed, but that on the basis of international and national legal provisions and earlier case law, the change of direction was a conscious choice of the Trial Chamber, as such not a necessity. Herewith, the Trial Chamber indirectly recognised that the application of the principle by the *ad hoc* tribunals in the past was not in contradiction with the principle, which as such was a clever move, because had the Trial Chamber contended that there was a clear recognition of command responsibility as a separate crime of omission, an act *sui generis* in international law, this would have disqualified all earlier decisions of these tribunals on this specific point.[24] The *Hadžihasanović* Trial Chamber opined that the reason why the 'object' of the superior's responsibility, either the crime resulting from his omission or the omission itself, had never been considered by the tribunal, was that the *Halilović* case was the first case in which the accused was charged on the basis of command responsibility only.[25] That it has not been done is correct, but it is difficult to see why the 'object' could not have been considered earlier, as it has been clear since the *Celebići* case that command responsibility is not about the superior's commission of a crime, but about his failure to prevent or punish his subordinates, and that this constitutes one of the elements that have to be proven in order to obtain a conviction.[26]

On the other hand, the *Halilović* Trial Chamber was right in holding that there are provisions, most notably Article 86(2) AP I, which do not explicitly state that the superior, when failing to prevent or punish crimes by subordinates, will himself be held responsible for an international crime. The wording of the relevant part of the provision is the following: 'The fact that a breach of the Conventions or of this Protocol was committed by a subordinate does not absolve his superiors from penal or disciplinary responsibility.' The responsibility could be penal or disciplinary, but there is no mention of the superior being held responsible for a certain international crime. Together with a few post-WW II cases which might be said to support the idea that only the failure to prevent or punish, i.e., the omission, is punished under the command responsibility principle, this provision shows that there is some basis for considering the command responsi-

[23] Ibid.

[24] Compare this reasoning with the *Hadžihasanović* TC Judgement which, while only being the second case to adopt this approach, states that command responsibility 'must be conceived as a type of personal responsibility for failure to act.' See *Hadžihasanović*, TC Judgement, para. 2075.

[25] See *Hadžihasanović*, TC Judgement, para. 69.

[26] It might be concluded that the reason why there was a direct need to consider whether command responsibility is responsibility for the international crime or an act *sui generis* in *Halilović*, was because the Chamber had to determine a sentence, without having the possibility of using an Art. 7(1) conviction as the basis for the length of the sentence.

bility principle as a concept which renders superiors criminally liable specifically for their failure to prevent or punish crimes by subordinates. When considering that also national legislation, in particular the German legislation, treats command responsibility as a separate crime of omission, it is understandable that this approach to applying the command responsibility principle has been well-received by scholars.[27]

The most appealing aspect of command responsibility as a separate crime of omission is that the superior is not seen as bearing responsibility for the international crime committed, and the culpability issue is thereby solved. The problem that arose with the *Yamashita* case concerning the requirement of personal guilt and that has been present ever since gets a satisfactory solution where the superior is only held liable for his own failure to act.[28] The concern that 'it appears inappropriate to associate an official superior with murderers, torturers, or rapists just because he negligently failed to realize that his subordinates are about to kill, torture or rape'[29] is also taken away at the international level, if the appropriateness of the superior's responsibility can be considered as separate from the culpability issue.

From this it follows that the *sui generis* approach opens possibilities for imposing sentences that are not dependent on the sentence that would be imposed on the perpetrators of the crime.[30] This is clearly to be seen in the *Hadžihasanović* case, where the accused holding superior positions were convicted on the basis of command responsibility only and were sentenced to the most lenient terms of imprisonment in the history of the *ad hoc* tribunals. As mentioned earlier, the Trial Chamber in this case upheld the view of the *Halilović* Trial Chamber that command responsibility should be treated as a crime *sui generis*. It also agreed with the finding in the *Halilović* judgement that the *sui generis* nature of the command responsibility principle allows for 'an even greater flexibility in the determination of sentence.'[31] The accused, Hadžihasanović and Kubura, were sentenced, on appeal, to three and a half years' and two years' imprisonment respectively.[32] Hadžihasanović had failed to prevent or punish cruel treatment during a period of around three months and had failed to punish cruel treatment

---

[27] For the discussion on the Geman Code of Crimes Against International Law, see *infra*. For support of the act *sui generis* approach, see B.I. Bonafé, 'Finding a Proper Role for Command Responsibility', 5 *Journal of International Criminal Justice* (2007) pp. 599-618, at pp. 603-604.

[28] Ambos 2002, 'Superior Responsibility', p. 847.

[29] Damaška, p. 466.

[30] 'The terminology of Article 7(1) and (3), however, shows a clear difference between the provisions, in that, under Article 7(1), the commander in our example would be held directly, individually responsible for the offence of ethnic cleansing, whilst, under Article 7(3), he would be deemed responsible, but to an unspecified extent, in respect of the offence committed by his subordinates. His offence under the latter would be failure in his duty as a commander, not murder as a crime against humanity. As he had no direct involvement in the commission of the killings, it may be thought that his share of the liability should be deemed less than if he was charged under Article 7(1).' See B.B. Jia, 'The Doctrine of Command Responbility: Current Problems', 3 *YIHL* (2000) pp. 131-165, at p. 143.

[31] See *Prosecutor* v. *Naser Orić*, Judgement, Case No. IT-03-68-T, 30 June 2006, para. 724.

[32] See *Prosecutor* v. *Enver Hadžihasanović et al.*, Appeal Judgement, Case No. IT-01-47-A, 22 April 2008, at VIII. Disposition.

during a period of about the same length. Kubura, in turn, had failed to punish the plundering of the town of Vareš that took place on 4 November 1993.[33] The Trial Chamber in the *Orić* case similarly sentenced the accused for his failure to prevent the occurrence of murder and cruel treatment, during a period of almost three months, to two years' imprisonment.[34] Compared to a conviction for some form of participation in the murder and cruel treatment during a period of three months or for plundering as a violation of the laws or customs of war, it is obvious that the crime of omission called 'failure to prevent or punish' is considered to be less severe than if the responsibility was for the crime committed.

As was suggested above, it is not appropriate to compare the superior who failed to prevent or punish crimes of his subordinates with a murderer or rapist or, in short, the direct perpetrator of the international crime. In addition, as was stated earlier, case law shows that those superiors who have been held responsible solely on the basis of their failure to prevent or punish crimes have been sentenced to relatively short terms of imprisonment. Nevertheless, a conviction of a high-level commander or superior for his failure only unavoidably raises the question of whether the end result, while perhaps being 'appropriate', will also be a satisfactory result. It is a fact that international criminal justice aims at, and the institutions applying it are only capable of prosecuting those most responsible for certain conflicts and crises around the world that are of concern to the international community. Where such high-level superiors, who are chosen for prosecution exactly because of their high rank, are only convicted on the basis of their failure to fulfil their duty as a superior, the question is whether justice is seen to be done.

Additional support for the *sui generis* approach can be found in national criminal law. In their article on the prosecution of international crimes according to German law, Werle and Nerlich pointed out that according to the German Code of Crimes Against International Law, in situations where the superior would have been able to prevent the crimes of his subordinates, the superior will not be prosecuted for an international crime, but for another kind of offence – his failure to perform a duty attached to his position of authority in relation to his subordinates. The omission on the part of the superior is a separate offence from the international crime that was committed by the subordinates.[35]

> 'Gemäß § 13 VStGB werden Befehlshaber und Vorgesetzte bestraft, die vorsätzlich oder fahrlässig ihre Aufsichtspflicht verletzt haben, sofern sie die Straftaten ihrer Untergebenen hätten erkennen und verhindern können. Nach § 14 VStGB machen sich Befehlshaber oder Vorgesetzte strafbar, die Völkerrechtsverbrechen ihrer Untergebenen nicht unverzüglich an die Strafvervolgungsbehörden melden. *Wiederum wird dem Befehlshaber oder Vorgesetzten nicht das Völkerrechtsverbrechen selbst, sondern*

[33] Ibid.

[34] *Orić*, TC Judgement, para. 782.

[35] *Bundesgesetzblatt* 2002 I, at 2254, 29 June 2002. The relevant provisions can be found in Sections 3, 13 and 14. A version of the document in English can be found on Professor Ambos' website, University of Göttingen, <http://lehrstuhl.jura.uni-goettingen.de/kambos/Forschung/doc/VStGB_BGBl_Englisch.doc> (accessed 16 July 2009).

> *eine Straftat eigener Art zur Last gelegt.* Das VStGB bringt damit – anders als Artikel 28 IStGH-Statut – zum Ausdruck, dass das Unrecht, das einem Befehlshaber oder Vorgesetzten bei einer Aufsichtspflichtverletzung oder bei der Nichtmeldung einer Straftat vorgeworfen wird, anderer Art und von geringerem Gewicht ist, als das vom Untergebenen begangene Kriegsverbrechen.'[36]

According to Cassese, the German approach seemed 'logically and theoretically more correct and also more consonant with general principles of justice (because of its consequences at the level of sentencing)',[37] than holding the superior responsible for the international crime itself.

Ambos in turn held that, 'Article 28 can be characterized as a genuine offence or separate crime of omission (*echtes Unterlassungsdelikt*), since it makes the superior liable only for a failure of proper supervision and control of his or her subordinates but not, 'at least not directly', for crimes they commit.'[38] He explained his argument by stating that, 'The underlying crimes of the subordinates are neither an element of the offence nor a purely objective condition of the superior's punishability.'[39] This interpretation of Article 28 seems to be in contradiction with the interpretation by Werle and Nerlich, who considered that while the German provisions define the liability as being the responsibility of the failure to act as a separate act, Article 28 provides a different definition. In other words, Werle and Nerlich were of the opinion that while German law provides for command responsibility as an *echtes Unterlassungsdelikt*, the provision in the ICC Statute does not. This possible contradiction in the reading of Article 28 is interesting. It is likely that these German authors all agree on the desirability of holding the superior responsible for an act of his own instead of the international crime committed, but because of the different perceptions of Article 28 discerned here, the question may be raised as to whether the existing international provisions actually do provide for command responsibility as an act *sui generis* or whether the desire to interpret the principle as such overrides any strict application of a provision, the formulation of which supports the idea of command responsibility as liability for the crime committed by subordinates.

The opponents of the *sui generis* approach have mainly found their arguments in the formulation of the doctrine in Article 28, which shows two main differences from the *ad hoc* tribunal provisions that are of direct relevance in the present discussion. First, there is the phrase 'shall be criminally responsible for crimes within the jurisdiction of the Court.' Triffterer has firmly argued that the ICC Statute is very explicit on this point and that superiors cannot therefore be held responsible for another crime, a crime *sui generis*.[40] In the opinion of Triffterer, the fact that some domestic legal systems have adopted this approach is not

---

36 G. Werle and V. Nerlich, 'Die Strafbarkeit von Kriegsverbrechen nach deutschem Recht', 3 *Humanitäres Völkerrecht* (2002) pp. 124-134, at p. 128 (emphasis added by MLN).

37 Cassese 2003, p. 206.

38 Ambos 2002, 'Superior Responsibility', p. 851.

39 Ibid.

40 Triffterer 2005, pp. 904-905 and 921. See also van der Wilt, 'Commentary', pp. 115-122, at p. 121.

a sufficient argument to consider command responsibility under the ICC Statute as an act *sui generis*, because '[i]international criminal law [...] punishes such conduct only when resulting in the commission of crimes within the jurisdiction of the Court by subordinates.'[41]

Secondly, Article 28 provides that responsibility arises where the crimes were committed by subordinates 'as a result of his or her failure to exercise control properly over such forces.' The phrase creates a causal link between the omission of the superior and the crimes,[42] which arguably proves that the superior's responsibility is based on a form of participation.[43]

It may also be asked what international legal basis the *sui generis* approach rests on. The study of the ICRC on Customary International Humanitarian Law confirms the customary law status of the command responsibility principle in its Rule 153, but discusses the principle as a commander's criminal responsibility for the crimes committed by his subordinates. As the customary law study was prepared prior to the *Halilović* case, it does not take into account the crime *sui generis* approach as developed in that and subsequent cases. On the other hand, had command responsibility as criminal liability for the failure to prevent or punish been established customary law in 2005 when the customary law study was published, the study, which refers to case law, national legislation and military manuals, would have referred to the principle as responsibility for a crime of omission. That this specific interpretation of the principle is established customary law is, thus, doubtful.[44]

It could also be argued that applying the *sui generis* approach does bring the principle back to its roots as set out in Chapter 3 of this book. When considering command responsibility in its original sense, not as a criminal law principle but as a military concept, it has served as a means to impose discipline throughout the hierarchy of the armed forces. It was in the interest of the commander to instruct and supervise his subordinates in accordance with applicable rules and practices because he knew that he would be held responsible where they misbehaved and he could have avoided that through supervision and disciplinary action. That the superior is now, under the *sui generis* approach, punished for his

---

[41] Triffterer 2005, p. 921.

[42] T. Weigend, 'Bemerkungen zur Vorgesetztenverantwortlichkeit im Völkerstrafrecht', 116 *Zeitschrift für die Gesamte Strafrechtswissenschaft* (2004) pp. 999-1027, at pp. 1017-1018. Weigend considers the 'as a result of' phrase as a sign of a causal link, but on the other hand he points out that the provision asks the impossible of the superior. He finds that having considered other options, 'bleibt eigentlich nur die Feststellung, dass eine Vorschrift, die die Vorgesetztenverantwortlichkeit anordnet für "crimes committed as a result of his or her failure … to submit the matter to the competent authorities for investigation or prosecution", von dem Vorgesetzten etwas logisch Unmögliches fordert, nämlich dass er eine Tat zur Verfolgung übergibt, die noch gar nicht begangen wurde. Bei richtiger Betrachtung kann es für den Fall der Nicht-Ahndung kein Kausalitätserfordernis geben: für das begangene Verbrechen aus logischen Gründen nicht, und für zukünftige Verbrechen deshalb nicht, weil der Vorgesetzte (jedefalls im Rahmen der völkerstrafrechtlichen Vorgesetztenverantwortlichkeit) nicht ihretwegen bestraft wird.' Ibid., p. 1021.

[43] Van der Wilt, pp. 115-122, at pp. 121-122.

[44] For a critical opinion on the status of international humanitarian law rules as customary law, see Heintschel von Heinegg, pp. 27-47.

failure to prevent or punish instead of as being partly responsible for the international crime committed, strengthens the thesis of command responsibility as a military principle primarily applicable to military superiors.

5.2.3 The bifurcated approach – Act *sui generis* and *sui generis* participation

In the previous sections arguments have been presented in favour of and against command responsibility as liability for a crime and as a *crimen sui generis*. There seems to be agreement that neither approach can satisfy all the demands of criminal law regarding the culpability of the superior and the causality between the omission of the superior and the crime committed. It is apparent that Article 28 ICC, with its requirements that deviate from those in Article 6(3) ICTR/7(3) ICTY, has complicated the issue rather than simplified it, at least when considering the command responsibility doctrine as a whole, not just its specific application by one tribunal or court.

Several authors now point to the possibilities of taking a bifurcated approach to the issue.[45] Command criminal responsibility would not be considered as one or the other, act *sui generis* or participation liability, but as a combination of both. This approach was applied in national criminal law and could be developed to suit the command responsibility doctrine in international criminal law, as well. As has been promoted throughout this book, the object and purpose of the command responsibility doctrine should be kept in mind when interpreting and applying it.

To put it more simply, the superiors who can be successfully prosecuted under the command responsibility doctrine are commanders, and in specific cases non-military superiors, who were not part of a plan to commit crimes, but at the time of the subordinates' crimes, did not pay attention to or did not care about what was going on. At most, he approved, in his mind, of the crimes and chose not act. Where crimes had been committed that he could not have prevented but that he could punish, he either did not pay attention to information about such crimes or did not care about making an effort to report the crimes. At most, he approved, in his mind, of the crimes and chose not to act.

Where the *mens rea* of the commander/superior was at the level of negligence (should have known), either at the stage of preventing or at the stage of punishment, the commander/superior would be held liable for command responsibility, an act *sui generis*. Where the *mens rea* of the commander/superior was at least at the level of 'consciously disregarded information which clearly indicated', i.e., 'higher' than negligence and implying some kind of intention on the part of the commander/superior, he would be held liable for aggravated command responsibility, a form of *sui generis* participation.[46]

---

[45] See K. Ambos, 'Remarks on the General Part of International Criminal Law', 4 *Journal of International Criminal Justice* (2006) pp. 660-673, at p. 672.

[46] For a categorisation of command responsibility which also pays attention to whether the superior acted negligently or had a higher level of *mens rea*, see V. Nerlich, 'Superior Responsibility under

First, holding a superior responsible for a crime *sui generis* where he 'should have known' about the crimes would satisfy the most sensitive issue involved in the discussion – that of liability that should correspond to the culpability of the superior. Although it may be argued that only the crimes under the jurisdiction of the court may be prosecuted and that international criminal law should not be concerned with crimes of this character, it is a fact that the underlying crimes were of concern to the international community, but that the omission to prevent or punish best describes the role of the accused. The question is what should be expected of the doctrine. It is interesting to note the formulation of Article 86(2) AP I in this respect. It provides as follows:

> 'The fact that a breach of the Conventions or of this Protocol was committed by a subordinate does not absolve his superiors from penal *or disciplinary responsibility, as the case may be.*'[47]

According to the Commentary on the Additional Protocols, this provision 'condemns failure to act of superiors in case of breaches which are not grave breaches as well as in case of grave breaches.'[48] The Commentary further explains that, 'In the first case the sanction can be disciplinary or penal, while universal jurisdiction understood as *aut dedere aut judicare* applies in the second case, i.e., in case of a grave breach.'[49] What makes this interpretation of the provision interesting in this context? By providing that a superior may incur penal *or* disciplinary responsibility, as the case may be, it seems that the drafters of Articles 86 and 87 of AP I wanted to emphasise the fact that the superior had a certain responsibility in relation to the crimes committed, rather than the nature of his responsibility – that he had either committed a separate crime of omission or participated in the crimes committed. As for the argument that only crimes under the jurisdiction of the ICC may be prosecuted, the ICC may borrow the above-mentioned argument from *Halilović*, according to which responsibility 'for' the crimes committed should not be understood as meaning sharing the responsibility of the subordinates. Rather, because of the crimes committed by the subordinates, the commander is to be held responsible for his failure to act.

As only military commanders or persons effectively acting as such are subjected to the 'should have known' standard under Article 28 ICC, applying command responsibility as a separate crime of omission to them where they only 'should have known' would reduce the concerns of those who saw participation liability as not corresponding to the culpability of the superior.

Secondly, the superior would be held liable for *sui generis* participation where he 'consciously disregarded information' or knowingly omitted to prevent or to punish. By *sui generis* participation is here meant that the mode of participation

---

Article 28 ICC Statute – For What Exactly is the Superior Held Responsible?', 5 *Journal of International Criminal Justice* (2007) pp. 665-682.

[47] Protocol Additional to the Geneva Conventions of 12 August 1949, and relating to the Protection of Victims of International Armed Conflicts (Protocol I), 8 June 1977, 1125 *UNTS* p. 3.

[48] Pilloud, p. 1012.

[49] Ibid.

does not have to meet the requirements of the other modes as provided for in provisions on individual criminal responsibility, at present most importantly in Article 25(3) ICC.[50] Triffterer pointed to the desirability of prosecuting superiors under Article 28 and not under the alternatives listed in Article 25(3). He stressed the 'great influence superiors have in hierarchically structured institutions', which generates 'a great responsibility for the prevention of such crimes.' As Article 28 only covers omissions and 'does not trigger responsibility for any active behaviour', this form of perpetration 'does not fit into the framework of Article 25 paragraph 3.'[51]

The idea that a superior could be held criminally responsible in relation to crimes committed by his subordinates on the basis of participation of its own kind has been elaborated and confirmed in Dutch case law and literature, as well as in other domestic legal systems.[52] In a comparison between the doctrine of command responsibility in international law and a form of criminal responsibility under Dutch law, according to which a superior may be held responsible for crimes committed by others within the framework of a legal person ('feitelijk leidinggeven' or 'functional liability'/functional perpetration[53]), it was considered as accepted that this form of responsibility in Dutch law, which despite its differences was founded on the same basis as the doctrine on the international level, could best be described as a special form of participation.[54] Treating the responsibility of a superior as a special form of participation, in the opinion of some Dutch authors, solves some of the inherent problems related to the responsibility of a person for crimes committed by someone else.[55] It was specifically pointed out, however, that one has to note the difference between the crimes, for example fraud, that are covered by this specific provision in Dutch criminal law, and the crimes covered by the command responsibility doctrine.[56] Another important difference should be noted. The 'should have known' standard as set out in Article 28 ICC sets a lower threshold for conviction than the threshold set by the Dutch 'feitelijk leidinggeven'.[57] For a conviction under the latter concept,

---

[50] A person shall be criminally responsible for a crime if the material elements are committed with intent and knowledge, as provided in Art. 30 ICC.

[51] Triffterer 2005, p. 922.

[52] J. de Hullu, *Materieel Strafrecht – Over algemene leerstukken van Strafrechtelijke aansprakelijkheid naar Nederlands recht* (Deventer, Gouda Quint 2000) pp. 478-483. See also Van Sliedregt 2003, pp. 200-201, who mentions similar solutions for the responsibility of the superior in other domestic legal systems.

[53] Van Sliedregt uses the term functional liability, while Van der Wilt discusses the phenomenon using the term functional perpetration. See H.G. van der Wilt, 'Joint Criminal Enterprise – Possibilities and Limitations', 5 *Journal of International Criminal Justice* (2007) pp. 91-108, at pp. 102-107.

[54] S.A.M. Stolwijk, ''Command responsibility' en 'strafbaar leidinggeven'. Beschouwingen over strafbaar leiderschap', in *Joegoslavië- en Rwanda-tribunalen: impact op het Nederlandse strafrecht* (Amsterdam, Leerstoelgroep Strafrechtswetenschappen Universiteit van Amsterdam 2002) p. 7. See also H.G. van der Wilt, 'Ontwikkeling van nieuwe deelnemingsvormen. Ben ik mijn broeders hoeder?', 37 *Delikt en Delinkwent* (2007) pp. 138-183, at p. 168.

[55] Stolwijk, p. 7.

[56] Ibid., p. 9.

[57] Van der Wilt, pp. 138-183, at p. 170.

more than negligence is required. The accused need not have been aware of the specific crimes he is charged with, but awareness is required at least in relation to criminal acts that are similar to and related to those with which the accused is charged.[58] As has been pointed out, there are some differences between the two concepts. Nevertheless, it has been held that the comparison just mentioned is justified because of the basis that is shared by both concepts.[59]

This view could combine the advantages of the *sui generis* approach and those of the approach considering command responsibility as responsibility for an international crime. As a form of participation of its own kind, the punishment would be defined as being more lenient as it is a separate form of participation, compared to those contained in the provisions on individual criminal responsibility. On the other hand, while calling 'aggravated command responsibility' a form of participation *sui generis*, the connection to the international crimes committed would remain.[60] As participation *sui generis*, the principle would require the same elements that have been set out as necessary for proving command responsibility.

5.3 Overlap between individual criminal responsibility and command responsibility?

5.3.1 **Introduction**

As set out in Chapter 2, the basis for criminal responsibility under international criminal law has been divided into individual criminal responsibility and command responsibility. While in principle the distinction between what constitutes individual criminal responsibility as opposed to command responsibility is clear, it is recognised that, 'The intricate relationship between Articles 7(1) and 7(3) inevitably means that there will be some overlap between the basis of liability imposed by them.'[61]

Command responsibility arises where a superior is liable for an omission to prevent or punish his subordinates. However, the case law of the *ad hoc* tribunals shows that in cases where the superior failed to act, showed passivity, and subordinates committed crimes under the jurisdiction of the tribunals, the act of omission has in certain cases led to criminal liability for participation in or a contribution to a joint criminal enterprise or for aiding and abetting a crime.

[58] De Hullu, p. 481.

[59] Stolwijk, p. 9.

[60] For the advantages of considering 'functional liability' as a mode of participation *sui generis*, see the commentary to the judgement of the Dutch Supreme Court in the *Slavenburg* case, 16 December 1986, NJ 1987, No. 321, p. 1205.

[61] See R. May and S. Powles, 'Command Responsibility – A New Basis of Criminal Liability in English Law?', *Criminal Law Review* (May 2002) pp. 363-378, at p. 373.

5.3.2 **Joint Criminal Enterprise**

5.3.2.1 *JCE – The concept*

With the Appeal Judgement in the *Tadić* case, individual criminal responsibility for participating in a common criminal purpose was introduced in the case law of the ICTY. What was needed for the existence of such a common criminal purpose, or in other words, the objective elements of this mode of participation were considered to be the following:

i) A plurality of persons;
ii) The existence of a common plan, design or purpose which amounts to or involves the commission of a crime provided for in the Statute; and
iii) Participation of the accused in the common design.[62]

While the Statute of the ICTY does not explicitly provide for this mode of participation in the crimes under the jurisdiction of the tribunal, the Appeals Chamber held that the object and purpose of the Statute was to enable the prosecution of 'all those who have engaged in serious violations of international humanitarian law, whatever the manner in which they may have perpetrated, or participated in the perpetration of those violations […].'[63] The reason for the introduction of the common purpose concept was that it, in the opinion of the Appeals Chamber, reflected the way in which most international crimes were committed, i.e., by a plurality of persons 'acting in pursuance of a common criminal design.'[64] The Appeals Chamber recognised that because the Statute did not specify the elements of this mode of participation, there was a need to identify these in customary international law. The question as to whether customary international law actually provides such elements was answered in the affirmative by the Appeals Chamber after having reviewed a number of post-WW II cases.[65] Cassese, a member of the *Tadić* Appeals Chamber, recently defended this view and pointed out that by referring to the common purpose doctrine, the tribunal only 'fulfilled its proper task of finding and interpreting the law', and did not resort to 'judicial creativity', as has been argued in the literature.[66]

Relying on the post-WW II cases, the *Tadić* Appeals Chamber identified three categories of cases that may constitute a common criminal purpose. Ambos nicely summarised the main aspects of the three categories as follows:

> '(i) the *basic* form, where the participants act on the basis of a 'common design' or 'common enterprise' and with a common 'intention';

---

[62] *Prosecutor* v. *Duško Tadić*, Appeal Judgement, Case No. IT-94-1-A, 15 July 1999, para. 227.
[63] Ibid., paras. 190-191.
[64] Ibid., para. 191.
[65] Ibid., para. 220.
[66] A. Cassese, 'The Proper Limits of Individual Responsibility under the Doctrine of Joint Criminal Enterprise', 5 *Journal of International Criminal Justice* (2007) pp. 109-133, at p. 114.

(ii) the *systemic* form, i.e. the so-called concentration camp cases where crimes are committed by members of military or administrative units such as those running concentration or detention camps on the basis of a common plan ('common purpose');
(iii) the so-called '*extended*' joint enterprise where one of the co-perpetrators actually engages in acts going beyond the common plan but his or her acts still constitute a 'natural and foreseeable consequence' of the realization of the plan.'[67]

While the objective elements (*actus reus*), as set out above, apply equally to all three forms of collective criminality, each of the categories requires a distinct subjective element (*mens rea*). As for the first category, the requirement is that the co-perpetrators all share the intent to perpetrate the crime. The second category requires knowledge of the system of ill-treatment and the intent to further this system. The *mens rea* requirement of the third category demands the intention to participate in and further the criminal activity or purpose of the group and to contribute to the commission of the crime by the group. With regard to the third category, it should be noted that a participant to the common criminal purpose can only incur responsibility in relation to crimes other than those covered by the common plan, if '(i) it was *foreseeable* that such a crime might be perpetrated by one or other members of the group and (ii) the accused *willingly took that risk*.'[68]

In subsequent judgements the idea of the common criminal purpose was acknowledged and applied, although the term used has been that of a 'joint criminal enterprise'.[69] The acceptance of the concept, however, has not been unanimous. Both the concept itself and certain aspects of its application have proven controversial among judges as well as among scholars.

The most fundamental controversy concerns the legitimacy of the concept. In the *Stakić* case, the Trial Chamber held the view that the traditional forms of participating in a crime should be preferred to applying the concept of 'joint criminal enterprise'.[70] In the opinion of the Trial Chamber, using co-perpetration instead of JCE corresponded more to what most legal systems understand by 'committing', a term used in the ICTY Statute, and it avoided creating the impression 'that a new crime not foreseen in the Statute of this Tribunal has been introduced through the backdoor.'[71] This attempt by the Trial Chamber to avoid the use of the concept, because it was not set out in the Statute, failed when the Appeals Chamber in its subsequent judgement faulted the decision of the Trial Chamber in this regard and returned to the interpretation of a JCE in the *Tadić* Appeal. A few months after the *Stakić* Trial Judgement was rendered, another rejection of the concept was expressed in the Separate and partly dissent-

[67] Ambos 2007, 'Joint Criminal Enterprise', p. 160.
[68] *Tadić*, AC Judgement, para. 228.
[69] See, for example, *Kvočka*, TC Judgement, para. 244.
[70] *Prosecutor* v. *Milomir Stakić*, Judgement, Case No. IT-97-24-T, 31 July 2003, para. 438.
[71] Ibid., para. 441.

ing opinion of Judge Lindholm in the *Simić et al.* case. Judge Lindholm dissociated himself from the concept and considered that in addition to having been a waste of time, the concept of JCE had neither benefited the work of the ICTY, nor the development of international criminal law.[72] In the *Lubanga* and *Katanga* cases brought before the ICC, the Pre-Trial Chamber clearly showed that it does not give preference to the concept of JCE, although it would have the possibility to build on the experience of the *ad hoc* tribunals.[73]

A greater nuance has been brought into the generally very critical analysis of the concept by scholars. Besides questioning the usefulness of the doctrine in prosecuting system criminality, scholars have generally recognised that it is only the extended joint criminal enterprise (JCE III) that causes serious concerns regarding the culpability of the accused.

5.3.2.2 *JCE and command responsibility*

In some cases that have come before the *ad hoc* tribunals, where the accused acted in a superior position and the alleged crimes were committed by their subordinates, the accused have been prosecuted under the concept of JCE.[74] As command responsibility also arises in cases of an omission to prevent or punish crimes committed by subordinates, the simultaneous application of JCE and command responsibility has been an invitation for critical comments and questions. Most interesting are the reasons behind the choice between either a JCE or command responsibility as the basis for criminal liability, where applying both bases seem feasible.

In the *Kvočka* case, the Prosecution had brought charges under both Article 7(1) and Article 7(3). Except for the accused Zigić, all the accused were charged under both 7(1) and 7(3). However, the Chamber found that because liability had already been established for the role of the accused in a joint criminal enterprise under Article 7(1), there was no need to further consider the issue of responsibility as a superior.[75] In relation to one of the accused, the Chamber held that, '[H]is participation in the joint criminal enterprise of Omarska camps renders him liable for crimes committed therein and arguably makes Article 7(3) liability duplicative.'[76] The Chamber did not elaborate on the reason for its decision. In other cases involving both Article 7(1) and 7(3) liability, the Chamber has made a similar assumption to the one in *Kvočka*, namely that responsibility under Article 7(1) makes a finding under Article 7(3) unnecessary.[77] All cases that have charged a superior both under the joint criminal enterprise theory and

[72] *Prosecutor* v. *Blagoje Simić, Miroslav Tadić and Simo Zarić*, Separate and Partly Dissenting Opinion of Judge Per-Johan Lindholm, Case No. IT-95-9-T, 17 October 2003, paras. 1-5.

[73] See the discussion in section 6.3 *infra*.

[74] See *Prosecutor* v. *Aloys Simba*, Judgement, Case No. ICTR-01-76-T, 13 December 2005. The accused was first charged under both Art. 6(1) and Art. 6(3), but at the end of its case, the prosecution withdrew the charge pursuant to Art. 6(3). Ibid., para. 4.

[75] See *Kvočka et al.*, TC Judgement, paras. 412, 466-467, 570 and 683.

[76] Ibid., para. 412.

[77] See *Stakić*, TC Judgement, para. 466. For a more detailed discussion, see section 4.3.4.2 *supra*.

under the provision on superior responsibility have resulted in a finding of liability for some kind of participation in a joint criminal enterprise, while the superior responsibility has been dismissed as superfluous or as only constituting an aggravating circumstance to be taken into account only for the purposes of sentencing.

The said cases have not provided a convincing reason for why superior responsibility has been dismissed as superfluous. This together with the fact that the notion of joint criminal enterprise has been dismissed by some judges as 'superfluous', in the sense that it does not add anything to the existing forms of participation as laid down in the provisions on individual criminal responsibility, creates that impression that the issue of superior responsibility in relation to joint criminal enterprise has not been satisfactorily clarified.

Some of the cases that have come before the *ad hoc* tribunals are cases of 'pure' command responsibility,[78] where the accused is a commander whose subordinates suddenly committed a crime which he should have prevented or punished. Such a case is the *Hadžihasanović* case, which according to the prosecution clearly concerned the failure to prevent or punish crimes, as responsibility under Article 6(1) was not even in the indictment.[79] Most cases, however, concern situations where the commander has been described as one of many 'actors' involved in the events during which a mass atrocity took place.[80] In such cases the role of the superior will not be as easily discernible and the prosecution will be inclined to include charges of both individual criminal responsibility and command responsibility in the indictment. The question is: What has caused the preference for JCE?

The view has been expressed that the use of the term 'joint criminal enterprise' in general gives more weight to the seriousness of a superior's role in the crimes committed.[81] The fact that a certain basis for liability sounds more serious than another mode of liability would, according to this view, stigmatise the perpetrators more than where the superior was convicted under that other heading.[82] This argument is not that foreign when considering that the *ad hoc* tribunals on several occasions have concluded that responsibility under the JCE doctrine best describes the role of the superior in the crimes committed, where command responsibility had also been established.[83] There is an obvious interest in showing that the superior is convicted for his share in the events, but it may be questioned whether a conviction under JCE is perceived as more serious than a conviction under the command responsibility doctrine. Another theory is that the incentives

[78] The term 'pure' command responsibility was used by Bonafé. See Bonafé, pp. 616-617.

[79] *Hadžihasanović*, TC Judgement, paras. 7-11.

[80] On mass atrocity and solutions for holding people accountable for such crimes, see M. Osiel, 'The Banality of Good: Aligning Incentives Against Mass Atrocity', 105 *Columbia Law Review* (2005) pp. 1751-1862.

[81] See A.M. Danner and J.S. Martinez, 'Guilty Associations: Joint Criminal Enterprise, Command Responsibility, and the Development of International Criminal Law', 93 *California Law Review* (2005) pp. 75-169, at p. 145; and Osiel 2005, pp. 1783-1784.

[82] Osiel 2005, p. 1784.

[83] See, for example, *Prosecutor* v. *Mladen Naletilić and Vinko Martinović* (*Tuta and Štela*), Judgement, Case No. IT-98-34-T, 31 March 2003, paras. 78-81.

of international prosecutors are, on the one hand, to gain convictions, in particular in cases against high-level accused, and on the other hand, to ensure the development of international criminal law and satisfy the standards set by it. According to this theory, by choosing JCE in the majority of cases – despite the fact that it raises culpability and legitimacy concerns – it seems clear that the most powerful incentive for international prosecutors has been the conviction of high-level accused.[84]

The more neutral and generally recognised reason for a preference for JCE to command responsibility is the 'effective control' argument. The concept of effective control is 'the threshold to be reached in establishing a superior-subordinate relationship for the purposes of Article 7(3) of the Statute.'[85] The 'effective control' requirement is intertwined with the 'material ability to prevent or punish' requirement, which should be established when proving that the superior took the necessary and reasonable measures to prevent or punish the crimes. The effective control concept does not require that the subordination be direct or formal, but the accused should either formally or informally have been in a hierarchically higher position than the perpetrators.[86] In *Halilović*, as in other cases, this requirement has been difficult to fulfil. Several scholars have drawn attention to the fact that the charges of command responsibility usually fail because of the 'effective control' requirement.[87] The perception of the concept of 'effective control' is at present not in line with the reality of actors in situations of armed conflict or mass atrocity. For the purposes of the command responsibility doctrine as presently interpreted, the parties are either being controlled or are themselves controlling others. In reality power relations between parties involved in situations where atrocities take place are not as clear-cut. A relationship may be asymmetrical while being based on mutual influence.[88]

It is rather obvious that because the prosecution is burdened with proving 'effective control', they prefer the JCE alternative, which does not encompass such a requirement. Consequently, where both command responsibility and JCE are included in the indictment in relation to the same facts, the command responsibility charge becomes a theoretical 'catch-all' provision, which is of importance for a conviction only where a JCE cannot be established. As JCE has proven easier to establish, the possibility that in some case JCE could not be established and command responsibility would be resorted to in order to ensure a conviction, is only theoretical.

---

[84] Osiel 2005, pp. 1822-1824.

[85] *Prosecutor* v. *Sefer Halilović*, Appeal Judgement, Case No. IT-01-48-A, 16 October 2007, para. 59.

[86] Ibid.

[87] Osiel 2005, pp. 1773-1783; H.G. van der Wilt, 'Halilović on Appeal: The Intricate Concept of 'Effective Control'', 2 *Hague Justice Journal* (No. 3, 2007) pp. 5-8; and Ambos 2007, 'Joint Criminal Enterprise', p. 177.

[88] See Osiel 2005, p. 1783, who discusses the effective control problem and the limits of the command responsibility doctrine in detail. See also Van der Wilt, 'Halilović on Appeal', p. 8.

There is an apparent preference for JCE at the *ad hoc* tribunals, but to what extent are JCE and command responsibility interchangeable in relation to crimes of omission by a superior? A look at the elements and the applicability of command responsibility as compared to the JCE concept reveals that command responsibility cannot simply be substituted by the JCE concept, as the two differ considerably. Ambos identified three distinguishing features of the two concepts. Identifying these distinctive features is useful in that most judgements and several commentators, when discussing JCE and command responsibility, consider specific cases and whether command responsibility should be subsumed where both JCE and command responsibility are being applied in that particular case. However, Ambos' identification of objective, distinctive features shows why a simultaneous application of the doctrines is both practically and theoretically troublesome, but at the same time possible in certain cases.

The first distinction between JCE and command responsibility concerns the 'act' of the superior, as JCE 'requires a *positive act* or contribution to the enterprise.'[89] This is the exact opposite of command responsibility, which is concerned with an *omission* of the superior. Considering this distinction, the simultaneous application of the two doctrines seems 'logically impossible'.[90] The second distinctive feature concerns the superior-subordinate relationship, which constitutes one of the required elements of the command responsibility doctrine. Under JCE I, members of the enterprise are considered as co-perpetrators, who normally act on the basis of coordination, not subordination. As regards JCE II and JCE III, however, the relationship between the members of the enterprise is less clear and may resemble that of the relationship required for command responsibility. Thirdly, JCE differs from command responsibility in the mental element or the *mens rea* required. For the purposes of JCE I, the participants share the *mens rea* to commit certain crimes and the *mens rea* regarding the goal of the enterprise. Although the other two forms of JCE are more lenient as to the shared *mens rea* of the members of the enterprise, even the lowest *mens rea* requirement for JCE III encompasses an awareness of the purpose of the JCE and of crimes as a foreseeable consequence of the activities of the JCE. As Ambos considers command responsibility an *echtes Unterlassungsdelikt*, a crime *sui generis*, the *mens rea* of the superior is required for the failure to act, but not in relation to the crimes committed by his subordinates.[91]

On the basis of these distinctions, a simultaneous application of the two doctrines does not seem realistic. However, as was recognised by Osiel and others, the flexibility of the JCE doctrine that makes it an interesting concept for international prosecutors and judges to apply erases some of the seeming differences between the doctrines,[92] as will be seen in the following.

[89] Ambos 2007, 'Joint Criminal Enterprise', p. 180.
[90] Ibid., pp. 179-180.
[91] Ibid., p. 180.
[92] See Osiel 2005, pp. 1786-1791; and Ambos 2007, 'Joint Criminal Enterprise', p. 180.

Cases in which the facts are such that charges can be instigated on the basis of JCE I are likely to never result in a simultaneous application of the two doctrines. As just mentioned, in JCE I cases the participants are usually connected to each other by a horizontal relationship, while command responsibility requires a vertical relationship. In addition, JCE I requires common intent on the part of the participants in the criminal enterprise in relation to the crimes committed and in this respect resembles co-perpetration. At the same time, because it is clear that the participants share the common purpose of the enterprise, this form of JCE does not coincide with command responsibility. Under the command responsibility doctrine the superior must fulfil the knowledge requirement but does not share the intent of the perpetrators. A simultaneous application is more likely in cases of JCE II and JCE III, where the participants in the JCE may act from hierarchically distinct positions. The accused could have had that superior relationship with the perpetrators of the crimes within a JCE II or JCE III, and therewith meet that requirement of a superior-subordinate relationship of the command responsibility doctrine. As far as the mental element of JCE II and JCE III is concerned, it comes closer to the *mens rea* requirement of command responsibility in that it does not expect the accused to have intended the commission of the crimes.[93] However, the *mens rea* requirements of JCE II and JCE II are disputed and, in fact, the Appeals Chamber in *Kvočka* held as follows: 'The Appeals Chamber affirms the Trial Chamber's conclusion that participants in a basic or systemic form of joint criminal enterprise must be shown to share the required intent of the principal perpetrators.'[94] If intent is required under JCE II, only JCE III, with its foreseeability standard which is 'neither precise nor reliable',[95] can theoretically come close to the same requirements as those of the command responsibility doctrine.

At the indictment stage the exact level of the *mens rea* of the accused will not necessarily be known and as a consequence, it will be a natural prosecutorial choice to use the basis for liability that causes the least evidentiary difficulties. In particular because of the 'effective control' requirement that has to be fulfilled for the purposes of the superior-subordinate relationship under the command responsibility principle, prosecution under JCE will be preferred.

Considering the requirement of intent in Article 25(3)(d) ICC, the question arises as to whether the overlap between JCE and command responsibility in practice, and theoretically, will be of a temporary nature. As participation in a 'common purpose' as provided in the ICC Statute should be intentional, the provision resembles that of participation under JCE I. The role of the superior in such cases will be a different one than in cases charging the accused under the command responsibility doctrine. Cassese made an attempt at expansively inter-

---

[93] See Ambos 2007, 'Joint Criminal Enterprise', pp. 172-176. In his view one possible interpretation is that JCE II only requires membership and foreseeability, which would more closely resemble responsibility under JCE III than JCE I.

[94] *Prosecutor* v. *Radislav Kvočka et al.*, Appeal Judgement, Case No. IT-98-33-A, 28 February 2005, para. 110.

[95] See Ambos 2007, 'Joint Criminal Enterprise', p. 174.

preting the intent requirement under Article 25(3)(d) ICC so as to include JCE III liability. In his view, a broad interpretation would be justified 'by the need to punish criminal conduct that otherwise would not be regarded as culpable.'[96] Considering the strong and broad resistance to JCE III liability, this attempt and the reason for its justification will hardly be given general support. The culpability of the accused is not well-founded under JCE III, and, as the argument goes, this is exactly why a person should not be held criminally liable.

From the point of view of the object and purpose of the command responsibility doctrine, the most important concern in this context is that the preference for JCE in cases of the simultaneous application of the two doctrines creates the impression that the concept 'invades the traditional ambit of command responsibility liability.'[97] If preference is given to JCE in all cases, even accused whose role was that of a superior failing to prevent or punish a crime will not be convicted under the command responsibility provision. The 'traditional ambit' of command responsibility and the 'threat' by other modes of liability will be considered more closely in Chapter 6.

5.3.3 **Aiding and abetting**

5.3.3.1 *Aiding and abetting – The concept*

The overlap between 7(1) and 7(3) responsibility is not limited to that between JCE and command responsibility, but is also discernible between aiding and abetting and command responsibility. The main difference is the fact that while JCE in itself constitutes a disputed concept, the idea behind aiding and abetting as a mode of participation is a well-known concept to criminal law in general.

International law, in particular as it has developed since the establishment of the *ad hoc* tribunals, recognises that a person may be held criminally responsible for a crime where he/she merely assisted the actual perpetrator in committing the crime and did not share the criminal intent of the perpetrator. The term used for this mode of participation is aiding and abetting. Aiding and abetting, like the other modes of participation applied in international criminal law, have been amply defined/described in the literature and its precise legal history and origin is not the focal point of this book. It suffices to say that aiding and abetting constitutes the 'weakest form of complicity',[98] which means that in order for an act to amount to aiding and abetting, it should in some way contribute to the commission of a crime or to the attempt to commit a crime.[99] The International Law

96 Cassese 2007, pp. 109-133, at p. 132.

97 Ambos 2007, 'Joint Criminal Enterprise', p. 159.

98 K. Ambos, 'Individual Criminal Responsibility – Article 25', in O. Triffterer, ed., *Commentary on the Rome Statute of the International Criminal Court – Observers' Notes, Article by Article* (Baden-Baden, Nomos 1999) pp. 475-492, at p. 481.

99 The *Kunarac* judgement nicely describes the *actus reus* and *mens rea* of aiding and abetting: 'As opposed to the "commission" of a crime, aiding and abetting is a form of accessory liability. The contribution of an aider and abettor may take the form of practical assistance, encouragement or moral support which has a substantial effect on the perpetration of the crime. The act of assistance need not

Commission in its 1996 Draft Code of Crimes against the Peace and Security of Mankind (the ILC's Draft Code of Crimes) considered that the contribution should be 'direct and substantial', which shows that a certain threshold has to be reached where criminal liability should be imposed.[100] Establishing where this threshold lies is in general the challenge in respect of this mode of participation.[101]

In the *Orić* Judgement of 30 June 2006, the ICTY Trial Chamber reaffirmed the position that an omission may constitute aiding and abetting a crime,[102] and made reference to a number of earlier judgements which took that opinion.[103] It is recognised that contributing to the commission of a crime may take the form of moral support[104] for the perpetrator or sympathy towards the commission of the crime.[105] On several occasions the *ad hoc* tribunals have considered whether the presence of a person at the scene of the crime without his active contribution to the crime may constitute aiding and abetting. In *Orić* the Trial Chamber held that presence at the crime scene does not *per se* constitute aiding and abetting, but may be considered as aiding and abetting by omission where the person in question had a duty to prevent the crime.[106] 'A bystander's position of authority as a superior or actual leader' may lead to the mere presence of the person being considered as constituting aiding and abetting. Or as found by the *Blaškić* Trial Chamber: '[T]he mere presence at the crime scene of a person with superior

have caused the act of the principal. It may consist of an act or an omission and take place before, during or after the commission of the crime.

The *mens rea* of aiding and abetting consists of the knowledge that the acts performed by the aider and abettor assist in the commission of a specific crime by the principal. The aider and abettor need not share the *mens rea* of the principal but he must know of the essential elements of the crime (including the perpetrator's *mens rea*) and take the conscious decision to act in the knowledge that he thereby supports the commission of the crime.' See *Prosecutor* v. *Dragljub Kunarac, Radomir Kovac and Zoran Vukovic*, Judgement, Case No. IT-96-23-T & IT-96-23/1-T, 22 February 2001, paras. 391-392.

[100] Draft Code of Crimes Against the Peace and Security of Mankind, UN GAOR, 51st Sess., Supp. No. 10, UN Doc. A/51/10 (1996), p. 24.

[101] Ambos 1999, 'Individual Criminal Responsibility', p. 481.

[102] See *Orić*, TC Judgement, para. 283. However, the Trial Chamber acquitted the accused under the Art. 7(1) charges for wanton destruction of cities, towns or villages not justified by military necessity. See ibid., para. 782.

[103] In the following case, aiding and abetting by omission was considered: *Prosecutor* v. *Milorad Krnojelac*, Judgement, Case No. IT-97-25-T, 15 March 2002, para. 88. Interestingly, in this case the Trial Chamber pointed out that the act of assistance, which may be an omission, can occur 'before, during or after the act of the principal offender'. Considering a possible overlap between aiding and abetting and command responsibility, this finding shows that an overlap does not necessarily only arise at the stage of preventing the crimes, but also where the omission took place after the fact. On aiding and abetting by omission, see also, among other cases:

Prosecutor v. *Mitar Vasiljević*, Judgement, Case No. IT-98-32-T, 29 November 2002, para. 70; *Kunarac*, TC Judgement, para. 391; *Brđanin*, TC Judgement, para. 271.

[104] Cassese 2003, p. 188.

[105] *Prosecutor* v. *Jean-Paul Akayesu*, Judgement, Case No. ICTR-96-4-T, 2 September 1998, para. 484.

[106] See *Prosecutor* v. *Naser Orić*, Judgement, Case No. IT-03-68-T, 30 June 2006, para. 283.

authority, such as a military commander, is a probative indication for determining whether that person encouraged or supported the perpetrators of the crime.'[107]

Accordingly, passivity does not equal an omission, which means that in order to consider the mode of participation of a person aiding and abetting, that person must have been under a duty to act.[108] As provided in the ILC's Draft Code of Crimes, the *ad hoc* tribunals have applied a requirement, according to which the act of assistance has to be of 'decisive' or 'substantial' effect, in order for the accused to incur liability for aiding and abetting the commission of a crime. As in the case of practical assistance, an act, constituting aiding and abetting, the aider and abettor should also have the necessary *mens rea* where his contribution to the crime consists of an omission.

5.3.3.2 *Aiding and abetting and command responsibility*

For the purposes of the present chapter, the interesting feature of aiding and abetting is its application to acts of omission. As in relation to JCE, if both individual and superior criminal responsibility could be established for an act of omission, there seems to be an overlap between two applicable concepts. Considering the requirements of an omission constituting aiding and abetting and the requirements of command responsibility, the question arises as to the kind of situations that may lead to the simultaneous application of both aiding and abetting and command responsibility. In other words, when does an overlap between the two occur?

As Van Sliedregt rightly pointed out, both crimes of a limited character, single crimes, and 'continuing crimes' or 'mass crimes', may create an impression of an overlap between aiding and abetting and command responsibility.[109] An example of the first category of crimes can be found in the *Furundžija* case. In this case one victim was tortured and another tortured and raped in the presence of the accused.[110] The presence of the accused at the crime scene, together with his position of authority, constituted aiding and abetting. The Trial Chamber held that, '[P]resence, when combined with authority, can constitute assistance in the form of moral support.'[111] On the face of it, this case justified charges under both the 'aiding and abetting' mode of participation and command responsibility. Both bases for responsibility require 'a status of authority, a failure to act, and an underlying crime committed by another person.'[112] *Furundžija* held a more superior position than the principal offender. He was present at the crime scene and

[107] *Prosecutor* v. *Tihomir Blaškić*, Appeal Judgement, Case No. IT-95-14-A, 29 July 2004, para. 47.

[108] *Prosecutor* v. *Blagoje Simić, Miroslav Tadić and Simo Zarić*, Judgement, Case No. IT-95-9-T, 17 October 2003, para. 162.

[109] Van Sliedregt 2003, p. 193.

[110] *Prosecutor* v. *Anto Furundžija*, Judgement, Case No. IT-95-17/1-T, 10 December 1998, paras. 266 and 273.

[111] Ibid., para. 209.

[112] Van Sliedregt 2003, p. 193.

failed to prevent the crimes from taking place. There is a *prima facie* overlap and some closer consideration is needed to confirm the overlap.

Secondly, there are the 'continuing crimes' or 'mass crime'. As found by Van Sliedregt: ''Continuing crimes' often connote the maintenance of a wrongful situation, for instance, cruel treatment in a concentration camp.'[113] Both categories of crimes concern situations where a multiplicity of crimes are committed, that may take place over time or in several places.[114] The *Čelebići* case may be used as an example of facts which point to the possibility of holding the accused liable for aiding and abetting and under the command responsibility provision. On one charge of the unlawful confinement of civilians in the Čelebići prison camp, the prosecution in its appeal challenged the acquittal of two of the accused, Delalić and Delić, both alleged commanders of the prison camp. The prosecution held that the two accused could have been held responsible both for aiding and abetting and under Article 7(3).[115] Where subordinates committed the crimes, the elements of command responsibility may be fulfilled here, while also aiding and abetting may be applicable, if the failure of the superior could be seen as support for or encouragement of the crime and the superior knew of the intent of the perpetrators.

There is reason to hold that both crimes on a limited scale and mass crimes may justify charges based on aiding and abetting and command responsibility. The character of the crime is not a determining factor when deciding how to go about the overlap. In the two cases discussed here, however, the overlap was only theoretical. In the *Furundžija* case, command responsibility was not included in the indictment. As to the specific charge in the *Čelebići* case, the Appeals Chamber acquitted the accused of both aiding and abetting and command responsibility. In the opinion of the prosecution, the Trial Chamber in relation to one of the accused had erred in finding that he did not possess the superior authority required for command responsibility.[116] That finding then had an additional effect in that the lack of authority gave the Trial Chamber a reason not to hold him liable for aiding and abetting. As the accused was not the principal perpetrator of the crimes and lacked superior authority, his participation could not have had the 'substantial effect' on the participation of the crimes, which is necessary for establishing aiding and abetting.[117]

Prima facie, both *Furundžija* and *Čelebići* satisfied the requirements of superior authority, *mens rea* and an omission that create the impression of an overlap. In cases where the facts show a conceivable overlap at the indictment stage, the decision as to the most suitable basis for responsibility is primarily made by the prosecution and, thus, is subjected to prosecutorial discretion. With regard to the ICC, also judicial discretion may come into play when deciding whether charges should be brought solely for aiding and abetting or command responsibil-

---

[113] Ibid.

[114] Ibid.

[115] *Čelebići*, AC Judgement, paras. 333 and 335.

[116] Ibid., para. 333.

[117] Ibid., para. 358.

ity, or for both. In the *Bemba* case, the Pre-Trial Chamber made a decision under Article 67(7)(c) ICC to adjourn the confirmation of charges hearing and to give the Prosecutor the possibility to submit an amended document containing charges under Article 28 ICC, i.e., command responsibility charges.[118] Similar decisions are equally conceivable where aiding and abetting is charged and where the facts of the case could also support charges of command responsibility.

Where the overlap appears at the indictment stage, the choice to keep both charges in the indictment will increase the burden of the prosecution to establish both aiding and abetting and command responsibility. On the other hand, there is no genuine overlap as long as it has not been proven beyond reasonable doubt that both bases for responsibility have been established. While at the indictment stage a superior position, *mens rea* and passivity will suffice to create the impression of an overlap, at the stage of a conviction the judges will have to consider which one of the two feasible situations has been established: a) The accused did not exercise effective control and, therefore, the elements of aiding and abetting were established but not those of command responsibility,[119] or alternatively, the elements of command responsibility were fulfilled but the omission of the accused did not have a substantial effect on the commission of the offences;[120] or b) The accused exercised effective control and the evidence supports a conviction under both provisions. Only with regard to the second situation can one speak of a true overlap.

The *Musema* case may be used as an illustration of situation (b) which, according to the Trial Chamber, justified a command responsibility conviction, while the circumstances of the case also provides support for a conviction under aiding and abetting. The Trial Chamber made the following finding:

> 'Considering that Musema was personally present at the attack sites, the Chamber is of the opinion that he knew or, at least, had reason to know that his subordinates were about to commit such acts or had done so. The Chamber notes that the Accused nevertheless failed to take the necessary and reasonable measures to prevent the commission of said acts by his subordinates, but rather *abetted in the commission of those acts*, by his presence and personal participation. Consequently, the Chamber finds that, for the acts committed by the employees of the Gisovu Tea Factory during the attack of 26 April 1994 on Gitwa Hill, Musema incurs individual criminal responsibility, as their superior, on the basis of the provisions of Article 6 (3) of the Statute.'[121]

The Trial Chamber even found that the omission showed that the accused abetted in the commission of the crimes, which shows that the command responsibility conviction was a conscious choice by the judges.

---

[118] *Prosecutor* v. *Jean Pierre Bemba Gombo*, Decision Adjourning the Hearing pursuant to Article 61(7)(c)(ii) of the Rome Statute, Case No. ICC-01/05-01/08-388, 3 March 2009.

[119] *Prosecutor* v. *Vidoje Blagojević and Dragan Jokić*, Judgement, Case No. IT-02-60-T, 17 January 2005, paras. 794-796.

[120] *Prosecutor* v. *Pavle Strugar*, Judgement, Case No. IT-01-42-T, 31 January 2005, para. 355.

[121] *Prosecutor* v. *Alfred Musema*, Judgement and Sentence, Case No. ICTR-96-13-T, 27 January 2000, para. 894 (italics added by MLN).

For the purpose of establishing in which situations a real overlap between aiding and abetting and command responsibility is conceivable, the cases where only command responsibility appears on the indictment are of interest. The following paragraph from the *Hadžihasanović* judgement concerns the co-accused Kubura:

> 'However, with regard to the plundering in the towns of Šusanj, Ovnak, Brajkovici and Grahovčici, the Trial Chamber is of the opinion that the Accused Kubura had knowledge of the plundering committed by the 7th Brigade military police in June 1993, and that he gave his consent to members of the 7th Brigade to share the plundered goods. The Accused Kubura failed to punish the perpetrators of these crimes.'[122]

The Trial Chamber found the accused responsible under Article 7(3) because of his failure to punish the perpetrators. A similar finding was made in the following statement by the Trial Chamber:

> 'The Trial Chamber is satisfied beyond reasonable doubt that, as of 4 November 1993, the Accused Kubura had information that his subordinates were plundering in Vares. It has been established that the Accused Kubura, in failing to take punitive measures against the perpetrators of the plundering committed in June 1993 of which he had knowledge, failed to prevent plundering in Vares in November 1993. Furthermore, the Accused Kubura also failed to take action against the perpetrators of these crimes and even organised the distribution of the plundered goods.'[123]

Similarly, the accused failed to punish his subordinates and thereby incurred responsibility under Article 7(3). With regard to both findings, the question is whether, had they been among the charges, the omissions of the superior Kubura could also have been considered as aiding and abetting the crimes of his subordinates. It should of course be kept in mind that because aiding and abetting was not among the charges, the Trial Chamber did not consider circumstances that would have been 'favourable' for aiding and abetting and so the theoretical reasoning here remains speculation, but serves a purpose, more specifically, the following.

The facts in the two examples referred to here, in which Kubura was found responsible, show that he both consented to sharing and organised the distribution of the plundered goods. Although these acts took place after the crimes had been committed, had aiding and abetting been prosecuted, the Trial Chamber might just as well have found that the omission to act on the part of Kubura could either have been considered as facilitating the commission of the crime or as being sympathetic to it. That the accused afterwards gave his approval for sharing the plundered goods is an indication not so much of his neglect and failure to prevent or punish his subordinates, but of his sympathy or encouragement of the crimes.[124]

---

[122] *Hadžihasanović*, Judgement Summary, at VII. D.

[123] Ibid.

[124] It should be noted here that with regard to the acts of plunder in Vareš, the Appeals Chamber found that Kubura had taken the necessary and reasonable measures to prevent the crimes, and did

In respect of the accused Hadžihasanović, the Trial Chamber made the following findings:

> 'Despite the real risk of his subordinates repeating their previous crimes, the Accused Hadzihasanovic decided in favour of passive negotiations with his subordinates to obtain the release of the abducted civilians. It has been established that the ABiH 3rd Corps never intended to use military means against the El Mujahed detachment. The Trial Chamber considers that the circumstances were such that, as of 20 October 1993, the 3rd Corps should have used force as the sole necessary and reasonable means to prevent the crimes committed at Orasac. The Trial Chamber concludes that the Accused Hadzihasanovic had the material capacity to use force against his subordinates and had sufficient time to put concrete and specific measures into effect in order to obtain the release of the abducted civilians.'[125]

The hypothesis here is that the accused was sympathetic to the subordinates' acts and transmitted this message to his subordinates by being passive and not effectively taking measures. Therefore, his act of omission contributed to the commission of the crime, and could have been considered as aiding and abetting.

> 'The Trial Chamber is furthermore of the opinion that, as soon as the El Mujahed detachment was incorporated into his forces, the Accused Hadzihasanovic had information allowing him to conclude that there was a real and reasonably foreseeable risk of violations by members of the El Mujahed detachment. He was familiar with their violent and dangerous behaviour. He did not instruct the members of the detachment in complying with the most basic rules of international humanitarian law. In spite of this alarming information, he decided to gain military advantage with the detachment although nothing compelled the 3rd Corps to use the Mujahedin in combat. It is clear, in the opinion of the Trial Chamber, that the Accused Hadzihasanovic put himself in a situation where he ran the risk of not being able to take appropriate measures as and when required. However, he will not be found guilty of having failed to punish the perpetrators of this crime since he only became aware of it on 6 November 1993 when he had already left his post.'[126]

Although not found guilty as a superior, the accused might have been held responsible for aiding and abetting the crimes committed by his subordinates. The omission to instruct members of his detachment to comply with the relevant rules of law, while aware of the risk of violations, could also have been considered as passive encouragement or being sympathetic and thereby abetting the violations by members of his detachment.

> 'The Trial Chamber considers that it has been established that, in spite of his knowledge of the cruel treatment of six prisoners of war in the Slavonija Furniture Salon and of the murder of one of them, the Accused Hadzihasanovic applied no more than disciplinary measures to punish the perpetrators of these crimes. In failing to take

not find him responsible in relation to those acts. See *Hadžihasanović*, AC Judgement, paras. 261-272.

[125] *Hadžihasanović*, Judgement Summary, at VII. D.

[126] Ibid.

> the necessary measures in this instance, the Trial Chamber believes that the Accused Hadzihasanovic failed to intervene in order to prevent any mistreatment from occurring after 18 August 1993 in the *Slavonija* Furniture Salon, the *Vojin Paleksic* Elementary School, the *Gimnazija* School Building and the FC *Iskra* Stadium.'[127]

Also in this example it could be considered that Hadžihasanović, by his omission, expressed his sympathies towards his subordinates and the crimes they were committing, without taking an active part therein. His passive support of the violations could have been considered as aiding or abetting.

The purpose of these examples is to indicate that almost any facts, on the basis of which superior responsibility can be proven, may also be used for proving aiding and abetting where individual criminal responsibility has been prosecuted. Passivity on the part of the superior could often be considered as a form of encouragement. However, what seems like an overlap between aiding and abetting and command responsibility, where both have been established, some closer consideration of the involvement of the accused might remove the overlap and justify a decision favouring either of the two possible forms of responsibility. The *Strugar* case could be mentioned in this regard. In that case, the Trial Chamber made an effort to explain why a finding based on aiding and abetting was not justified, and decided in favour of command responsibility.[128] It was established that the accused did not take all necessary and reasonable measures to stop an unlawful attack on the Old Town of Dubrovnik, but evidence showed that he issued a ceasefire order and, thus, did not remain entirely inactive. The accused did not initiate an investigation into the events, but, on the other hand, the Trial Chamber found that the fact that the accused did not take steps to investigate, could not have had a 'direct and substantial effect on the commission of the offences.'[129] The fact that the accused did not remain entirely inactive, which could be seen as silent encouragement, and that not investigating did not have a substantial effect on the commission of the crimes, together with the fact that the evidence did not satisfy the intent requirement, led to the finding that command responsibility more properly reflected the role of the accused in the events.[130]

On the basis of the above, it can be concluded that the existing case law confirms the overlap between the field of applicability of aiding and abetting, on the one hand, and superior responsibility, on the other. The way in which this overlap is treated in the judgements gives reason for the following statement: The case law, in particular where the accused is a civilian in a position of superior authority, illustrates that an omission by the accused may easily be brought under the aiding and abetting mode of liability where both individual and superior criminal responsibility are charged for the same offence. Accordingly, where there is reason to indict a superior under individual and superior responsibility, there would in fact be no need to pursue the charges under the superior responsibil-

[127] Ibid.

[128] *Prosecutor* v. *Pavle Strugar*, Judgement, Case No. IT-01-42-T, 31 January 2005, para. 355.

[129] Ibid.

[130] Ibid.

ity provision, as it would anyway be covered by aiding and abetting. That would limit the applicability of superior responsibility to cases where the prosecution decides not to press charges of individual criminal responsibility, for example, because there was no evidence of the superior instigating or ordering the crimes. Taking this thought a step farther, there would be no need to use the superior responsibility provision as a 'catch-all' provision, as resort could always be had to aiding and abetting.

As in those cases where both JCE and command responsibility are applicable, the cases charging aiding and abetting give reason for questions as to the role of command responsibility. Case law shows that command responsibility in cases of simultaneous applicability leads to its being subsumed under the individual criminal responsibility conviction. According to Van Sliedregt, 'the nature of superior responsibility as the *specialis* of the *generalis* individual responsibility is expressed' by what seems to be the prosecutorial aim to primarily establish individual criminal responsibility and, secondly, to establish command responsibility.[131] However, if it is true that even the cases where charges were brought only under the command responsibility provision would have led to a conviction under aiding and abetting, had that been on the indictment, then command responsibility, again, seems to be a conscious choice, first on the part of the Prosecutor and secondly on the part of the judges. In *Krnojelac*[132] and in *Musema*, the Trial Chambers chose in favour of command responsibility.

5.3.4 **Cumulative conviction or aggravating circumstance**

The two previous sections have discussed the overlap between modes of individual criminal responsibility and command responsibility in cases where the superior has showed 'passivity' in relation to the crimes committed or to be committed by principal perpetrators who were his subordinates. An overlap as discussed in these sections resulted in a possibility to choose the basis for liability. The present section is concerned with the overlap that occurs at the stage of a conviction, where enough evidence has been adduced to establish both the individual criminal responsibility and the command responsibility of the superior.

Early case law from the *ad hoc* tribunals did not find cumulative conviction under both individual criminal responsibility and command responsibility problematic, and paid more attention to the concern that an accused should not be cumulatively convicted of two crimes, where the charges were essentially based on the same facts.[133] In fact, in the *Aleksovski* case, the Trial Chamber made the following finding:

---

[131] Van Sliedregt 2003, p. 194.

[132] See section 5.3.5 *infra*. *Prosecutor* v. *Milorad Krnojelac*, Judgement, Case No. IT-97-25-T, 15 March 2002, para. 316.

[133] See, for example, *Čelebići*, AC Judgement, para. 412; and *Prosecutor* v. *Dragljub Kunarac, Radomir Kovac and Zoran Vukovic*, Appeal Judgement, Case No. IT-96-23 & IT-96-23/1-A, 12 June 2002, para. 168.

'The Trial Chamber therefore considers that the accused is responsible under Articles 7(1) and 7(3) for the physical detention conditions and the mistreatment to which the prisoners were subjected within the Kaonik compound.'[134]

This conviction was not altered on appeal,[135] and the case is in this respect not at all unique, as several cases have resulted in similar cumulative convictions.[136] It is important to note that the present discussion concerns what may be called 'true cumulations', that is conviction under both the individual criminal responsibility and command responsibility provisions in relation to the same facts, as opposed to 'false cumulation', where there is a conviction on the basis of both provisions, but in relation to separate crimes.[137] In the *Blaškić* Appeal Judgement, a cumulative conviction entered by the Trial Chamber was reversed. In the opinion of the Appeals Chamber, a conviction pursuant to both Article 7(1) and 7(3) 'in relation to the same count based on the same facts', i.e., a 'true cumulation', constituted a legal error.[138] This approach has been accepted and applied by the *ad hoc* tribunals in more recent case law, the general acceptance being based primarily on the 'logical argument' that a person who committed a crime cannot at the same time be held responsible for omitting to prevent or punish the same crime.[139] This argument is connected to the *ne bis in idem* argument, which is convincing in that a conviction under Article 7(1) and 7(3) would hold the accused liable twice in relation to the same facts.[140]

In the literature, there has been very little disagreement with the rejection of cumulative convictions pursuant to Article 7(1) and 7(3). Nevertheless, it is interesting to pay some attention to the views of Henquet who does question the decision by the *ad hoc* tribunals to rule out cumulative convictions. Henquet recognises that where the 'speciality test' that was formulated by the *Čelebići* Appeals Chamber in relation to the cumulation of substantive offences is applied, a conviction will be entered only on the basis of the one offence that contains 'an additional materially distinct element'.[141] But where no distinct element could be found, the Chamber could, instead of deciding in relation to which crime a conviction should be entered, enter a conviction under both provisions. In Henquet's opinion, if the 'speciality test' were to be applied to cumulation pursuant to Article 7(1) and 7(3), a conviction under both provisions would be precluded because of the additional elements of a positive act and criminal intent that are required for individual criminal responsibility. The argument is as such

---

[134] *Aleksovski*, TC Judgement, para. 138.

[135] *Aleksovski*, AC Judgement.

[136] See, for example, *Kayishema and Ruzindana*, TC Judgement, paras. 568-569.

[137] T. Henquet, 'Convictions for Command Responsibility under Articles 7(1) and 7(3) of the Statute of the International Criminal Tribunal for the Former Yugoslavia', 15 *LJIL* (2002) pp. 805-834, at pp. 815-825.

[138] *Blaškić*, AC Judgement, paras. 91-92.

[139] *Blaškić*, TC Judgement, para. 337.

[140] For reflections on cumulative convictions pursuant to Art. 7(1) and 7(3) and the conceivable double jeopardy concerns, see Henquet, pp. 821-825.

[141] *Čelebići*, AC Judgement, para. 413.

not well elaborated, as an overlap only arises where there is an omission, and at most, knowledge in relation to the crimes.[142] However, he rightly draws attention to the distinct elements of importance for the cumulation of substantive offences. If applying the same reasoning to individual and command responsibility, where no materially distinct element can be found, the Chamber could enter a conviction pursuant to both provisions. The justification for doing so is the argument that the substantive offences represent different interests and values, despite the fact that under the 'speciality test' the offences may not contain materially distinct elements.[143] For example, wilfully causing great suffering or serious injury and the crime of torture are distinguished by the purpose of the perpetrator of the torture. According to Judges Hunt and Bennouna in their Separate and Dissenting Opinion to the *Čelebići* Appeal Judgement, this specific feature of the crime of torture would under the speciality test not be considered as a distinct element, although the violation of specific interests and values is expressed by the particular purpose of the perpetrator of the torture.[144] The same is true for individual and command responsibility. Borrowing from Henquet, '[N]either form of responsibility can properly express the criminal conduct of the accused under the other.'[145] In other words:

> 'The conduct under each provision is criminal because it violates distinct norms under international humanitarian law: a commander is responsible for his own criminal conduct (first norm) *and* that of his subordinates (second norm). A conviction only for the violation of the first norm does not show that the commander also violated the second norm. Therefore, a conviction under both Articles 7(1) and Article 7(3) must be permissible.'[146]

The Trial Chamber in *Orić* refuted this argument by holding that:

> '[P]articipation in the crime means to have made a causal contribution to the impairment of the protected interest, whereas the failure as a superior need not necessarily contribute to the injury as such, but may merely involve the omission of his duty, as is particularly evident in the case of failure to punish.'[147]

---

142 Henquet, pp. 826-827.

143 Ibid., p. 830.

144 *Prosecutor* v. *Zejnil Delalić et al.*, Separate and Dissenting Opinion of Judge David Hunt and Judge Mohamed Bennouna, Case No. IT-96-21-A, 20 February 2001, paras. 38-39. The judges were not in favour of cumulative convictions but were nevertheless of the opinion that, 'A rigidly imposed preference for the crime charged under a particular Article of the Statute will obviously be less time consuming and more convenient. However, the rigidly imposed choice [...], made in isolation from the relevant conduct to be criminalized in the particular case, will not necessarily always produce the result which must be the ultimate function of criminal proceedings: to recognise and penalise with the most appropriate conviction the proven criminal conduct of an accused.' Ibid., para. 39.

145 Henquet, p. 830.

146 Ibid., p. 834.

147 *Orić*, TC Judgement, para. 342.

Nevertheless, the attempt to justify cumulative convictions or dual liability – to distinguish it from the substantive offences[148] – is valuable for the present study, as it puts emphasis on the need to recognise that command responsibility represents other values and interests, as compared to individual criminal responsibility.[149] With regard to the *ne bis in idem* principle, mentioned above, the approach favouring dual liability could circumvent this difficulty at the sentencing stage. According to Henquet the Chamber should consider the 'absorption' of the conduct which underlies the accused's command responsibility by the conduct that gives rise to individual criminal responsibility.[150] What is suggested is that the overlap between the two bases for responsibility would not be weighed twice at the sentencing stage, and as a consequence the sentence would correspond to the culpability of the accused, while at the same time the command responsibility of the accused would be recognised.

Applying 'absorption' to reduce the sentence to correspond to culpability is the opposite of applying aggravating circumstances where an overlap between individual and command responsibility occurs at the stage of a conviction.

As such, the process of considering aggravating and mitigating circumstances at the sentencing stage of a criminal case is a well-known trait of criminal law and the practice has been present since the first judgement rendered by the *ad hoc* tribunals.[151] In the *Tadić* case, the aggravating circumstances taken into account did not concern the superior position of the accused, but rather his willingness to engage in crimes and other factors.[152] In the *Blaškić* case, the Trial Chamber expressed the view that the position of the commander should always be considered as an aggravating factor at the sentencing stage.

> 'Therefore, when a commander fails in his duty to prevent the crime or to punish the perpetrator thereof he should receive a heavier sentence than the subordinates who committed the crime insofar as the failing conveys some tolerance or even approval on the part of the commander towards the commission of crimes by his subordinates and thus contributes to encouraging the commission of new crimes. It would not in fact be consistent to punish a simple perpetrator with a sentence equal or greater to that of the commander. From this viewpoint, the Trial Chamber recalls that in the *Tadic* case the Appeals Chamber found that a prison sentence above twenty years would be excessive given the relatively low rank of Dusko Tadic within the command structure. Command position must therefore systematically increase the sentence or at least lead the Trial Chamber to give less weight to the mitigating circumstances, independently of the issue of the form of participation in the crime.'[153]

---

[148] The term dual liability, which seems like a more appropriate term, was used in the *Orić* case. See *Orić*, TC Judgement, para. 341.

[149] See Chapter 3 *supra*.

[150] Henquet, p. 834.

[151] See *Prosecutor* v. *Duško Tadić*, Judgement, Case No. IT-94-1-T*bis*-R117, 11 November 1999, paras. 19-20.

[152] Ibid.

[153] *Blaškić*, TC Judgement, para. 789.

This approach, which has been repeatedly accepted by both *ad hoc* tribunals, is based on the view that the superior position of the accused automatically justifies a harsher punishment, in comparison with a perpetrator in a hierarchically lower position. In the judgements of the *ad hoc* tribunals, the result has been that where an overlap between individual and command responsibility has been established, or where at least individual criminal responsibility and the superior position of the accused have been established,[154] the punishment has been harsher than it would have been had the accused not held such a superior position. Considering the superior position of the accused as an aggravating circumstance at the sentencing stage has even been considered an obligation.[155] At first glance, this practice seems both logical and in accordance with one of the overarching goals of all international courts and tribunals, to ensure the accountability of those who bear the most responsibility for the crimes committed.

For the purposes of the command responsibility doctrine, however, this practice is unfortunate, in so far as it concerns established liability under both forms of responsibility, after which command responsibility is subsumed and consequently used as an aggravating circumstance at the sentencing stage. Where established command responsibility is considered as an aggravating circumstance at the sentencing stage and, in fact, equals a harsher punishment on conviction, the interests, values or the message involved in a conviction pursuant to the command responsibility doctrine are not expressed. The practical effect or message of these cases to victims, societies and the international community is simply that the accused were convicted on the basis of their individual criminal responsibility for the crimes. However, the role and behaviour of the accused in the events does not find expression in such convictions. That a conviction is ensured and that the sentence is harsher because of this aggravating circumstance called command responsibility are factors that do satisfy the aim of retribution in the individual case, but that do not contribute to the legitimacy of the decision or the institution which rendered the judgement.[156] Neither does such a conviction contribute to a correct remembrance of the events, which arguably is an important factor for deterrence, more so than the actual conviction of one particular person.[157]

The case law on this issue is unclear. While it is generally accepted that a superior position may or should be considered as an aggravating circumstance in sentencing, the reasoning used to justify it is not consistent. There are three issues that have to be addressed in order to make a well-reasoned argument as to the use of the superior position of the accused as an aggravating circumstance in relation to cumulative convictions or established dual liability. First, the question arises as to whether it is the superior position itself or the abuse of authority by the accused that should form the basis for the aggravation. On several occasions,

---

[154] *Orić*, TC Judgement, para. 343.

[155] *Kajelijeli*, AC Judgement, paras. 91 and 317.

[156] See the discussion and reference to Osiel in section 5.3.3.2 *supra*.

[157] This argument was inspired by views expressed during a presentation by M. Cherif Bassiouni, Professor, DePaul University, 'Reflections on the Darfur Case', Supranational Criminal Law Lecture Series, T.M.C. Asser Institute, The Hague, 1 October 2008.

the *ad hoc* tribunals have pointed out that it is not the superior position as such that constitutes an aggravating circumstance. It was clearly stated in the *Babić* case that:

> '[A] Trial Chamber has the discretion to take into account, as an aggravating circumstance, the seniority, position of authority, or high position of leadership held by a person criminally responsible under Article 7(1) of the Statute. A high rank in the military or political field does not, in itself, merit a harsher sentence. But a person who abuses or wrongly exercises power deserves a harsher sentence. Consequently, what matters is not the position of authority taken alone, but the position coupled with the manner in which the authority is exercised.'[158]

Whereas a policy decision like this is logical and in accordance with Article 24 of the Statute, the more difficult question is which breaches should be considered as an abuse of power. Is the crime for which the accused is prosecuted at the same time an abuse of his power? If so, it seems that the fact that a person who committed a crime while in a position of authority is at the same time an aggravation of that same offence. Consider the *Kvočka* case in this regard, where the Trial Chamber stated as follows:

> 'His experience and integrity can be viewed as both mitigating and aggravating factors – his job was to maintain law and order and, although he apparently did a fine job of this prior to working in the camp, he failed seriously to perform his duty to uphold the law during his time spent in Omarska camp. Holding a position of respect and trust in the community, his failure to object to crimes and maintaining indifference to those committed in his presence was likely viewed as giving legitimacy to the criminal conduct.'[159]

Kvočka was, in fact, prosecuted for his role in the crimes that took place in the Omarska prison camp. Holding that these breaches constituted an aggravating factor seems to be duplicative. Various Chambers maintain that they do not use the same factors both to establish responsibility for the crimes and to harshen the sentence of the accused,[160] but in his Opinion to the *Galić* Trial Judgement, Judge Nieto-Navia submitted that where it was established that the accused had ordered the crimes proved at trial, his position as a military commander could not be considered as an aggravating factor. The majority in this case held that, '[T]he fact that General Galić occupied the position of VRS Corps commander, and repeatedly breached his public duty from this very senior position, is an aggravating factor.' However, in Nieto-Navia's view 'considering his position as a military

[158] *Prosecutor* v. *Milan Babić*, Judgement on Sentencing Appeal, Case No. IT-03-72-A, 18 July 2005, para. 80.

[159] *Kvočka et al.*, TC Judgement, para. 716.

[160] *Prosecutor* v. *Stanislav Galić*, Appeal Judgement, Case No. IT-98-29-A, 30 November 2006, para. 412.

commander as an aggravating circumstance is analogous to concluding that being a husband is an aggravating circumstance with respect to the crime of uxoricide.'[161]

Secondly, it is of importance to consider whether it is the superior position (including the abuse of power) or established command responsibility that constitutes the aggravating factor. For instance in the *Kajelijeli* case, the Appeals Chamber confirmed the view expressed in earlier cases that where an accused has been convicted under the requirements of both Article 7(1) and 7(3) in relation to the same facts, a conviction should be entered on the basis of Article 7(1) only, and the superior position should be considered as an aggravating circumstance in the sentencing. But, in addition, the Appeals Chamber reaffirmed that only matters that are proved beyond reasonable doubt may be taken into account as an aggravating factor, which means that where the superior position of the accused is used as a ground for a harsher sentence, that superior position must have been proven at trial.[162] The consequence of this is that where Article 7(3) responsibility has been established at trial, the superior position has been proven beyond reasonable doubt. Where that is not the case, the superior position will have to be proven separately. In *Stakić*, the Trial Chamber stated that, '[T]he aggravating effect is identical whether the accused is found to have fulfilled the requirements for responsibility under Article 7(3) or is simply proved to have held superior positions.'[163]

This brings the discussion to the third issue, which is actually an assessment of the consequences of this practice by the *ad hoc* tribunals to three possible scenarios to which an aggravating circumstance is applied. In the first case (a) the accused is convicted under Article 7(1) only. As discussed above, a breach of his position of authority may be considered as an aggravating factor, in so far as the breach is not the crime for which the accused is convicted. In the second scenario, (b) the accused is convicted under Article 7(3) only. In the judgements in the *Hadžihasanović* and *Delić* cases, the Chambers held that, '[I]n the context of a conviction under Article 7(3) of the Statute, use of the superior's position of authority as an aggravating circumstance would be inappropriate since it is itself an element of criminal liability.'[164] Accordingly, established command responsibility cannot be used as an aggravating factor. Only 'the superior's abuse of that level of authority' in addition to established command responsibility could be so used.[165] Having applied this reasoning, Hadžihasanović was convicted under Article 7(3), his superior position having been established, but he did not receive a harsher sentence because no other abuse of authority was claimed.[166] For the third category (c), where dual liability (both 7(1) and 7(3)) is established, this finding leads to the conclusion that it is not correct to refrain from cumulatively

[161] *Prosecutor* v. *Stanislav Galić*, Separate and Partially Dissenting Opinion of Judge Nieto-Navia, Case No. IT-98-29-T, 5 December 2003, para. 121.

[162] *Kajelijeli*, AC Judgement, para. 82.

[163] *Prosecutor* v. *Milomir Stakić*, Judgement, Case No. IT-97-24-T, 31 July 2003, para. 912.

[164] See *Hadžihasanović*, AC Judgement, para. 320; and *Prosecutor* v. *Rasim Delić*, Judgement, Case No. IT-04-83-T, 15 September 2008, para. 569.

[165] See *Hadžihasanović*, AC Judgement, para. 320.

[166] Ibid.

convicting the accused in favour of subsuming Article 7(3) responsibility under Article 7(1) liability, and subsequently to use established command responsibility as an aggravating circumstance. The Appeals Chamber in *Hadžihasanović* and the Trial Chamber in *Delić* were right in pointing out that the use of the superior position as an aggravating factor where command responsibility has been established is inappropriate. This finding gives credit to the opinion, stated above, that command responsibility represents other values and interests than those expressed by a conviction under Article 7(1), these not being well recognised where the responsibility is reduced to an aggravating factor of the individual criminal responsibility of the accused.

5.3.5 **Conclusion**

In some cases the judges have justified their preference for Article 7(1) liability by saying that this basis best describes the role of the superior in the crimes committed.[167] However, the latest development does not even require this justification but assumes that the Article 7(3) liability is anyway subsumed under the individual criminal responsibility finding.[168] This approach removes the possibility, or at least the obligation, that the judges would have to consider the 'traditional ambit' of the command responsibility principle and give preference to command responsibility as the basis for liability where the case indeed falls within that – obviously more restrictive – category of cases.

At least two cases, the *Aleksovski* case and the *Krstić* case, have been mentioned by commentators in relation to which a different approach favouring command responsibility could have been useful.[169] In relation to the *Aleksovski* case, Jia found that while the crimes and the situation fitted under Article 7(1), a command responsibility conviction would have been more suitable.[170] The following finding by Jia is interesting:

> 'At no time in his term of office was he a mere individual. His participation in the offences of his subordinates may be no more than secondary in terms of importance to his failure to prevent the offences from being committed within his sight by others under his control. From a practical point of view, to prosecute him mainly as a commander would not lead to a different result in terms of sentence than if he was convicted under Article 7(1), with his command position as the aggravating factor. However, this possibly alternative approach has to be balanced by the fact that the ICTY in its practice follows the opposite approach.'[171]

---

[167] See *Tuta and Štela*, TC Judgement, paras. 78-81.

[168] See *Prosecutor* v. *Dragomir Milošević*, Judgement, Case No. IT-98-29/1-T, 12 December 2007, para. 984, which refers to a number of judgements sharing that view: *Blaškić* (AC); *Krštić* (TC and AC); *Kordić and Čerkez* (AC); *Kvočka* (AC); *Kajelijeli* (AC); and *Naletilić and Martinović* (*Tuta and Štela*) (AC).

[169] See Jia, p. 145; and Danner and Martinez, p. 153.

[170] The *Aleksovski* judgement was rendered before the *Tadić* Appeals Chamber introduced the JCE concept, but as the accused acted as a warden in a prison camp, a JCE charge could have been expected, had the accused stood trial at a later date.

[171] See Jia, p. 145.

Jia favours an approach by which preference is given to command responsibility, despite the possibility of a conviction under Article 7(1), and finds that such an approach would not necessarily lead to harsher or more lenient sentences. This form of 'affirmative action' was also considered in relation to the *Krstić* case.[172] Consider the following opinion of Danner and Martinez:

> 'Given the Appeals Chamber's obvious discomfort with the broad liability Krstić incurred under a JCE theory, it is even more curious why the court concluded that Krstić's conduct amounted to aiding and abetting the JCE when it could have recast his liability on a command responsibility theory, which had been included in his indictment. Since the Appeals Chamber viewed General Krstić's principal fault as failing to take steps to prevent troops under his command from participating in the genocidal plan hatched by other, command responsibility – rather than aiding and abetting – seems to capture more accurately the basis for the liability that the Appeals Chamber found.'[173]

The role of the accused was such as to allow a finding under Article 7(1), but according to these authors, the emphasis should have been put on his responsibility under the command responsibility principle. Whether the role of Krstić was indeed one that would fall within the 'traditional ambit' of command responsibility is a separate issue,[174] but the example illustrates the different approach that may be taken in cases that charge both individual and command responsibility.

In fact, the Trial Chamber in the *Krnojelac* case took that other approach. The judges made the following finding:

> 'With respect to aiding and abetting liability pursuant to Article 7(1), the Trial Chamber is satisfied that the Accused knew of the beatings and that, by failing to take any appropriate measures which, as the warden, he was obliged to adopt, he encouraged these acts, at least in respect of his subordinates. The Trial Chamber is satisfied therefore that the Accused's liability for aiding and abetting the beatings pursuant to Article 7(1) has been established. The Trial Chamber considers, however, that, in view of the nature of the Accused's participation, the more appropriate basis of liability in relation to the beatings is his responsibility as a superior pursuant to Article 7(3) of the Statute. As the Trial Chamber is of the view that it is inappropriate to convict under

---

172 *Prosecutor* v. *Radislav Krstić*, Appeal Judgement, Case No. IT-98-33-A, 19 April 2004.

173 Danner and Martinez, p. 153.

174 In a footnote the Appeals Chamber gave the following 'explanation' with regard to the issue of the superior responsibility of Krstić: 'The Appeals Chamber's determination that General Krstić is responsible as an aider and abettor is also based on Article 7(1). Even if General Krstić is also found to be responsible as a Commander, the Appeals Chamber concludes, as did the Trial Chamber, that the mode of liability under Article 7(1) best encapsulates General Krstić's criminality. This is because the most he could have done as a Commander was to report the use of his personnel and assets, in facilitating the killings, to the VRS Main Staff and to his superior, General Mladić, the very people who ordered the executions and were active participants in them. Further, although General Krstić could have tried to punish his subordinates for their participation in facilitating the executions, it is unlikely that he would have had the support of his superiors in doing so.' See *Prosecutor* v. *Radislav Krstić*, Appeal Judgement, Case No. IT-98-33-A, 19 April 2004, n. 250.

both heads of responsibility based on the same acts, it will enter a conviction under Article 7(3) only.'[175]

While it had established that the accused incurred responsibility under Article 7(1), the Trial Chamber found that also the elements of command responsibility had been proven and that the principle should be used for the facts in this case. The subsequent reasoning by the judges serves as an example of the kind of situations to which command responsibility is, indeed, applicable:

> 'In respect of the actions of the guards of the KP Dom, the Accused is responsible as their superior under Article 7(3) of the Statute. As warden of the KP Dom, the Accused was the *de jure* superior of the guards, and he knew, for the reasons given above, that they were involved in the beating of non-Serb detainees. Not only did the Accused personally see one of his subordinates beat a detainee, he also heard about such incidents, and it must have been clear that, considering that the guards were in direct contact with and controlled the detainees, some of them were involved.'[176]

These examples confirm that with regard to the relationship between individual and command responsibility the challenge is not so much whether there is a basis for the simultaneous application of individual and command responsibility, as it is to find out what the command responsibility should achieve. This broader question will be addressed in Chapter 6.

5.4 The nature of the crime underlying the charges of command responsibility

5.4.1 **Introduction**

Another factor that influences the application of the command responsibility doctrine is the nature of the crime underlying the charges of command responsibility. While the statutes of the presently active international(ised) tribunals and courts set out the applicability of the command responsibility doctrine in relation to all international crimes under their jurisdictions, the specific definitions of certain international crimes necessitate some closer consideration of the applicability of the doctrine to these violations.

With regard to the application of the command responsibility doctrine to war crimes and crimes against humanity, neither case law nor legal writings have identified problems specifically related to the nature of these crimes. As concerns the crime of genocide, the situation is a little different. The crime of genocide is unique in that in its definition it requires *mens rea* on the part of the perpetrator 'to destroy, in whole or in part, a national, ethnical, racial or religious group, as

[175] *Prosecutor* v. *Milorad Krnojelac*, Judgement, Case No. IT-97-25-T, 15 March 2002, para. 316.
[176] Ibid., para. 318.

such.'[177] In relation to the application of the command responsibility doctrine this specific intent requirement is generally considered as very problematic, considering the fact that the superior charged under the command responsibility doctrine is not himself the physical perpetrator of the crime. The case law produced shows inconsistencies, which are troubling from the perspective of the jurisprudence of the *ad hoc* tribunals but also for the future decision-making of the ICC and other international courts applying the same doctrine. Depending on which approach regarding the nature of the command responsibility doctrine itself is taken, the applicability of the doctrine to the crime of genocide raises various questions that will be addressed in section 5.4.2.

While not yet defined for the purposes or nor applied by the ICC, the crime of aggression has also been a source for debates and negotiations. An aspect which is unsettled and which will be addressed below is aggression and its relationship with command responsibility. Although the two crimes – genocide and aggression – are challenging in different ways, they both raise some questions regarding the significance of the nature of the crime underlying the charges of command responsibility. Can all crimes be charged on the basis of command responsibility?

This question goes further than the crime of genocide and crimes against humanity. As command responsibility is considered to apply to all crimes under the jurisdictions of the various international tribunals, the question may be asked whether the applicability is restricted to international crimes. At present, many states participate in peacekeeping missions all over the world that may not be qualified as armed conflicts. There are situations in which the state is faced with violations that do not qualify as war crimes, but show similarities with cases in which the commander, had the crime been an international crime, could have been charged under the command responsibility doctrine. Is there something in the nature of international crimes that makes the command responsibility doctrine particularly suitable for liability for these crimes, or could commanders in cases of any unlawful military use of force be tried under this doctrine? This issue will also be briefly addressed below.

5.4.2 **Genocide**

5.4.2.1 *Applicability*

The present definition of genocide applied by international courts and tribunals stems from the Convention on the Prevention and Punishment of the Crime of Genocide. Having been included in the initial Draft Code of Crimes Against the Peace and Security of Mankind in 1950 and in the subsequent versions of the Draft Code, the crime of genocide was naturally incorporated in the statutes of the *ad hoc* tribunals and in the Rome Statute of the ICC.[178] The Genocide

[177] See Art. 2 of the Convention on the Prevention and Punishment of the Crime of Genocide of 9 December 1948, 78 *UNTS* p. 277.

[178] W. Schabas, *Genocide in International Law: The Crime of Crimes* (Cambridge, Cambridge University Press 2000) pp. 81-101.

Convention was considered to have become part of international customary law and, therefore, satisfied the requirement set for the *ad hoc* tribunals that they could only apply humanitarian law which had beyond any doubt become part of international customary law.[179]

Applying the genocide definition as laid down in international customary law is generally recognised as problematic, due to the special intent requirement, without which there cannot be criminal liability for the crime of genocide.[180] The 'special intent' concept is in itself increasingly contested,[181] and raises specific concerns in relation to command responsibility. As stated by Schabas, a special intent crime 'requires performance of the *actus reus* but in association with an intent or purpose that goes beyond the mere performance of the act.'[182] The difficulties arise when assessing the role of the accused in the perpetration of the crime of genocide. Where in the genocidal machinery should the special intent be found? If only the physical perpetrator/principal offender/'the one who pulled the trigger' should possess the special intent to destroy one of the specified groups or part of it, the nature of the crime of genocide is not well understood. Schabas noted that in relation to the crime of genocide, the principal offender is often 'a small cog in the machine', while the accomplice is 'the real villain'.[183] That same consideration springs to mind when assessing the crime of genocide in combination with the command responsibility doctrine, as the 'object' of command responsibility, the commander/superior, is not the physical perpetrator of the crime.[184]

There are two relevant questions to be asked here. The first concerns the nature of command responsibility, as discussed earlier in this chapter. The second concerns the applicability of command responsibility to all international crimes included in the various statutes. In relation to the first question, several authors have struggled with the fact that if command responsibility leads to criminal liability for the crime itself, for genocide, also the special intent of the commander/superior will have to be proven.[185] Most authors hold the view, based on convincing arguments, that if command responsibility is to be applied to geno-

---

179 See *Report of the Secretary-General Pursuant to Paragraph 2 of Security Council Resolution 808 (1993)*, UN Doc. S/25704 (1993), reprinted in 32 *ILM* (1993) p. 1163, paras. 34-35.

180 See, for example, Schabas 2000, pp. 206-256; L. van den Herik and E. van Sliedregt, 'Ten Years Later, the Rwanda Tribunal still Faces Legal Complexities: Some Comments on the Vagueness of the Indictment, Complicity in Genocide, and the Nexus Requirement for War Crimes', 17 *LJIL* (2004) pp. 537-557; H.G. van der Wilt, 'Genocide, Complicity in Genocide and International v. Domestic Jurisdiction – Reflections on the *van Anraat* Case', 4 *Journal of International Criminal Justice* (2006) pp. 239-257; C. Eboe-Osuji, ' ""Complicity in Genocide" versus "Aiding and Abetting Genocide" – Construing the Difference in the ICTR and ICTY Statutes', 3 *Journal of International Criminal Justice* (2005) pp. 56-81; and C. Kress, 'The Darfur Report and Genocidal Intent', 3 *Journal of International Criminal Justice* (2005) pp. 562-578.

181 Van der Wilt, 'Genocide, 2006, pp. 239-257.

182 Schabas 2000, p. 218.

183 Ibid., p. 286.

184 On command responsibility in relation to genocide, see Schabas 2000, pp. 304-313.

185 See, for example, Cassese 2003, p. 108; Schabas 2000, pp. 311313; and Zahar 2001, pp. 614-616.

cide in the first place, there has to be a lower requirement of the level of intent than the possession of special intent.[186] Where special intent on the part of the commander/superior can be proven, '[T]he commander comes within the easy grasp of Article 6(1)/7(1) and superior-liability charges are redundant.'[187] Schabas came to the conclusion that it is difficult to reconcile the negligent behaviour of a superior with a crime that requires 'the highest level of intent'.[188] In fact, he could not offer any other solution to the applicability problem, except to 'create an evidentiary presumption by which a commander is deemed to have participated in genocide if his or her subordinates committed the crime.'[189] This answer to the problem can hardly become an option, as liability is then founded on the position of the accused as the superior of those who committed the genocide. This option has repeatedly been rejected, as it comes close to the strict liability of the superior.[190] According to Zahar, the problem with Schabas' conclusion is that he treats command responsibility as a negligence crime.[191] In Zahar's view, command responsibility is clearly 'a special form of *complicity*',[192] which in contrast to negligence offences contains a knowledge requirement.[193] While the lack of genocidal intent led Schabas to conclude that it is illogical to apply command responsibility to genocide with the evidentiary presumption, Zahar held that there can be a number of forms of participation in the crime of genocide and did not see why the superior could not be convicted under the command responsibility provision for genocide. In his view: 'Genocide was, after all, the only crime which the defendant superior, by his or her deliberate acts of omission, associated himself or herself with.'[194]

The views of these authors, formulated prior to the great amount of new *ad hoc* tribunal case law of the past few years and influenced by the existing case law at the time, very well illustrate the challenges facing command responsibility for the crime of genocide. Cassese briefly addressed the issue of command responsibility in relation to the crime of genocide, but noted that the commander/superior may possess various levels of *mens rea*, and that any consideration as to the applicability of the command responsibility doctrine in relation to genocide should be seen in light of this finding.[195] The levels of *mens rea* were extracted from categories of command responsibility set out in the German Criminal Code,

---

[186] P. Akhavan, 'The Crime of Genocide in the ICTR Jurisprudence', 3 *Journal of International Criminal Justice* (2005) pp. 989-1006, at p. 993.

[187] Zahar 2001, p. 615.

[188] Schabas 2000, p. 312.

[189] Ibid., p. 313.

[190] See, for example, *Kayishema and Ruzindana*, TC Judgement, para. 229, where the Trial Chamber pointed out that for the purposes of command responsibility, only 'those superiors who exercise effective control over their subordinates' may incur liability. It is the material ability that constitutes 'the touchstone' of Art. 6(3) responsibility. See ibid. It would not be justified to hold that the fact that the accused happened to be a superior creates a presumtion of participation in genocide.

[191] Zahar 2001, p. 615.

[192] Ibid., p. 614.

[193] Ibid., p. 615.

[194] Ibid.

[195] See Cassese 2003, p. 108.

which were discussed earlier in this chapter.[196] In Cassese's view, there may arguably be a possibility to find command responsibility in relation to genocide, but only in those cases where the commander/superior 'knows that genocide is about to be perpetrated, or is being committed, and deliberately refrains from forestalling the crime or stopping it.'[197] Where he failed to punish subordinates who had committed genocide, according to Cassese, the commander could not be held responsible, regardless of whether the breach of his duties was intentional, reckless or negligent.[198]

Allowing a lower level of *mens rea*, in keeping with that described by Cassese, certainly offers an outcome to the cases of 'aggravated command responsibility', as discussed previously in this chapter.[199] In these cases the commander is indifferent to or silently approves of the commission of crimes by his subordinates and his liability is based on a form of participation *sui generis*. To require that the commander 'knows that genocide is about to be perpetrated, or is being committed' seems like a workable solution. However, instead of completely rejecting the applicability in cases of negligence on the part of the commander, as suggested by Cassese, the 'act *sui generis*' option, at least theoretically, offers possibilities to apply command responsibility to genocide in this second category of cases.

It has been held that where command responsibility is considered an act *sui generis*, there may be possibilities for broadening the applicability of the command responsibility principle.[200] Where command responsibility is seen as an act *sui generis*, the superior will be held responsible for the failure to act, regardless of the character of the crime which triggers the responsibility. The fact that subordinates commit the crime of genocide and necessarily must have special intent in order to incur responsibility for that crime does not create any requirements with regard to the *mens rea* of the superior, as his responsibility only concerns the failure to act. The only *mens rea* requirement in relation to the superior is whether he knew or 'had reason to know' of an unlawful act by the subordinates. In cases where there is no 'aggravated command responsibility', the *sui generis* option offers a more justifiable solution than command responsibility as criminal liability for the actual crimes committed by subordinates. Accordingly, applying the two-category approach to command responsibility is a somewhat better way to approach the difficulties caused by the special intent requirement in the definitions on genocide. The inherent incompatibility between genocide and the command responsibility principle remains, despite the theoretical efforts to combine the two.

---

196 See section 5.2.2 *supra*.
197 See Cassese 2003, p. 108.
198 Ibid.
199 See section 5.2.2 *supra*.
200 Swart, p. 234.

5.4.2.2 *Case law*

The considerations regarding the crime of genocide of this and other authors, as mentioned earlier, have been influenced and inspired by the case law produced by, mainly, the *ad hoc* tribunals. The issue of command responsibility for the crime of genocide has been addressed in several judgements, primarily in the cases before the ICTR, but also in some important decisions of the ICTY.

One of these cases was the *Krstić* case. General Krstić was the commander of the Drina Corps, which was involved in crimes of terror committed at Potocari, the subsequent forcible transfer of women, children and the elderly and the mass execution of military-aged Muslim men from Srebrenica, which constituted genocide.[201] The Trial Chamber first found the accused criminally liable as a principal perpetrator in a JCE aimed at committing genocide. In this context the Trial Chamber found the accused to have had genocidal intent.[202] The Trial Chamber subsequently considered whether the accused could also be found liable under Article 7(3) and concluded that all the elements of command responsibility, the effective control, the *mens rea* and the failure to prevent or punish, had been shown.[203] With regard to the *mens rea* requirement, the Trial Chamber concluded that the accused knew of the ongoing killing campaign and had to have been aware of the genocidal objectives. In the opinion of the Trial Chamber, Krstić could have incurred superior responsibility for the crime of genocide, but instead it held that, 'General Krstić's responsibility for the participation of his troops in the killings is sufficiently expressed in a finding of guilt under Article 7(1)',[204] and did not enter a conviction based on superior responsibility. On appeal the issue of Krstić's superior responsibility under Article 7(3) was not as such considered, but it was nevertheless mentioned in the context of the findings of responsibility by the Appeals Chamber. The basis for the liability of the accused was changed on appeal from participation in a joint criminal enterprise to aiding and abetting the crime of genocide.[205] In a footnote, the Appeals Chamber agreed with the Trial Chamber that an Article 7(3) conviction would not have encapsulated the criminality of the accused as well as liability under Article 7(1). The reasoning was as follows:

> 'This is because the most he could have done as a Commander was to report the use of his personnel and assets, in facilitating the killings, to the VRS Main Staff and to his superior, General Mladić, the very people who ordered the executions and were active participants in them. Further, although General Krstić could have tried to punish his subordinates for their participation in facilitating the executions, it is unlikely that he would have had the support of his superiors in doing so.'[206]

---

[201] *Prosecutor* v. *Radislav Krstić*, Judgement, Case No. IT-98-33-T, 2 August 2001, para. 606.
[202] Ibid., para. 644.
[203] Ibid., paras. 647-648.
[204] Ibid., para. 652.
[205] *Prosecutor* v. *Radislav Krstić*, Appeal Judgement, Case No. IT-98-33-A, 19 April 2004, n. 250.
[206] Ibid.

The *Krstić* case is of value in this context because of its command responsibility charges in relation to genocide. However, the findings are more interesting for the discussion previously in this chapter regarding the overlap between individual criminal responsibility and command responsibility, as the dismissal of the command responsibility charges were not related to the fact that the crimes committed by the subordinates constituted genocide. Neither was there any explanation regarding the relevance of the knowledge of the accused as to the genocidal objectives of the killing campaign. Something that deserves to be mentioned is the note by the Appeals Chamber that the accused, in his position as a commander, would not have been able to prevent or punish because his superiors were involved 'in the plot'. If this statement had been made only in relation to the crime of genocide, it could support the view that genocide presupposes the involvement of the highest officials and makes command responsibility inapplicable. A similar statement was made regarding imprisonment as a crime against humanity in the *Krnojelac* case, which shows that this argument is not unique to genocide.[207] For the command responsibility doctrine in general, the argument in *Krnojelac* and in *Krstić* is interesting, as it could create a presumption of the inapplicability of the command responsibility both in relation to crimes against humanity and genocide. The commander would be hindered in his possibilities to prevent or punish because he would not get support from his superiors. It should be recognised, of course, that this view was expressed in a small minority of the cases.

As in the *Krstić* case, one of the accused in the '*Media case*' (ICTR) was acquitted under Article 6(3) charges of genocide, because an Article 6(1) finding had been made.[208] This finding by the Appeals Chamber reversed the finding by the Trial Chamber, according to which the accused, Barayagwiza, had:

> '[S]uperior responsibility over members of the CDR[209] and its militia, the *Impuzamugambi*,[210] as President of CDR at Gisenyi Prefecture and from February 1994 as President of CDR at the national level. He promoted the policy of CDR for the extermination of the Tutsi population and supervised his subordinates, the CDR members and *Impuzamugambi* militia, in carrying out the killings and other violent acts. For his active engagement in CDR, and his failure to take necessary and reasonable measures to prevent the killing of Tutsi civilians by CDR members and *Impuzamugambi*, the Chamber [found] Barayagwiza guilty of genocide pursuant to Article 6(3) of its Statute.'[211]

---

207 *Prosecutor* v. *Milorad Krnojelac*, Judgement, Case No. IT-97-25-T, 15 March 2002, para. 127.

208 *Nahimana et al.*, AC Judgement, para. 667.

209 The *Coalition pour la Défense de la République* party, of which Barayagwiza was a founding member. See *Nahimana et al.*, TC Judgement and Sentence, para. 7.

210 'Those who have the same goal'; Name of the youth wing of the CDR, according to the glossary included in the judgement.

211 *Nahimana et al.*, TC Judgement and Sentence, para. 977. Barayagwiza was also held responsible for incitement to commit genocide pursuant to Art. 6(1).

The Chamber established that the accused had the genocidal intent necessary to find him guilty of genocide, concluding the following: 'From his words and deeds, Barayagwiza's ruthless commitment to the destruction of the Tutsi population as a means by which to protect the political gains secured by the Hutu majority from 1959 is evident.'[212] The Appeals Chamber did not pronounce on the need, under the command responsibility doctrine, to establish that the superior had genocidal intent. The finding goes against the views, as expressed above, that proven genocidal intent brings the accused within the reach of the individual criminal responsibility provisions. Such responsibility had already been established in this case.

The *Serushago* case was decided following a guilty plea by the accused, in which he admitted being guilty of genocide and crimes against humanity, crimes that had taken place in the Gisenyi prefecture in Rwanda between April and July 1994.[213] The accused acknowledged that he had been one of the leaders of the *Interahamwe* in Gisenyi and the head of a group of militiamen, over which he exercised authority and control.[214] In light of the admissions by the accused, the Trial Chamber noted that it had been admitted by the Defence that:

> 'Omar Serushago, in the commission of the crimes for which he has been found guilty, played a leading role and that he therefore incurs individual criminal responsibility under the provisions of Article 6(3) of the Statute.'[215]

The outcome of the case has rightly been considered ambiguous.[216] Although the findings were based on a guilty plea, the accused should not have been convicted under Article 6(3) for genocide, as he had already pleaded guilty to the commission of genocide. Similarly, the Trial Chamber in the *Kambanda* case accepted the guilty plea of the accused and found him guilty of genocide by virtue of both Article 6(1) and 6(3).[217] The accused was the Prime Minister of the Interim Government of Rwanda during the period that the genocide took place and exercised *de jure* and *de facto* authority over both senior civil servants as well as senior officers in the military. The accused pleaded guilty under Article 6(1) but also admitted that he 'knew or should have known that persons for whom he was responsible were committing crimes of massacre upon Tutsi and that he failed to prevent them or punish the perpetrators.'[218]

Further, in the case against Clément Kayishema and Obed Ruzindana the Trial Chamber established liability for genocide pursuant to Article 6(3), in addition to its finding of liability under Article 6(1), in relation to one of the accused,

---

[212] Ibid.

[213] *Prosecutor v. Omar Serushago*, Decision Relating to a Plea of Guilty, Case No. ICTR-98-39-T, 14 December 2003, para. 25.

[214] Ibid.

[215] Ibid., para. 28.

[216] Schabas 2000, p. 310.

[217] *Prosecutor v. Jean Kambanda*, Judgement and Sentence, Case No. ICTR-97-23-S, 4 September 1998, para. 40.

[218] Ibid., para. 39.

Kayishema. At the time, Kayishema exercised both *de jure* and *de facto* control over all or most of the perpetrators of the crimes. The Trial Chamber found that Kayishema both 'knew that his subordinates were about to attack and failed to take reasonable and necessary measures to prevent them, when he had the material ability to do so.'[219] The number of victims, the pattern or methodology with which the crimes were committed and the utterances of the accused showed Kayishema's genocidal intent.[220] This case, like *Serushago* and *Kambanda*, is one of the earlier cases decided by the *ad hoc* tribunals. Judgements of a later date have rejected cumulative convictions under Articles 6(1)/7(1) and 6(3)/7(3).

On the basis of these examples, it seems justified to conclude that both *ad hoc* tribunals have recognised that superiors may be held liable under the superior responsibility provision for genocide.[221] Regrettably, thorough reasoning as to the applicability of the command responsibility doctrine in relation to the crime of genocide is still lacking.

5.4.2.3 *Desirability*

The two previous sections discussed the applicability in theory and in case law of the command responsibility doctrine in relation to the crime of genocide. In the present section, the desirability of applying command responsibility in relation to genocide will be discussed.

By removing the special intent from the superior charged with command responsibility in relation to genocide, as discussed earlier, the application of this doctrine to the crime of genocide becomes more acceptable. As to the desirability of allowing an interpretation which makes a conviction on the basis of command responsibility for genocide conceivable, the nature of the command responsibility doctrine and its purpose should be reiterated.[222] For the purposes of the present discussion, it is useful to consider which purpose the command responsibility doctrine was not intended to serve. On the basis of the elements of command responsibility as defined and applied, it is not meant to apply to facts which support a finding that the commander planned, instigated or incited his subordinates to commit crimes. As regards genocide, this is exactly what is expected of a superior. Consider the following statement:

---

[219] *Kayishema and Ruzindana*, TC Judgement, para. 555.

[220] Ibid., paras. 531-540. The judgement was not altered by the Appeals Chamber on this point. See *Kayishema and Ruzindana*, AC Judgement.

[221] Also in more recent cases, such as the *Cyangugu* case, the accused have, at first instance, been found liable under the command responsibility provision. For reasons other than the applicability of command responsibility in relation to genocide, the Appeals Chamber has overturned these convictions. See, for example, *Ntagerura et al.*, TC Judgement and Sentence, *inter alia*, paras. 694-695; and *Ntagerura et al.*, AC Judgement, paras. 164-165. On this case, see also S. Kagan, 'The 'Media case' before the Rwanda Tribunal: The *Nahimana et al.* Appeal Judgement', 3 *Hague Justice Journal* (2008) pp. 83-91, at pp. 87-88.

[222] See Chapter 3 *supra*.

'The difficulty with genocide is that it tends to be committed along a chain of command. At the top of the chain, the point at which the planning, instigating and directing occurs, the special intent is most evident. But those who plan may not be involved in the commission of a basic act. In contrast, at the bottom of the chain, the point at which the basic acts are committed, it may be difficult to infer special intent.'[223]

First, under command responsibility the superior is not the one who planned or directed the commission of the crimes. Secondly, the subordinates of the superior, usually those who committed the basic acts, may not have special genocidal intent. On the basis of these findings, it may be held that the doctrine does not lend itself to application in relation to the crime of genocide. Nevertheless, there are at least two important factors that have an impact on the continuing attempts to apply the doctrine and to try to justify its application in cases of genocide. The first factor to keep in mind is the prosecutors and their attitude towards command responsibility in relation to genocide. Statements made by prosecutors at the various tribunals create the impression that genocide may well be charged on the basis of the command responsibility provision and, despite the development of the doctrine in a slightly different direction, that command responsibility is a significant tool when prosecuting 'local or central leaders' in relation to 'crimes of great magnitude'.[224] Also relatively recent indictments indicate that prosecutors consider command responsibility as a desirable legal basis for liability in relation to genocide.[225]

The second factor is the fact that the statutes of the various courts and tribunals have not specified the applicability of the command responsibility provision to certain crimes. As command responsibility can arise for all crimes mentioned in the statutes, it has been considered that this should not be any different with regard to genocide, or to incitement to commit genocide, and accordingly that, '[E]ven if subordinates merely 'directly and publicly incite others to commit genocide', superiors can be held responsible and liable for punishment for Command Responsibility with regard to genocide, when all the other elements also can be established.'[226] Consequently, where the superior failed to prevent

[223] N.H.B. Jørgensen, 'The Definition of Genocide: Joining the Dots in Light of Recent Practice', 1 *International Criminal Law Review* (2001) pp. 285-313, at p. 309.

[224] C. Del Ponte, 'Prosecuting the Individuals Bearing the Highest Level of Responsibility', 2 *Journal of International Criminal Justice* (2004) pp. 516-519, at p. 517. The same impression was also created during lectures delivered by Stephen Rapp, Chief Prosecutor of the Special Court, 'The Legal Challenges of Prosecuting National Leaders for Violations of International Humanitarian Law for Sierra Leone', Occasional Guest Lecture Series, T.M.C. Asser Institute, The Hague, 28 February 2008; and Brenda J. Hollis, Principal Trial Attorney SCSL/OTP, 'Lessons Learned from International Criminal Courts and Tribunals', Supranational Criminal Law Lecture Series, Grotius Centre for International Legal Studies, The Hague, 11 March 2009.

[225] See *Prosecutor* v. *Michel Bagaragaza*, Amended Indictment, Case No. ICTR-2005-86-I, 1 December 2006; and *Prosecutor* v. *Dominique Ntawukuriryayo*, Indictment, Case No. ICTR-2005-82-I, 26 May 2005.

[226] O. Triffterer, 'Command Responsibility, Article 28 Rome Statute, an Extension of Individual Criminal Responsibility for Crimes Within the Jurisdiction of the Court – Compatible with Article 22, *nullum crimen sine lege*?', in O. Triffterer, ed., *Gedächtnisschrift für Theo Vogler* (Heidelberg, Müller 2004) pp. 213-262, at p. 242.

or punish the incitement, he could be held responsible. In that case, those who perpetrated or were incited to commit the crime of genocide need not have been the subordinates of the superior who is being held liable. Accepting that there may be superior responsibility for all crimes defined, including in relation to genocide, the responsibility of the superior and his failure to act is stressed, rather than the difference between the specific crimes.

Taking the view that the command responsibility doctrine should be applied restrictively, it could be argued that such responsibility goes too far in that it does not reflect the actual culpability of the superior in a crime of such great magnitude.[227] Regardless of the nature of command responsibility, the crime of genocide requires an intent to destroy, in whole or in part, a religious, ethnic or other group of people. Accordingly, a certain group is being killed or seriously harmed with the intent to destroy that group or there is an imminent threat that that is going to happen. In the cases in the past, where the occurrence of genocide was established, the scale of the killing or the harm was very extensive. As the critics in the cases decided by the ICTR have rightly observed, it is difficult to imagine that in such circumstances the superior could fulfil the elements of command responsibility without playing a more active or facilitative role in those large-scale events. This line of thinking is corroborated by the fact that in the ICTR genocide cases the superiors incurring command responsibility have also been found to have, in some way, actively participated in the events (for the purposes of Article 6(1)).

The question remains as to whether there are situations in which the superior could incur command responsibility for genocide, where the special intent of the crime of genocide itself was not required. Imagine the following situation: Killings of a certain group have been carried out over a large area and members of this group are internally displaced. Arriving at a town these persons are brought to a sports complex and the superior and his subordinates are ordered to keep guard. Because he knows that some of his subordinates share the sentiment of those who have killed members of the group with intent being to destroy that group, the superior reminds his subordinates that they are there simply to keep guard, but decides to spend the evening at a bar in the town centre. In the meantime, several persons are taken out of the complex and killed by his subordinates. Because of the unrest in the area, the people are moved to another location the next morning and the superior, together with his subordinates, are reassigned and leave. The superior does not have time to make inquiries into the events of the evening.

In relation to the superior in the present example, the elements of command responsibility could be said to have been fulfilled, for the failure to act, that is. Applying the '*sui generis* option', there would be no requirement of a special intent for the purposes of genocide on the part of the superior. The application of the command responsibility principle in relation to genocide in such a specific

[227] Whereas the present discussion concerns the crime of genocide, applying command responsibility to crimes against humanity may raise similar concerns, as this category of crimes requires that violations were widespread and systematic and, thus, of a great magnitude.

case is conceivable. However, the above example does not correspond to the facts in the majority of the genocide cases tried so far. Because of the scale on which the crime of genocide usually takes place, the most suitable basis for trying a superior will be an act, rather than an omission, on the part of the superior. Even where command responsibility was considered as an 'act *sui generis*', the removed special intent requirement would not change the difficulty of combining command responsibility and genocide, not least in relation to purely civilian superiors.

Are we to regret this conclusion, or in other words, is it desirable that superiors incur command responsibility in relation to the crime of genocide? Regardless of whether the superior is a military superior or a civilian, command responsibility does not constitute the most suitable basis for responsibility in situations where the crime of genocide has been committed. The lack of a requirement of special intent on the part of the superior would not change the fact that the circumstances under which genocide may occur are such that command responsibility purely as a crime of omission is not the best way of describing the responsibility of the superior.

The command responsibility provisions in the statutes of the *ad hoc* tribunals and of the ICC apply to all crimes included in the statutes, i.e., also to genocide, and have been applied by the *ad hoc* tribunals in relation to that crime. However, future criticism is avoided only by treating command responsibility in relation to genocide as a theoretical option to other ways of prosecuting alleged criminals, with the understanding that it is only in highly exceptional cases that charges under that principle would be justified, not least in relation to civilian superiors.[228]

5.4.3 **Aggression**

An aspect of the command responsibility discussion which is still not definitely solved is whether the principle and in particular the provision on superior responsibility in the ICC Statute can and should be applied to the crime of aggression. As no case law exists at the international level where a superior has been charged under the command responsibility principle in relation to the crime of aggression, the issue has most notably arisen in the context of the Special Working Group on the Crime of Aggression (SWGCA), which was set up at the first session of the Assembly of States Parties to the Rome Statute of the International Criminal Court.[229] In its negotiations on different issues pertaining to the crime of aggression, the SWGCA, which is 'open on an equal footing to all States Members of the United Nations',[230] recognised the need to discuss the applicability of Article 28 ICC, i.e., the superior responsibility provision, in relation to the crime of aggression. Participants at the SWGCA have expressed the view that superior responsibility is 'not applicable by virtue of both the essence and the nature of

[228] See the discussion in section 6.2.3 *infra*.

[229] Official Records of the Assembly of States Parties to the Rome Statute of the International Criminal Court, First Session, 3-10 September 2002, Resolution ICC-ASP/1/Res.1.

[230] Ibid.

the crime'[231] of aggression, or that at most the principle is 'of rather theoretical relevance for the crime of aggression.'[232] Accordingly, while the definition or description of the crime of aggression is subject to difficult negotiations, it seems clear that the crime of aggression can only be committed by the highest superiors, which means that there is no higher hierarchical level to prosecute under the command responsibility provision.

A practical application of command responsibility in relation to the crime of aggression could be possible if the definition of aggression were to be formulated so that the crime could be committed without the orders of the top officials of the relevant state or other group committing the crime of aggression.

Participants at the SWGCA have expressed a preference to formulate a specific provision which rules out the application of the command responsibility principle to the crime of aggression. For the purposes of the ICC, such a provision would render it unnecessary to further theorise about the applicability of command responsibility in relation to the crime of aggression.

5.4.4 Acts not qualifying as international crimes

The two previous sections discussed the applicability of command responsibility in relation to genocide and aggression, two international crimes with distinct features that make the application of command responsibility arguably less straightforward than where the subordinates committed war crimes. The present section addresses acts not qualifying as international crimes and the question why command responsibility does not constitute the best basis for criminal liability in relation to such crimes. For the purposes of the present discussion, by acts not qualifying as international crimes are meant violations that are committed in or are connected to an armed conflict or mass atrocities, but that do not belong to the core crimes – genocide, crimes against humanity, war crimes and aggression. The aim of this chapter is not to broaden the applicability of the doctrine to crimes committed in other, mostly civilian settings, or to compare it to other forms of responsibility, like the responsibility of corporate officers.[233]

At present, the command responsibility doctrine as developed in international law applies primarily to international crimes, but to a limited number of international crimes. As explained by Schabas, the concept of 'international crimes' is far from new and covers more crimes than those included in the Rome Statute, such as piracy and trafficking in women and children.[234] The crimes included in

[231] Official Records of the Assembly of States Parties to the Rome Statute of the International Criminal Court, Fourth Session, 28 November – 3 December 2005, ICC-ASP/4/32, Annex II, para. 47.

[232] Official Records of the Assembly of States Parties to the Rome Statute of the International Criminal Court, Sixth Session, 30 November – 14 December 2007, ICC-ASP/6/20, Annex III, para. 13.

[233] On this and other analogous concepts, see, for example, Van Sliedregt 2003, pp. 199-209.

[234] Discussing the criminal responsibility of individuals in the post-WW II period, Woentzel said the following about international crimes: '[A]n act is an international crime, if it causes grave harm to the international community.' See R.K. Woentzel, *The Nuremberg Trials in International Law with a Postlude to the Eichmann Trial* (London, Stevens and Sons 1962) p. 110.

the Rome Statute are international 'because their heinous nature elevates them to a level where they are of 'concern' to the international community.'[235] There is, however, no provision in international law which limits the applicability of the command responsibility doctrine to these international crimes. The Statutes of the SCSL and the Special Tribunal for Lebanon (STL) both provide for the applicability of command responsibility to the crimes under their respective jurisdictions, although not all of the violations qualify as international crimes, as set out in the Rome Statute.[236] Had it not been for the lack of support for the inclusion of certain other international crimes during the negotiation process leading to the adoption of the Rome Statute, also the ICC could have applied the command responsibility doctrine to crimes other than the international core crimes now included.[237] There have also been suggestions to amend the Rome Statute to allow the command responsibility doctrine to cover crimes more generally:

> '[A] superior is criminally responsible for failure to take such measures as are reasonable to prevent his subordinates from committing such crimes which are reasonable foreseeable in the circumstances of the armed conflict.'[238]

At the international level there seems to be an acceptance of command responsibility as a doctrine which is applicable to those crimes which are considered important enough to be included in the statute of an international tribunal. From a criminal law point of view, the argument that the command responsibility doctrine extends the criminal liability of the subordinates committing the crime to the superior has led authors to consider whether command responsibility should primarily remain a basis for criminal liability for international crimes. Damaška, who in his article expressed very critical views regarding the applicability of command responsibility as such, most importantly because, in his view, it deviates from the culpability principle in domestic criminal law, asked the following question:

> 'Is there something peculiar in the circumstances in which international criminal tribunals operate, in the nature of massive human rights violations, or in the criminal liability for outcomes of complex organisations, that calls for and justifies the exceptional severity of imputed forms of command responsibility?'[239]

---

235 Schabas 2004, p. 29.

236 In addition to international crimes, the Statute of the SCSL contains crimes under Sierra Leonean Law, including 'Offences relating to the abuse of girls'. See Art. 5 of the SCSL Statute. Art. 2 of the STL Statute states that the tribunal is to apply 'provisions of the Lebanese Criminal Code relating to the prosecution and punishment of acts of terrorism, crimes and offences against life and personal integrity, illicit associations and failure to report crimes and offences.'

237 Schabas 2004, pp. 34-35.

238 C. Eboe-Osuji, 'Rape and Superior Responsibility: International Criminal Law in Need of Adjustment', Guest Lecture Series of the Office of the Prosecutor of the International Criminal Court, The Hague, 20 June 2005, p. 9, available at <http://www.icc-cpi.int/library/organs/otp/050620_Chile_presentation.pdf> (accessed 15 July 2009).

239 Damaška, p. 471.

Damaška considered that in spite of reasons such as the deterrent or preventive effect or the symbolic function of international criminal law,[240] which may be different for international crimes than for common crimes, there will have to be a 'gradual refinement' of international criminal rules, in order to reach the same level of acceptance under domestic criminal law.[241] This concerns in particular the rule on command responsibility.

Many states have implemented the command responsibility doctrine as being applicable to international crimes in new provisions in their domestic penal codes or as a separate law on international crimes. That, of course, does not mean that they consider the command responsibility doctrine to be applicable to crimes not qualifying as international crimes. The United Kingdom has accepted the doctrine and has included it in the 2004 *Manual of the Law of Armed Conflict* of the United Kingdom Ministry of Defence, which contains the following wording in relation to the responsibility of commanders:

> 'Military commanders are responsible for preventing violations of the law (including the law of armed conflict) and for taking the necessary disciplinary action.'[242]

Reference is made to the Fourth Hague Convention, to the Geneva Conventions and to Additional Protocol I, which all set out the general responsibility of the contracting parties to suppress acts contrary to the provision of the conventions.[243] The Manual does not refer exclusively to preventing international crimes, but seems to remind the commanders of their duty to take action in relation to all violations. In accordance with recent developments of international law, the Manual also points out that a failure to prevent such breaches will lead to criminal responsibility. The commander may be held criminally responsible even where the act of the subordinates did not amount to an international crime. The Manual continues with an explanation of the command responsibility doctrine as developed in international law and does not provide for another basis of the criminal responsibility of the commander where the crime was not an international crime. The Manual seems to accept that the applicability of the doctrine of command responsibility is not restricted to international crimes and could be applicable to situations where commanders fail to prevent violations of the law or fail to take disciplinary action. As such, the obligation of the commanders to take action is in accordance with Article 87AP I.[244] The fact that the obligation leads to command criminal responsibility suggests a possibility to apply the command responsibility

[240] Ibid, pp. 471-483. For an analysis of Damaška's views, see H.G. van der Wilt, 'Why International Criminal Lawyers Should Read Mirjan Damaška', in *Future Perspectives on International Criminal Justice* (The Hague, T.M.C. Asser Press 2010).

[241] Damaška, p. 496.

[242] UK Ministry of Defence, *The Manual of the Law of Armed Conflict* (Oxford, Oxford University Press 2004) p. 436.

[243] The Manual refers to 1907 HC IV, Art. 3; GC I, Art. 49; GC II, Art. 50; GC III, Art. 129; GC IV, Arts. 29 and 146; and AP I, Art. 91.

[244] See Rogers, pp. 201-203.

doctrine to commanders under domestic law, for acts not qualifying as international crimes.

However, the question is whether the applicability of the command responsibility doctrine as a basis for criminal responsibility for crimes not falling under the law of armed conflict is accepted in practice, as well. May and Powles concluded that regardless of the fact that the responsibility of commanders for acts of their subordinates was recognised in English law, there had not been any cases in the United Kingdom of prosecuting commanders for their failure to prevent or punish crimes, international or other crimes, of their subordinates.[245] On the basis of this, just one example of the lack of practice, it is not possible to draw any conclusions. It is, however, interesting to note that a recognition of the idea that a commander bears responsibility for the acts of his subordinates has not translated into a practice of prosecuting superiors for their failure to act. In addition, May and Powles, who considered that responsibility for a failure to prevent or punish constitutes a new basis for liability in English law, introduced after the adoption of the Rome Statute, held that the reason why such an extension was admitted into the law after the Rome Statute was the extreme character of the crimes.[246] Following their reasoning, offences not constituting crimes against the law of armed conflict should not lead to superior responsibility.

Damaška may be right when arguing that command responsibility as presently applied raises issues in relation to the culpability of the accused, the commander, an issue which is completely unacceptable under domestic criminal law. But could it also be the case that both in the past and at present, there is and perhaps should be concerns on the part of the armed forces towards the criminalisation of the general command responsibility of commanders. As argued by May and Powles, the legislation including the command responsibility provision 'is not aimed at commanders who make a misjudgement in the agony of the moment, during battle.'[247] While not concerned with command responsibility, a commentary to a Dutch case, the case against Eric O., explains why command responsibility in relation to violations not qualifying as international crimes may be difficult to introduce in the domestic setting.[248] In this case, the accused allegedly fired his weapon during a peacekeeping mission, which allegedly led to the death of a civilian. The circumstances of the case were such that the prosecutor could have charged the accused with a dereliction of duty or, alternatively, murder or manslaughter.[249] The prosecutor chose the latter and the accused was acquitted. The case caused general indignation and led to the fear, among members of the armed forces, that any use of force by military personnel may lead to a crimi-

[245] May and Powles, pp. 363-378, at p. 377.

[246] Ibid., p. 378.

[247] Ibid.

[248] G.L. Coolen, 'Eric O. en de slapende mariniers', in M.M. Dolman, P.D. Duyx and H.G. van der Wilt, eds., *Geleerde lessen. Liber amicorum Simon Stolwijk* (Nijmegen, Wolf Legal Publishers 2007) pp. 13-26, at pp. 13-20.

[249] Ibid., pp. 14-15.

nal prosecution.[250] Extending the command responsibility doctrine to crimes not qualifying as international crimes may lead to similar concerns.

5.5 Conclusion

The present chapter has addressed questions in relation to the application of the command responsibility doctrine that have regularly been raised and debated both in judgements, dissenting opinions of the judges and in scholarly writings. The approach in this chapter, as in the whole book, has been respect for the origin and purpose of the command responsibility doctrine when finding a solution to contested issues or when making a choice out of several possible ways of applying the doctrine. Section 5.2 elaborated on the nature of command criminal responsibility. While the case law of the *ad hoc* tribunals during the first ten years of their existence suggests that command responsibility was interpreted as liability for an international crime, more recent judgements insist on applying command responsibility as an act *sui generis*. The disadvantage of command responsibility as liability for an international crime is the lack of intent on the part of the superior in relation to the crimes committed. Considering command responsibility as a crime of its own kind would remove this disadvantage because it does not require such intent. Considering the situations in which command responsibility can/should be applied, i.e., where the superior did not know but should have known about the crimes, or where he silently approved of the crimes, the suggestion in the present chapter is to apply a bifurcated approach to command responsibility. Where the superior ignored or, in fact, approved of the crimes, his omission would be considered as *sui generis* participation in the crimes. The causal link with the crimes would stay but command responsibility would not be considered as one of the other forms of participation. The sentence could reflect the severity of the crimes committed. Where the superior should have known, but did not know about the crimes, he would be held responsible for his failure to act as an act *sui generis*. His lower level of culpability would be reflected by conviction for an act of its own kind, the failure to prevent or punish.

Section 5.3 concerned the overlap between individual criminal responsibility and command responsibility. The overlap is most prevalent where facts allow for charges of participation in a JCE and command responsibility at the same time, or where aiding and abetting and command responsibility can be cumulatively charged. With regard to JCE and command responsibility, it may be argued that only certain cases of JCE may be considered to overlap with command responsibility. The same applies to aiding and abetting. In cases where both bases are established beyond reasonable doubt, a choice should be made between the two. In the opinion of the present author, the choice should not be made automatically in favour of individual criminal responsibility. Rather, it should reflect the involvement of the superior in the events. The choice could, therefore, be made in

---

[250] Ibid., p. 14.

favour of command responsibility. This could increase the role of the command responsibility doctrine in present and future cases, a desirable result as more and more emphasis is laid on individual criminal responsibility. The same attitude should be taken when considering cumulative convictions and command responsibility as an aggravating factor in sentencing.

Section 5.4 discussed the nature of the crime underlying the charges of command responsibility and more specifically the question whether command responsibility may be applied to all crimes, regardless of the specific elements contained in some crimes. With regard to the crime of genocide, case law supports the applicability of the command responsibility doctrine in relation to this crime. For convincing reasons this application is seriously criticised, most importantly because the nature of the crime of genocide and the required elements of command responsibility can only be joined with difficulty. The application of command responsibility in relation to aggression is only a theoretical option and having regard to the development of a definition of aggression for the purposes of the ICC, application will most likely remain a theoretical exercise. With regard to crimes not qualifying as international crimes, but resembling international crimes because of their place in the statutes of internationalised tribunals, the applicability of the command responsibility doctrine seems to be accepted. Where crimes resemble international crimes because of the conflict situation in which the crimes take place, the forum for applying the doctrine is a national court. Whereas command responsibility could be the logical consequence of crimes committed by soldiers during, for instance, a peacekeeping mission, the fact that the command responsibility doctrine extends criminal liability to a commander for his omission to an unacceptable degree is not acceptable to domestic criminal law.

Chapter 6

Synthesis – Justified differentiation between military and civilian superiors?

6.1 Introduction

This study has presented aspects of the command responsibility doctrine that are essential to the present and future application of the doctrine but that have received less attention than they merit in the otherwise rich legal literature on the topic. The aim of the author has been to grasp the essence of the concept by putting it in its evolutionary perspective, without gearing attention exclusively on the authority of the existing case law. The research has focussed on the question which approach should be taken when applying command responsibility to civilian superiors. Another central question was whether a differentiation between military and civilian superiors is justified when applying the command responsibility doctrine.

Chapters 2 and 3 of this book elaborated on the legal basis for the principle of command responsibility and the origin of the concept of command responsibility in the military context. Chapters 4 and 5 addressed the application of the principle, in particular to civilians and to the contentious issues still hampering the consistent use of the command responsibility principle at the international level. What remains in this chapter is to elaborate on the question whether a differentiation between civilian and military superiors offers a solution to the application of the command responsibility principle in practice. Accordingly, does the command responsibility principle need an explicit distinction between military and civilian superiors, or is the distinction rather an academic or artificial one? Having discussed arguments in favour of and against an explicit distinction between civilian superiors and military commanders, and the consequences thereof, the concluding chapter finally addresses selected issues of interest to the application of the command responsibility doctrine in the future, expressing the views of the present author.

6.2 Justified differentiation between military and civilian superiors?

6.2.1 The ICC provision and the *ad hoc* tribunal case law differentiation

The main thesis/underlying message of this study is that when applying the command responsibility doctrine, the origin and purpose of the concept should be kept in mind. This approach is of specific importance when considering the applicability of command responsibility to civilian superiors, as discussed in detail in Chapter 4. A question that was left open in Chapter 4 was whether an explicit differentiation between civilian and military superiors in the codified provisions of the doctrine, as most significantly exemplified by Article 28 ICC, should be considered justified. Despite the meagre result in cases where command responsibility has been applied to civilian superiors by the *ad hoc* tribunals,[1] these tribunals, in accordance with their statutes, did not find a reason to differentiate between civilian and military superiors by way of developing separate elements for the two groups of superiors.

While the *ad hoc* tribunals have realised the practical differences between civilian and military superiors and the complications these add to the applicability of command responsibility, they did not need an explicit provision to point out the distinction. The explicit division of superiors into two categories in Article 28 ICC focuses on the need for two different knowledge requirements when command responsibility is applied either to military commanders or to civilian superiors. Such an explicit provision aims at creating a higher standard of proof when the superior is a civilian. While a higher standard could arguably be a necessary measure to diminish the possibilities of convicting civilian superiors under the command responsibility doctrine, this measure emphasises an aspect of the doctrine which will not contribute, at least not on its own, to a more coherent application of the doctrine. A consistent and justified application of the command responsibility principle at the international level is dependent on several factors, among which is the realisation of the object and purpose of the principle.

As many other provisions in the Rome Statute, the command responsibility provision was the result of a compromise. The distinction between military commanders and so-called other superiors in Article 28 ICC came about as a result of a desire expressed by the United States that there should be a higher level of proof for the prosecution of civilian superiors for crimes under the jurisdiction of the ICC.[2] The treaty entered into force some years later, but before the negotiations on Article 28, no judgement had been rendered at the international level on charges of command responsibility since the post-WW II period. Accordingly, prior to Article 28 ICC, a differentiation between military and civilian superiors had not been of practical importance.[3] Of course, what had been recognised was the applicability, in theory, of the command responsibility principle to both civilian and military superiors. In fact, it was the United States that, after the adoption of Security Council Resolution 827, expressed the understanding that the principle was to be understood as being applicable to superiors, both civilian and military.[4]

---

[1] See Chapter 4 *supra*.

[2] Ambos 2002, 'Superior Responsibility', p. 848.

[3] See section 2.2.2 *supra*.

[4] See *Security Council Provisional Verbatim Record of the Three Thousand Two Hundred and Seventeenth Meeting*, UN Doc. S/PV. 3217, 25 May 1993, p. 16. See also *Čelebići*, TC Judgement, para. 356.

Although the *ad hoc* tribunals had not had an opportunity to decide command responsibility cases before the adoption of Article 28 ICC, they were aware of the existence of separate elements for civilian superiors in the ICC provision when deciding their first cases. In the *Čelebići* case the Defence pointed out that there is a distinction between civilian and military superiors and that this form of criminal liability should not be applied to civilian superiors.[5] The applicability of the command responsibility doctrine to civilian superiors was confirmed by the Trial Chamber, however, and the three elements that according to the Chamber needed to be proven for the superior to be held liable, were applicable to all superiors alike.[6] In the same case, the Appeals Chamber held that

> 'Civilian superiors undoubtedly bear responsibility for subordinate offences under certain conditions, but whether their responsibility contains identical elements to that of military commanders in not clear in customary law.'[7]

If we accept that the question of identical elements for military and civilian superiors is not settled in customary law, is the differentiation in Article 28 ICC to be considered useful or even justified?

a) Arguments in favour of a differentiation

Let us first consider the arguments supporting the Article 28 ICC differentiation. This study has shown that there is a fundamental distinction between military commanders and civilians. It is inherent in the profession of a commander that they have to exercise 'general command responsibility' over their subordinates and that along with this duty comes another duty, that of ensuring that the conduct of hostilities is in accordance with existing rules and regulations. In complete agreement with the purpose of having the distinction between civilians and those who take part in hostilities, most civilians are not in a position to exercise general command responsibility over their subordinates. Accordingly, their relationship with their subordinates is a significantly different one.[8] Considering this fact and the possibility that civilian superiors, despite the different position they are in, could be charged under the command responsibility doctrine, it is understandable that states agreed to separate elements for civilian superiors and, in particular, accepted a higher *mens rea* standard for civilian superiors. Civilians should not necessarily have the same duty to know about the acts of others as the military commander whose hierarchical military organisation enables the commander to acquire knowledge.[9] Looking at the higher *mens rea* standard from the

---

[5] *Čelebići*, TC Judgement, para. 352.

[6] Ibid., para. 354.

[7] *Čelebići*, AC Judgement, para. 240.

[8] See the discussion in Chapters 3 and 4 *supra*.

[9] H.G. van der Wilt, 'The Duty to Know. Enkele beschouwingen over het leerstuk van command responsibility', in G.J.M. Corstens and M.S. Groenhuijsen, eds., *Rede en Recht – Opstellen ter gelegenheid van het afscheid van Prof. mr. N. Keijzer van de Katholieke Universiteit Brabant* (Deventer, Gouda Quint 2000) pp. 123-135, at p. 133.

perspective of criminal law, support for the differentiation can be found in the argument that liability for omissions should be introduced and handled with great care. The duties of the military commander have a firm basis in military tradition and in law, which makes it easier to justify criminal liability for their omissions than for the omissions of civilian superiors. Although there might be a desire to attain doctrinal consistency, the caution needed in cases concerning criminal liability for omissions should arguably take precedence.[10] In *Kayishema*, the Trial Chamber supported this view. It held as follows:

> 'On this issue, the Chamber finds the distinction between military commanders and other superiors embodied in the Rome Statute an instructive one. In the case of the former it imposes a more active duty upon the superior to inform himself of the activities of his subordinates when he, "knew or, owing to the circumstances at the time, should have known that the forces were committing or about to commit such crimes." This is juxtaposed with the *mens rea* element demanded of all other superiors who must have, "[known], or consciously disregarded information which clearly indicated, that the subordinates were committing or about to commit such crimes."
>
> The Trial Chamber agrees with this view insofar that it does not demand a *prima facie* duty upon a non-military commander to be seized of every activity of all persons under his or her control. In light of the objective of Article 6(3) which is to ascertain the individual criminal responsibility for crimes as serious as genocide, crimes against humanity and violations of Common Article 3 to the Geneva Conventions and Additional Protocol II thereto, the Chamber finds that the Prosecution must prove that the accused in this case either knew, or consciously disregarded information which clearly indicated or put him on notice that his subordinates had committed, or were about to commit acts in breach of Articles 2 to 4 of this Tribunal's Statute.'[11]

While the differentiation was not explicitly set out in the elements, the ICTR here required the higher *mens rea* standard as set out in Article 28 ICC. It may be argued that the idea of establishing a higher *mens rea* requirement for civilians superior and, thus, a differentiation between civilian and military superiors, is understood and supported by other international tribunals.

b) Arguments against a differentiation

The desirability of having separate elements for civilian and military superiors has not met with consensus among legal scholars. The thesis of Vetter was that:

> '[T]he civilian command responsibility standard codified in article 28(2) of the ICC Statute reduces the efficacy of the permanent international criminal court. This argument rests on the premise that the new civilian standard is less strict than the ICC military standard and perhaps less strict than the prior law of command responsibility as applied to civilians. It also rests on the presumption that individual accountability

[10] H.G. van der Wilt, 'Elies van Sliedregt, The Criminal Responsibility of Individuals for Violations of International Humanitarian Law, diss.', 167 *Rechtsgeleerd Magazijn Themis* (2006) pp. 19-23, at p. 23.

[11] *Kayishema and Ruzindana*, TC Judgement, paras. 227-228.

in the ICC will help deter human rights abuses and that a less strict standard allows a civilian superior to either exercise less diligence in controlling subordinates, or have less fear of being convicted when intentionally allowing or encouraging subordinates to commit human rights abuses.'[12]

Vetter's rejection of two separate standards is based on the expected consequence that the provision will have. The threshold for the prosecution to prove the *mens rea* element of the civilian superior will be higher, which will lead to fewer civilian superiors being convicted or to a lesser deterrent effect on civilian leaders. The concern may be valid, but in the opinion of the present author, the reasoning is not sufficient to abolish the separate standards. The efficacy of the ICC, i.e., the ability of the Court to produce the desired results – according to Vetter the deterrence and accountability of civilian superiors – cannot be more valuable than a fair standard to which the civilian superior is held criminally responsible.

Also Van Sliedregt expressed her regret at the differentiation between civilian and military superiors, in particular through the distinct knowledge requirement, but her criticism was based on the premise that the difference between civilian and military superiors lies in the scope of their duty to know. Where this difference in scope is acknowledged by the judges, the same knowledge formula can be applied. This approach leaves the decision regarding the scope of the superior's duty to know to the judges. The more limited scope of the civilian superior's duty to know will be established on a case by case basis, but where it has been established that that particular civilian superior had the duty to know, the civilian will be held to the same knowledge standard as the military superior. As such, there is nothing new to this approach, as the *ad hoc* tribunals have had to apply the same knowledge standard to both categories of superiors. The previous section showed that there are also convincing arguments as to why the starting point should be that civilian superiors have a more limited duty to know or acquire information and that this is best expressed by applying different knowledge standards to the two categories of superiors.

Although there are well elaborated reasons as to why there should or should not be a differentiation between civilian and military superiors in the command responsibility provision, focussing on the issue of whether the *mens rea* of all superiors should be the same will make it difficult to decide whether the arguments against a differentiation in Article 28 ICC are outweighed by arguments in favour of the separate elements. The central issue is another one. The formulation of Article 28 ICC in its present form created the idea that it might, indeed, be more accurate to require a higher *mens rea* standard for civilian superiors. Concentrating on the differentiation in Article 28 ICC, however, the discussion has laid the focus of the whole command responsibility debate on the issue of whether civilian superiors should be tried subject to conditions that are different from those for military colleagues, and whether they should be tried under the command responsibility doctrine in the first place, instead of focusing on the object and purpose of the command responsibility doctrine. Considering what

[12] Vetter, pp. 89-141, at p. 103.

should be achieved by applying the existing command responsibility provisions will provide a more convincing answer as to the necessity of the differentiation between civilian and military superiors in the legal provision. The next section will discuss the 'traditional ambit' of command responsibility, a discussion which encompasses the object and purpose of command responsibility.

6.2.2 The 'traditional ambit' of command responsibility

In Chapter 5 of this book, reference was made to the 'traditional ambit' of the command responsibility principle. This term was used by Ambos in the context of the overlap between JCE and command responsibility.[13] Ambos discussed the fact that a JCE conviction has prevailed in cases where the elements of command responsibility have also been fulfilled and that JCE thereby invades the 'traditional ambit' of command responsibility. But what exactly is the 'traditional ambit' of command responsibility? In Ambos' article the concept of this 'traditional ambit' seems simply to represent those cases where the elements of command responsibility have been fulfilled, or in other words, the cases in which the command responsibility doctrine could be applied. In the opinion of the present author, it may be very useful to refer to the 'traditional ambit' of command responsibility when discussing the doctrine, but with the understanding that the phrase refers to a specific type of case, the traditional case, to which the command responsibility doctrine has been applied. Knowing the 'traditional ambit' as just explained could give a framework to the application of the command responsibility doctrine.

Chapter 3 of this book analyses command responsibility and its origin as a military concept, but if we take international case law as a starting point for defining the traditional ambit of command criminal responsibility, the result will be disappointing. In the opinion of this author, there is no such thing. From the first judgements onwards, the overlap between individual and command responsibility has caused confusion and the challenge has been to actually find the ambit of what is best described as 'belonging' to command responsibility.

It is suggested here that the solution to the overlap between certain modes of liability and command responsibility can only be offered if the 'traditional ambit' of command responsibility is defined. This issue is completely separate from the question so often discussed as to whether the aim of holding high military and political leaders responsible for international crimes can be reached by using either JCE or command responsibility or some other mode of participation. The following finding by Van Sliedregt clarifies the issue:

> 'Accordingly, superior responsibility is not the most appropriate concept to prosecute or even convict military and political superiors. This has already been recognised at the ICTY where joint criminal enterprise has become its alternate. The application of

[13] Ambos 2007, 'Joint Criminal Enterprise', p. 159.

the latter concept is welcomed, if only to *allow superior responsibility to have its own place in war crimes law.*'[14]

The key here is to 'find the traditional ambit of command responsibility', which could mean the same as to 'allow superior responsibility to have its own place in war crimes law'.

The aspects of the command responsibility doctrine analysed in Chapters 3, 4 and 5 together provide the necessary directions for forming an opinion and drawing some conclusions on the kinds of situations and cases that the doctrine best applies to or should apply to.

The conclusion in Chapter 3 was that the military concept of command responsibility and the doctrine as applied in international criminal law have to be compatible if the command responsibility doctrine is to serve the purposes of international criminal law, in particular accountability and deterrence. Based on the findings in Chapter 3, it was concluded that military commanders will only take the doctrine seriously if it is felt that the provision allows for the effective and efficient conduct of war. For the purposes of discovering the 'traditional ambit' of command responsibility, this means that charges and convictions on the basis of the command responsibility provision should take the reality of military commanders in warfare into account. Accordingly, the principle should be more closely associated with situations and relationships to which the 'general command responsibility', as mentioned in Chapter 3, applies. Case law from the *ad hoc* tribunals provides some, but in fact a limited number of examples of cases which take the compatibility issue mentioned in Chapter 3 into account.[15] Of interest in this respect is the *Hadžihasanović* case, which has been regularly mentioned in the previous chapters. This is a case of 'pure' command responsibility, i.e., a case where only charges under Article 7(3) were brought against the accused.[16]

In this context it is of interest to consider the facts of this case and the role of the accused. The fact that in the *Hadžihasanović* case, both Hadžihasanović himself and his co-accused Kubura were military commanders who were not even charged under Article 7(1), resulted in both the Trial and the Appeal judgement focussing primarily on whether the accused fulfilled the elements of command responsibility, instead of concentrating on the weight of the active and passive role of the superiors, as has been the impression created in cases containing charges under both Article 7(1) and 7(3). In particular the Appeal Judgement is commendable in that it puts the elements of command responsibility, while already weighed by the Trial Chamber, to an additional test. The Appeals Chamber clearly took the reality of the military commander into account in its deliberations. In the grounds of appeal raised by Hadžihasanović each of the three elements of the doctrine were present and crucial to the findings. With regard to the murder and cruel treatment committed by the *El Mujahedin* detachment, the

[14] Van Sliedregt 2003, p. 359.

[15] See, for example, *Strugar*, TC Judgement, para. 355.

[16] Bonafé, pp. 616-617.

Appeals Chamber considered the first element (the superior-subordinate relationship) between the accused and the perpetrators and contrary to the findings of the Trial Chamber, the Appeals Chamber did not find the relationship to be one of subordination. It found that the only way of control was by attacking the *El Mujahedin* detachment 'as if they were a distinct enemy force.'[17] That the findings differed from those of the Trial Chamber does of course not provide a sufficient reason to say that the Trial Chamber did not take the reality of the commander into consideration; it simply shows the intricacies of the circumstances under which the military commander acts. These were brought more to the forefront by the Appeals Chamber.

As to the second element (the knowledge requirement), the Appeals Chamber considered that the fact that the accused knew of mistreatment at a certain location did not constitute sufficient evidence to say that he also had the requisite *mens rea* for mistreatment that took place later in time at another location. The geographic proximity of the locations was also insufficient proof of the *mens rea* of the accused.[18] The Appeals Chamber here implicitly stressed the importance of the personal liability of the commander.

The Appeals Chamber also put the third element (necessary and reasonable measures to prevent or punish) to the test when it reversed the Trial Chamber's finding, according to which the accused did not take sufficient measures to punish his subordinates for one murder and cruel treatment. According to the Appeals Chamber, the accused could not be held responsible, as he had identified, arrested and imprisoned the perpetrators. They were brought before a military disciplinary organ and the crimes were reported to the municipal public prosecutor. While admittedly the crimes could have been reported to a more appropriate authority, in the opinion of the Appeals Chamber the accused had taken the necessary and reasonable measures to punish the perpetrators, considering the circumstances prevailing at the time.[19] As has been shown by these findings on the separate elements, the Appeals Chamber clearly put emphasis on the factual circumstances in which the commander operated. It should be noted, however, that the Appeals Chamber confirmed the conviction of the accused in relation to other crimes.

On the basis of the facts of the case and the role played by the accused, as exemplified through the above discussion on findings relating to the elements, the *Hadžihasanović* case seems like a case that would typically be decided on the basis of the command responsibility doctrine. From the perspective of the origin of the doctrine in a military concept, this case could be one that exemplifies the typical command responsibility case that respects the realities of warfare when applying the criminal law doctrine of command responsibility.

The question is if the traditional ambit can be discerned by using case law which has convicted superiors under the command responsibility principle only, can the traditional ambit or the object and purpose of the command responsibility principle be considered to encompass civilian superiors? Chapter 4 concluded

[17] *Hadžihasanović*, AC Judgement, para. 230. See also ibid., para. 231.

[18] Ibid., paras. 161-163.

[19] Ibid., paras. 149-155.

with the finding that in practice the elements of command responsibility have been very difficult to establish where the accused was a civilian leader. Nevertheless, it is undisputed that the command responsibility doctrine in international law allows for command responsibility as a basis for criminal liability in relation to superiors other than those qualifying as military commanders. In the opinion of this author, the application of the doctrine in relation to civilian superiors should be done in the spirit of the following findings by the ILC in its commentaries to the Draft Code of Crimes against the Peace and Security of Mankind:

> 'The reference to "his superiors" [in Article 6 of the Draft Code] indicates that this principle applies *not only to the immediate superior of a subordinate, but also to his other superiors in the military chain of command or the governmental hierarchy if the necessary criteria are met.* The reference to "superiors" is sufficiently broad to cover military commanders or other civilian authorities who are in a similar position of command and exercise a similar degree of control with respect to their subordinates.'[20]

At first glance, the ILC Draft Code contains nothing that has not been discussed before. The ILC recognises the applicability of the doctrine to civilian superiors. But, in fact, what the ILC does is to discuss the applicability of the doctrine in the context of the crimes. The commentary points out that where crimes have been committed the doctrine is not limited to the immediate superior of the perpetrator. Higher superiors may also incur responsibility, where it can be shown that the perpetration of the crimes by the subordinates and the omission by the immediate superior should have been known to the higher superior and he, too, omitted to prevent or punish either the immediate superior or the perpetrators or both, as the case may be. This approach is logical in that it ensures accountability also at the higher levels and in that it is in accordance with the hierarchical structure of the armed forces and their relationship to the highest political officials of the state. What should not be read into this recognition of the applicability of the doctrine to civilian superiors is that it, by definition, should apply to civilians and that, therefore, it is necessary to provide for a separate category of superiors, as was done in Article 28 ICC.

Adherence to this approach means ruling out cases like *Musema* and *Nahimana, Barayagwiza and Ngeze* from the traditional ambit of command responsibility, as the above reasoning does not apply to them. Could the criterion 'who are in a similar position of command and exercise a similar degree of control' encompass these superiors? No. This criterion should be exclusively reserved for superiors who were 'part of a *prima facie* legitimate quasi-martial organization, such as a prison-camp, or in control of a militia-like unit with a *prima facie* legitimate role, such as a police force.'[21] These groups of superiors, while not belonging to the armed forces, are subjected to a military-like hierarchy, with

---

[20] Draft Code of Crimes Against the Peace and Security of Mankind, UN GAOR, 51st Sess., Supp. No. 10, UN Doc. A/51/10 (1996), p. 26.

[21] A. Zahar and G. Sluiter, *International Criminal Law – A Critical Introduction* (Oxford, Oxford University Press 2008) p. 271.

similar duties and responsibilities. Whereas these superiors are called civilians, the superior-subordinate relationships in which they act are not typically civilian. Rather, they are non-military superiors because their organisation does not form part of the armed forces. With the changing character of armed conflicts and parties to an armed conflict, the role of these persons 'effectively acting as a military commander'[22] is increasingly important.

In order to fall within the traditional ambit of the command responsibility doctrine, cases brought against civilians should concern superiors who, except for an official position as a military commander, should have the characteristics of a military commander.[23] Referring to the requirements of the legal notion of effective control as set out in the *Čelebići* case, Zahar and Sluiter said the following:

> 'While this proposition does not distinguish between military and non-military superiors, it incorporates the principle that the position of the latter will in practice have to be very similar to that of the former. Several attempts by defence teams to help the ICTY/ICTR Appeals Chamber to see the point have not removed the intellectual blind spot.'[24]

The lack of realisation that in practice the civilian superior and the military commander charged should be rather similar may perhaps be referred to as an intellectual blind spot on the part of the judges. It could also be held that so far the right focus – on the origin and purpose of the command responsibility doctrine – has been lacking.

Discovering the traditional ambit of command responsibility, the fact that some cases are being charged under both the command responsibility provision and under modes of liability such as JCE or aiding and abetting cannot be ignored. The possible overlap between individual criminal responsibility and command responsibility was discussed in Chapter 5, and the conclusion was that unless a conscious choice is made in favour of command responsibility, both at the indictment stage and at the stage of convicting the accused, the liability will almost without exception be based on JCE. However, to think that where available, the prosecutor would not try to apply JCE or aiding and abetting, is not realistic because of their evidentiary advantages.[25] Stopping the invasion by JCE of all cases of command responsibility will, therefore, depend on the understanding by the judges of the necessity of finding the traditional ambit of command responsibility or, in other words, the essence of the principle. On the other hand, having regard to the *Hadžihasanović* case, as an example of a case which definitely falls within the traditional ambit of command responsibility, consideration should be given to the question whether typical cases of command responsibility encompass cases that *prima facie* give the impression of a superior whose contribution to the commission of the crimes was more substantial than the role of the

[22] Art. 28 ICC.
[23] In other words, without calling it a duck, it should walk like a duck and swim like a duck and quack like a duck.
[24] Zahar and Sluiter, p. 265.
[25] Bonafé, p. 615.

superior under the command responsibility doctrine, and thereby justifies that the superior is charged with individual criminal responsibility. A fundamental element of the command responsibility doctrine is the omission by the superior. At most the omission is combined with a higher *mens rea* than mere negligence – aggravated command responsibility, but the omission will not necessarily be of substantial effect to the commission of the crimes. Where the evidence at the indictment stage shows that the involvement of the superior in the events was more important than the pure failure to prevent or punish the perpetrators, the case should at least not be considered as a typical case of command responsibility. It is conceivable that in some cases charges on the basis of both individual and command responsibility are justified in relation to separate facts or events. In the opinion of this author, however, alarm bells should be ringing where the superior was also actively involved in the events resulting in the commission of international crimes, as the basis for command responsibility charges falls apart where the superior is clearly involved in violations of IHL. Even where the charges concern separate events, the argument that the superior was simply negligent or reckless in relation to some crimes committed by his subordinates, while on another occasion he planned, ordered or aided the commission of other crimes, is not a credible one. The key issue as regards the typical case of command responsibility is the attitude of the superior towards the conflict.[26] Did he generally conduct hostilities to the best of his knowledge and ability under the orders of his superiors or did he act with the understanding that in reaching the higher goal of his superiors, violations of IHL were an inherent part of the acts?

The discussion in Chapter 5 concerning the applicability of the command responsibility doctrine to cases involving the crime of aggression or the crime of genocide is of importance to the discussion on the traditional ambit of the command responsibility doctrine. It was concluded that the application of command responsibility to the crime of aggression is a hypothetical exercise, necessitated by the incorporation of this crime into the ICC Statute, but without any real practical importance. Chapter 5 also presented arguments to the effect that the crime of genocide, in particular its requirement of special intent, is not easily combined with the requirements of the command responsibility doctrine. What remains for the typical case of command responsibility are cases concerning crimes against humanity and war crimes. While not elaborated in detail in the previous chapter, it was noted that the widespread and systematic character of crimes against humanity is shared, although not by definition, with the crime of genocide.[27] With regard to genocide, the fact that crimes are planned and committed on a very large scale makes it more difficult to believe that the role of the superior was limited to a failure to prevent or punish the perpetrators. This incompatibility between genocide and command responsibility is shared by crimes against humanity in relation to command responsibility. Cases concerning

---

[26] Here the use of the term attitude seems more suitable that using the term *mens rea*, as the attitude of the superior refers to his mindset in general, rather than his state of mind in relation to one specific crime or event.

[27] See section 5.4.2.3 *supra*. See also Schabas 2000, p. 10.

crimes against humanity should not be considered as typical cases of command responsibility, but the existing case law encompasses several cases of convictions on the basis of command responsibility in relation to crimes against humanity.[28] Most importantly, convictions on the basis of command responsibility in relation to crimes against humanity should concern incidents or violations of a more limited scope within the broader events that, taken together, are widespread and systematic, if the role and the attitude of the superior are to fit the requirements of command responsibility.

The most suitable cases to fall within the traditional ambit of command responsibility are those concerning war crimes.[29] While not necessarily less grave than crimes against humanity, the lack of the requirement of their widespread character is important. Where crimes were committed that were not necessarily part of a plan to carry out a series of atrocities, it is easier to think of possible situations where the role of the superior, his acts or omissions, did not have a substantive effect on the commission of the crime, but where he failed to prevent or punish the perpetrators in accordance with the requirements of the command responsibility doctrine.[30]

The consequence of the search for the 'traditional ambit' of the command responsibility doctrine would be a command responsibility principle which is more limited than it is presently assumed to be. The aim of the present section has not necessarily been to set such strict limits to the application of the doctrine, but to show that having established what could be the typical cases of command responsibility, any application of the doctrine to cases not falling within the 'traditional ambit' of command responsibility should be accompanied with the awareness that other cases are atypical to the command responsibility doctrine and, therefore, should be done with respect to the origin and purpose of the doctrine.

As an interesting note to this discussion, the sentencing trends by the *ad hoc* tribunals, as analysed by Judge Harhoff, may be mentioned, most importantly because they seem to offer support for the finding that the cases falling within the 'traditional ambit' of command responsibility and not high-level civilian leaders have found responsibility on the basis of this doctrine. Considering the sentences imposed, Harhoff found that while lower-level and higher-level accused tend to be given harsher sentences, more lenient sentences tend to be imposed on

[28] See, for example, the RUF case before the Special Court for Sierra Leone, *Prosecutor* v. *Issa Hassan Sesay, Morris Kallon and Augustine Gbao*, Judgement, Case No. SCSL-04-15-T, 25 February 2009, at IX. Disposition.

[29] War crimes are here the crimes set out in Art. 8 ICC, but could in general encompass at least Violations of Article 3 Common to the Geneva Conventions and of Additional Protocol II (Art. 2 ICTR), Grave breaches of the Geneva Conventions of 1949 (Art. 2 ICTY) and Violations of the laws or customs of war (Art. 3 ICTY).

[30] See *Prosecutor* v. *Pavle Strugar*, Judgement, Case No. IT-01-42-T, 31 January 2005, para. 456. Strugar was charged pursuant to both Art. 7(1) and Art. 7(3), but was only convicted on the basis of Art. 7(3). The accused was convicted in relation to 'devastation not justified by military necessity', 'unlawful attacks on civilian objects', and some other crimes constituting violations of the laws and customs of war, under Art. 3 ICTY. Ibid., paras. 477-479.

the accused at the middle level. The more lenient sentences are not errors in the sentencing policy, but a consequence of convictions under Article 7(3). Typically, the lower-level accused are direct perpetrators, whereas the middle-level accused are responsible military commanders or civilian superiors who pursued a plan or followed directions from the higher-level accused, who are either military commanders at the highest level or the highest civilian leaders. Lenient sentences tend to be imposed for Article 7(3) responsibility, which again corresponds to the sentences of the middle-level accused who neither physically committed nor planned the atrocities.[31]

6.3 Where does this leave the civilian superior?

The study shows that in practice the command responsibility doctrine does not lend itself particularly well for the prosecution of civilian superiors. Cases, and more importantly convictions, against civilian superiors are to be considered as exceptional. In order not to be heavily criticised for an unjust interpretation of the doctrine, there should be an additional argument, or the facts should be such that the case against this specific civilian superior is motivated, for example because the role of the civilian superior was similar to that of a military commander that it justifies charges under the command responsibility provision.

The fact remains that where atrocities are committed, more often than not those who did not physically commit the crimes but are seen as being responsible for them are civilians. If command responsibility is not the most suitable basis for holding these leaders criminally liable, what other options are there to ensure that they are held accountable? This section briefly discusses some alternatives to the command responsibility doctrine where civilian superiors are the accused in relation to international crimes.

The discussion regarding the best possibilities for dealing with system criminality through international criminal law, where the 'big fish' usually never physically commit crimes themselves, has been ongoing since the *Tadić* case and the advantages and disadvantages of the JCE doctrine are quite well-known.[32] With regard to civilian leaders, JCE I and II certainly offer more possibilities for the prosecution than the command responsibility doctrine in that they do not require the vertical superior-subordinate relationship between the accused and the perpetrators. As JCE III may show an overlap with command responsibility and at the same does not require a superior-subordinate relationship, this could, in theory, be a better alternative for civilian superiors. However, the general resistance towards JCE III, based on legality concerns, does not make this a practical alternative.

---

[31] F. Harhoff, 'Sense and Sensibility in Sentencing – Taking Stock of International Criminal Punishment', in O. Engdahl and P. Wrange, eds., *Law at War – The Law as it Was and the Law as it Should Be* (Leiden, Koninklijke Brill 2008) pp. 121-140, at pp. 135-137.

[32] JCE was discussed previously in this book, see section 5.3.2 *supra*.

Some of those who expressed their objection to the JCE doctrine sought an alternative to this doctrine in the traditional forms of complicity.[33] In particular aiding and abetting can serve as an alternative where the accused is a civilian superior.[34] Aiding and abetting requires that the act or omission had a substantive effect on the commission of the crime, and as a basis for liability this form of participation has resulted in quite harsh sentences of more than 10 years' imprisonment. The term aiding and abetting itself points out that this form of participation is not sufficiently representative of the responsibility of the 'big fish', often civilian superiors. An interesting option for prosecuting those most responsible is functional perpetration as applied under Dutch law.[35] Interestingly, the *Organisationsherrschaftslehre* known to German law has been offered as another mode of liability suitable for these purposes.[36] The doctrine is referred to as 'the control over the crime approach' and was interpreted by Pre-Trial Chamber I of the ICC as having been incorporated into the framework of the ICC Statute, in two of the cases pending before the court.[37] The main advantage of this approach is that the accused could be considered a principal to the crime, without having physically committed the crime. The Pre-Trial Chamber put it as follows:

> '[P]rincipals to the crime are not limited to those who physically carry out the objective elements of the offence, but also include those who, in spite of being removed from the scene of the crime, control or mastermind its commission because they decide whether and how the offence will be committed.'[38]

While no judgements have been rendered in these cases and, thus, no definite statement has been made by the ICC on this mode of liability, it may constitute one of the alternatives for successfully prosecuting civilian superiors, where they did not physically commit the crimes themselves. Of course, this approach was immediately criticised for not offering a good enough alternative to JCE. The criticism was mainly based on the argument that the German concept focuses too much on hierarchical top-down organisations, an approach which does not correspond to the realities of present-day armed conflicts.[39]

---

[33] Reference to this issue was made previously in this book, see section 5.3.2 *supra*.

[34] See section 5.3.3 *supra*.

[35] See section 5.2.3 *supra*.

[36] Ambos 2002, 'Superior Responsibility', p. 854. See also A. Singh, 'Criminal Responsibility for Non-State Civilian Superiors Lacking *De Jure* Authority: A Comparative Review of the Doctrine of Superior Responsibility and Parallel Doctrines in National Criminal Laws', 28 *Hastings International and Comparative Law Review* (2005) pp. 267-297, at pp. 294-297.

[37] *Prosecutor* v. *Germain Katanga and Mathieu Ngudjolo Chui*, Decision on the Confirmation of Charges, Case No. ICC-01/04-01/07-717, 30 September 2008, para. 501; and *Prosecutor* v. *Thomas Lubanga Dyilo*, Decision on the Confirmation of Charges, Case No. ICC-01/04-01/06-803-tEN, 29 January 2007, paras. 330 et seq.

[38] *Prosecutor* v. *Thomas Lubanga Dyilo*, Decision on the Confirmation of Charges, Case No. ICC-01/04-01/06-803-tEN, 29 January 2007, para. 330.

[39] M. Osiel, 'Perpetration by Hierarchical Organization', Guest Lecture Series of the Office of the Prosecutor of the ICC, The Hague, 22 April 2009.

That being said, what should not be lost sight of in this discussion is the core of the matter, the origin and the purpose of the command responsibility doctrine, as mentioned in the section on the 'traditional ambit' of the command responsibility doctrine. What has just been presented as alternatives to the command responsibility doctrine for the prosecution of civilian superiors in fact constitute the existing possibilities for finding those most responsible criminally liable under international criminal law. Strictly speaking, where an alternative to command responsibility is sought for civilian superiors, the focus should be on situations of pure omissions to prevent or repress by the civilian superior, as this is what the command responsibility doctrine is concerned with. The purpose of the command responsibility doctrine is not necessarily to provide for the liability of those 'most responsible'. In this regard, it is interesting to note that the drafting history of the Rome Statute contains a provision on *actus reus* in addition to the provision on *mens rea*, which is now Article 30 of the ICC Statute. This article on the *actus reus* never ended up in the final version of the Rome Statute, although it was included in the Zutphen Draft and the Decisions Taken by the Preparatory Committee at its Session held 11 to 21 February 1997. The provision was to regulate conduct that constituted either an act or an omission. At the drafting stage this provision included several optional versions in brackets, and removing some of the alternatives, one version could have read as follows:

> '[A] person may be criminally responsible and liable for punishment for an omission where the person has the ability, but intentionally or knowingly fails to avoid the result of an offence where: (a) The omission is specified in the definition of the crime under this Statute; or (b) In the circumstances, the result of the omission corresponds to the result of a crime committed by means of an act, and the person is either under a pre-existing obligation to avoid the result of such crime or creates a particular risk or danger that subsequently leads to the commission of such crime.'[40]

This provision, while one of many possible alternatives, is interesting in that it provides for criminal liability in relation to an omission, without being restricted by the history and purpose that any interpretation of the command responsibility doctrine carries with it. As was previously mentioned,[41] it is recognised in national criminal law that certain omissions may be criminal and, thus, the insertion of a provision on omissions would not have been groundbreaking. A provision similar to the ones suggested in the drafts to what became the Rome Statute would constitute a possibility to hold any accused, regardless of his civilian or military status, liable for an omission. Of course, it should be recognised that omissions both in national and in international criminal law constitute a cumbersome basis for criminal liability and should be applied with great care. In international courts the prosecution of omissions could create an additional diffi-

---

[40] M. Cherif Bassiouni, ed., *The Legislative History of the International Criminal Court*, Vol. 2: *An Article-by-Article Evolution of the Statute from 1994-1998* (Ardsley, Transnational Publishers 2005) pp. 195 and 199.

[41] See section 5.2.1 *supra*.

culty to the already existing problems of international trials.[42] The question is also whether the accused responsible for an omission would be considered important enough for trial by an international court. The importance of pointing to this draft article lies in the fact that whether prosecuted under this provision or on the basis of command responsibility, omissions constitute a specific type of conduct and should not be mistaken for or mixed up with the conduct of those who control or mastermind the commission of crimes behind the scene of the crime.

6.4 Future perspective on command responsibility

The application of the command responsibility doctrine to civilian superiors under international criminal law and in particular the explicit codification of the applicability of the doctrine to civilians in Article 28 ICC have led to the implementation in national legislation of command responsibility provisions similar to that contained in the ICC Statute. The existence of national legal provisions theoretically increases the possibilities of national prosecutions against civilian superiors for their failure to prevent or repress international crimes. It has even been suggested that by expanding the command responsibility provision under national law, the same principle could be applied to civilian superiors even in relation to other crimes than the atrocities covered by the ICC Statute.[43] Potentially, the existing legal basis and a positive attitude towards an extension of the doctrine to other crimes in the civilian sphere could lead to prosecutions in a number of states, even in states which have not recently been faced with mass atrocities but on which territory persons suspected of international crimes are presently living.

Whereas the application of the doctrine to civilian superiors is explicitly recognised in Article 28 ICC, the idea of an expansion to other crimes in the civilian sphere, unrelated to the armed conflict or the mass atrocities, does not correspond to the idea expressed in the ICC Statute, according to which arguably it should be more difficult to hold a civilian responsible under the command responsibility doctrine. An expansion seems to express the opposite view. Whereas it is recognised that in some circumstances a civilian exercises the same kind of authority over his subordinates as does a military superior, both the ICC Statute and the *ad hoc* tribunal jurisprudence express reluctance as to civilian superior responsibility. It was the reluctance of certain delegations at the Rome Conference to expand the superior responsibility principle that led to the stricter definition of the superior responsibility of civilians.[44]

At least at the international level, there is a great likelihood that this reluctance towards the command responsibility of civilian superiors will continue. The present author agrees with Bonafé, who found that:

[42] Danner and Martinez, p. 168.

[43] N. Keijzer and E. van Sliedregt, 'Collectieve aansprakelijkheid in het strafrecht', in M.S. Groenhuijsen and J.B.H.M. Simmelink, eds., *Glijdende schalen, Liber amicorum J. de Hullu* (Nijmegen, Wolf Legal Publishers 2003) p. 240.

[44] Ambos 2002, 'Superior Responsibility', p. 848.

> '[D]espite its very broad scope, command responsibility is successfully applied only in more traditional military-like contexts, where, it is easier to demonstrate command responsibility and guarantee a strict adherence to the principle of individual criminal responsibility at the same time.'[45]

Bonafé bases her conclusion on her calculation that of the approximately 100 accused before the *ad hoc* tribunals, and out of 54 prosecuted under the principle of command responsibility, only 10 persons were convicted on an Article 7(3)/6(3) basis.[46] The finding strengthens the position of the present author, which promotes a very limited applicability of the principle to civilian superiors, and the application of the command responsibility doctrine to military commanders and other military-like superiors with respect for the purpose of the doctrine only.

An issue for the future of command responsibility is the challenges posed by the changing means and methods of warfare. An illustration of this can be found in the warrants of arrest issued by the ICC, when taken as a whole. So far, no arrest warrant has included charges of command responsibility.[47] As mentioned previously in this book, the Pre-Trial Chamber in the *Bemba* case recently requested the amendment of the charges against the accused to include command responsibility.[48] This could partly be due to the changing perception of the doctrine and the realisation that only specific cases are suitable for command responsibility charges. Certainly the answer to why no such charges have been included is at least partly that the situations that are of concern to the ICC at the moment, have not emerged from the classic conflict between states, nor have the conflicts seen organised armed forces opposing each other in the traditional way. The atrocities have been committed in conflicts that are representative of modern warfare – mostly asymmetric and often carried out between armed groups that do not correspond to the organised armed forces as described in IHL.

---

[45] Bonafé, p. 602.

[46] Ibid. It should be noted that the article was published in 2007 and so does not include judgements rendered by the *ad hoc* tribunals since then. The cases rendered later do not considerably alter the balance between the number of accused, those charged on the basis of command responsibility and those actually convicted under this provision.

[47] *Prosecutor* v. *Jean Pierre Bemba Gombo*, Warrant of Arrest, Case No. ICC-01/05-01/08-1, 23 May 2008; *Prosecutor* v. *Thomas Lubanga Dyilo*, Warrant of Arrest, Case No. ICC-01/04-01/06-2, 10 February 2006; *Prosecutor* v. *Bosco Ntaganda*, Warrant of Arrest, Case No. ICC-01/04-02/06-2, 22 August 2006; *Prosecutor* v. *Germain Katanga*, Warrant of Arrest, Case No. ICC-01/04-01/07-1, 2 July 2007; *Prosecutor* v. *Mathieu Ngudjolo Chui*, Warrant of Arrest, Case No. ICC-01/04-01/07-260, 6 July 2007; *Prosecutor* v. *Joseph Kony*, Warrant of Arrest, Case No. ICC-02/04-01/05-53, 27 September 2005; *Prosecutor* v. *Vincent Otti*, Warrant of Arrest, Case No. ICC-02/04-01/05-54, 8 July 2005; *Prosecutor* v. *Okot Odhiambo*, Warrant of Arrest, Case No. ICC-02/04-01/05-56, 8 July 2005; *Prosecutor* v. *Dominic Ongwen*, Warrant of Arrest, Case No. ICC-02/04-01/05-57, 8 July 2005; *Prosecutor* v. *Ahmad Harun*, Warrant of Arrest, Case No. ICC-02/05-01/07-2, 27 April 2007; *Prosecutor* v. *Ali Kushayb*, Warrant of Arrest, Case No. ICC-02/05-01/07-3, 27 April 2007; *Prosecutor* v. *Omar Hassan Ahmad Al Bashir*, Warrant of Arrest, Case No. ICC-02/05-01/09-1, 4 March 2009; *Prosecutor* v. *Bahr Idriss Abu Garda*, Warrant of Arrest, Case No. ICC-02/05-01/05-2, 27 April 2007.

[48] See section 5.3.3.2 *supra*.

According to Schmitt, unfortunately 'most law applicable in today's conflicts was designed for yesterday's.'[49] The question is whether that can also be said of the command responsibility principle. Schmitt found that in asymmetrical warfare, the party with the technological advantage is not inclined to act in violation of IHL. However, the disadvantaged party to the conflict is likely to do so in order to ensure survival, first, and secondly, its victory over the advantaged party. Lacking the technology, the disadvantaged party will try to use all other means to attain victory, including unlawful ones.[50] This is where the applicability of the command responsibility principle to modern conflicts will be put to the test. Where the opposing party in modern asymmetric conflicts is a non-state actor, that party is more likely to have committed violations of IHL and, therefore, may at least theoretically face charges under international law. Lacking the hierarchy of state armed forces, the application of the command responsibility doctrine to these cases will prove difficult, as is shown by the ICC arrest warrants, mentioned above.

This, however, is of course not to say that military officers should not continue to be held accountable under the command responsibility doctrine under international law or under domestic law, as held by Schmitt.[51] Reactions to situations such as that in the Abu Ghraib prison facilities in Iraq in 2004, where prisoners were abused and humiliated and there was a failure to punish senior officers for these violations, could involve prosecutions under the command responsibility doctrine.[52]

Authors of legal writings who have a military background urge an understanding of the position of the military commander and of the circumstances in which they operate by the civilian jurists who act as prosecutors or judges in cases where international humanitarian law is applied. There is a concern that civilians who do not have 'in-depth knowledge of the operational art' fall short in this regard.[53] While these concerns have been expressed in relation to the application of various principles of the laws of war, they are certainly relevant for the discussion on the command responsibility doctrine, as well.[54] While the application of international humanitarian law rules and principles by international courts and tribunals may have given more reasons for concern during the last few

---

[49] M. Schmitt, '21st Century Conflict: Can the Law Survive?', 8 *Melbourne Journal of International Law* (2007) pp. 443-476, at p. 460.

[50] Ibid., p. 462.

[51] Ibid., p. 475.

[52] Knoops, pp. 781-783.

[53] M.L. Kramer and M.N. Schmitt, 'Lawyers on Horseback? Thoughts on Judge Advocates and Civil-Military Relations', 55 *UCLA Law Review* (2008) pp. 1407-1436, at p. 1435.

[54] T. Stein, 'Collateral Damage, Proportionality and Individual International Criminal Responsibility', in W. Heintschel von Heinegg and V. Epping, eds., *International Humanitarian Law Facing New Challenges: Symposium in Honour of Knut Ipsen* (Berlin, Springer 2007) pp. 157-161, p. 160. Discussing the assessment of proportionality by international tribunals, Stein held that the tribunal would 'have to put itself as best as it can in the position of the commander or soldier concerned, taking all the surrounding circumstances into account, so as to appraise the situation as experienced in real time, before considering the question of culpability. How many judges would be in a position to do that? Would any proper judgement demand that they had witnessed similar situations in place?' Ibid.

decades, the sentiments of military officers in relation to the command responsibility doctrine are not new and do not seem to have changed much over the past decades. Describing the situation in the 1980s, Eckhardt stated the following:

> 'Modern law of war is driven by an idealistic internationally minded community. The soldier sees his iron law of war sweetened, lawyerized, politicalized, third-world-ized, and made much less practical.'[55]

That any future application of the command responsibility doctrine should be more limited and correspond to the reality of the 'soldier' is preferable for several reasons was illustrated by Darcy who discussed the implications of imputed criminal liability on the goals of international criminal justice. Darcy stated the following:

> 'Convicting major figures on the basis of the more controversial aspects of joint criminal enterprise liability or superior responsibility could undermine the contribution of international judgements to the record of history.'[56]

If one of the goals of international criminal justice is to provide a historical record, the 'truth' about a certain period or event, the conviction of the 'big fish' only on the basis of a failure, not requiring intention on the part of the accused, could give reasons for those who doubted the guilt of the leader in the first place, to deny the role of this person in the atrocities and, ultimately, to deny the occurrence of the atrocities.[57]

Still considering the goals of international criminal justice, command responsibility charges against and the conviction of high-level accused could, for those who consider the accused their hero, have a lower level of psychological impact, as the direct involvement of the accused was not established. The psychological impact of a conviction of a specific leading actor for his personal involvement in the events could hopefully lead to the acceptance of the responsibility for the crimes of one or a few individuals and not of the entire ethnic or other group, and thereby serve one of the goals of international criminal justice - reconciliation.[58] Accordingly, the furtherance of the goals of international criminal justice is served by a command responsibility doctrine that does not focus on the top-level, often civilian, superiors.

Another aspect that will remain of importance in the future is the recognition of the distinction between the superior's, and more specifically the commander's, moral responsibility and criminal liability. The relevance of this distinction may be illustrated by a few examples. The first example is a situation which was described by Best and concerned the Pacific War. It is recognised that despite the strict discipline applied to the Japanese armed forces during the Pacific War,

---

[55] Eckhardt, p. 3.

[56] S. Darcy, 'Imputed Criminal Liability and the Goals of International Justice', 20 *LJIL* (2007) pp. 377-404, at p. 400.

[57] Ibid., pp. 400-401.

[58] Ibid., p. 397.

crimes, both war crimes and ordinary crimes, were committed. Crimes were ordered to be committed, but breaches were also being committed spontaneously.[59] The latter phenomenon is interesting in that the Japanese forces were very well disciplined, and nevertheless they committed more self-directed crimes than the German armed forces.[60] Several reasons have been found that could explain the difference in behaviour, but most interesting is the question that Best formulated as a consequence of these historical findings: '[W]ere commanders whose men did these things culpable for not having trained them better and for not having ordered them *not* to commit atrocities?'[61]

Best did not give an answer to the question that concerned the specific case of the Pacific War. He only stated that omissions to prevent were condemned in the subsequent *Yamashita* case, something that does not provide an answer to this question. What was being asked was whether commanders, despite the fact that their forces were well disciplined, were criminally responsible for inadequate training and for their failure to order their forces *not* to commit crimes.

There are two issues involved here. The first is whether duties falling under the commander's general command responsibility are part of command criminal responsibility. This issue is intertwined with the second one, which is the feeling that it should have been his responsibility. Case law from the ICTY reveals that there is no simple answer to the problem.

The criminal responsibility is based on the omission of the commander to prevent the crimes. However, when it comes to the stage that precedes the immediate, necessary and reasonable preventive measures, the international tribunals have encountered some difficulties. While the *Čelebići* Trial Chamber did away with the question by stating that an *in abstracto* definition of what measures have to be taken by a commander would not be meaningful,[62] Chambers in subsequent cases have felt a necessity to consider to what extent the commander's responsibility extends to the training of their subordinates.[63] The conclusion that has been drawn is that where a commander fails in the training of his subordinates, he does not fulfil his responsibilities as a commander, and he may be subjected to disciplinary sanctions. However, it is not possible to draw the conclusion that a failure of the commander to train or control his troops at an earlier stage leads to criminal command responsibility.[64] Nonetheless, the *Hadžihasanović* Trial Chamber underlined the importance of these measures of the commander by stating that the 'general measures', or in other words the fulfilment of his responsibilities as a commander, may be taken into consideration in the factual analysis of the case at hand.[65] At the same time, the Chamber pointed out that the fact that where the opposite is true, where the commander has taken all so-called general

[59] Best, p. 191.
[60] Ibid.
[61] Ibid.
[62] *Čelebići*, TC Judgement, paras. 394-395.
[63] *Halilović*, TC Judgement, paras. 81-88; and *Hadžihasanović*, TC Judgement, paras. 145-151.
[64] *Halilović*, AC Judgement, paras. 61-65.
[65] *Halilović*, TC Judgement, para. 88; and *Hadžihasanović*, TC Judgement, para. 151.

measures, but where crimes nevertheless occur, the commander cannot avoid criminal responsibility by referring to his fulfilment of the general measures. On the basis of the *Hadžihasanović* case it may be concluded that the failure to train soldiers in general does not fall under command criminal responsibility. Just as in the Pacific War example, this solution leaves an observer or the prosecutor with the feeling that although it might not be command criminal responsibility, the commander is in some other way responsible.

It is evident that the whole discussion, from that concerning the *Yamashita* case to the reasoning in the more recent case law, concerns the moral responsibility of the commander. It is felt that it should at least be the moral obligation of the commander to ensure the training of his subordinates in accordance with the laws of war. The problem is that the moral component of command responsibility, the moral obligation of a commander, should not be mistaken for command criminal responsibility, as this is likely to create confusion when applying the principle of command responsibility.

The next question is how to deal with the moral responsibility of the commander in a case concerning command responsibility. In the *Hadžihasanović* case, the Trial Chamber of the ICTY held that because the accused, Hadžihasanović, had trained his subordinates in the laws of war and had worked to enforce the rules of international humanitarian law, these 'general measures' should be considered in the evaluation of the mitigating circumstances.[66] Accordingly, the fact that the commander had in general fulfilled his duties as a commander meant that he had, except for the occasions when the relevant crimes were committed, acted in accordance with his general command responsibility. The Chamber considered that he should be given credit for this, although one should bear in mind that the *Blaškić* Trial Judgement pointed out that in respect of the criminal responsibility of an accused, the mitigating circumstances 'do not in any event mitigate the seriousness of the offence.'[67] Nevertheless, the Hadžihasanović Trial Chamber considered a reward appropriate for his generally speaking appropriate behaviour.

The basis for the reward is a moral consideration. There was nothing morally reprehensible about his behaviour in general. However, considering the characteristics of a moral rule as set out earlier,[68] the *Blaškić* reasoning is important to keep in mind. As pointed out earlier, compliance with a moral rule is a matter of course and not a matter of praise. The ICTY has usually considered a variety of personal circumstances in mitigation at the sentencing stage. Nevertheless, the reward by the Trial Chamber in the *Hadžihasanović* case does not do away with the reprehensibility of the acts which constituted the basis for the conviction of the commander under the command responsibility principle.

To sum up, the future of command responsibility should preferably be and is likely to be more sober and low key than its recent past. Despite the possibilities of increasing prosecution, also of civilian superiors, under national law, the

---

[66] *Hadžihasanović*, TC Judgement, paras. 151 and 2080.

[67] *Blaškić*, TC Judgement, para. 765.

[68] See Chapter 3 *supra*.

doctrine under international criminal law will be more focussed on the purpose of the doctrine, which will be of assistance when facing challenges to the doctrine, such as new methods and means of warfare. While not necessarily limited only to cases falling within the 'traditional ambit' of command responsibility, as discussed in the previous section, a doctrine which is less focussed on the leaders of atrocities could contribute to attaining the goals of international criminal justice. An important aspect of a successful future for the command responsibility doctrine is the understanding of the distinction between the moral and the criminal responsibility of the superior.[69]

6.5 Final observations

Is there a difference between military and civilian superiors? There certainly is. It is this difference which has complicated the practical application of a doctrine which in theory applies to all superiors subject to the condition that the required elements of the doctrine have been established. What this study has attempted to show is that case law and the voluminous literature on the subject of command responsibility provide us with well elaborated and convincing arguments on the various aspects of the doctrine, not least on the aspect of the applicability of the command responsibility doctrine to civilians. According to this author the missing link in the discussion between the various contentious aspects of the application of the doctrine is a focus on the origin of the doctrine and the possibilities of combining this with the criminal law doctrine as it is today.

The lack of focus could be attributed to the fact that the command responsibility doctrine can be viewed from at least three perspectives. Each of these perspectives has its own focus, which makes the common focus difficult to achieve. First, there is the more theoretical perspective of the international community, international law, and in particular human rights. The emphasis on these aspects actually brought the command responsibility doctrine where it is today. Of course, without the codification of the doctrine and the UN Security Council resolutions on the establishment of the *ad hoc* tribunals, the doctrine would not have developed into its present shape. This perspective sometimes seems to confuse moral responsibility with criminal liability and the purpose that the command responsibility doctrine serves/should serve. Looked at from this perspective, the most important goal of the codified provision is to ensure the accountability of those responsible for human rights abuses. The focus is on the desire for an appropriate reaction to human rights abuses through international law. Secondly, there is the more practical criminal law perspective. Viewed from this perspective, command responsibility is a provision laid down in statutes and conventions that has to be applied in a criminal court. The focus is on a fair and just process and the interpretation of the law. Thirdly, there is the perspective and the concern of the military and civilian actors in the field who have to act in accordance with the law.

[69] E. van Sliedregt, 'Criminal Responsibility in International Law – Liability Shaped by Policy Goals and Moral Outrage', 14 *EJIL* (2006) pp. 81-114, at pp. 103-104.

This is not so much about the deterrent effect of the doctrine on the acts of military commanders as about the practicality of international law/criminal law rules. If rules are meant to contribute to the conduct of warfare in accordance with IHL, they should be practical. A successful future development and application of the command responsibility doctrine can only be achieved if the importance of all three perspectives is acknowledged.

Annex I

Interview with Colonel Richard van Harskamp, The Hague, 22 October 2008

General command responsibility vs. command criminal responsibility

Command responsibility as criminal responsibility is clearly a consequence of responsible command or general command responsibility. Although IHL is not geared towards sanctioning, there is an expectation that commanders act in accordance with the rules. The ability to do that, to carry out your responsibility as a commander is something that is a part of you, or is not. In the latter case, you are not suitable as a commander. Inherent in your position as a commander is the fact that there are no guarantees. You can carry out your responsibilities to the best of your ability and still acts may occur which cause situations that you did not expect or desire. Here the distinction between the general command responsibility and the command criminal responsibility is clearly visible. Even in situations that were not planned or expected and caused by a subordinate on whatever level, the commander is responsible for what has happened, in the sense of his general command responsibility. This responsibility could be compared to Hart's role responsibility, and should not be confused with liability responsibility.[1]

A more difficult issue is the commander's guilt or liability in such cases. The command (criminal) responsibility principle is problematic because of the difficulty of establishing exactly at which level of the hierarchy liability should be found. A directly related question is which procedure should be used in order to establish possible blameworthy behaviour on the part of the commander. States seem to use different methods for the establishment of the responsibility when an incident has occurred. Some years ago, when a US soldier was filmed shooting a person who was lying on the ground,[2] the commander of that soldier's unit was immediately called back to the US. The process of finding out whether the commander had acted in accordance with the applicable rules and regulations followed. Such a procedure implicitly gives the impression of blameworthy behaviour on the part of the commander and requires that if the commander was not to be blamed, his good reputation will have to be restored. As such there is nothing wrong with this procedure, but it is questionable whether this procedure

[1] Hart 1968, pp. 210-222.

[2] Associated Press, 'TV Report Says Marine Shot Prisoner', published at NYTimes.com, 16 November 2004. Available at <http://www.nytimes.com/2004/11/16/international/middleeast/16marine.html?_r=1&scp=2&sq=fallujah%202004%20us%20kills%20unarmed&st=cse&oref=slogin> (accessed 15 July 2009).

is suitable for all cultural contexts. As a comparison, the Dutch investigation into the incident would directly concern the possibly wrongful act of the soldier. The commander's responsibility (role responsibility and liability responsibility) would only arise if wrongfulness on the part of the soldier was established. This example may serve to show two things; first, it proves the difficulty of establishing whether somewhere in the chain of command there was wrongful behaviour or whether the wrongfulness was on the part of the one 'who pulled the trigger'. Secondly, there seems to be a very thin line between the general command responsibility of the commander and his command criminal responsibility. Was the threat felt by the soldier understandable and his behaviour justifiable, or was his shooting a consequence of the commander's failure to supervise?

The deterrent effect of the command responsibility doctrine

From a commander's point of view, regardless of the command responsibility doctrine, you will always command from your heart. Of course, as a commander, you are supported and restricted by various rules and regulations. The way you carry out an assigned mission will depend on the Rules of Engagement and other established criteria as to when and how you can act. As a commander you should also be able to estimate which impact the three components (conceptual, mental and physical component) of your military ability will have on your task. So while having to take these things into account as a commander, your exercise of command cannot use a legal framework as your starting point. This would lead to a situation where your priority is the rules and your 'men' come second. Exercising command in this way is bound to be unsuccessful.

Based on this view, it seems that the command responsibility doctrine does not have a direct deterrent effect on the commander. From a commander's perspective, if the doctrine were to have a preventive effect it would need to be determined who at which level was to be held responsible in the event that something went wrong. As a commander, it seems strange that an accused (before an international tribunal) is charged and tried for his command responsibility before an investigation has shown at which level the responsibility lies. That means that responsibility could be found at each level of the hierarchy.

On the elements of command responsibility (superior-subordinate relationship; knowledge requirement; and necessary and reasonable measures to prevent or punish)

As mentioned earlier, it is inherent in the position of a commander that there are no guarantees, or in other words that regardless of the measures taken, there is always a possibility of some kind of violation, although the procedure when giving orders and keeping abreast of what is happening, as well as the authority to take the necessary and reasonable measures are geared towards the certainty of compliance with the rules.

Orders usually depend on two kinds of operations to be carried out – framework operations and specific operations (gerichte operaties). In the second case, the order is very specific, for instance: 'We are going to blow up that house'. There is little room for interpretation and input from a subordinate (commander). Concerning framework operations, the order is more general, for instance: 'Make sure that the area is secure', and the subordinate commander is expected to consider how the task should be carried out. Clearly, when such an order is given, there is a bigger chance that the commander who gave the order may not know the exact acts of those carrying out the order, despite a reporting procedure.

With regard to orders, a subordinate commander is asked to report back on the measures taken to carry out the order, the effect of the order, the means used etc. This is done at several points in time. To a larger extent than concerning specific operations, orders regarding framework operations are dependent on the mental capacities of the subordinate commander. Despite the reporting, it may be concluded that the commander at this level has to face more uncertainty as to the effect of the order.

Daily contact with subordinate commanders is to make sure that the commander is aware of possible violations that are to be committed or have been committed. A complicating factor in keeping informed is a situation where a violation has occurred, but there is agreement among subordinates that the violation will not be reported to the commander. Such a violation could be of a lesser character, not amounting to a criminal act, and concern the rules set up by the commander of that mission, but shows the possibility of the commander's lack of knowledge.

It is certainly true that a commander serves as an enabling factor, which means that most acts depend on the commander and that the authority of the commander makes the subordinates able to do what they are supposed to do (including killing).[3] To say that without a commander's order or knowledge, things would not happen, is one step too far. The phenomenon called 'strategic corporal effect', which means that at each level of the hierarchy someone may decide to take action on his own, should not be underestimated. It may be impossible for the commander to know of the sudden or planned acts of the individual soldier. The following could serve as an example: If a young man fulfils the requirements concerning education and physical and mental fitness, he will be accepted into the armed forces. The fact that his father is an immigrant and belongs to one of the tribes involved in a conflict to which the armed forces are sent on a mission, will probably not constitute a sufficient reason for not sending the young soldier on that mission, if the soldier is considered sufficiently trained for it. You cannot assume that the commander had knowledge that such a soldier would act in violation of the rules, but there is always a possibility of that 'strategic corporal effect'.

[3] This was discussed in section 3.2.6 *supra*.

With regard to the necessary and reasonable measures to prevent or punish a crime, the commander has far-reaching authority. In a situation where a crime is about to be committed by a subordinate, the commander may use force to prevent the subordinate from committing a crime. On the other hand, that authority is also an obligation of every serviceman. Even where someone holding a higher rank is about to commit a crime, the subordinate has an obligation to prevent him from doing so.

From a commander's point of view, it is clear that also a failure to punish violations may lead to criminal responsibility. In cases like that against Hadžihasanović (ICTY),[4] where the commander assumed command after the crimes had taken place, it should be the commander's obligation to take measures to punish the violators, if he found out that violations had occurred. Another example could be the events at My Lai, where the crimes were covered up. The commander (Capt. Medina)[5] should have been held criminally responsible for not taking any measures to prevent or punish the crimes.

COMMAND RESPONSIBILITY AND CIVILIAN SUPERIORS

As mentioned above, the responsibility of the commander for his men must be an integral part of you as a commander. In this regard, the relationship between a military commander and his subordinates may be unique. However, from a commander's perspective, the possibilities of taking the necessary and reasonable measures to prevent or punish violations in a conflict situation are not so different for a civilian superior than the possibilities of a military commander. Consider the following example: Where a mayor of a city under emergency law has the authority over the local police and possibly even paramilitary units, he can use his authority to order the police to put a stop to any violations taking place. If the police participate in the violations, the mayor, as any military commander, has the possibility of turning to his superiors for assistance. The same could apply to other civilian superiors. Where the superior did not take action, it could be justified to hold him criminally responsible on the same basis as the military commander who did not take the necessary and reasonable measures.

The same reasoning may be applied to military staff officers. While they do not have a position in the line of command, in case of a violation they have roughly the same possibilities to stop a violation and to refer the perpetrators to their superiors. It should not be forgotten that although staff officers do not have hierarchical superiority, they do have functional superiority.

[4] *Hadžihasanović*, Decision on Interlocutory Appeal Challenging Jurisdiction in Relation to Command Responsibility, paras. 37-57.

[5] See Friedman, Vol. I, pp. 1729-1737.

The effect of 'new warfare' on command responsibility

The effect of new forms of warfare may be considered as having an indirect effect on command responsibility. Consider the following example: A truck drives in the direction of a group of soldiers/a base at full speed. There may be several reasons for this. The sunset hinders the driver's visibility; the driver needs immediate help and approaches the soldiers etc. The instructions or procedure followed by the commander in such a situation, and more specifically the permission to shoot at the driver, is changing now that in some conflicts suicide bombing has become a method of warfare by some decentralised fighting organisations. While in traditional warfare the instructions may have been to consider the various reasons for the truck driving into the soldiers, the high risk of suicide bombings has forced the regular armed forces to reconsider their instructions. When is the decision by a soldier to shoot a reasonable measure as opposed to a violation, possibly leading to liability on the part of the commander as a consequence of his failure to prevent (supervise) the soldier?

An even more illustrative example of how new warfare may affect command responsibility is the case of the soldier who shot a person lying on the ground. Was the commander to be held liable for not properly instructing soldiers not to kill persons *hors de combat* (in the case of an enemy soldier) or can you not blame the commander for having instructed the soldiers always to take out the enemy in case of a suspected suicide bomber?

Marta Nybondas-Maarschalkerweerd
24 October 2008

Annex II

Interview with Major-General Patrick C. Cammaert, The Hague, 27 October 2008

General command responsibility vs. command criminal responsibility

As an illustration of the relationship between general command responsibility and command criminal responsibility, the example of a ship, a frigate that sails on the Pacific Ocean at night, may be used. The commander of the ship is sleeping in his cabin and the officer of the watch is on the bridge. At a certain moment the ship collides with a Japanese trawler, causing the death of several people on board the fishing vessel. The commander is responsible for the ship and all activities on board at all times, even where the authority to exercise command and control is temporarily transferred to a subordinate officer. An investigation into the event will look into the responsibility of the commander – using the terminology of Hart[1] – both his role responsibility and his liability responsibility. Also the responsibility of the officer of the watch will be the subject of the inquiries. While the commander bears overall responsibility, the question of his guilt is a different one. Where the officer of the watch had the required training and certificates to carry out the duties of that specific officer, but fell asleep while on duty, the commander of the ship will not be liable for the acts that occurred. Where the commander had allowed someone without the required training to carry out the tasks of an officer of the watch, the commander will be liable/held responsible, regardless of whether the officer of the watch fell asleep or not.

While the liability responsibility here is not strictly speaking the command responsibility as defined in international criminal law, from a commander's point of view this example shows the difference between general command responsibility and command criminal responsibility. The example shows that the commander can only delegate authority, not responsibility. The responsibility remains the same, but liability may be avoided where the commander has fulfilled his supervisory and other duties as a commander.

The distinction between general command responsibility and command criminal responsibility also becomes evident when considering the case of sexual exploitation and abuse by UN soldiers on a peace-mission in the Democratic Republic of Congo.[2] In an area two and a half times the territory of France, the commander of the UN mission was responsible for more than 15,000 troops of

[1] Hart 1968, pp. 210-222.

[2] 'UN soldiers arrested in DR Congo', BBC News, 13 February 2005, available at <http://news.bbc.co.uk/2/hi/africa/4262743.stm> (accessed 15 July 2009).

38 nationalities. While responsible for the acts of his men, the question has to be asked whether actual liability responsibility on the part of the commander arises when soldiers have sexually exploited Congolese women and girls. Of a commander of 15,000 men and women, it cannot be expected that he is aware of every act by every soldier. The hierarchical and even the physical distance between the commander and the perpetrator is too great. Commanders on a lower level are responsible for the supervision of, in this case, the soldiers committing the crimes. However, it will be considered whether the commander had not been negligent in his duties, allowing for a culture tolerating such behaviour to exist.

The same applies in a hypothetical example of soldiers on patrol, who bump into some Congolese and one of the soldiers opens fire. Two people die. No order to open fire had been given. The lieutenant will be asked how he had supervised his subordinates in order to see whether there was liability on his part. Of course, in such a case the liability of the superior/the commander, if there is any, is reduced the higher up in the ranks you go.

From a commander's point of view, when assessing the blameworthiness of the commander, two factors seem to increase the blame that can be attributed to him. First, was the event an incident? If so, there may have been very little that the commander could do about the behaviour of the subordinates at that specific moment. If the acts occur regularly, a good commander will come to know about them. By a firm reaction to the misbehaviour the commander will avoid liability responsibility. Where the acts take place regularly, the blameworthiness of the commander increases if his inaction proves to be a toleration of the behaviour. The guilt of the commander increases even further where the use of language shows that the commander approves of such behaviour. However, to say that where a high-level commander was negligent in not acting when informed of crimes or misbehaviour, he permitted such acts is going too far. Secondly, the commander is increasingly guilty when, using an example from the ICTR, the commander was present at the scene of the crimes and did nothing.[3] It is a commander's responsibility to ensure that subordinates are acting in accordance with the laws of war. His omission to prevent the crimes was a breach of this duty. Through his inaction he put the trust invested in him to shame. By permitting the acts he also made an escalation of the crimes possible. By acting he could also have prevented a further continuation of the crimes. In other words, his inaction was an abuse of power.

On the basis of the examples, it is clear that from a commander's point of view, the liability responsibility of a commander increases where the possibilities to act increase. It is not for a commander to say where the dividing line lies between command responsibility for an omission and individual criminal responsibility for permitting the crime.

[3] See, for example, *Ntagerura et al.*, TC Judgement and Sentence, para. 654. Imanishimwe was later acquitted by the Appeals Chamber under Art. 6(3) in relation to the Gashirabwoba massacre because the prosecution had failed to specify these charges in the Indictment. See *Ntagerura et al.*, AC Judgement, paras. 164-165.

THE DETERRENT EFFECT OF THE COMMAND RESPONSIBILITY DOCTRINE

As it never serves the interest of a commander to cause unnecessary suffering, a commander tries to avoid unnecessary violence being used or violations of the laws of war being caused, regardless of the existence or non-existence of provisions on criminal responsibility of the commander. In other words, the command responsibility doctrine does not change the way the commander exercises command and, thus, does not seem to have a deterrent effect.

ON THE ELEMENTS OF COMMAND RESPONSIBILITY (SUPERIOR-SUBORDINATE RELATIONSHIP; KNOWLEDGE REQUIREMENT; AND NECESSARY AND REASONABLE MEASURES TO PREVENT OR PUNISH)

The nature of the conflict, whether a war in which you defend your own country or a conflict in which you participate as part of a peacekeeping mission, does not seem to affect the relationship between the commander and his subordinates. A peacekeeping mission has the same effect on people and their behaviour. Based on experience with commanders of different nationalities, the way commanders view their general command responsibility seems universal. There are no differences worth mentioning.

At the level of a division commander, orders are given that inform subordinate commanders what is to be done, not how the order is to be carried out. Where a written order is given, the intention of the mission is stated in the order. 'In order to' is an expression frequently used in written orders, to clarify the intention of the order. It is the task of the subordinate to act in accordance with the spirit of the commander, 'to be in his mind'. The subordinate commander should be able to foresee what the commander 'two levels up' expects to be done.

With regard to information gathering, the commander has the possibility of being either reactive or proactive. The first method includes taking account of reports and other pieces of information that are being brought to your attention. The most effective way of keeping abreast of what is happening is acting proactively. As a commander you should keep your ear to the ground and try to find out what is happening by talking to various people. Listen and talk. The more experience you have, the easier it will be to hear and see things that are not being expressly spelled out. As a commander you should also try to create an atmosphere of trust in your unit. When subordinates trust their commander they will more easily confide in him. It will be easier for the commander to anticipate when things are developing in the wrong direction.

A 'golden triangle' in a unit consists of the commander, the doctor and the priest. Although both the doctor and the priest, and to some extent also the commander, are bound by professional confidentiality, a good relationship between the three persons is essential for a good unit. If these three people communicate and work well together, they know what is happening within their unit, which is of great support to the commander.

With regard to preventing crimes by subordinates, the most important measures include training, instructing and talking to your people. They should be aware of the code of conduct applicable to the situation. When instructing a subordinate commander does not lead to improved behaviour, sending him back home from a peacekeeping mission may be the only option. These measures have been taken and, thus, the example is not a hypothetical one. When it comes to preventing imminent crimes from occurring everyone, regardless of their rank, has the obligation to stop someone else from committing a crime. One may argue that a commander who fails to prevent a subordinate is bears a greater degree of guilt than a person who holds the same or a lower rank than the perpetrator and fails to prevent the violation.

Command responsibility and civilian superiors

From a commander's point of view, it seems that a civilian superior has more or less the same possibilities of taking measures to prevent or punish crimes as military commanders. For instance, a mayor can give orders to the police to prevent the commission of crimes. He also has the possibility to turn to his superiors, such as a governor or the president. Also a minister has power, even where the perpetrators are not his direct subordinates. That a minister of foreign affairs was tried by the IMTFE for not preventing or punishing crimes committed by the Japanese[4] is understandable, as you can expect that a person in his position should have acted. As a minister, you always have the option of resigning when you do not agree with the policy of the government. Admittedly, there is a certain difference between the civilian superior and the military commander, although both may have the possibilities to take measures to prevent crimes. Two things may be pointed out. First, the military commander always operates in situations of violence and misery, which has an effect on the subordinates of the commander and his relationship with them. Secondly, while the civilian superior may have access to law enforcement agencies, there is not the same command relationship between him and the commander of that agency as that between the military commander and his subordinates. For instance the mayor may instruct the military police to act, but is more dependent on the willingness of that commander to carry out his request, than the military commander would be when giving an order.

The effect of 'new warfare' on command responsibility

With regard to the changing character of armed conflicts, peacekeeping missions certainly constitute a more difficult kind of conflict. Three reasons may be men-

[4] See the case against Hirota, International Military Tribunal for the Far East (IMTFE), 29 April 1946–12 November 1948, The Tokyo War Crimes Trial (Tokyo Judgement), in Friedman, Vol. I, p. 1134.

tioned. First, in a traditional armed conflict, you knew who the enemy was. In present conflicts, you often do not know who the opponents are and what they look like. Secondly, peacekeeping missions are governed by more rules than the traditional war – Rules of Engagement etc. Finally, while the traditional armed conflict aimed at (simply stated) the destruction of the enemy, the aim of a peacekeeping mission is to attain peace. A commander in a peacekeeping mission constantly has to consider how much force is needed to stop the violence. The commander of a peacekeeping mission has to be proactive in this regard and balance more things in his mind, as he will be held accountable for the decisions he makes. At the stage of trying a commander under the command responsibility provision, these new requirements in relation to the decision-making process of the commander should be taken into account when considering whether he is criminally liable for violations committed by subordinates.

Maria Nybondas-Maarschalkerweerd
3 November 2008

BIBLIOGRAPHY

'Doctrine of Command Responsibility in U.S. Human Rights Cases', 96 *AJIL* (2002) pp. 719-723.

Interpretive Guidance on the Notion of Direct Participation in Hostilities under International Humanitarian Law (ICRC, Geneva 2009).

Leidraad Commandovoering, LD I (The Hague, Doctrinecommissie van de Koninklijke Landmacht 2000).

Militaire Doctrine, LDP I (The Hague, Doctrinecommissie van de Koninklijke Landmacht 1996).

Akhavan, P., 'The Crime of Genocide in the ICTR Jurisprudence', 3 *Journal of International Criminal Justice* (2005) pp. 989-1006.

Alford, S., 'Some Thoughts on the Trial of Saddam Hussein: The Realities of the Complementarity Principle', 8 *International Criminal Law Review* (2008) pp. 463-475.

Ambos, K., 'Joint Criminal Enterprise and Command Responsibility', 5 *Journal of International Criminal Justice* (2007) pp. 159-183.

Ambos, K., 'Remarks on the General Part of International Criminal Law', 4 *Journal of International Criminal Justice* (2006) pp. 660-673.

Ambos, K., *Der Allgemeine Teil des Völkerstrafrechts – Ansätze einer Dogmatisierung* (Berlin, Duncker & Humblot 2002).

Ambos, K., 'Superior Responsibility', in A. Cassese, P. Gaeta and J.R.W.D. Jones, eds., *The Rome Statute of the International Criminal Court: A Commentary*, Vol. I (Oxford, Oxford University Press 2002) pp. 823-872.

Ambos, K., 'General Principles of Criminal Law in the Rome Statute', 10 *Criminal Law Forum* (1999) pp. 1-32.

Ambos, K., 'Individual Criminal Responsibility – Article 25', in O. Triffterer, ed., *Commentary on the Rome Statute of the International Criminal Court – Observers' Notes, Article by Article* (Baden-Baden, Nomos 1999) pp. 475-492.

Ambrose, S.E., *Band of Brothers – E Company, 506th Regiment, 101st Airborne from Normandy to Hitler's Eagle's Nest* (New York, Simon & Schuster 2001).

Ashworth, A., *Principles of Criminal Law*, 5th edn. (Oxford, Oxford University Press 2006).

Bantekas, I., *Principles of Direct and Superior Responsibility in International Humanitarian Law* (Manchester, Manchester University Press 2002).

Bantekas, I., 'The Interests of States versus the Doctrine of Superior Responsibility', 82 *IRRC* (2000) pp. 391-401.

Bantekas, I., 'The Contemporary Law of Superior Responsibility', 93 *AJIL* 3 (1999) pp. 573-595.

Bassiouni, M. Cherif, *The Legislative History of the International Criminal Court*, Vol. 2: *An Article-by-Article Evolution of the Statute from 1994-1998* (Ardsley, Transnational Publishers 2005).

Best, G., *War and Law since 1945* (Oxford, Oxford University Press 1994).

Boister, N. and R. Cryer, eds., *Documents on the Tokyo International Military Tribunal – Charter, Indictment and Judgments* (Oxford, Oxford University Press 2008).

Bonafé, B.I., 'Finding a Proper Role for Command Responsibility', 5 *Journal of International Criminal Justice* (2007) pp. 599-618.

BORN, H., and D. VERWEIJ, 'Het hobbesiaanse karakter van zogeheten "nieuwe oorlogen"', 55 *Internationale Spectator* (2001) pp. 23-29.

BROWNLIE, I., *Principles of Public International Law*, 7th edn. (Oxford, Oxford University Press 2008).

CASSESE, A., 'The Proper Limits of Individual Responsibility under the Doctrine of Joint Criminal Enterprise', 5 *Journal of International Criminal Justice* (2007) pp. 109-133.

CASSESE, A., *International Law*, 2nd edn. (Oxford, Oxford University Press 2005).

CASSESE, A., *International Criminal Law* (Oxford, Oxford University Press 2003).

COOLEN, G.L., 'Eric O. en de slapende mariniers', in M.M. Dolman, P.D. Duyx and H.G. van der Wilt, eds., *Geleerde lessen. Liber amicorum Simon Stolwijk* (Nijmegen, Wolf Legal Publishers 2007) pp. 13-26.

COOLEN, G.L., *Militair straf- en strafprocesrecht*, 4th edn. (Deventer, Kluwer 2004).

CRYER, R., 'The Boundaries of Liability in International Criminal Law, or "Selectivity by Stealth"', 6 *Journal of Conflict and Security Law* (2001) pp. 3-31.

DAMAŠKA, M., 'The Shadow Side of Command Responsibility', 49 *American Journal of Comparative Law* (2001) pp. 455-496.

DANNER, A.M., and J.S. MARTINEZ, 'Guilty Associations: Joint Criminal Enterprise, Command Responsibility, and the Development of International Criminal Law', 93 *California Law Review* (2005) pp. 75-169.

DARCY, S., 'Imputed Criminal Liability and the Goals of International Justice', 20 *LJIL* (2007) pp. 377-404.

DE HULLU, J., *Materieel Strafrecht – Over algemene leerstukken van Strafrechtelijke aansprakelijkheid naar Nederlands recht* (Deventer, Gouda Quint 2000) pp. 478-483.

DEL PONTE, C., 'Prosecuting the Individuals Bearing the Highest Level of Responsibility', 2 *Journal of International Criminal Justice* (2004) pp. 516-519.

DUFF, R.A., *Answering for Crime – Responsibility and Liability in the Criminal Law* (Oxford, Hart Publishing 2007).

EBOE-OSUJI, C., '"Complicity in Genocide" versus "Aiding and Abetting Genocide" – Construing the Difference in the ICTR and ICTY Statutes', 3 *Journal of International Criminal Justice* (2005) pp. 56-81.

EBOE-OSUJI, C., 'Rape and Superior Responsibility: International Criminal Law in Need of Adjustment', Guest Lecture Series of the Office of the Prosecutor of the International Criminal Court, 20 June 2005, The Hague, available at <http://www.icc-cpi.int/library/organs/otp/050620_Chile_presentation.pdf> (accessed 15 July 2009).

ECKHARDT, W.G., 'Command Criminal Responsibility: A Plea for a Workable Standard', 97 *Military Law Review* (1982) pp. 1-33.

FENRICK, W.J., 'Article 28', in O. Triffterer, ed., *Commentary on the Rome Statute* (Baden-Baden, Nomos 1999) pp. 515-522.

FLETCHER, G.P., *Basic Concepts of Criminal Law* (New York, Oxford University Press 1998).

FRIEDMAN, L., *The Law of War: A Documentary History*, Vol. I/Vol. II (New York, Random House 1972).

GAETA, P., 'The Defence of Superior Orders: The Statute of the International Criminal Court versus Customary International Law', 10 *EJIL* (1999) pp. 172-191.

GILL, T.D., 'The "Genocide" Case: Reflections on the ICJ's Decision in Bosnia and Herzegovina v. Serbia', 2 *Hague Justice Journal* (2007) pp. 43-47.

GOODHART, A.L., 'The Legality of the Nuremberg Trials', in G. Mettraux, ed., *Perspectives on the Nuremberg Trial* (Oxford, Oxford University Press 2008) pp. 626-637.

GROSSMAN, D., *On Killing – The Psychological Cost of Learning to Kill in War and Society* (New York, Back Bay Books/Little, Brown and Company 1995).

GROTIUS, H., *De Jure Belli Ac Pacis* (1646), Vol. 2, transl. by F.W. Kelsey et al. (New York/London, Oceana Publications Inc./Wildy & Son 1964).

HARHOFF, F., 'Sense and Sensibility in Sentencing – Taking Stock of International Criminal Punishment', in O. Engdahl and P. Wrange, eds., *Law at War – The Law as it Was and the Law as it Should Be* (Leiden, Koninklijke Brill 2008) pp. 121-140.

HART, H.L.A., *Punishment and Responsibility* (Oxford, Clarendon 1968).

HART, H.L.A., *The Concept of Law* (Oxford, Oxford University Press 1984).

HEINTSCHEL VON HEINEGG, W., 'Criminal International Law and Customary International Law', in A. Zimmermann, ed., *International Criminal Law and the Current Development of Public International Law* (Berlin, Duncker & Humblot 2003) pp. 27-47.

HENCKAERTS, J.-M., and L. DOSWALD-BECK, *Customary International Humanitarian Law*, Vol. I (Cambridge, Cambridge University Press 2005).

HENQUET, T., 'Convictions for Command Responsibility Under Articles 7(1) and 7(3) of the Statute of the International Criminal Tribunal for the Former Yugoslavia', 15 *LJIL* (2002) pp. 805-834.

HOLLEY, I.B., Jr., 'Concepts, Doctrines, Principles: Are You Sure You Understand These Terms?', 35 *Air University Review* (July – August 1984), available at <http://www.au.af.mil/au/cadre/aspj/airchronicles/aureview/1984/jul-aug/holley.html> (accessed 26 May 2009).

HOLMES ARMSTEAD, J., 'The Chain of Command', in L. Rothfield, ed., *Antiquities under Siege – Cultural Heritage Protection after the Iraq War* (Lanham, Rowman & Littlefield Publishers 2008) pp. 117-124.

JAREBORG, N., *Allmän kriminalrätt* (Uppsala, Iustus Förlag 2001).

JIA, B.B., 'The Doctrine of Command Responbility: Current Problems', 3 *YIHL* (2000) pp. 131-165.

JØRGENSEN, N.H.B., 'The Definition of Genocide: Joining the Dots in Light of Recent Practice', 1 *International Criminal Law Review* (2001) pp. 285-313.

KAGAN, S., 'The "Media case" before the Rwanda Tribunal: The *Nahimana et al.* Appeal Judgement', 3 *Hague Justice Journal* (2008) pp. 83-91, available at <https://www.haguejusticeportal.net> (accessed 9 July 2009).

KALDOR, M., 'Old Wars, Cold Wars, New Wars, and the War on Terror', 42 *International Politics* (2005) pp. 491-498.

KEEGAN, J., *The Mask of Command – A Study of Generalship* (London, Pimlico 2004).

KEIJZER, N., *The Military Duty to Obey* (Amsterdam, Vrije Universiteit 1977).

KEIJZER, N., and E. VAN SLIEDREGT, 'Collectieve aansprakelijkheid in het strafrecht', in M.S. Groenhuijsen and J.B.H.M. Simmelink, eds., *Glijdende schalen. Liber amicorum J. de Hullu* (Nijmegen, Wolf Legal Publishers 2003) pp. 225-245.

KEUNING, D., and D.J. EPPINK, *Management & Organisatie: Theorie en toepassing* (Groningen, Wolters-Noordhoff 2004).

KNOOPS, G.G.J., 'De Abu Ghraib vervolgingen. Strafrechtelijke "victor's justice" voor militaire leiders?', *Nederlands juristenblad* (2005) pp. 778-783.

KOSKENNIEMI, M., 'The Pull of the Mainstream', 88 *Michigan Law Review* (1990).

KRAMER, M.L., and M.N. SCHMITT, 'Lawyers on Horseback? Thoughts on Judge Advocates and Civil-Military Relations', 55 *UCLA Law Review* (2008) pp. 1407-1436.

KRESS, C., 'The Darfur Report and Genocidal Intent', 3 *Journal of International Criminal Justice* (2005) pp. 562-578.

LIPPMAN, M., 'The Evolution and Scope of Command Responsibility', 13 *LJIL* (2000) pp. 139-170.

MALANCZUK, P., ed., *Akehurst's Modern Introduction to International Law*, 7th rev. edn. (London, Routledge 1997).

MAY, R., and S. POWLES, 'Command Responsibility – A New Basis of Criminal Liability in English Law?', *Criminal Law Review* (May 2002) pp. 363-378.

May, R., and M. Wierda, *International Criminal Evidence* (Ardsley, Transnational Publishers Inc. 2002).

McDonald, A., 'Dogs of War Redux? Private Military Contractors and the "New Mercenarism"', 7 *Militair Rechtelijk Tijdschrijft* (2007), pp. 210-228.

Meron, T., 'The Geneva Conventions as Customary Law', 81 *AJIL* (1987) pp. 348-370.

Mettraux, G., *The Law of Command Responsibility* (Oxford, Oxford University Press 2009).

Milgram, S., *Obedience to Authority* (New York, Harper Collins Publishers 2004).

Nerlich, V., 'Superior Responsibility under Article 28 ICC Statute – For What Exactly is the Superior Held Responsible?', 5 *Journal of International Criminal Justice* (2007) pp. 665-682.

Osiel, M., 'The Banality of Good: Aligning Incentives Against Mass Atrocity', 105 *Columbia Law Review* (2005) pp. 1751-1862.

Osiel, M.J., *Obeying Orders* (New Brunswick, Transaction Publishers 1999).

Parks, W.H., 'Command Responsibility for War Crimes', 62 *Military Law Review* (1973) pp. 1-104.

Pilloud, C. et al., *Commentary on the Additional Protocols of 8 June 1977 to the Geneva Conventions of 12 August 1949* (Dordrecht, Nijhoff 1987).

Post, H.H.G., 'The Role of State Practice in the Formation of Customary International Humanitarian Law', in I.F. Dekker and H.H.G. Post, eds., *On the Foundation and Sources of International Law* (The Hague, T.M.C. Asser Press 2003) pp. 129-147.

Reid, N., 'Bridging the Conceptual Chasm: Superior Responsibility as the Missing Link between State and Individual Responsibility under International Law', 18 *LJIL* (2005) pp. 795-828.

Roberts, K., 'The Use of the Tokyo Trial in Determining the Applicability of the Doctrine of Command Responsibility to Civilians', in K. Koufa, *The New International Criminal Law*, 2001 International Law Session, Thesaurus Acroasium, Vol. XXXII (Thessaloniki, Sakkoulas Publications 2003) pp. 1045-1063.

Rogers, A.P.V, *Law on the battlefield*, 2nd edn. (Manchester, Manchester University Press 2004).

Röling, B.V.A., 'Criminal Responsibility for Violations of the Laws of War', 12 *Revue belge de droit international* (1976) pp. 8-26.

Röling, B.V.A. and C.F. Rüter, eds., *The Tokyo Judgment: The International Criminal Tribunal for the Far East (IMTFE), 29 April 1946 – 12 November 1948*, Vol. II (Amsterdam, APA – University Press Amsterdam 1977) p. 1064.

Roxin, C., *Täterschaft und Tatherrschaft*, 7th edn. (Berlin, De Gruyter 2000).

Schabas, W., *Introduction to the International Criminal Court*, 2nd edn. (Cambridge, Cambridge University Press 2004).

Schabas, W., 'Commentary', in A. Klip and G. Sluiter, eds., *Annotated Leading Cases of International Criminal Tribunals*, Vol. 2 (Antwerp, Intersentia/Hart 2001) pp. 539-554.

Schabas, W., *Genocide in International Law: The Crime of Crimes* (Cambridge, Cambridge University Press 2000).

Schmitt, M.N., '21st Century Conflict: Can the Law Survive?', 8 *Melbourne Journal of International Law* (2007) pp. 443-476.

Schmitt, M.N., 'Humanitarian Law and Direct Participation in Hostilities by Private Contractors or Civilian Employees', 5 *Chicago Journal of International Law* (2004) pp. 511-546.

Schmitt, M.N., 'Targeting and Humanitarian Law: Current Issues', 34 *Israel Yearbook on Human Rights* (2004) pp. 59-104.

Shraga, D., and R. Zacklin, 'The International Criminal Tribunal for the Former Yugoslavia', 5 *EJIL* (1994) pp. 360-380.

Singh, A., 'Criminal Responsibility for Non-State Civilian Superiors Lacking *De Jure* Authority: A Comparative Review of the Doctrine of Superior Responsibility and Parallel Doctrines in National Criminal Laws', 28 *Hastings International and Comparative Law Review* (2005) pp. 267-297.

Skilbeck, R., 'Defending the Khmer Rouge', 8 *International Criminal Law Review* (2008) pp. 423-445.

Stein, T., 'Collateral Damage, Proportionality and Individual International Criminal Responsibility', in W. Heintschel von Heinegg and V. Epping, eds., *International Humanitarian Law Facing New Challenges: Symposium in Honour of Knut Ipsen* (Berlin, Springer 2007) pp. 157-161.

Stolwijk, S.A.M., '"Command responsibility" en "strafbaar leidinggeven". Beschouwingen over strafbaar leiderschap', in *Joegoslavië- en Rwanda-tribunalen: impact op het Nederlandse strafrecht* (Amsterdam, Leerstoelgroep Strafrechtswetenschappen Universiteit van Amsterdam 2002) pp. 1-10.

Sun-Tzu, *The Art of War* (transl. by R.D. Sawyer, Westview Press, Oxford 1994).

Swart, A.H.J., 'De strafrechtelijke aansprakelijkheid van meerderen in het internationale humanitaire recht', in M.M. Dolman, P.D. Duyx and H.G. van der Wilt, eds., *Geleerde lessen. Liber amicorum Simon Stolwijk* (Nijmegen, Wolf Legal Publishers 2007) pp. 213-234.

Swart, B., and A. Klip, eds., *International Criminal Law in the Netherlands* (Freiburg im Breisgau, Ed. iuscrim, Max-Planck-Institut für ausländisches und internationales Strafrecht 1997).

Triffterer, O., '"Command Responsibility" – *Crimen sui generis* or Participation as "otherwise provided" in Article 28 Rome Statute?', in J. Arnold et al., eds., *Menschengerechtes Strafrecht – Festschrift für Albin Eser zum 70. Geburtstag* (München, Beck 2005) pp. 901-924.

Triffterer, O., 'Command Responsibility, Article 28 Rome Statute, an Extension of Individual Criminal Responsibility for Crimes Within the Jurisdiction of the Court – Compatible with Article 22, *nullum crimen sine lege*?', in O. Triffterer, ed., *Gedächtnisschrift für Theo Vogler* (Heidelberg, Müller 2004) pp. 213-262.

Van Baarda, Th.A., 'Ethiek, commandantenverantwoordelijkheid en enkele dilemma's bij militaire operaties', in Th.A. van Baarda, A.H.M. van Iersel and D.E.M. Verweij, eds., *Praktijkboek Militaire Ethiek* (Budel, DAMON 2004) pp. 73-123.

Van Creveld, M., *Command in War* (Cambridge, Harvard University Press 1985).

Van Creveld, M., *The Art of War – War and Military Thought* (London, Cassell & Co 2000).

van den Herik, L., and E. van Sliedregt, 'Ten Years Later, the Rwanda Tribunal still Faces Legal Complexities: Some Comments on the Vagueness of the Indictment, Complicity in Genocide, and the Nexus Requirement for War Crimes', 17 *LJIL* (2004) pp. 537-557.

Van der Kruit, P., 'Noodzakelijke regulering van Private Military Compagnies [sic!]. Enkele mogelijkheden', 7 *Militair Rechtelijk Tijdschrift* (2007) pp. 252-263.

Van der Wilt, H.G., 'Why International Criminal Lawyers Should Read Mirjan Damaška', in *Future Perspectives on International Criminal Justice* (The Hague, T.M.C. Asser Press 2010).

Van der Wilt, H.G., 'Commentary', in A. Klip and G. Sluiter, eds., *Annotated Leading Cases of International Criminal Tribunals*, Vol. XIV (Antwerp, Intersentia 2008) pp. 115-122.

Van der Wilt, H.G., 'Halilović on Appeal: The Intricate Concept of "Effective Control"', 2 *Hague Justice Journal* (No. 3, 2007) pp. 5-8.

Van der Wilt, H.G., 'Joint Criminal Enterprise – Possibilities and Limitations', 5 *Journal of International Criminal Justice* (2007) pp. 91-108.

Van der Wilt, H.G., 'Ontwikkeling van nieuwe deelnemingsvormen. Ben ik mijn broeders hoeder?', 37 *Delikt en Delinkwent* (2007) pp. 138-183.

Van der Wilt, H.G., 'Elies van Sliedregt, The Criminal Responsibility of Individuals for Violations of International Humanitarian Law, diss.', 167 *Rechtsgeleerd Magazijn Themis* (2006) pp. 19-23.

VAN DER WILT, H.G., 'Genocide, Complicity in Genocide and International v. Domestic Jurisdiction – Reflections on the *van Anraat* Case', 4 *Journal of International Criminal Justice* (2006) pp. 239-257.

VAN DER WILT, H.G., 'Commentary on Judgement, Prosecutor v. Delalić et al., Case No. IT-96-21-T, 16 November 1998', in A. Klip and G. Sluiter, eds., *Annotated Leading Cases of International Criminal Tribunals*, Vol. 3 (Antwerp, Intersentia/Hart 2001).

VAN DER WILT, H.G., 'The Duty to Know: Enkele beschouwingen over het leerstuk van command responsibility', in G.J.M. Corstens and M.S. Groenhuijsen, eds., *Rede en recht. Opstellen ter gelegenheid van het afscheid van Prof. mr. N. Keijzer van de Katholieke Universiteit Brabant* (Deventer, Gouda Quint 2000) pp. 123-135.

VAN EGMOND, C.P.M., 'Leiderschap in the praktijk', in TH.A. van Baarda, A.H.M. van Iersel and D.E.M. Verweij, eds., *Praktijkboek Militaire Ethiek* (Budel, DAMON 2004) pp. 49-71.

VAN SLIEDREGT, E., 'Criminal Responsibility in International Law – Liability Shaped by Policy Goals and Moral Outrage', 14 *EJIL* (2006) pp. 81-114.

VAN SLIEDREGT, E., *The Criminal Responsibility of Individuals for Violations of International Humanitarian Law* (The Hague, T.M.C. Asser Press 2003).

VERDROSS, A., 'Entstehungsweisen und Geltungsgrund des universellen völkerrechtlichen Gewohnheitsrechts', 29 *Zeitschrift für ausländisches öffentliches Recht und Völkerrecht* (1969).

VETTER, G.R., 'Command Responsibility of Non-Military Superiors in the International Criminal Court', 25 *Yale Journal of International Law* (2000) pp. 89-141.

VON CLAUSEWITZ, C., 'Ethics and Military Strategy', in G.M. Reichberg, H. Syse and E. Begby, eds., *The Ethics of War* (Malden, Blackwell Publishing 2006) pp. 553-561.

WEIGEND, T., 'Bemerkungen zur Vorgesetztenverantwortlichkeit im Völkerstrafrecht', 116 *Zeitschrift für die Gesamte Strafrechtswissenschaft* (2004) pp. 999-1027.

WERLE, G., 'General Principles of International Criminal Law', in A. Cassese, ed., *The Oxford Companion to International Criminal Justice* (Oxford, Oxford University Press 2009) pp. 54-62.

WERLE, G., and V. NERLICH, 'Die Strafbarkeit von Kriegsverbrechen nach deutschem Recht', 3 *Humanitäres Völkerrecht* (2002) pp. 124-134.

WOENTZEL, R.K, *The Nuremberg Trials in International Law with a Postlude to the Eichmann Trial* (London, Stevens and Sons 1962).

ZAHAR, A., 'Command Responsibility of Civilian Superiors for Genocide', 14 *LJIL* (2001) pp. 591-616.

ZAHAR, A., and G. SLUITER, *International Criminal Law – A Critical Introduction* (Oxford, Oxford University Press 2008).

ZARATE, J.C., 'The Emergence of a New Dog of War: Private International Security Companies, International Law, and the New World Disorder', 34 *Stanford Journal of International Law* (1998) pp. 75-162.

ZEGVELD, L., *Armed Opposition Groups in International Law: The Quest for Accountability*, Ph.D. Dissertation, Utrecht University 2000.

ZHU, W., 'The Doctrine of Command Responsibility as Applied to Civilian Leaders: The ICTR and the *Kayishema* Case', in S. Yee and W. Tieya, eds., *International Law in the Post-Cold War World, Essays in Memory of Li Haopei* (London, Routledge 2001).

TABLE OF TREATIES AND DOCUMENTS

TREATIES AND AGREEMENTS

1907 Regulations Respecting the Laws and Customs of War on Land, annexed to the 1907 Hague Convention (IV) Respecting the Laws and Customs of War on Land, 100 *BFSP* 338, reprinted in 2 *AJIL* (1908) Supp. p. 90.

1948 Convention on the Prevention and Punishment of the Crime of Genocide of 9 December 1948, 78 *UNTS* p. 277 (entered into force 12 January 1951).

1949 Geneva Convention III of 12 August 1949, 75 *UNTS* p. 135.

1951 Convention Relating to the Status of Refugees, 189 *UNTS* p. 137.

1968 Convention on the Non-Applicability of Statutory Limitations to War Crimes and Crimes Against Humanity of 26 November 1968, 754 *UNTS* p. 73.

1977 Protocol Additional to the Geneva Conventions of 12 August 1949, and relating to the Protection of Victims of International Armed Conflicts (Protocol I), 8 June 1977, 1125 *UNTS* p. 3.

1998 Rome Statute of the International Criminal Court, UN Doc. A/CONF.183/9 (1998), 17 July 1998, 37 *ILM* (1998) p. 999.

2002 Statute of the Special Court for Sierra Leone, annexed to the Agreement between the United Nations and the Government of Sierra Leone on the establishment of a Special Court for Sierra Leone, 16 January 2002, 2178 *UNTS* p. 137.

2007 Statute of the Special Tribunal for Lebanon, annexed to the Agreement between the United Nations and the Lebanese Republic on the establishment of a Special Tribunal for Lebanon, 22 January 2007.

OTHER DOCUMENTS

ICC

Elements of Crimes, ICC-ASP/1/3(part II-B), 9 September 2002.

Official Records of the Assembly of States Parties to the Rome Statute of the International Criminal Court, First Session, 3-10 September 2002, Resolution ICC-ASP/1/Res.1.

Official Records of the Assembly of States Parties to the Rome Statute of the International Criminal Court, Fourth Session, 28 November – 3 December 2005, ICC-ASP/4/32, Annex II.

Official Records of the Assembly of States Parties to the Rome Statute of the International Criminal Court, Sixth Session, 30 November – 14 December 2007, ICC-ASP/6/20, Annex III.

ILC

Draft Code of Offences Against the Peace and Security of Mankind, UN GAOR, 9th Sess., Supp. No. 9, UN Doc. A/2693 (1954).
Draft Code of Crimes Against the Peace and Security of Mankind, UN GAOR, 51st Sess., Supp. No. 10, UN Doc. A/51/10 (1996).

United Nations

Final Report of the Commission of Experts Established pursuant to Security Council Resolution 780 (1992), UN Doc. S/1994/674, 27 May 1994, Annex.
Report of the Secretary General Pursuant to Paragraph 2 of Security Council Resolution 808 (1993), UN Doc. S/25704 (1993), reprinted in 32 *ILM* (1993) p. 1163.
Security Council Provisional Verbatim Record of the Three Thousand Two Hundred and Seventeenth Meeting, UN Doc. S/PV. 3217, 25 May 1993.
Statute for the International Criminal Tribunal for the former Yugoslavia, 32 *ILM* (1993) p. 1159.
Statute for the International Criminal Tribunal for Rwanda, 33 *ILM* (1994) p. 1598.
Statute of the International Court of Justice, San Fransisco, 26 June 1945, 145 *BFSP* 832.

Versailles Peace Conference 1919

Commission on the Responsibility of the Authors of the War and on the Enforcement of Penalties, Report Presented to the Preliminary Peace Conference, Versailles, 29 March 1919, reprinted in 14 *AJIL* (1920) pp. 95-154.

Finland

RP 55/2007 rd, Regeringens proposition till Riksdagen med förslag till ändring av strafflagens bestämmelser om krigsförbrytelser och brott mot humaniteten samt vissa lagar som har samband med den; Government Act No. 55/2007 proposing changes to the provisions of the Penal Code concerning war crimes and crimes against humanity and some laws connected thereto (translation by MLN), Law enacted on 11 April 2008, Entered into force on 1 May 2008, Finlands FörfS. (Statutes of Finland) 212/2008.

Germany

Code of Crimes Against International Law (CCAIL), 'Gesetz zur Einführung des Völkerstrafgesetzbuches', 26 June 2002, *Bundesgesetzblatt Jahrgang* 2002 Teil II, Nr. 42, 2254.

Militär-Strafgesetzbuch für das Deutsche Reich, Vom 20. Juni 1872. Original source: Deutsches Reichsgesetzblatt, Band 1872, Nr. 18, Seite 174-204. Cited source: <http://www.documentarchiv.de/ksr/1872/militaerstrafgesetzbuch_deutsches-reich.html> (accessed 1 September 2008).

Netherlands

'International Crimes Act', 9 June 2003, Stb. 2003, No. 270.

Peru

Corte Suprema de Justicia de la República, Sala Penal Especial, *Caso Fujimori*, Asuntos Varios 0019-2001 (Barrios Altos, Cantuta, Sotanos SIE), Sentencia: Fundamentos y fallo, 7 April 2009, at Parte IV – Decisión, § 4. La autoría mediata y la responsabilidad del superior en el Derecho Penal Internacional.

United Kingdom

The Manual of the Law of Armed Conflict, UK Ministry of Defence (Oxford, Oxford University Press 2004).

Lectures

Bassiouni, M. Cherif, Professor, DePaul University, 'Reflections on the Darfur case', Supranational Criminal Law Lecture Series, T.M.C. Asser Institute, The Hague 1 October 2008.

Hollis, B.J., Principal Trial Attorney SCSL/OTP, 'Lessons learned from international criminal courts and tribunals', Supranational Criminal Law Lecture Series, Grotius Centre for International Legal Studies, The Hague, 11 March 2009.

Osiel, M., 'Perpetration by hierarchical organization', Guest Lecture Series of the Office of the Prosecutor of the ICC, The Hague, 22 April 2009, available at <http://www.icc-cpi.int/NR/rdonlyres/9FCE9732-65A3-4997-B74E-A4B3ABE144CF/280431/PresentationMOsiel.pdf> (accessed 13 July 2009).

Rapp, S., Chief Prosecutor of the Special Court, 'The legal challenges of prosecuting national leaders for violations of International Humanitarian Law for Sierra Leone', Occasional Guest Lecture Series, T.M.C. Asser Institute, The Hague, 28 February 2008.

Media

'Judge Allows Abu Ghraib Lawsuit Against Contractor', available at <http://www.washingtonpost.com/wp-dyn/content/article/2007/11/06/AR2007110602025.html> (Accessed 12 December 2008).

'TV Report Says Marine Shot Prisoner', Associated Press, published at NYTimes.com, 16 November 2004 available at <http://www.nytimes.com/2004/11/16/international/middleeast/16marine.html?_r=1&scp=2&sq=fallujah%202004%20us%20kills%20unarmed&st=cse&oref=slogin> (Accessed 15 July 2009).

'UN soldiers arrested in DR Congo', BBC News, 13 February 2005, available at <http://news.bbc.co.uk/2/hi/africa/4262743.stm> (Accessed 15 July 2009).

Others

'ICTR Detainees – Status on 2 December 2008', available at <http://69.94.11.53/ENGLISH/factsheets/detainee.htm> (accessed 18 December 2008).

NATO Glossary of Terms and Definitions, available at <http://www.nato.int/docu/stanag/aap006/aap-6-2009.pdf>, p. 2-C-9 (accessed 2 July 2009).

TABLE OF CASES

INTERNATIONAL COURTS

International Court of Justice

International Status of South-West Africa, Advisory Opinion, Separate Opinion by Sir Arnold McNair, ICJ Reports 1950.
Asylum Case (Colombia/Peru), Judgement, ICJ Reports 1950.
Continental Shelf Case (Libyan Arab Jamahiriya/Malta), Judgement, ICJ Reports 1985.
Case Concerning Armed Activities on the Territory of the Congo (DRC v. Uganda), Judgement, ICJ Reports 2005.

International Criminal Court

Bemba

Prosecutor v. *Jean Pierre Bemba Gombo*, Warrant of Arrest, Case No. ICC-01/05-01/08-1, 23 May 2008.
Prosecutor v. *Jean Pierre Bemba Gombo*, Decision Adjourning the Hearing pursuant to Article 61(7)(c)(ii) of the Rome Statute, Case No. ICC-01/05-01/08-388, 3 March 2009.

Lubanga

Prosecutor v. *Thomas Lubanga Dyilo*, Warrant of Arrest, Case No. ICC-01/04-01/06-2, 10 February 2006.
Prosecutor v. *Thomas Lubanga Dyilo*, Decision on the Confirmation of Charges, Case No. ICC-01/04-01/06-803-tEN, 29 January 2007.

Katanga and Ngudjolo Chui

Prosecutor v. *Germain Katanga*, Warrant of Arrest, Case No. ICC-01/04-01/07-1, 2 July 2007.
Prosecutor v. *Mathieu Ngudjolo Chui*, Warrant of Arrest, Case No. ICC-01/04-01/07-260, 6 July 2007.
Prosecutor v. *Germain Katanga and Mathieu Ngudjolo Chui*, Decision on the Confirmation of Charges, Case No. ICC-01/04-01/07-717, 30 September 2008.

Ntaganda

Prosecutor v. *Bosco Ntaganda*, Warrant of Arrest, Case No. ICC-01/04-02/06-2, 22 August 2006.

Kony, Otti, Odhiambo and Ongwen

Prosecutor v. *Vincent Otti*, Warrant of Arrest, Case No. ICC-02/04-01/05-54, 8 July 2005.
Prosecutor v. *Okot Odhiambo*, Warrant of Arrest, Case No. ICC-02/04-01/05-56, 8 July 2005.
Prosecutor v. *Dominic Ongwen*, Warrant of Arrest, Case No. ICC-02/04-01/05-57, 8 July 2005.
Prosecutor v. *Joseph Kony*, Warrant of Arrest, Case No. ICC-02/04-01/05-53, 27 September 2005.

Harun and Kushayb

Prosecutor v. *Ahmad Harun*, Warrant of Arrest, Case No. ICC-02/05-01/07-2, 27 April 2007.
Prosecutor v. *Ali Kushayb*, Warrant of Arrest, Case No. ICC-02/05-01/07-3, 27 April 2007.

Al Bashir

Prosecutor v. *Omar Hassan Ahmad Al Bashir*, Warrant of Arrest, Case No. ICC-02/05-01/09-1, 4 March 2009.

Abu Garda

Prosecutor v. *Bahr Idriss Abu Garda*, Warrant of Arrest, Case No. ICC-02/05-01/05-2, 27 April 2007.

International Criminal Tribunal for Rwanda

Akayesu

Prosecutor v. *Jean-Paul Akayesu*, Amended Indictment, Case No. ICTR-96-4-I, 17 June 1997.
Prosecutor v. *Jean-Paul Akayesu*, Judgement, Case No. ICTR-96-4-T, 2 September 1998.
Prosecutor v. *Jean-Paul Akayesu*, Sentence, Case No. ICTR-96-4-T, 2 September 1998.

Bagambiki and Imanishimwe

Prosecutor v. *Emmanuel Bagambiki and Samuel Imanishimwe*, Indictment, Case No. ICTR-97-36-I, 13 October 1997.

Bagaragaza

Prosecutor v. *Michel Bagaragaza*, Amended Indictment, Case No. ICTR-2005-86-I, 1 December 2006.

Bagilishema

Prosecutor v. *Ignace Bagilishema*, Amended Indictment, Case No. ICTR-95-1A-I, 17 September 1999.
Prosecutor v. *Ignace Bagilishema*, Judgement, Case No. ICTR-95-1A-T, 7 June 2001.
Prosecutor v. *Ignace Bagilishema*, Appeal Judgement, Case No. ICTR-95-1A-A, 3 July 2002.

Gacumbitsi

Prosecutor v. *Sylvestre Gacumbitsi*, Indictment, Case No. ICTR-01-64-I, 20 June 2001.
Prosecutor v. *Sylvestre Gacumbitsi*, Judgement, Case No. ICTR-01-64-T, 17 June 2004.
Prosecutor v. *Sylvestre Gacumbitsi*, Appeal Judgement, Case No. ICTR-01-64-A, 7 July 2006.

Kajelijeli

Prosecutor v. *Juvénal Kajelijeli*, Amended Indictment pursuant to the Tribunal Order Dated 25 January 2001, Case No. ICTR-98-44A-I, 25 January 2001.
Prosecutor v. *Juvénal Kajelijeli*, Judgement and Sentence, Case No. ICTR-98-44A-T, 1 December 2003.
Prosecutor v. *Juvénal Kajelijeli*, Appeal Judgement, Case No. ICTR-98-44A-A, 23 May 2005.

Kambanda

Prosecutor v. *Jean Kambanda*, Indictment, Case No. ICTR-97-23-I, 28 October 1997.
Prosecutor v. *Jean Kambanda*, Judgement and Sentence, Case No. ICTR-97-23-S, 4 September 1998.

Kayishema and Ruzindana

Prosecutor v. *Clément Kayishema and Obed Ruzindana*, First Amended Indictment, Case No. ICTR-95-1-I.
Prosecutor v. *Clément Kayishema and Obed Ruzindana*, Judgement, Case No. ICTR-95-1-T, 21 May 1999.
Prosecutor v. *Clément Kayishema and Obed Ruzindana*, Appeal Judgement, Case No. ICTR-95-1-A, 1 June 2001.

Musema

Prosecutor v. *Alfred Musema*, Case No. ICTR-96-13-T, Judgement and Sentence, 27 January 2000.

Nahimana, Barayagwiza and Ngeze

Prosecutor v. *Ferdinand Nahimana, Jean-Bosco Barayagwiza and Hassan Ngeze*, Judgement and Sentence, Case No. ICTR-99-52-T, 3 December 2003.
Prosecutor v. *Ferdinand Nahimana, Jean-Bosco Barayagwiza and Hassan Ngeze*, Appeal Judgement, Case No. ICTR-99-52-A, 28 November 2007.

Ntagerura, Bagambiki and Imanishimwe

Prosecutor v. *André Ntagerura*, Amended Indictment, Case No. ICTR-96-10-I, 29 January 1998.
Prosecutor v. *André Ntagerura, Emmanuel Bagambiki and Samuel Imanishimwe*, Judgement and Sentence, Case No. ICTR-99-46-T, 25 February 2004.
Prosecutor v. *André Ntagerura, Emmanuel Bagambiki, and Samuel Imanishimwe*, Appeal Judgement, Case No. ICTR-99-46-A, 7 July 2006.

Ntawukuriryayo

Prosecutor v. *Dominique Ntawukuriryayo*, Indictment, Case No. ICTR-2005-82-I, 26 May 2005.

Rugambarara

Prosecutor v. *Juvénal Rugambarara*, Decision on the Prosecution Motion to Amend the Indictment, Case No. ICTR-00-59-T, 28 June 2007.
Prosecutor v. *Juvénal Rugambarara*, Amended Indictment, Case No. ICTR-2000-59-I, 2 July 2007.
Prosecutor v. *Juvénal Rugambarara*, Judgement and Sentence, Case No. ICTR-00-59-T, 16 November 2007.

Rutaganira

Prosecutor v. *Vincent Rutaganira*, Judgement and Sentence, Case No. ICTR-95-1C-T, 14 March 2005.

Semanza

Prosecutor v. *Laurent Semanza*, Judgement, Case No. ICTR-97-20-T, 15 May 2003.

Serugendo

Prosecutor v. *Joseph Serugendo*, Corrigendum of Indictment, Case No. ICTR-2005-84-I, 21 July 2005.
Prosecutor v. *Joseph Serugendo*, Judgement and Sentence, Case No. ICTR-2005-84-I, 12 June 2006.

Serushago

Prosecutor v. Omar Serushago, Decision Relating to a Plea of Guilty, Case No. ICTR-98-39-T, 14 December 2003.

Simba

Prosecutor v. *Aloys Simba*, Judgement, Case No. ICTR-01-76-T, 13 December 2005.

International Criminal Tribunal for the former Yugoslavia

Aleksovski

Prosecutor v. *Zlatko Aleksovski*, Judgement, Case No. IT-95-14/1-T, 25 June 1999.
Prosecutor v. *Zlatko Aleksovski*, Appeal Judgement, Case No. IT-95-14/1-A, 24 March 2000.

Babić

Prosecutor v. *Milan Babić*, Judgement on Sentencing Appeal, Case No. IT-03-72-A, 18 July 2005.

Blagojević and Jokić

Prosecutor v. *Vidoje Blagojević and Dragan Jokić*, Judgement, Case No. IT-02-60-T, 17 January 2005.

Blaškić

Prosecutor v. *Tihomir Blaškić*, Judgement, Case No. IT-95-14-T, 3 March 2000.
Prosecutor v. *Tihomir Blaškić*, Appeal Judgement, Case No. IT-95-14-A, 29 July 2004.

Boškoski and Tarčulovski

Prosecutor v. *Ljube Boškoski and Johan Tarčulovski*, Judgement, Case No. IT-04-82-T, 10 July 2008.

Brđanin

Prosecutor v. *Radoslav Brđanin*, Judgement, Case No. IT-99-36-T, 1 September 2004.

Delalić et al. (*Čelebići*)

Prosecutor v. *Zejnil Delalić et al.*, Judgement, Case No. IT-96-21-T, 16 November 1998.
Prosecutor v. *Zejnil Delalić et al.*, Appeal Judgement (*Čelebići* Appeal Judgement), Case No. IT-96-21-A, 20 February 2001.
Prosecutor v. *Zejnil Delalić et al.*, Separate and Dissenting Opinion of Judge David Hunt and Judge Mohamed Bennouna, Case No. IT-96-21-A, 20 February 2001.

Delić

Prosecutor v. *Rasim Delić*, Judgement, Case No. IT-04-83-T, 15 September 2008.

Erdemović

Prosecutor v. *Drazen Erdemović*, Sentencing Judgement, Case No. ICTY-96-22-T, 29 November 1996.

Furundžija

Prosecutor v. *Anto Furundžija*, Judgement, Case No. IT-95-17/1-T, 10 December 1998.

Galić

Prosecutor v. *Stanislav Galić*, Separate and Partially Dissenting Opinion of Judge Nieto-Navia, Case No. IT-98-29-T, 5 December 2003.
Prosecutor v. *Stanislav Galić*, Appeal Judgement, Case No. IT-98-29-A, 30 November 2006.

Hadžihasanović

Prosecutor v. *Hadžihasanović et al.*, Decision on Joint Challenge to Jurisdiction, Case No. IT-01-47-PT, 12 November 2002.
Prosecutor v. *Hadžihasanović et al.*, Decision on Interlocutory Appeal Challenging Jurisdiction in Relation to Command Responsibility, Case No. IT-01-47-AR72, 16 July 2003.
Prosecutor v. *Hadžihasanović et al.*, Judgement Summary, Case No. IT-01-47-T, 15 March 2006.
Prosecutor v. *Hadžihasanović et al.*, Judgement, Case No. IT-01-47-T, 15 March 2006.
Prosecutor v. *Hadžihasanović et al.*, Appeal Judgement, Case No. IT-01-47-A, 22 April 2008.

Halilović

Prosecutor v. *Sefer Halilović*, Indictment, Case No. IT-01-48-I, 12 September 2001.
Prosecutor v. *Sefer Halilović*, Judgement, Case No. IT-01-48-T, 16 November 2005.
Prosecutor v. *Sefer Halilović*, Appeal Judgement, Case No. IT-01-48-A, 16 October 2007.

Karadžić and Mladić

Prosecutor v. *Radovan Karadžić and Ratko Mladić*, Review of Indictment Pursuant to Rule 61 of the Rules of Procedure and Evidence, Case No. IT-95-5-R61, IT-95-18-R61, 11 July 1996.

Kordić and Čerkez

Prosecutor v. *Dario Kordić and Mario Čerkez*, Judgement, Case No. IT-95-14/2-T, 26 February 2001.

Krnojelac

Prosecutor v. *Milorad Krnojelac*, Judgement, Case No. IT-97-25-T, 15 March 2002.

Krstić

Prosecutor v. *Radislav Krstić*, Judgement, Case No. IT-98-33-T, 2 August 2001.
Prosecutor v. *Radislav Krstić*, Appeal Judgement (*Krstić* Appeal Judgement), Case No. IT-98-33-A, 19 April 2004.

Kunarac

Prosecutor v. *Dragljub Kunarac, Radomir Kovac and Zoran Vukovic*, Judgement, Case No. IT-96-23-T &IT-96-23/1-T, 22 February 2001.
Prosecutor v. *Dragljub Kunarac, Radomir Kovac and Zoran Vukovic*, Appeal Judgement, Case No. IT-96-23 & IT-96-23/1-A, 12 June 2002.

Kvočka et al.

Prosecutor v. *Radislav Kvočka et al.*, Judgement, Case No. IT-98-33-T, 2 November 2001.
Prosecutor v. *Radislav Kvočka et al.*, Appeal Judgement, Case No. IT-98-33-A, 28 February 2005.

Milošević, Dragomir

Prosecutor v. *Dragomir Milošević*, Judgement, Case No. IT-98-29/1-T, 12 December 2007.

Slobodan Milošević

Prosecutor v. *Slobodan Milošević*, Amended Indictment, Case No. IT-02-54-T, 22 November 2002.

Naletilić and Martinović (Tuta and Štela)

Prosecutor v. *Mladen Naletilić and Vinko Martinović* (Tuta and Štela), Judgement, Case No. IT-98-34-T, 31 March 2003.

Orić

Prosecutor v. *Naser Orić*, Judgement, Case No. IT-03-68-T, 30 June 2006.

Plavšić

Prosecutor v. *Biljana Plavšić*, Amended Consolidated Indictment, Case No. IT-00-39&40-PT, 7 March 2002.
Prosecutor v. *Biljana Plavšić*, Plea Agreement, Case No. IT-00-40-PT, 30 September 2002.
Prosecutor v. *Biljana Plavšić*, Factual Basis for Plea of Guilt, Case No. IT-00-39&40-PT, 30 September 2002.
Prosecutor v. *Biljana Plavšić*, Sentencing Judgement, Case No. IT-00-39&40/1, 27 February 2003.

Prlić et al.

Prosecutor v. *Jadranko Prlić et al.*, Second Amended Indictment, Case No. IT-04-74-T, 11 June 2008.

Sikirica et al.

Prosecutor v. *Duško Sikirica et al.*, Second Amended Indictment, Case No. IT-95-8-PT, 3 January 2001.

Simić, Tadić and Zarić

Prosecutor v. *Blagoje Simić, Miroslav Tadić and Simo Zarić*, Judgement, Case No. IT-95-9-T, 17 October 2003.

Prosecutor v. *Blagoje Simić, Miroslav Tadić and Simo Zarić*, Separate and Partly Dissenting Opinion of Judge Per-Johan Lindholm, Case No. IT-95-9-T, 17 October 2003.

Stakić

Prosecutor v. *Milomir Stakić*, Judgement, Case No. IT-97-24-T, 31 July 2003.

Strugar

Prosecutor v. *Pavle Strugar*, Judgement, Case No. IT-01-42-T, 31 January 2005.

Tadić

Prosecutor v. *Duško Tadić*, Judgement, Case No. IT-94-1-T, 7 May 1997.

Prosecutor v. *Duško Tadić*, Appeal Judgement, Case No. IT-94-1-A, 15 July 1999.

Prosecutor v. *Duško Tadić*, Judgement, Case No. IT-94-1-T*bis*-R117, 11 November 1999.

Todorović

Prosecutor v. *Stevan Todorović*, Second Amended Indictment, Case No. IT-95-9-PT, 25 March 1999.

Prosecutor v. *Stevan Todorović*, Sentencing Judgement, Case No. IT-95-9/1-S, 31 July 2001.

Vasiljević

Prosecutor v. *Mitar Vasiljević*, Judgement, Case No. IT-98-32-T, 29 November 2002.

International Military Tribunal

Trial of Major War Criminals before the International Military Tribunal, *The Nuremberg Judgement* (1945-46), in L. Friedman, ed., *The Law of War: A Documentary History*, Vol. II, (New York, Random House 1972) pp. 922-1026.

International Military Tribunal for the Far East

The Tokyo Judgment, The International Criminal Tribunal for the Far East, 29 April – 12 November 1948, Vol. II, B.V.A. Röling and C.F. Rüter, eds., (Amsterdam, APA – University Press Amsterdam 1977) p. 1064.

Special Court for Sierra Leone

RUF case

Prosecutor v. *Issa Hassan Sesay, Morris Kallon and Augustine Gbao*, Judgement, Case No. SCSL-04-15-T, 25 February 2009.

Taylor

Prosecutor v. *Charles Ghankay Taylor*, Amended Indictment, Case No. SCSL-03-01-I, 16 March 2006.

Supreme Court of Leipzig

Judgement in the Case of Emil Müller, 30 May 1921, 16 *AJIL* (1922) p. 684.

United States Military Tribunals at Nuremberg

Brandt et al. (the *Medical* case), Judgement, TWC, Vol. II, pp. 171-300.
Flick et al., Opinion and Judgement, TWC, Vol. VI, p. 1187-1223, in L. Friedman, ed., *The Law of War: A Documentary History*, Vol. II, (New York, Random House 1972) pp. 1281-1302.
The High Command Case, Opinion and Judgement of United States Military Tribunal at Nuremberg in United States vs. Wilhelm von Leeb et al., in L. Friedman, ed., *The Law of War: A Documentary History*, Vol. II, (New York, Random House 1972) pp. 1421-1470.
The Hostage Case, Opinion and Judgement of the United States Military Tribunal at Nuremberg in United States vs. Wilhelm List et al., in L. Friedman, ed., *The*

Law of War: A Documentary History, Vol. II (New York, Random House 1972) pp. 1303-1343.

Pohl et al. (*Pohl* case), TWC, Vol. V, pp. 958-1163, in L. Friedman, ed., *The Law of War: A Documentary History*, Vol. II, (New York, Random House 1972) pp. 1254-1280.

The UNWCC Trials

United Nations War Crimes Commission, *Law Reports of Trials of War Criminals* (UNWCC), Vols. I-XV (London, HMO 1947-1949).

Abbaye Ardenne case, UNWCC, Vol. IV, pp. 97-112.
Masao case, UNWCC, Vol. XI, pp. 56-61.
Sakai case, UNWCC, Vol. XIV, pp. 1-7.
Schonfeld and Nine Others, UNWCC, Vol. XI, pp. 64-73.
Yamashita, UNWCC, Vol. IV, pp. 1-96.

NATIONAL COURTS

Bosnia and Herzegovina

Prosecutor's Office of Bosnia and Herzegovina v. *Mitar Rašević and Savo Todović*, Verdict, Case No. X-KR/06/275, 28 February 2008.
Prosecutor's Office of Bosnia and Herzegovina v. *Paško Ljubičić*, Verdict, Case No. X-KR-06/241, 29 April 2008.

Netherlands

Slavenburg case, Dutch Supreme Court, 16 December 1986, *NJ* 1987, No. 321.

United States of America

In re *Yamashita*, 327 US 1 (1946).

INDEX

MIX
Papier aus verantwortungsvollen Quellen
Paper from responsible sources
FSC® C105338

If you have any concerns about our products,
you can contact us on
ProductSafety@springernature.com

In case Publisher is established outside the EU,
the EU authorized representative is:
Springer Nature Customer Service Center GmbH
Europaplatz 3, 69115 Heidelberg, Germany

Printed by Libri Plureos GmbH
in Hamburg, Germany